CAPABLANCA'S BEST CHESS ENDINGS

J. R. Capablanca

CAPABLANCA'S BEST CHESS ENDINGS

60 Complete Games

by

Irving Chernev

Dover Publications, Inc.
New York

This book is dedicated to
my dear wife Selma, with love

Copyright © 1978 by Irving Chernev.
All rights reserved under Pan American and International Copyright Conventions.

Published in Canada by General Publishing Company, Ltd., 30 Lesmill Road, Don Mills,
Toronto, Ontario.
Published in the United Kingdom by Constable and Company, Ltd., 10 Orange Street,
London WC2H 7EG.

This Dover edition, first published in 1982, is an unabridged republication of the work
originally published by Oxford University Press, Oxford, in 1978 with the title *Capablanca's
Best Chess Endings*. The frontispiece portrait of Capablanca in the present edition is not the
same as that in the original edition.

International Standard Book Number: 0-486-24249-8

Manufactured in the United States of America
Dover Publications, Inc.
180 Varick Street
New York, N.Y. 10014

Library of Congress Cataloging in Publication Data

Capablanca, José Raúl, 1888-1942.
  Capablanca's best chess endings.

  Reprint. Originally published: Oxford, Eng.: Oxford University Press, 1978.
  Bibliography: p.
  Includes index.
  1. Chess—End games. 2. Capablanca, José Raúl, 1888-1942. 3. Chess—Collections of
games. I. Chernev, Irving, 1900-   . II. Title. III. Title: Best chess endings.
GV1450.7.C34 1982   794.1′24   81-17311
ISBN 0-486-24249-8   AACR2

The accent is on the ending!

The opening of a game is important—and hundreds of books are written on the opening. The opening leads to the midgame.

The midgame is important—and hundreds of books are written on the midgame. The midgame leads to the endgame.

The endgame is important—and *no books are written on the endgame*!

Yes, there are books, but they concern themselves with composed endings, or with theoretical (and for the most part artificial) positions.

The composed endings are admittedly beautiful, but they are of limited value, as they have no relationship to practical play.

Of the theoretical positions, many have their uses, but one must sift the wheat from the chaff. To what use can we put such knowledge as the procedure for mating with a Knight and Bishop, or with the two Bishops, when an opportunity to do so may not occur in a lifetime? And why burden our minds with the manner of forcing mate with three Knights (believe-it-or-not) or winning with four minor pieces against a Queen (sans Pawns) when such positions as these have never yet been seen on land or sea?

Capablanca himself says, 'In order to improve your game, you must study the endgame before anything else; *for whereas the endings can be studied and mastered by themselves, the middle game and the opening must be studied in relation to the endgame.*'

There are no books on endings from real life, no books from the practice of masters in actual play, let alone from the practice of a single master.

This fact alone is enough to justify this book of endings, selected from the tournament and match play of the greatest endgame virtuoso the world has ever seen—the immortal Capablanca.

Here are wondrous endings to enchant the reader, endings of breath-taking artistry.

Here are endings of astonishing accuracy, whose relentless logic will inspire the earnest student to emulate a similar technique—the technique of seeking a clear-cut, efficient win, instead of a display of fireworks.

The games are given in full, in order to show how a slight advantage, acquired in the early stages, is carried forward and exploited in the endgame.

I have annotated the endings in detail (a consideration they have rarely received before) for the better appreciation of the fine points of Capablanca's play, and have given credit to those who have anticipated my findings.

San Francisco   *Irving Chernev*

And there for an hour, or maybe two, we shall
enter into that rapturous realm where the
Knight prances and the Bishop lurks with his
shining sword, and the Rooks come crashing
through in double file.   *A. E. Gardiner*

Books by Irving Chernev

The Golden Dozen: the Twelve
   Greatest Players of All Time
Capablanca's Best Chess Endings
Wonders and Curiosities of Chess
The most Instructive Games of
   Chess ever Played
Logical Chess, Move by Move
The 1000 Best Short Games of
   Chess
Combinations: the Heart of Chess
The Bright Side of Chess
Chessboard Magic!

The Chess Companion
Practical Chess Endings
The Russians Play Chess
Winning Chess Traps
An Invitation to Chess (with
   Kenneth Harkness)
The Fireside Book of Chess (with
   Fred Reinfeld)
Winning Chess (with Fred Reinfeld)
Chess Strategy and Tactics (with
   Fred Reinfeld)
Curious Chess Facts

Contents

Contents

Contents

CAPABLANCA'S BEST CHESS ENDINGS

The endings

GAME 1

White J. R. Capablanca
Black J. Corzo
Ninth Match Game, Havana, 1901

Dutch Defence

Despite the importance of the occasion, this being a match for the Championship of Cuba, the 12-year-old Capablanca breezes through the entire game in phenomenally quick time, taking only 24 minutes for the entire 59 moves, an average of less than half a minute per move!

The two players whizz through the opening, skip the midgame, and arrive at the ending in less than 20 moves!

The ending is absorbing enough, though, to make up for anything else that is lacking.

1   d2-d4   f7-f5

The Dutch Defence has been favoured by aggressive players, from Morphy to Alekhine.

Morphy won two beautiful games from Harrwitz with the Dutch, demonstrating in each of them incidentally his skill in the endgame.

Alekhine, needing a win to capture first prize in the Hastings 1922 Tournament, chose the Dutch as a fighting weapon against Bogolyubov. His faith was not misplaced, as he won the game in

glorious style (the details of which can be found in *The Golden Dozen* on page 265).

Botvinnik, a connoisseur of this defence, used it in his game against Steiner at Groningen in 1946. He launched an irresistible King-side attack when he obtained the initiative, and demolished his opponent in 28 moves.

2   e2-e4   f5xe4

3   Nb1-c3   Ng8-f6

4   Bc1-g5

White has a good alternative here in the Staunton Gambit, beginning with 4 f2-f3, when the play might go as follows: 4 . . . e4xf3 5 Ng1xf3 g7-g6 6 Bf1-d3!, and 7 h2-h4 followed by 8 h4-h5 offers prospects of an attack for the Pawn.

4   . . .   c7-c6

Black does not make the mistake of protecting the Pawn by 4 . . . d7-d5, as that allows 5 Bg5xf6 followed by 6 Qd1-h5+, and White recovers the Pawn with advantage.

Nimzowitsch against Johner at Carlsbad in 1929 proceeded with 4 . . . b7-b6 5 f2-f3 e4-e3 6 Bg5xe3

e7-e6 7 Qd1-d2 d7-d5 8 0-0-0
c7-c5 9 Bf1-b5+ Bc8-d7
10 Bb5xd7+ Qd8xd7 11 Ng1-h3
Nb8-c6 12 Rh1-e1 0-0-0
13 Qd2-e2 c5-c4, and won a fine
game.

5	Bg5xf6	e7xf6
6	Nc3xe4	d7-d5
7	Ne4-g3	Qd8-e7+
8	Qd1-e2	Qe7xe2+
9	Bf1xe2	Bf8-d6
10	Ng1-f3	0-0
11	0-0	Bc8-g4
12	h2-h3	Bg4xf3
13	Be2xf3	Bd6xg3
14	f2xg3	Nb8-d7

Corzo has relinquished any advantage the two Bishops might have
given him, and seems to be playing
for a quick draw.

To his sorrow he learns that one
does not arrive at a quick draw with
Capablanca by exchanging pieces. It
was in the handling of the consequent positions that Capablanca
was unrivalled: they often turned
out to be not so simple as they
appeared.

15	Rf1-e1	Ra8-e8
16	Kg1-f1	f6-f5
17	Re1xe8	Rf8xe8
18	Ra1-e1	Re8xe1+
19	Kf1xe1	Nd7-f6
20	Ke1-d2	Nf6-e4+
21	Kd2-e3	Ne4-d6

If 21 . . . Ne4xg3 22 Ke3-f4 Ng3-f1
(ready to meet 23 Kf4xf5 with
23 . . . Nf1-e3+ winning a Pawn for
Black) 23 Bf3-e2 N1-d2

24 Kf4xf5, and White's King has
gained ground.

22 Bf3-e2   Kg8-f7

A preferable course was
22 . . . g7-g5, to keep White's King
at bay.

23 Ke3-f4   Kf7-f6

Ending 1

Position after 23 . . . Kf7-f6
Corzo

Capablanca to move

The position may look drawish, but
it is to Capablanca's liking; he often
manages to squeeze a win out of a
theoretical draw.

In discussing the relative worth
of Knight and Bishop, Capablanca
once remarked, 'The weaker the
player, the more terrible the Knight
is to him, but as a player increases
in strength the value of the Bishop
becomes more evident to him, and
of course there is, or should be, a
corresponding decrease in the value
of the Knight as compared to the
Bishop.'

24 h3-h4

Clearly, this is to prevent
24 . . . g7-g5+.

24 . . . g7-g6

Not at once 24 . . . h7-h6 (to support 25 . . . g7-g5+) as 25 h4-h5
stops that little scheme.

25 g3-g4 h7-h6

Still intent on advancing the Knight
Pawn, but he gets no chance to do
so.

26 g4-g5+ h6xg5+
27 h4xg5+ Kf6-e7
28 g2-g4 f5xg4
29 Be2-d3! Nd6-f5

This results in White's getting an
outside passed Pawn—an advantage,
as its threat to move on ties down
Black's pieces.

David Hooper suggests
29 . . . Ke7-f7 instead, when
30 Kf4xg4 Nd6-b5 31 c2-c3 Nb5-c7
offers good drawing chances.

30 Kf4xg4 Nf5xd4

After 30 . . . Ke7-e6 31 Bd3xf5+
g6xf5+ 32 Kg4-f4, Black will have
to abandon the Pawn as soon as his
Queen-side Pawns run out of moves.

31 Bd3xg6 c6-c5
32 Kg4-h5 Nd4-e6

Black must bring his pieces over to
the King-side to prevent the passed
Pawn from pushing on.

33 Kh5-h6 Ke7-f8
34 Bg6-f5 Ne6-g7

Black must be cautious. If he
becomes ambitious and moves the
Knight to d4, this could result:
35 Bf5-d7 Nd4xc2 36 g5-g6

(threatens 37 Kh6-h7) Kf8-g8
38 Bd7-e6+ Kg8-h8 39 g6-g7 mate.
     Or if 34 . . . Ne6-d4 35 Bf5-d7
Nd4-f3 (to get back to the King-
side) 36 g5-g6 Nf3-e5 37 g6-g7+
Kf8-g8 38 Bd7-e6+ Ne5-f7+
39 Kh6-g6, and White mates next
move.

35 Bf5-c8 b7-b6
36 g5-g6 d5-d4
37 b2-b3

This prevents the c-Pawn from advancing.

37 . . . Kf8-g8
38 a2-a4

And this holds back the b-Pawn.

38 . . . Kg8-f8
39 Bc8-g4 Ng7-e8
40 Kh6-h7 Ne8-g7
41 Kh7-h6 Ng7-e8
42 Bg4-e2 Ne8-g7
43 Be2-c4 Ng7-e8
44 Kh6-g5 Kf8-e7

If 44 . . . Kf8-g7 45 Bc4-b5 Ne8-d6
46 Bb5-d3 Nd6-e8 47 Kg5-f5, and
the King wanders over to the
Queen-side to pick up some Pawns,
his own passed Pawn being protected.

45 Kg5-f5 Ne8-g7+
46 Kf5-e5 Ng7-h5

Black dare not shift forces to the
Queen-side. If 46 . . . Ke7-d7 for
example, there follows 47 Ke5-f6
Ng7-e8+ 48 Kf6-f7 Ne8-d6+
49 Kf7-f8, and Black must give up
his Knight for the passed Pawn.

47 Bc4-e2 Nh5-g7
48 Ke5-d5 Ng7-e8

Game 2

On 48 . . . Ke7-d7 49 Be2-g4+ forces the King to an unpleasant decision: moving to e7 will lose the Queen-side Pawns, while moving to c7 will cost the Knight his life.

This is the position:

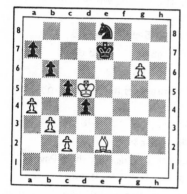

Position after 48 . . . Ng7-e8

49	Kd5-c6	Ne8-g7
50	Kc6-b7	Ke7-d6
51	Kb7xa7	Kd6-c7

52	Ka7-a6	Ng7-e8
53	Be2-f3	Ne8-g7
54	Bf3-d5	Ng7-e8

Or 54 . . . Ng7-f5 55 Bd5-e4 Nf5-g7 56 Ka6-b5 Ng7-e8 57 a4-a5 Ne8-d6+ 58 Kb5-a6 Nd6xe4 59 a5xb6+ Kc7-b8 60 g6-g7 Ne4-f6 61 Ka6-b5 Kb8-b7 62 Kb5xc5 Nf6-g8 63 Kc5xd4 and White wins (Hooper).

55	Bd5-f7	Ne8-g7

By this time the Knight must be heartily sick of moving from e8 to g7 and back again.

56	Ka6-b5	Ng7-f5
57	a4-a5	Nf5-d6+
58	Kb5-a6	b6xa5

No better is 58 . . . Nd6-f5 (to head off the Pawn) as 59 a5xb6+ Kc7-b8 60 Ka6-b5 breaks down all resistance.

59	g6-g7	**Black Resigns**

GAME 2

White J. R. Capablanca
Black J. Corzo
Eleventh Match Game, Havana, 1901

Queen's Pawn Opening

'Considering my age and experience,' says Capablanca, 'this game is quite remarkable; even the endgame was very well played by me.'

Señor Capablanca is unduly modest. The game is one of the most remarkable of his entire career. It surpasses any accomplishment by such other prodigies as Morphy, Reshevsky, and Fischer.

There is a beautiful Queen sacrifice in the midgame, but it is not meant to startle the natives. *The Queen is sacrificed as the quickest and most effective means of reaching a favourable endgame!* Truly a magnificent concept!

The endgame is conducted with elegance and accuracy—characteristics of Capablanca's play.

An impressive feature of this 60-move masterpiece is that it was dashed off in the singularly short time of 42 minutes!

1	d2-d4	d7-d5
2	Ng1-f3	c7-c5
3	e2-e3	Nb8-c6
4	b2-b3	e7-e6
5	Bc1-b2	Ng8-f6
6	Nb1-d2	c5xd4

There was no hurry to make this exchange. The recipe called for more development by 6 . . . Bf8-e7 or 6 . . . Bf8-d6.

| 7 | e3xd4 | Bf8-d6 |
| 8 | Bf1-d3 | 0-0 |

Black plays mechanically, and thereby misses a good opportunity. With 8 . . . Qd8-e7! he threatens to force a break in the center by 9 . . . e6-e5, as well as to get rid of White's potentially strong Queen Bishop by 9 . . . Bd6-a3.

| 9 | 0-0 | Nf6-h5 |

The object of this move is to induce the reply 10 g2-g3 (which does White no harm) but it loses time. Black should centralize instead by 9 . . . Nc6-b4 10 Bd3-e2 Nf6-e4 followed by 11 . . . f7-f5.

| 10 | g2-g3 | f7-f5 |
| 11 | Nf3-e5 | Nh5-f6 |

Of course not 11 . . . Bd6xe5 12 d4xe5 g7-g6 (on 12 . . . Qd8-e8 13 Bb2-a3 Nc6-e7 14 Ba3xe7 wins a piece for White) and Black's position has deteriorated, the black squares near his King being irremediably weak, while his remaining Bishop is virtually imprisoned by the many Pawns standing on white squares.

| 12 | f2-f4 | Bd6xe5 |
| 13 | f4xe5 | Nf6-g4 |

Or 13 . . . Nf6-e4 14 Bd3xe4 f5xe4 (but not 14 . . . d5xe4 when 15 Nd2-c4, threatening to plant itself at d6, is too painful to bear) 15 Rf1xf8+ Qd8xf8 16 Qd1-e2, and White maintains the pressure.

14	Qd1-e2	Qd8-b6
15	Nd2-f3	Bc8-d7
16	a2-a3	

This wards off the menace of 16 . . . Nc6-b4 followed by removing one of the Bishops.

16	. . .	Kg8-h8
17	h2-h3	Ng4-h6
18	Qe2-f2	Nh6-f7
19	Kg1-g2	g7-g5

Strange as it may seem, this move renders Black's King vulnerable to attack on the long diagonal by the Bishop hidden away at b2.

| 20 | g3-g4! | Nc6-e7 |

This is better than 20 . . . f5-f4, when 21 h3-h4 opens up the Rook file for the benefit of White's pieces.

21	Qf2-e3	Rf8-g8
22	Ra1-e1	Ne7-g6
23	g4xf5	Ng6-f4+
24	Kg2-h2	Nf4xd3
25	Qe3xd3	e6xf5
26	c2-c4!	

Blacks' Queen Pawn must be destroyed! Once it is gone, White's pieces can release their pent-up power.

26	...	Qb6-e6
27	c4xd5	Qe6xd5
28	e5-e6!	

Begins a grand combination. To checkmate? No, checkmate appears in the notes. The point of the combination, which includes a Queen sacrifice, is to clear away some pieces, and leave White with the superior endgame.

| 28 | ... | Bd7-b5 |

Black avoids the capture by 28 ... Bd7xe6, when 29 Re1xe6 Qd5xe6 30 d4-d5 dis.ch is the grievous consequence.

| 29 | Qd3xb5! | |

Beautiful!

29	...	Qd5xb5
30	d4-d5+	Rg8-g7
31	e6xf7	h7-h6
32	Nf3-d4	Qb5xf1

If 32 ... Qb5-d7 (so that the Queen stays on the diagonal leading to e8) the win would be achieved, according to Capablanca, by 33 Nd4xf5 Qd7xf7 34 Bb2xg7+ Kh8-h7 35 Re1-e7 Qf7xd5 36 Bg7-e5+ Kh7-g6 37 Re7-g7+ Kg6-h5 38 Nf5-g3+ Kh5-h4 39 Rf1-f4+ g5xf4 40 Rg7-g4 mate! (Exquisite!)

33	Re1xf1	Rg7xf7
34	Rf1xf5	Rf7xf5
35	Nd4xf5+	Kh8-h7

Ending 2

Position after 35 ... Kh8-h7
Corzo

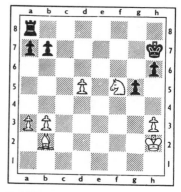

Capablanca to move

Capablanca conducts the ending with the refined technique of a mature master.

He has a slight material advantage with two minor pieces against a Rook, while the passed Pawn is a positional advantage, as its advance must be prevented at all cost.

Capablanca plans to keep Black's King from approaching the Pawn, while his own King will move towards the center to assist its advance.

| 36 | Nf5-e7! | |

Cuts the King off from the center. The Knight and Bishop control all the exits, in fact.

| 36 | ... | Ra8-f8 |

Threatens to win a piece by 37 ... Rf8-f2+.

If 36 ... Ra8-e8 instead, 37 d5-d6 Re8-d8 38 Bb2-e5, and White brings his King up the board.

| 37 | Kh2-g2 | h6-h5 |

38	d5-d6	g5-g4
39	h3xg4	h5xg4
40	Bb2-e5	

It would not do to attack the Pawn, as after 40 Kg2-g3 Rf8-f3+ 41 Kg3xg4 Rf3xb3, and Black has vigorous counterplay.

| 40 | ... | Kh7-h6 |

Now 40 ... Rf8-f3 has little effect. There could follow 41 Be5-d4 Rf3-d3 42 Ne7-f5 Kh7-g6 (or 42 ... Rd3-f3) 43 d6-d7, and White wins.

| 41 | d6-d7! | |

Threatens 42 Be5-c7 and 43 d7-d8 (Q), winning the Rook for the Pawn.

| 41 | ... | Rf8-d8 |

Does this win the precious Pawn?

| 42 | Ne7-g8+! | |

Not quite, as we shall see. Corzo himself says of this move, 'Otra jugada de maestro!'

| 42 | ... | Rd8xg8 |

Or 42 ... Kh6-g6 43 Ng8-f6 Kg6-f7 44 Be5-c7, and Black must give up his Rook.

43	Be5-c7	Kh6-g6
44	d7-d8(Q)	Rg8xd8
45	Bc7xd8	b7-b5
46	Kg2-f2	

Did Capablanca miss a quicker win? If 46 Kg2-g3 Kg6-f5 47 b3-b4 Kf5-e4 48 Kg3xg4 Ke4-d4 49 Kg4-f4 Kd4-c3 50 Kf4-e4 Kc3-b3 51 Ke4-d4 Kb3xa3 52 Bd8-a5, and White wins.

Perhaps he did, but Capablanca saw one line of play leading to a

win, and that was enough. There was no reason to look for another way.

46	...	Kg6-f5
47	Kf2-e3	Kf5-e5
48	Ke3-d3	Ke5-d5
49	Kd3-c3	g4-g3
50	Bd8-h4	g3-g2
51	Bh4-f2	

Clearly, the Bishop is to restrain the passed Pawn, while the King will try to get to Black's Q-side Pawns.

| 51 | ... | a7-a5 |
| 52 | b3-b4 | Kd5-e4 |

Or 52 ... a5-a4 53 Kc3-d3 Kd5-e5 54 Bf2-g1 Ke5-d5 55 Bg1-d4 Kd5-e6 56 Kd3-e4 Ke6-d6 57 Bd4-e5+ Kd6-e6 58 Be5-h2 Ke6-d7 59 Ke4-d5, and White wins the Q-side Pawns.

| 53 | Bf2-b6 | |

White is not tempted into capturing hastily, for if 53 b4xa5 Ke4-d5 follows and White cannot win, as his Bishop does not control the Queening square a8.

53	...	Ke4-d5
54	Kc3-d3	Kd5-c6
55	Bb6-g1	Kc6-d5
56	Bg1-h2	Kd5-c6
57	Kd3-d4	a5-a4

Corzo has failed to tempt his opponent into taking the Rook Pawn, but he still has a little trick up his sleeve.

| 58 | Kd4-e5 | Kc6-b6 |
| 59 | Ke5-d5 | Kb6-a6 |

Corzo's last hope is that Capablanca

will make the natural move
60 Kd5-c6, when the reply forces a
draw thus: 60 . . . g2-g1(Q)
61 Bh2xg1, and Black is stalemated!

But Capablanca was not to be
caught by traps, neither as a child
prodigy, nor in his adult chess career.

| 60 | Kd5-c5! | **Black Resigns** |

It is worth repeating that Capablanca
took less than a minute per move
for the whole of this astonishing
game, Queen sacrifice and all!

GAME 3

White F. J. Marshall
Black J. R. Capablanca
Fifth Match Game, New York,
1909

Queen's Gambit Declined
Nobody but nobody ever used the
tactical weapon of *zwischenzug* to
such good effect as Capablanca.

This witty interposition of an
unexpected move before making an
obvious reply (such as a recapture)
usually changes the state of affairs.
There may be no intent to discon-
cert the opponent, but it often gives
him a bit of a jolt.

Capablanca's games abound in
these clever little *zwischenzüge*, and
they offer evidence of the thought
he gave to even the most natural
moves before making them.

1	d2-d4	d7-d5
2	c2-c4	e7-e6
3	Nb1-c3	Ng8-f6
4	Bc1-g5	Bf8-e7
5	e2-e3	Nf6-e4

Capablanca knew little opening
theory at that time, but was
impressed by Lasker's success with
this move against Marshall, and
decided to try it himself.

| 6 | Bg5xe7 | Qd8xe7 |
| 7 | Bf1-d3 | |

A better course was 7 c4xd5
Ne4xc3 8 b2xc3 e6xd5
9 Qd1-b3, and White's pressure on
the Knight file makes it difficult for
Black to develop his Bishop.

7	. . .	Ne4xc3
8	b2xc3	Nb8-d7
9	Ng1-f3	0-0
10	Qd1-c2	h7-h6
11	0-0	c7-c5
12	Rf1-e1	d5xc4
13	Bd3xc4	b7-b6
14	Qc2-e4	

Capablanca points out that this
attractive-looking move not only
gains White no advantage, but
practically compels Black to post
his pieces to good effect—his
Bishop at b7, the Knight at f6, and
the Rooks at c8 and d8, from
which squares they can attack the
center.

14	. . .	Ra8-b8
15	Bc4-d3	Nd7-f6
16	Qe4-f4	Bc8-b7
17	e3-e4	Rf8-d8
18	Ra1-d1	Rb8-c8

'Black's moves are timed,' says Hermann Helms, 'with a precision that discloses the mind of a master player.'

19   Re1-e3

White's position looks imposing, but a few sharp moves by Capablanca expose the weaknesses.

19	. . .	c5xd4
20	c3xd4	Rc8-c3
21	Bd3-b1	g7-g5!
22	Nf3xg5	

Rather than submit tamely to the loss of a Pawn by 22 Qf4-g3 Rc3xe3 23 f2xe3 Nf6xe4, Marshall takes his chances on stirring up an attack by giving up a Knight for two Pawns.

But, as the old novelists used to say, he reckons without his host.

22	. . .	Rc3xe3
23	Qf4xe3	

On 23 f2xe3 Nf6-h5 followed by 24 . . . Qe7xg5 wins quickly.

23	. . .	Nf6-g4
24	Qe3-g3	Qe7xg5
25	h2-h4	

If 25 Qg3-c7 Rd8-c8 26 Qc7xb7 Rc8-c1 27 Qb7-b8+ Kg8-g7 28 Rd1-f1 Qg5-d2, and the threats of mate by 29 . . . Qd2xf2+, or by 29 . . . Rc1xf1+, cannot both be parried.

25	. . .	Qg5-g7

26	Qg3-c7	Rd8xd4

Although this pretty move led to a win, Capablanca commented objectively that the better move, overlooked by all the analysts, was 26 . . . Qg7-f6, whereby the King is provided with a flight-square at g7. This would have spared him some trouble.

'I was highly praised,' says he, 'because of the excellence of my play in this position, while in reality I could have done better.'

27	Qc7-b8+	Kg8-h7
28	e4-e5+	Bb7-e4
29	Rd1xd4	Be4xb1
30	Qb8xa7	

Ending 3

Position after 30 Qb8xa7

Capablanca to move

Marshall

Black has a bit of material advantage, with Knight and Bishop against a Rook.

He will try to initiate an attack on the King, while keeping a

Ending 3

weather eye open on White's potentially dangerous Queen Rook Pawn.

30 ... Ng4xe5

Threatens 31 ... Ne5-f3+ winning a whole Rook.

31 Rd4-f4 Bb1-e4

Now the idea is 32 ... Ne5-f3+ 33 Kg1-f1 (if 33 Kg1-h1, Qg7-a1 mate) 33 ... Qg7-a1+ 34 Kf1-e2 Qa1-e1 mate.

Meanwhile the Bishop is tabu, as after 32 Rf4xe4, there follows 32 ... Ne5-f3+ 33 Kg1-f1 (if 33 Kg1-h1, Qg7-a1+ and mate next) 33 ... Nf3-d2+, and the Rook comes off.

32 g2-g3 Ne5-f3+
33 Kg1-g2 f7-f5
34 Qa7xb6

An attempt to simplify instead by exchanging Queens leads to disaster, thus: 34 Qa7xg7+ Kh7xg7 35 Rf4xf3 Kg7-g6, and White is in *zugzwang*. Sooner or later he will have to play g3-g4, when the reply ... f5-f4 or ... f5xg4 will win the pinned Rook.

34 ... Nf3xh4+
35 Kg2-h2

If 35 Kg2-h3, Qg7-a1 would win at once (Capablanca).

35 ... Nh4-f3+
36 Rf4xf3

White decides to fight it out with a passed Pawn against a Bishop, the alternative being 36 Kh2-g2 Nf3-g5+ followed by 37 ... Qg7-a1 winning.

36 ... Be4xf3
37 Qb6xe6 Bf3-e4
38 f2-f3 Be4-d3

39 Qe6-d5 Qg7-b2+
40 Kh2-g1 Bd3-b1

This pretty problem-like move provides a hiding place for the Queen at a1.

'It is from now on' says Capablanca, 'that it can be said that I played well. The ending is worth studying.'

41 a2-a4 Qb2-a1

The Queen now attacks the passed Pawn, and at the same time threatens to win the Queen by a discovered check.

42 Qd5-b7+

But not 42 Qd5-f7+, as 42 ... Qa1-g7 forces an exchange of Queens or wins the g-Pawn.

42 ... Kh7-g6
43 Qb7-b6+

White checks at this square and not at c6 for two reasons: (a) he wants the Queen on a black square, out of range of a possible discovered attack by the Bishop, and (b) he wants to protect his Rook Pawn when it moves up a square.

The importance of the fact that the Queen is now at b6 and not at c6 will be seen later, and is proof that *Marshall did not miss a forced mate.*

43 ... Kg6-h5
44 Kg1-h2 Bb1-a2

This is the situation:

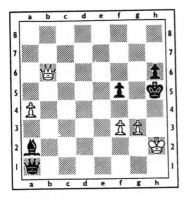

Position after 44 ... Bb1-a2

It is at this point that the critics, *placing White's Queen erroneously at c6,* stated that Marshall missed a mate or win of the Queen by 45 Qc6-e8+ Kh5-g5 46 f3-f4+ Kg5-g4 (or 46 ... Kg4-f6 47 Qe8-h8+) 47 Qe8-e2 mate.

The position appeared in *Chess Review* in June 1933 in Brand's column *Mistakes of the Masters*, in Du Mont's *Basis of Combination,* in Gutmayer's *Schach-Praktiker,* in *Chess* for March of 1951, in Abrahams's *The Chess Mind,* in Alexander's *Penguin Book of Chess Positions*, and I have no doubt in many other chess books and chess columns.

Typical is such a reaction as that of Abrahams for example, who said, 'Thus we find Marshall ruining one of the few opportunities given him by Capablanca.'

It struck me as strange that Capablanca should fall into a mate, and just as strange that Marshall should miss it. For Marshall had as

keen an eye for a mate in five as anyone that ever lived. I have seen him solve in a twinkling problems that baffled other masters.

It would seem that critics copy from one another, without looking up the original score of the games before finding fault with the players concerned.

For the sake of the record: Marshall never missed a golden opportunity to checkmate Capablanca, as the latter never gave him the chance to do so.

Now, back to New York in 1909, and the fifth game of the match . . .

45   Qb6-b5

Now there is a threat of 46 Qb5-e8+ leading to mate, as well as the brutal one of instant mate by 46 Qb5xf5+.

45	...	Kh5-g6
46	a4-a5	Qa1-d4
47	Qb5-c6+	Qd4-f6
48	Qc6-e8+	Qf6-f7
49	Qe8-a4	Qf7-e6
50	a5-a6	

White has no more checks, and this is all that's left.

50   ...   Qe6-e2+

But Black has a powerful check on tap, and he uses it.

51	Kh2-h3	Ba2-d5
52	a6-a7	Bd5xf3
53	**White Resigns**	

There are still no checks, and mate in two is threatened.

'In the handling of this endgame,' says Hermann Helms in the *American Chess Bulletin*, 'Capablanca has provided a rare treat.'

GAME 4

White F. J. Marshall
Black J. R. Capablanca
Twenty-third Match Game, New York, 1909

Queen's Gambit Declined
Capablanca makes it look easy! With the smooth effortless skill of a born magician, Capablanca makes a few deft passes, and the position on the board changes right before your eyes!

In just a few brief moves, Capablanca manages to obtain a Queen-side majority of Pawns. This slight positional advantage is enough, in his talented hands, to be decisive.

The Pawns advance at every opportunity, and their steady progress eventually compels Marshall to give up a piece to prevent one of them from Queening.

The continuation from that point on is unusually interesting. In only fourteen more moves, Capablanca, who has won a Bishop for two Pawns, weaves an air-tight mating net around Marshall's King.

1	d2-d4	d7-d5
2	c2-c4	e7-e6
3	Nb1-c3	c7-c5

Highly recommended by Tarrasch, this defence was used to good effect by Mieses in his second match game with Rubinstein.

4	c4xd5	e6xd5
5	Ng1-f3	Nb8-c6
6	g2-g3	Bc8-e6

Improving on Capablanca may be lèse-majesté, but I would suggest instead the development of the K-side by 6 . . . Ng8-f6 7 Bf1-g2 Bf8-e7 8 0-0 0-0, as preferable.

7	Bf1-g2	Bf8-e7
8	0-0	Ng8-f6
9	Bc1-g5	

The stronger line, discovered years later, is 9 d4xc5 Be7xc5 10 Nc3-a4 Bc5-e7 11 Bc1-e3 0-0 12 Nf3-d4, and White's position is superior.

9	. . .	Nf6-e4!

A good move which frees Black's game.

10	Bg5xe7	Qd8xe7

'Would anyone defending against the Queen's Gambit want a better position than this after ten moves?' says Tarrasch proudly in justification of his pet line, the Tarrasch Defence.

11	Nf3-e5	

But not 11 d4xc5 Ne4xc3 12 b2xc3 Qe7xc5, and White's Q-side is broken up.

In the Rubinstein-Mieses game, White's 11 Ra1-c1 led to play which enabled Mieses to exploit his positional advantages—pressure on the open file, and a Q-side Pawn majority. The continuation is interesting, the more so as Rubinstein the Giant-killer is not often beaten so quickly and decisively.

The game (after 11 Ra1-c1) went

on like this: 11 . . . Ne4xc3
12 Rc1xc3 c5-c4 13 Nf3-e5 0-0
14 b2-b3 Qe7-b4! 15 Qd1-d2
Ra8-c8 16 Rf1-d1 b7-b5 17 f2-f4
Nc6xe5 18 f4xe5 a7-a5 19 b3xc4
Rc8xc4 20 Rc3-b3 (if 20 Rc3xc4
Qb4xd2 21 Rd1xd2 d5xc4, and
Black will soon have two connected
passed Pawns) 20 . . . Qb4-a4
21 e2-e3 Rf8-c8 22 Bg2-f1 Rc4-c2
(the almighty seventh rank!)
23 Qd2-e1 b5-b4 24 Bf1-d3
Qa4xa2!, and White resigned in
view of what might follow:
25 Bd3xc2 Rc8xc2 26 Rd1-b1
Rc2-g2+ 27 Kg1-f1 Be6-h3, and
White is helpless to ward off the
threats of mate.

| 11 | . . . | Nc6xd4! |

This is better than trying to break
up White's Pawns by 11 . . . Ne4xc3
12 b2xc3 Nc6xe5 13 d4xe5 Qe7-d7
14 f2-f4 0-0 15 Qd1-c2, and White
has a respectable game.

| 12 | Nc3xe4 | d5xe4 |
| 13 | e2-e3 | |

But not 13 Bg2xe4 Be6-h3, and
suddenly three of White's pieces are
attacked.

13	. . .	Nd4-f3+
14	Ne5xf3	e4xf3
15	Qd1xf3	0-0
16	Rf1-c1	

Marshall avoids 16 Qf3xb7, as after
16 . . . Qe7xb7 17 Bg2xb7 Ra8-b8
18 Be7-e4 Rb7xb2 Black has a
passed Pawn, and a Rook on the
seventh.

| 16 | . . . | Ra8-b8 |
| 17 | Qf3-e4 | |

Threatens 18 Bg2-h3, which would
either lead to an exchange of
Bishops, or induce a weakening of
Black's Pawn structure by
18 . . . f7-f5.

| 17 | . . . | Qe7-c7 |
| 18 | Rc1-c3 | |

Ending 4

Position after 18 Rc1-c3

Capablanca to move

Marshall

Capablanca has a slight positional
advantage for the endgame in his
Queen-side Pawn majority—in most
cases a more effective weapon than
a King-side Pawn majority.

Black plans to get his Queen-side
Pawns rolling at every opportunity.
An exchange of Pawns leaves two
Pawns to one, and a further
exchange will leave him with one
Pawn to none.

This last Pawn might then either
promote to a Queen, or cost the
opponent a piece to prevent it from
doing so.

18 ... b7-b5

Capablanca starts playing out his trumps—the Queen-side Pawn majority. From now on the Pawns will push on every chance they get.

19 a2-a3

Not only to prevent 19 . . . b5-b4, when 20 a3xb4 Rb8xb4 21 Qe4xb4 would be the penalty, but in order to mobilize the Queen Rook.

19 ... c5-c4

20 Bg2-f3

White avoids 20 b2-b3, when 20 . . . Qc7-a5 attacks the Rook and also threatens to capture the b-Pawn. White would be compelled to advance by 21 b3-b4, leaving his opponent with a protected passed Pawn.

20 ... Rf8-d8

Takes command of the only open file. So small an advantage is hardly enough to be decisive, but it is the accumulation of these little advantages that brings an opponent to the breaking point and forces capitulation.

21 Ra1-d1 Rd8xd1+

22 Bf3xd1 Rb8-d8

Capablanca has full command of the board. His play is an example of how slight advantages should be utilized (Lasker).

23 Bd1-f3 g7-g6

A necessary precaution, as the King may require air sooner or later.

It also renders feasible the continuation 24 . . . Be6-f5 followed by 25 . . . Rd8-d2. Lacking the Pawn move, there is this dreadful

possibility: 23 . . . Rd8-d2 24 Rc3-c2 Be6-d5 25 Qe4-e8 mate.

24 Qe4-c6

Of course not 24 Rc3-c2 (to prevent invasion of the seventh rank by the enemy Rook) as 24 . . . Be6-f5 wins a whole live Rook.

24 ... Qc7-e5!

Black avoids the immediate exchange of Queens, as he must then lose a move in protecting his b-Pawn.

25 Qc6-e4 Qe5xe4

26 Bf3xe4

According to the authorities, White should have the superior position, as his Bishop controls squares of a different colour than do his Pawns.

Black, in violation of the precepts, has a Bishop hampered by his Pawns, nearly all of which occupy squares of the same colour.

Theory is theory, but life, alas, refuses to conform. The great master relies on his own instincts, makes his own rules, and opens up new worlds.

26 ... Rd8-d1+!

The Rook swoops down, to get behind the enemy Pawns.

27 Kg1-g2 a7-a5

The Queen-side Pawns move ahead every chance they get. Notice that Black maintains a strong initiative, even though Queens are off the board.

28 Rc3-c2 b5-b4

29 a3xb4 a5xb4

30 Be4-f3

If White tries 30 Kg2-f3 (centralizing his King, and threatening to
drive the Rook off) he might fall
victim to this strange contretemps:
30 . . . b4-b3 31 Rc2-e2 Be6-h3!,
when suddenly his Rook faces
capture by 32 . . . Bh3-f1, and has
no saving move!

30   . . .   Rd1-b1

31   Bf3-e2

Anticipates 31 . . . c4-c3 32 b2xc3
b4-b3 33 Rc2-d2 b3-b2 (threatens
to Queen in a hurry by
34 . . . Rb1-g1+, sacrificing the
Rook and then pushing the Pawn)
34 Be2-d3, and the precious Pawn
is lost.

But . . .

31   . . .   b4-b3!

This is the proper Pawn push!

32   Rc2-d2

Marshall avoids 32 Rc2-c3 Rb1xb2
33 Be2xc4, as 33 . . . Rb2-c2 wins
by a neat sleight of hand.

32   . . .   Rb1-c1

With the powerful threat of
33 . . . Rc1-c2, a move which must
be prevented at all cost.

33   Be2-d1

This seems to do the trick. But
Capablanca has two strings to his
bow in the (potential) passed
Pawn's lust to expand.

33   . . .   c4-c3!

34   b2xc3   b3-b2!

And now the Rook must abandon
his Bishop, as the dangerous Pawn
must be destroyed.

35   Rd2xb2

Restraining the Pawn instead by
35 Bd1-c2 loses instantly by the
capture 35 . . . Rc1xc2.

35   . . .   Rc1xd1

36   Rb2-c2

Capablanca's treatment of the ending from this point on is a revelation.

While keeping White busy in the
defence of his passed Pawn, Capablanca whips up an attack which
drives the King into a mating net.

All this, done with so little
material, and in so few moves,
makes this ending the very best of
its kind. It will repay study by
master as well as by amateur.

This is the position:

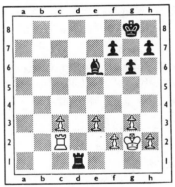

Position after 36 Rb2-c2

36   . . .   Be6-f5

Banishes the Rook from the Bishop
file—and the protection of the
Pawn . . .

37   Rc2-b2   Rd1-c1

And enables Black to occupy the
file—and attack the Pawn.

38   Rb2-b3

The Rook must assume a passive

position, in order to save the Pawn.

| 38 | ... | Bf5-e4+ |

39 Kg2-h3

There is no choice, as 39 f2-f3 Rc1-c2+ costs White a Pawn.

| 39 | ... | Rc1-c2 |

The Rook is in an ideal position— on the seventh rank, and behind the passed Pawn.

| 40 | f2-f4 | h7-h5 |

Every move a picture!

This begins the hemming-in process, and institutes a threat of sudden mate by 41 ... Be4-f5+ 42 Kh3-h4 Rc2xh2+ 43 Kh4-g5 Kg8-g7.

41	g3-g4	h5xg4+
42	Kh3xg4	Rc2xh2
43	Rb3-b4	f7-f5+
44	Kg4-g3	

Or 44 Kg4-g5 Kg8-g7, and mate by 45 ... Rh2-h5 will follow.

| 45 | ... | Rh2-e2 |

| 45 | Rb4-c4 | Re2xe3+ |
| 46 | Kg3-h4 | Kg8-g7 |

Obviously intending to surround the King.

| 47 | Rc4-c7+ | Kg7-f6 |

Relentlessly precise to the last! On 47 ... Kg7-h6, the reply 48 Rc7-e7 pins the Bishop. If then 48 ... Re3xc3, 49 Re7-e6 Be4-g2 50 Re6xg6+!, and White either forces a draw by stalemate or wins the Bishop.

48	Rc7-d7	Be4-g2
49	Rd7-d6+	Kf6-g7
50	White Resigns	

If 50 Rd6-d7+, Kg7-h6 followed by 51 ... Re3-h3 is mate, or if 50 Kh4-g5, Re3-g3+ 51 Kg5-h4 Rg3-g4 is mate.

Capablanca himself says of this game, 'I was able to wind up the match with one of the most accurate games I have ever played.'

GAME 5

White J. R. Capablanca
Black A. Kreymbourg
New York, 1910

Queen's Pawn Opening

Capablanca plays so quiet an opening that it would require a miracle to make something out of it.

Somehow a miracle does appear! Capablanca exchanges a piece here, and a piece there, when ... lo and behold! The scene has changed, and the position on the board transformed to an endgame with all four Rooks assuming the principal roles while Capablanca, as befitting to the magician in charge, is endowed with a slight advantage.

| 1 | d2-d4 | d7-d5 |
| 2 | Ng1-f3 | Ng8-f6 |

3   Bc1-f4

The development of this Bishop is usually delayed until the opponent has played . . . e7-e6, locking in his Queen Bishop.

The masters discovered long ago, though, that the most aggressive moves do not always bring about the best results. A move that is fairly good (such as this one) but less analyzed, is likely to throw the opponent on his own resources, and increase one's winning prospects.

3   . . .   e7-e6

But this is too meek! Black should try to seize the initiative by 3 . . . c7-c5, with this likely continuation: 4 e2-e3 Qd8-b6 (with unremitting pressure on the Queen-side) 5 Qd1-c1 Nb8-c6 6 c2-c3 Bc8-f5 7 d4xc5 (in order to develop the Queen Knight with gain of time) Qb6xc5 8 Nb1-d2 Ra8-c8 9 Nd2-b3 Qc5-b6 10 Qc1-d2 e7-e6 11 Bf1-d3 Bf5-e4, with equality at least, as Maroczy (with Black) demonstrated in his game against Capablanca at New York in 1924.

4	e2-e3	c7-c5
5	c2-c3	Nb8-c6
6	Bf1-d3	Bf8-d6
7	Bf4xd6	Qd8xd6
8	Nb1-d2	e6-e5
9	d4xe5	Nc6xe5
10	Nf3xe5	Qd6xe5
11	Bd3-b5+	Bc8-d7
12	Qd1-a4	Qe5-c7

Necessary in order to castle. Clearly Black must not play 12 . . . Bd7xb5, as 13 Qa4xb5+ costs him a Pawn.

13	0-0-0	0-0
14	Bb5xd7	Nf6xd7

And here if 14 . . . Qc7xd7 15 Qa4xd7 Nf6xd7 16 Nd2-e4 d5xe4 (otherwise a Pawn is lost) 17 Rd1xd7, and White has a Rook on the seventh and winning chances.

15	Nd2-f3	Qc7-c6

This looks plausible enough, as the alternative 15 . . . Nd7-f6 condemns Black to wait passively for his opponent to work up an attack.

16	Qa4xc6	b7xc6
17	Nf3-d2	Nd7-e5

With a little threat of winning the exchange by 18 . . . Ne5-d3+ followed by 19 . . . Nd3xf2, striking at both Rooks.

18	Kc1-c2	c5-c4
19	Rh1-f1	f7-f5
20	Nd2-f3	Ne5xf3

Black should have accepted the challenge and played 20 . . . Ne5-d3, as it offered more practical chances than did a simplified position, in which Capablanca was supremely eminent. The Knight could not be easily dislodged, any such attempt involving certain risks.

A likely continuation was this: 21 b2-b3 Ra8-b8 22 b3xc4 d5xc4 23 Rd1-b1 (to stop mate on the move) Rb8xb1 24 Rf1xb1 Nd3xf2 25 Nf3-e5 Nf2-g4 26 Ne5xc4 Ng4xh2 27 Rb1-b7 Rf8-f7, and White can either take the draw by 28 Rb7-b8+ Rf7-f8 29 Rb8-b7 Rf8-f7, or try for a risky win by 28 Rb7xf7 Kg8xf7 29 Nc4-e5+ Kf7-e6 30 Ne5xc6.

21   g2xf3   Ra8-e8

Ending 5

Position after 21 . . . Ra8-e8
Kreymbourg

Capablanca to move

Material is even, but White has a positional advantage:

(a) His King stands closer to the center.

(b) His Rooks have more potential for attack. One Rook bears down on Black's center Pawns, the other is ready to seize an open file.

(c) His Pawn position is superior, Black's center Pawns being unable to move without loss.

Capablanca plans to activate his Rooks, break up the enemy Pawn structure, and then bring strong pressure to bear on the isolated Queen Rook Pawn.

22   Rd1-d4!

The first step is to prevent 22 . . . f5-f4, which could now be met by 23 e3-e4, followed by 24 Rf1-d1.

22   . . .   Rf8-f6

Evidently to continue with 23 . . . Rf6-g6, and then on to the seventh rank.

23   b2-b3   c4xb3+

24   a2xb3   Kg8-f7

25   Kc2-d3

Apparently with the idea of breaking up the center Pawns, but Capablanca has something else in mind.

25   . . .   Re8-e7

26   Rf1-a1   Kf7-e6

A natural move, which Capablanca terms a mistake. He recommends instead an attack on the Rook Pawn by 26 . . . g7-g5 (not at once 26 . . . Rf6-h6, which could be met by 27 h2-h4) followed by 27 . . . Rf6-h6

27   Ra1-a6

Fixes one Pawn (at a7) whilst attacking another (at c6).

27   . . .   Re7-c7

But not 27 . . . Ke6-d6, when 28 c3-c4 wins a Pawn—or two.

28   Rd4-a4   g7-g5

Initiates a counter-attack on the K-side.

The defensive 28 . . . Rf6-f7 instead would allow 29 f3-f4 in reply, paralyzing Black's position completely.

29   h2-h4!

Much better than 29 Ra6xa7 Rc7xa7 30 Ra4xa7 Rf6-h6, and Black regains his Pawn with advantage.

29   . . .   g5-g4

It would be fatal to play

29 . . . g5xh4, then 30 Ra4xh4 would render Black's game desperate. His King could not retreat without the loss of the King Rook Pawn, and his Rooks could do little. His Pawns? If he continued with 30 . . . h7-h6, White's response would be 31 b3-b4. The threat of winning a Pawn by 32 b4-b5, supplemented by 33 Kd3-d4 if need be, and the further entrance of the King at c5 or e5 should be decisive.

30   Kd3-e2   g4xf3+

As good as there is. Attacking the Rook Pawn is out of the question, as after 30 . . . Rf6-h6 31 f3xg4 Rh6xh4 32 g4xf5+ wins the unfortunate Rook, while 30 . . . h7-h5 is countered with 31 f3-f4, tying Black up completely.

(a) His Pawns would be unable to move.

(b) His Rooks would be tied to the defence of the Queen Rook Pawn.

(c) His King could not retreat without breaking the line of communication of his Rooks.

Capablanca's winning procedure (after 30 . . . Rf6-f7) could be 31 b3-b4, threatening to win a Pawn by 32 b4-b5, or 31 Ke2-d3 followed by 32 Kd3-d4, in preparation for the Pawn push.

31	**Ke2xf3**	**Rf6-f7**
32	**Kf3-e2**	**Ke6-d6**
33	**b3-b4**	**Rc7-b7**
34	**h4-h5**	

A slight inaccuracy, according to Capablanca himself. He should have played (he says) 34 f2-f4, and if

then 34 . . . Rf7-g7 35 h4-h5 Rg7-g2+ 36 Ke2-d3 Rg2-h2 37 Ra6xa7 Rb7xa7 38 Ra4xa7 Rh2xh5 39 Ra7-a6, with winning chances.

This is the position:

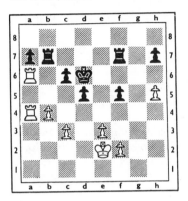

Position after 34 h4-h5

34	**. . .**	**h7-h6**

Black misses an opportunity to draw by 34 . . . f5-f4. If then 35 e3xf4, Rb7-e7+ 36 Ke2-f1 Rf7xf4 37 Ra6xa7 Re7-e3!

35	**f2-f4**	**Rf7-g7**
36	**Ke2-d3**	**Rg7-e7**
37	**Ra4-a1**	**Re7-g7**
38	**Kd3-d4**	**Rg7-g2**

Actually threatening (believe it or not) mate on the move!

Such is the power of an aggressive Rook!

39	**Ra6-a2**	**Rb7-g7**
40	**Kd4-d3!**	**Rg2xa2**
41	**Ra1xa2**	**Rg7-e7**

There is no hope in 41 . . . Rg7-g1 42 Ra2-a6! Rg1-d1+ 43 Kd3-c2 Rd1-h1 44 b4-b5 Rh1xh5 45 Ra6xc6+ Kd6-d7 46 Rc6-a6, and the rest is an easy win for White.

42	Ra2-g2	Re7-e6
43	Rg2-g7	

After all its threatening gestures on the Q-side, White's energetic Rook rushes to force a decision on the K-side.

43	. . .	Re6-e7
44	Rg7-g8	c6-c5

Practically throwing himself on the sword, but he cannot save his Pawns.

The threat is 45 Rg8-h8 Re7-e6 46 Rh8-f8 winning the King Bishop Pawn. If Black defends his Rook Pawn by 44 . . . Re7-h7 (a dreadful

spot for the Rook) 45 Rg8-g6+ Kd6-d7 46 Rg6-f6 still wins the Bishop Pawn.

45	Rg8-g6+	Re7-e6
46	b4xc5+	Kd6-d7
47	Rg6-g7+	Kd7-c6

Loses quickly, but there is no hope in 47 . . . Re6-e7 48 c5-c6+ Kd7-d6 (or 48 . . . Kd7-d8 49 Rg7-g6, and the threats of 50 Rg6xh6, or 50 Rg6-d6+ or 50 Rg6-f6 are too much to meet) 49 Rg7-g6+ Re7-e6 50 c6-c7!, and Black must give up his Rook.

48	Rg7xa7	Kc6xc5
49	Ra7-f7	Black Resigns

A highly instructive Rook ending.

GAME 6

White J. R. Capablanca (blindfold)
Black J. Corzo, R. Blanco &
R. Portela
Havana, 1910

Center Counter Defence
Capablanca rarely played blindfold chess, but when he did so he produced games that crackled with original ideas.

Clever little combinations mark the midgame play, while the ending is conducted with the casual elegance characteristic of his style.

1	e2-e4	d7-d5
2	e4xd5	Qd8xd5
3	Nb1-c3	Qd5-a5
4	Bf1-c4	Ng8-f6
5	d2-d3	Bc8-g4

6	f2-f3!	

Better than 6 Ng1-f3, as this Pawn and the g-Pawn will cut down the Bishop's mobility, while the King Knight can develop at e2.

6	. . .	Bg4-f5
7	Ng1-e2	c7-c6

Black clears a way for the return home of his Queen, whose safety is threatened by 8 Bc1-d2 followed by 9 Nc3-d5 Qa5-c5 (on 9 . . . Qa5-a4 10 Bc4-b5+ Qa4xb5 11 Nd5xc7+ does the trick)

10 Bd2-b4 Qc5-c6 11 Bc4-b5 and
the Queen is caught, as
11 . . . Qc6xb5 allows the Knight
fork by 12 Nd5xc7+.

8	g2-g4!	Bf5-c8

Dispirited, the Bishop goes back
home.

9	Bc1-d2	Qa5-c7

The Queen, too, prudently retreats.

10	Ne2-g3	e7-e6
11	Qd1-e2	Nb8-d7
12	g4-g5!	Nf6-g8

Surprisingly enough, the Knight too
must turn back. Moving to d5
instead loses a Pawn after
13 Bc4xd5 c6xd5 14 Nc3xd5, and
Black may not recapture.

13	f3-f4	b7-b5
14	Bc4-b3	Nd7-c5
15	Nc3-e4	Nc5xb3

White has lost a stalwart Bishop,
but in return he gains an open file
for the use of his Queen Rook.

16	a2xb3	Ng8-e7
17	Ng3-h5!	Ne7-f5
18	Nh5-f6+	g7xf6
19	Ne4xf6+	Ke8-e7

The only move, as 19 . . . Ke8-d8
allows a pin of the Queen by
20 Bd2-a5.

20	Bd2-b4+	Nf5-d6

Again the only move, as
20 . . . c6-c5 loses the Queen by
21 Nf6-d5+, a pretty blending of
pin and Knight fork.

21	Qe2-e5	

Threatens the powerful 22 Nf6-e4,
uncovering an attack on the King

Rook, and striking a third time at
the pinned Knight.

21	. . .	Bf8-g7

Black of course pins the dangerous
beast.

22	Rh1-f1	a7-a5
23	f4-f5!	

More energetic than 23 Bb4-c5,
this will open the Bishop file for
the Rook.

23	. . .	a5xb4

Or 23 . . . Rh8-d8 24 Bb4-c5
Ke7-f8 25 Nf6xh7+ Kf8-g8
26 Nh7-f6+ Kg8-f8 27 f5xe6
Bc8xe6 28 g5-g6!, and Black's
position falls apart.

Black decides to give up the
exchange to get rid of the troublesome Bishop.

24	Ra1xa8	Nd6-e8
25	Qe5-c5+	Qc7-d6
26	Ra8-a7+	Ke7-f8

Naturally if 26 . . . Bc8-d7
27 Ra7xd7+ snaps the Bishop off,
while interposing the Knight is even
worse, as 27 Ra7xc7+ removes the
Knight, after which the Bishop falls,
then the Queen, and finally the
King himself suffers mate.

27	Qc5xd6+	

'Characteristically,' say Hooper
and Brandreth in *The Unknown
Capablanca*, 'Capablanca's brilliant
play leads neither to mate nor to
material gain, but to the endgame.'

27	. . .	Ne8xd6
28	Nf6-e4!	Nd6xe4

One would expect 28 . . . Nd6xf5,
but it loses by some pretty play,
thus: 29 Ra7-c7 Nf5-e7 (if

29 ... Bc8-a6 30 Ne4-c5 traps the unfortunate Bishop) 30 Ne4-d6 Bc8-a6 31 Rf1xf7+ Kf8-g8 32 Rc7xe7, and White wins quickly.

| 29 | d3xe4 | Kf8-e8 |

Ending 6

Position after 29 . . . Kf8-e8

Allies

Capablanca to move

Black's two Bishops against a Rook give him a slight superiority in material. This is outweighed, though, by White's positional advantage. His Rooks enjoy a freedom of movement which contrasts strongly with the undeveloped state of his opponent's pieces.

Capablanca concocts a little combination to transform the position into a Rook-and-Pawn ending. The plan thereafter is to effect a breakthrough by means of some clever Pawn moves, and create a passed Pawn against which the enemy Rook will be helpless.

| 30 | f5-f6 | Bg7-f8 |

Black's pieces seem fated to short careers in the outer world.

| 31 | Ke1-e2 |

Clearance for 32 Rf1-d1 next move —a move of paralyzing effect. Black would be completely powerless to prevent 33 Ra7-a8 and mate in two.

| 31 | ... | e6-e5 |
| 32 | Ke2-f3 |

Not at once 32 Rf1-d1, as 32 . . . Bc8-g4+ would come like a shot.

| 32 | ... | Bf8-c5 |

The attempt to get the Rook into play by 32 . . . h7-h6 fails after 33 g5-g6 (threatens 34 g6-g7) f7xg6 34 f6-f7+ and White wins.

| 33 | Ra7-c7 | Bc8-d7 |

Alternative defences succumb quickly:

(a) 33 . . . Bc8-a6 34 Rc7xc6, and Black loses one of the unprotected Bishops.

(b) 33 . . . Bc8-e6 34 Rf1-a1 Ke8-d8 35 Rc7xc6 Bc5-d4 (if 35 . . . Bc5-f8 36 Ra1-a8+ Kd8-d7 37 Rc6-c8 wins) 36 Rc6xe6 f7xe6 37 Ra1-a8+ wins easily.

34	Rf1-d1	Bc5-d4
35	c2-c3	b4xc3
36	b2xc3	Ke8-d8
37	Rc7xd7+	Kd8xd7
38	c3xd4	e5xd4
39	e4-e5!	

A very fine move! It is considerably stronger than the natural recapture of the Pawn with check, viz: 39 Rd1xd4+ Kd7-e6 40 Kf3-f4 h7-h6 41 e4-e5 (threatens mate on

the move) h6xg5+ 42 Kf4-e4
Rh8-h4+ 43 Ke4-e3 Ke6xe5, and
White's Pawns fall.

39	...	c6-c5
40	Kf3-e4	Kd7-c6
41	e5-e6!	

Another fine move by the e-Pawn!
The automatic 41 Ke4-f5 runs into
trouble after 41 . . . Kc6-d5
42 h2-h4 Rh8-e8 43 Rd1-e1 c5-c4,
and Black has two dangerous connected passed Pawns.

41	...	f7xe6
42	Ke4-e5	Kc6-d7

But not 42 . . . Rh8-e8, after which
43 f6-f7 Re8-d8 44 Ke5xe6
Rd8-d6+ 45 Ke6-e7 Rd6-d7+
46 Ke7-e8 forces Black to give up
his Rook for the f-Pawn.

43	b3-b4	Rh8-g8

44	h2-h4	Rg8-c8

There is a chance in a million (or
perhaps less) that Capablanca will
fall into 45 b4xc5 Rc8xc5+
46 Ke5xd4 Rc5-d5+ losing his
Rook, but Capablanca even blindfold does not go astray.

45	h4-h5	Black Resigns

After 45 . . . Rc8-g8 46 g5-g6
h7xg6 47 f6-f7 Rg8-f8
48 h5xg6 Kd7-e7 49 Rd1-a1
(faster than 49 g6-g7) d4-d3
50 Ra1-a7+ Ke7-d8 51 g6-g7, and
mate follows in two more moves.

A great blindfold performance.

The Pawn sacrifices are reminiscent of the classic Pillsbury-
Gunsberg ending that crowned the
former's great performance at
Hastings in 1895.

GAME 7

White J. R. Capablanca   *Black*
Black D. Janowsky
San Sebastian, 1911

Queen's Pawn Opening
Strange things happen in this
exciting game!

Janowsky outplays his formidable opponent in the midgame complications.

Janowsky spurns four opportunities to draw by perpetual check—
two at each side of the board.

Janowsky misses a win by check-
ing at the wrong square—nearer the
King instead of at the end of the
board!

Capablanca rallies from a near-
knockout, springs back like the
giant Antaeus after touching the
earth, and demolishes his opponent
in the endgame.

The ending, highlighted by remarkable Queen and Knight combinative play, is equal in power and
beauty to any in the entire literature of chess.

1	d2-d4	d7-d5
2	e2-e3	

Game 7

Cautious play, but this was Capablanca's first International Tournament, and he may have been self-conscious, and perhaps awed by the reputations of these great masters whom he was meeting for the first time.

2	...	Ng8-f6
3	Ng1-f3	c7-c5
4	c2-c4	e7-e6
5	Nb1-c3	Bf8-e7

This loses a tempo, as the Bishop will have to recapture the c-Pawn after White plays 6 d4xc5.

He might have tried 5 ... Nb8-c6 6 a2-a3 Nf6-e4, the line with which Marshall beat him brilliantly at Cambridge Springs in 1904.

6	d4xc5	0-0
7	a2-a3	Be7xc5
8	b2-b4	Bc5-e7

One would expect Janowsky to play the more aggressive 8 ... Bc5-d6.

| 9 | Bc1-b2 | a7-a5 |
| 10 | b4-b5 | b7-b6 |

Black's last two moves assure him control of the square c5.

| 11 | c4xd5 | e6xd5 |

Black has compensation for his isolated Queen Pawn in the pressure it exerts on the squares c4 and e4, and in his two active Bishops.

| 12 | Nf3-d4! | |

Blockades the Queen Pawn, and prevents as well the development by Black of 12 ... Bc8-f5.

| 12 | ... | Be7-d6 |
| 13 | Bf1-e2 | |

Capablanca explains that 13 g2-g3

seemed the proper continuation, but this being his first big tournament, he feared being criticized for creating such a formation of Pawns on the King side: 'hence the selection of this bad move against my better judgement.'

| 13 | ... | Bc8-e6 |
| 14 | Be2-f3 | Ra8-a7! |

This unusual (but good) deployment of the Queen Rook is found often in Reshevsky's games.

15	0-0	Ra7-c7
16	Qd1-b3	Nb8-d7
17	Rf1-d1	

The tempting 17 Nd4-c6 loses two pieces for a Rook by 17 ... Rc7xc6! 18 b5xc6 d5-d4 19 Nc3-d5 Be6xd5 20 Bf3xd5 Nd7-c5 21 Qb3-a2 Nf6xd5 (there's a lot of activity at d5!) and White may not play 22 Qa2xd5 as 22 ... Bd6xh2+ would win his Queen.

17	...	Nd7-e5
18	Bf3-e2	Qd8-e7
19	Ra1-c1	Rf8-c8

Capablanca now decides to simplify the position to relieve the pressure. He saw the coming combination, but was confident of being able to weather the storm.

20	Nc3-a4	Rc7xc1
21	Rd1xc1	Rc8xc1+
22	Bb2xc1	Nf6-e4!
23	Bc1-b2	

On 23 Na4xb6 instead, 23 ... Qe7-c7 would be painful.

| 23 | ... | Ne5-c4! |

What centralization!

24	Be2xc4	Bd6xh2+

Much better than 24 . . . d5xc4
25 Qb3-c2, and White has equalized.
This assures Black of a draw at least,
by perpetual check.

25	Kg1xh2	Qe7-h4+
26	Kh2-g1	Qh2xf2+
27	Kg1-h2	Qf2-g3+
28	Kh2-g1	

Carefully avoiding 28 Kh2-h1, when
28 . . . Be6-h3 29 Bc4-f1 Ne4-f2+
30 Kh1-g1 Nf2-g4 forces mate.

28	. . .	d5xc4
29	Qb3-c2	Qg3xe3+
30	Kg1-h2	Qe3-g3+
31	Kh2-g1	Qg3-e1+
32	Kg1-h2	Qe1-g3+
33	Kh2-g1	Qg3-e1+
34	Kg1-h2	Ne4-f6

Disdaining the draw, the ingenious
Janowsky finds other ways to
renew the attack. Now he threatens
35 . . . Nf6-g4+ 36 Kh2-h3 Ng4-e3+
winning the Queen.

35	Nd4xe6	

Kills off one tormenter.

35	. . .	Qe1-h4+
36	Kh2-g1	Qh4-e1+
37	Kg1-h2	Qe1-h4+
38	Kh2-g1	Nf6-g4!
39	Qc2-d2	

The only move, as 39 Qc2-c3 (to
guard the e1 square) allows
39 . . . Qh4-f2+ and mate next
move, while 39 Bb2-c3 (again to
guard e1) loses after
39 . . . Qh4-h2+ 40 Kg1-f1
Ng4-e3+, and the Queen falls.

39	. . .	Qh4-h2+
40	Kg1-f1	Qh2-h1+
41	Kf1-e2	Qh1xg2+
42	Ke2-d1	Ng4-f2+
43	Kd1-c2	Qg2-g6+
44	Kc2-c1	Qg6-g1+
45	Kc1-c2	Qg1-g6+
46	Kc2-c1	Nf2-d3+

Antony: 'I thrice presented him a
kingly crown, Which he did thrice
refuse.'

47	Kc1-b1	f7xe6
48	Qd2-c2	

Of course not 48 Na4xb6 Qg6-g1+
winning the Knight.

Capablanca says that 48 Kb1-a2,
instead of the text, would have
given him a draw.

48	. . .	h7-h5

Black has a flock of Pawns for the
piece, including a dangerous King
Rook Pawn which threatens to run
to the eighth square.

That Capablanca should be able
to save the game (let alone win it)
borders on the miraculous.

Ending 7

Position after 48 ... h7-h5

Janowsky

Capablanca to move

The situation does not seem to be in White's favour. He is faced with impending disaster by threats of discovered attack, and he must cope with a wicked-looking Rook Pawn on its way to become a Queen.

All the more reason to admire (psychologically) Capablanca's *sangfroid*, and (technically) the skilful way in which he combines attack and defence in a difficult endgame.

49 Bb2-d4!

The Bishop not only attacks the Knight Pawn, but prepares to restrain the ambitious Rook Pawn.

The alternatives are found wanting: 49 Na4xb6 loses by 49 ... Qg6-g1+ followed by removing the Knight, while 49 Qc2xc4 is met by 49 ... h5-h4, and if then

50 Qc4xh4, the reply
50 ... Nd3-b4+ forces quick mate.

49 ...   h5-h4

50 Bd4xb6

Now White has a passed Pawn too, to add to the excitement.

50 ...   h4-h3

51 Bb6-c7   e6-e5

Blocks the path of the Bishop, and faces White with the threat of 52 ... Qg6-g1+ followed by 53 ... h3-h2.

52 b5-b6

A win-or-lose move. Capablanca underestimated the strength of Black's position, or he would have played the safer 52 Qc2xc4+, when 52 ... Kg8-f8 53 Bc7-d6+ Qg6xd6 54 Qc4-c8+ followed by 55 Qc8xh3 would probably have led to a draw.

52 ...   Qg6-e4!

This is the position:

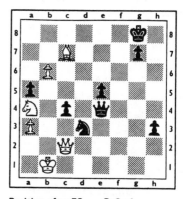

Position after 52 ... Qg6-e4

'This move I had not properly considered,' says Capablanca, 'though it was the only one to win.'

Strangely enough, Janowsky had

remarked at this point, 'This is the only move,' but missed the right continuation afterward.

Janowsky's multi-purpose move prevents the advance of White's passed Pawn, protects his own Bishop Pawn, and keeps White's Knight on the sidelines, out of the game.

If 53 Na4-b2 h3-h2 54 Qc2xh2 Qe4-e1+ 55 Kb1-a2 (if 55 Nb2-d1, Qe1xd1+ 56 Kb1-a2 Qd1-b3+ 57 Ka2-a1 Nd3-e1 wins for Black) 55 . . . Nd3-c1+ 56 Ka2-b1 Nc1-b3+ 57 Kb1-c2 Qe1-c1 is mate.

Or if 53 Na4-c3 h3-h2! 54 Nc3xe4 (on 54 Qc2xh2 Qe4-e1+ wins the Knight) 54 . . . h2-h1(Q)+ 55 Kb1-a2 Qh1xe4, and if 56 b6-b7 Nd3-b4+ wins the Queen and then the King.

53   Bc7xe5   Qe4-e1+

Janowsky was so intent on this check (the key-move in the two previous variations) that he checks at the wrong square.

The right way was to check at h1, whence the Queen could keep a tight surveillance on White's passed Pawn. Janowsky apparently missed the point completely; he analyzed the position (after the game) for two hours, never saw where he made the error, and had to be told by the other masters.

54   Kb1-a2

And now Janowsky has a fourth opportunity to draw by perpetual check! He can do so by 54 . . . Nd3-c1+ 55 Ka2-b1 Nc1-d3+ 56 Kb1-a2 Nd3-c1+, but . . .

54   . . .   Nd3xe5

. . . he does not take it! And with that goes his last chance.

'Before continuing,' says Capablanca, 'I should add that the coming endgame is perhaps the finest of its kind ever played, and that for some unknown reason it has not been properly appreciated. It is a masterpiece, one of which I am very proud, and which should be carefully studied.'

55   b6-b7   Ne5-d7
56   Na4-c5!

An important move. The subsequent play will show why this is superior to 56 Na4-b6.

56   . . .   Nd7-b8
57   Qc2xc4+   Kg8-h8
58   Nc5-e4!

The Knight is beautifully centralized. It guards White's King against annoying checks by the Queen, and is also in perfect position to take part in combination play against Black's King and Queen.

For example, if 58 . . . h3-h2 59 Qc4-c8+ Kh8-h7 60 Qc8-h3+ Kh7-g8 (if 60 . . . Kh7-g6 61 Qh3-e6+ followed by 62 Ne4-f6+ wins the Queen) 61 Qh3-e6+ Kg8-h8 (if 61 . . . Kg8-f8 62 Qe6-d6+, or if 61 . . . Kg8-h7 62 Ne4-g5+ wins the Queen) 62 Qe6-e8+ Kh8-h7 63 Ne4-g5+ and White wins the Queen (Schlechter).

58   . . .   Kh8-h7
59   Qc4-d3   g7-g6

If 59 . . . Qe1-h4 60 Ne4-g5+

Kh7-h6 61 Ng5-f7+ Kh6-h5
62 Qd3-f5+ g7-g5 63 Nf7-e5, and
wins (Capablanca).

Or if 59 . . . h3-h2 60 Ne4-g5+
Kh7-h6 61 Ng5-f7+ Kh6-h5
62 Qd3-f5+ Kh5-h4 63 Qf5-f4+
Kh4-h3 64 Nf7-g5+ Kh3-g2
65 Qf4-f3+ Kg2-g1 66 Ng5-h3
mate! (Schlechter).

All this is elegant endgame play,
quite like a Rinck composition.

60	Qd3xh3+	Kh7-g7
61	Qh3-f3!	Qe1-c1

Hoping desperately for a fifth try at
a perpetual check.

But opportunity has tired of
knocking.

62	Qf3-f6+	Kg7-h7
63	Qf6-f7+	Kh7-h6

If 63 . . . Kh7-h8 64 Qf7-f8+
Kh8-h7 65 Ne4-f6 mate.

64	Qf7-f8+	Kh6-h5
65	Qf8-h8+	Kh5-g4
66	Qh8-c8+	

Forces an exchange of Queens,
the promotion of the Pawn to a
Queen, and the end of resistance.

66	. . .	**Black Resigns**

A magnificent game, with an
original opening, an exciting midgame and an artistic conclusion.

GAME 8

White P. S. Leonhardt
Black J. R. Capablanca
San Sebastian, 1911

Queen's Gambit Declined

At his 9th move Leonhardt either
sacrifices a Pawn, or overlooks its
loss.

Capablanca removes the Pawn,
completes his development, exchanges the superfluous pieces, gets
his King-side Pawns rolling, and
proceeds to win a fascinating ending in clear-cut methodical style.

1	d2-d4	d7-d5
2	c2-c4	e7-e6
3	Nb1-c3	c7-c5

The Tarrasch Defence, strongly
advocated by the Old Master as a
specific for the cramped positions

resulting from the Orthodox
Defence to the Queen's Gambit,
had fallen away into innocuous
desuetude, as it had few supporters.

It has been revived recently to
good enough effect to help Spassky
win the World Championship in
1969.

4	e2-e3

Solid, and recommended as best by
Tarrasch. The vigorous continuation
is to isolate the Queen Pawn, blockade it, and then remove it from the
board, as Spassky did many years
later against Yanofsky at Siegen in

1970, thus: 4 c4xd5 e6xd5
5 Ng1-f3 Nb8-c6 6 g2-g3 (the
Schlechter-Rubinstein variation,
which almost put the Tarrasch
Defence out of business, and with
which Rubinstein defeated Capablanca in the same San Sebastian
1911 Tournament) 6 . . . Ng8-f6
7 Bf1-g2 Bf8-e7 8 0-0 0-0
9 Bc1-e3 c5xd4 (good chances are
offered by 9 . . . Bc8-g4! 10 d4xc5
Bg4xf3 11 Bg2xf3 d5-d4!
12 Bf3xc6 d4xe3 13 Bc6xb7
e3xf2+ 14 Kg1-g2 Be7xc5, with a
vigorous counter-attack) 10 Nf3xd4
h7-h6 11 Ra1-c1 Nc6-a5 12 b2-b3!
Na5-c6 13 Qd1-d3 Nc6-e5
16 Qd3-c2 Qd8-a5 15 Nc3-b5
Bc8-d7 16 Qc2-c7! Qa5xc7
17 Nb5xc7 Ra8-d8 18 Nc7xd5,
and White won on the 42nd move.

4	. . .	Ng8-f6
5	Ng1-f3	Nb8-c6
6	Bf1-d3	d5xc4
7	Bd3xc4	Bf8-e7
8	0-0	0-0
9	Qd1-e2	

Played hastily, this sacrifice of a
Pawn does not yield White an
advantage in position.

Theoretically, Black now has a
won game. But winning a won game
is not an automatic process. It is an
art in itself—as Capablanca now
demonstrates.

9	. . .	c5xd4
10	e3xd4	Nc6xd4
11	Nf3xd4	Qd8xd4
12	Rf1-d1	Qd4-g4
13	f2-f3	Qg4-h5

14   Nc3-e4

This only speeds up matters, as it
brings about exchanges, instead of
the complications which White
should be seeking.

Straightforward development by
14 Bc1-f4 was more to the point.

14	. . .	Qh5-e5
15	Ne4xf6+	Be7xf6
16	Qe2xe5	Bf6xe5

'Each side has difficulty in developing his Queen Bishop,' observes
Tarrasch.

17	a2-a4	b7-b6
18	a4-a5	Bc8-b7
19	a5xb6	

This only helps the opponent.
Better prospects were offered by
the aggressive 19 Bc1-e3

19	. . .	a7xb6
20	Ra1xa8	Rf8xa8

For the Rook file, which White
took the trouble to pry open, is in
Black's possession.

21	b2-b3	

The more courageous 21 f3-f4
Be5-f6 22 Rd1-d7, posting the
Rook on the seventh rank, was
called for.

21	. . .	Bb7-c6

This keeps the Rook from reaching
the seventh rank, and posing any
threats.

22	Bc1-e3	b6-b5
23	Bc4-e2	f7-f6

Prepares to bring his King to the
center.

24	Rd1-c1	

Ending 8

Position after 24 Rd1-c1

Capablanca to move

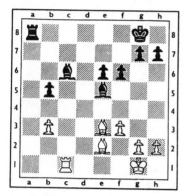

Leonhardt

Black has an extra Pawn as material advantage.

He plans to exploit this advantage by maneuvers on the King-side (where he has four Pawns to three) which should enable him to emerge with a passed Pawn.

Promoting this Pawn would still require careful play, in view of the resistance offered by White's long-range Bishops.

24	...	Ra8-a1

First the Rooks must come off, to clarify the position.

25	Rc1xa1	Be5xa1

Now we have a four-Bishop ending, a rare occurrence in practical play.

26	Kg1-f2	Kg8-f7
27	Kf2-e1	e6-e5

Gangway for the King!

28	Ke1-d2	Kf7-e6
29	Be2-d3	g7-g6

30	h2-h4	

'The Pawns of the weaker side should rarely advance,' says Tarrasch, 'as they offer better targets of attack, and facilitate the creation (by the opponent) of a passed Pawn.

30	...	f6-f5
31	b3-b4	e5-e4!
32	f3xe4	Bc6xe4

This is superior to capturing with the Pawn.

33	Bd3xb5	

White prefers to activate the Bishop rather than defend with the meek 33 Bd3-f1.

33	...	Be4xg2
34	Bb5-a6	

Makes way for the passed Pawn, which might give Black some trouble.

34	...	Ba1-f6
35	Be3-f2	Bf6-e5

This Bishop is now centralized, and controls the Queening square of White's passed Pawn.

36	b4-b5	h7-h6

On 36 ... Bg2-f1 (to pin the Pawn) White frees himself by 37 Ba6-c8+ followed by 38 b5-b6.

37	b5-b6	g6-g5
38	h4xg5	h6xg5

Part of the plan has been carried out, and Capablanca has two connected passed Pawns, which he intends to advance as quickly as possible. As for the opponent's passed Pawn, that can be blockaded by the dark-squared Bishop when it advances to the seventh rank.

39	Ba6-c8+	Ke6-f6
40	Kd2-e2	

A deceptive waiting move. The precipitate reply 40 . . . g5-g4 would be penalized by 41 Be1-h4+ Kf6-g6 42 Bh4-d8 followed by 43 Bd8-c7, after which Black would have to give up a Bishop for the Pawn.

40	. . .	Bg2-c6
41	Ke2-f1	Bc6-d5
42	Kf1-e2	Bd5-c4+
43	Ke2-d2	f5-f4

This increases the scope of White's Bishop, but Black will soon appropriate this fine diagonal for his own use.

44	Bc8-g4	Bc4-e6
45	Bg4-f3	g5-g4
46	Bf3-e4	g4-g3

The Pawns become more and more menacing with every step they take.

47	Bf2-c5	Be6-g4
48	Kd2-e1	f4-f3
49	Bc5-e3	

Great care must still be taken before either Pawn moves on.

For example, if 49 . . , f3-f2+, the reply 50 Be3xf2 snaps off the Pawn and draws, while advancing the Knight Pawn could lead to this: 49 . . . g3-g2 50 b6-b7 Be5-h2 51 Be3-g1! Bh2xg1 52 Be4xf3! Bg1-h2 (or 52 . . . Bg4xf3 53 b7-b8(Q)) 53 Bf3xg2, and again White forces a draw.

49	. . .	Be5-d6
50	b6-b7	Kf6-e5
51	Be4-c6	

There is a pretty win after 51 Be3-a7

instead, by 51 . . . Ke5xe4 52 b7-b8(Q) Bd6xb8 53 Ba7xb8 f3-f2+ 54 Ke1-f1 Ke4-f3 55 Bb8xg3 Bg4-h3 mate!

51	. . .	Bd6-b8

Quick, before White plays 52 Be3-a7!

52	Ke1-f1	Bg4-h5
53	Kf1-g1	Ke5-f5
54	Bc6-d5	Kf5-g4
55	Bd5-e6+	Kg4-h4
56	Be3-c5	

'Instead of this, ' says Tarrasch, 'White could set his opponent more problems by deploying his Bishop to g1, as follows: 56 Kg1-f1 Bh5-g4 57 Be6-d5 Kh4-h3 58 Be3-g1 g3-g2+ 59 Kf1-e1 Kh3-g3 60 Bd5-c6 (a move by the other Bishop allows 60 . . . Kg3-h2, while a King move is met by 60 . . . f3-f2) 60 . . . Bb8-e5 (the only way to win, the threat being 61 . . . Be5-c3+ 62 Ke1-d1 f3-f2+) 61 Bg1-d4! Be5xd4! 62 b7-b8(Q)+ Kg3-h3, and Black wins.

56	. . .	Bh5-g4
57	Be6xg4	

White must exchange Bishops, as otherwise there follows 57 . . . Kh4-h3 58 . . . g3-g2 59 . . . Bb8-h2+ and 60 . . . g2-g1 (Q)+ and mate.

57	. . .	Kh4xg4
58	Kg1-f1	Kg4-h3
59	Bc5-g1	

Or 59 Kf1-g1, when Black wins neatly by 59 . . . g3-g2 60 Kg1-f2 Kh3-g4 61 Kf2-g1 (else there

follows 61 . . . Bb8-g3+)
61 . . . Kg4-g3 62 Bc5-b6 (the
stalemate try 62 Bc5-d6+ fails after
62 . . . Bb8xd6 63 b7-b8(Q)
f3-f2 mate) 62 . . . f3-f2+!
63 Bb6xf2+ Kg3-h3 64 Bf2-c5,
Bb8-h2+ 65 Kg1-f2 g2-g1(Q)+,
and it's all over.

| 59 | ... | Bb8-c7 |
| 60 | Bg1-a7 | |

White is virtually in *zugzwang*, a
King move (60 Kf1-e1) succumbing
to 60 . . . Kh3-g2 61 Bg1-c5 f3-f2+,
and Black gets a new Queen.

| 60 | ... | Kh3-h2 |
| 61 | b7-b8(Q) | |

So White is first to Queen his Pawn!

| 61 | ... | g3-g2+ |

Of course not 61 . . . Bc7xb8
62 Ba7xb8 f3-f2 (on 62 . . . Kh2-h3
63 Bb8xg3 Kh3xg3 64 Kf1-g1
forces an elementary draw)
63 Bb8-c7 Kh2-h3 64 Bc7-b8 (but
not 64 Bc7xg3 Kh3xg3 which loses
for White), and Black can make no
progress.

62 White Resigns

White is convinced. The further
course could be: 62 Kf1-e1 Bc7xb8
63 Ba7xb8+ Kh2-h1 64 Bb8-a7
g2-g1(Q)+ 65 Ba7xg1 Kh1xg1, and
the last Pawn will reach the last
square to become a Queen.

A much-admired Capablanca
endgame, absorbing throughout its
length.

GAME 9

White L. Carranza
Black J. R. Capablanca (Exhibition Game)
Buenos Aires, 1911

Three Knights Game
It is a common delusion that the
way to draw against a great player
is to exchange as many pieces as
possible.

It just does not work, especially
against Capablanca, who always
seems to emerge with a slight
advantage after every exchange.

The old adage still holds true,
'If you want to get a draw, play to
win!'

1	e2-e4	e7-e5
2	Ng1-f3	Nb8-c6
3	Nb1-c3	d7-d6

Rather quiet, the energetic
3 . . . Bf8-b4 is usually preferred.
Still more modern is the fianchetto of the King Bishop, to bear
down on the center, thus:
3 . . . g7-g6 4 d2-d4 e5xd4
5 Nc3-d5 Bf8-g7 6 Bc1-g5 Nc6-e7!
(but not 6 . . . Ng8-e7 7 Nf3xd4
Bg7xd4 8 Qd1xd4 Nc6xd4
9 Nd5-f6+ Ke8-f8 10 Bg5-h6 mate)
7 Nf3xd4 c7-c6 8 Nd5-c3 h7-h6
9 Bg5-f4 d7-d5, and Black has a
fine, free game.

| 4 | Bf1-b5 | Ng8-e7 |

5	d2-d4	f7-f6

Dr. Tarrasch would have shuddered at this 'ugly' move, but it does maintain the strong point at e5.

6	d4xe5	

But this eases the pressure, and provides Black (after castling) with an open file for his Rook.

6	. . .	f6xe5
7	Bc1-g5	Bc8-g4
8	Qd1-d3	a7-a6
9	Bb5-a4	h7-h6
10	Bg5xe7	Bf8xe7
11	Nc3-d5	0-0
12	Ba4xc6	

This move, and his next, release whatever pressure White has had on the position.

A spirited alternative is offered by Capablanca in *La Prensa*, as follows: 12 Qd3-b3! Kg8-h7 13 Qb3xb7 Bg4xf3 14 Ba4xc6 Ra8-b8 15 Qb7xc7 Qd8xc7 16 Nd5xc7 Bf3xg2 17 Rh1-g1 Bg2-h3 18 Rg1-g3 Bh3-c8, and he considers Black to have enough compensation for the sacrificed Pawn.

12	. . .	b7xc6
13	Nd5xe7+	Qd8xe7
14	Nf3-d2	Bg4-e6

The beginning of centralization, and the establishment of a Pawn roller.

15	0-0	

It is of such mechanical development that Botvinnik, commenting on his game against Sokolsky, said, 'It is gradually becoming apparent that White (Sokolsky) has no plan whatever, and is occupied only with "development" of his pieces. Perhaps this was sufficient fifty years ago, but in our day, when at the sixth to eight move every master formulates his plan for the middle-game, there is no "better" way of getting a cramped and passive position than by aiming only at development.'

More to the point than the text move, was 15 c2-c4, to make Black fight for occupation of the center.

15	. . .	d6-d5!
16	f2-f3	Qe7-c5+
17	Kg1-h1	a6-a5!

Intending 18 . . . a5-a4 next, to keep the Knight out of the square b3.

18	Nd2-b3	Qc5-b6
19	Qd3-c3	d5-d4

Forced, as the King Pawn was attacked, and forcing, as the Queen must exchange or retreat.

20	Qc3-c5	

White is happy to exchange Queens, as a means of obtaining a draw.

20	. . .	Be6xb3
21	Qc5xb6	c7xb6
22	a2xb3	c6-c5
23	Kh1-g1	

The position would now be called a draw by most players, but Black has an infinitesimal advantage—and that's all that Capablanca needs!

The endgame that follows is one of the most delightful ever played by Capablanca, with enough Pawn play to gladden the heart of a Philidor.

Ending 9

Position after 23 Kh1-g1

Capablanca to move

Carranza

Black has a positional advantage in that his Pawns have great potential to expand. His Queen Pawn may, with care, be converted to a passed Pawn, and there is some prospect of gaining control of the Queen Rook file.

This may seem nebulous, but watch the meticulous manipulations of Capablanca's fine Cuban hand!

| 23 | ... | Kg8-f7! |

White poses no danger in 24 f3-f4, as after 24 ... e5xf4 25 Rf1xf4+ Kf7-e6 26 Ra1-f1 Rf8xf4 27 Rf1xf4 a5-a4!, and Black wins.

24	Kg1-f2	Kf7-e6
25	Kf2-e2	b6-b5
26	Ke2-d2	g7-g5
27	h2-h3	h6-h5

This prepares for a possible breakthrough by ... g5-g4.

| 28 | g2-g4 | |

Squashes that little idea! But Capablanca has other resources.

28	...	h5-h4
29	Kd2-e2	Rf8-f7
30	Rf1-f2	Rf7-a7
31	Ke2-d3	a5-a4

Threatens 32 ... a4xb3 33 Ra1xa7 Ra8xa7 34 c2xb3 Ra7-a1 35 Rf2-h2 (to save the Rook Pawn) 35 ... Ra1-b1 36 Kd3-c2 (any other King move loses the Rook, and any Rook move loses the Rook Pawn) 36 ... Rb1-f1, and Black wins the Bishop Pawn, after which the King Pawn or the Rook Pawn falls.

32	b3xa4	c5-c4+
33	Kd3-d2	Ra7xa4
34	Ra1-b1	Ra4-a1
35	Rf2-f1	Ra1xb1
36	Rf1xb1	Ra8-a2

Rook on the seventh! The magic winning move!

37	Kd2-d1	b5-b4
38	Kd1-d2	Ke6-d6
39	Kd2-d1	Kd6-c5
40	b2-b3	

This lets Black win in beautiful style. The alternative 40 Kd1-d2 leads to this neat finish: 40 ... Ra2xb2! 41 Rb1xb2 c4-c3+ 42 Kd2-c1 c3xb2+ 43 Kc1xb2 Kc5-c4 44 Kb2-c1 d4-d3 45 c2xd3+ Kc4xd3 46 f3-f4 (otherwise 46 ... Kd3-e3 wins at once) 46 ... e5xf4 47 e4-e5 f4-f3, and Black wins.

| 40 | ... | c4-c3 |

41	Rb1-c1	d4-d3!
42	c2xd3	

Two other moves allow amusing Pawn forks:

(a) 42 Rc1-b1 d3xc2+ winning the Rook.

(b) 42 Kd1-e1 d3-d2+ winning the Rook.

42	...	Ra2-h2
43	Rc1-c2	

Any other move by King or Rook loses the Rook instantly.

43	...	Rh2-h1+
44	Kd1-e2	Kc5-d4!

This is the position:

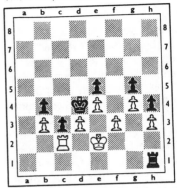

Position after 44 ... Kc5-d4

White is in *zugzwang*! Any move by King or Rook loses the Rook.

45 White Resigns

A picturesque conclusion by a great artist.

GAME 10

White J. R. Capablanca
Black D. Janowsky
New York, 1913

Four Knights Game
Capablanca chooses a safe, solid opening that offers little winning chances—except against Janowsky, who would hardly be content to draw by going into a symmetrical variation.

Thus it is that Capablanca emerges from the opening with a slight initiative. But this smidgen of advantage is all Capablanca needs, as he knows how to carry it over skilfully into the ending, in this case a superb specimen of Rook and Pawn play.

1	e2-e4	e7-e5
2	Ng1-f3	Nb8-c6
3	Nb1-c3	Ng8-f6
4	Bf1-b5	a7-a6

Janowsky tries to induce 5 Bb5-a4 in reply, switching over to the Ruy Lopez.

The strongest defence 4 ... Nc6-d4 had just about then been discovered by Rubinstein, but could not have been known to Janowsky, who never opened a chess book in his life.

5	Bb5xc6	d7xc6
6	0-0	

A more aggressive line is this:
6 Nf3xe5 Nf6xe4 7 Nc3xe4
Qd8-d4 8 0-0 Qd4xe5 9 d2-d4
Qe5-f5 10 Rf1-e1 (threatens
11 Ne4-f6+ and mate next) Bc8-e6
11 Bc1-g5 Bf8-d6 (the better move
is 11 . . . h7-h6) 12 g2-g4 Qf5-g6
(but not 12 . . . Qf5xg4+
13 Qd1xg4 Be6xg4 14 Ne4xd6+,
winning a piece) 13 f2-f4 f7-f5
14 Ne4xd6+, c7xd6 15 d4-d5!, and
White wins a piece (or more) as in
the game Znosko-Borovsky against
Rubinstein at Ostend in 1907.

6	. . .	Bc8-g4
7	h2-h3	Bg4-h5
8	Qd1-e2	Bf8-d6
9	d2-d3	Qd8-e7
10	Nc3-d1	0-0-0

Lasker's suggestion for obtaining
counter-play by 10 . . . Nf6-d7
11 Nd1-e3 Bh5xf3 12 Qe2xf3
g7-g6, would not have interested a
two-Bishop man like Janowsky.

11	Nd1-e3	Bh5-g6
12	Nf3-h4	Rh8-g8
13	Ne3-f5	Qe7-e6
14	f2-f4!	

With the tactical threat 15 Nf5xd6+
Qe6xd6 16 f4-f5 Bg6-h5
17 g2-g4 trapping the Bishop, and
the strategical threat of opening the
Bishop file for the convenience of
the Rooks, who will bear down on
it with their full weight.

14	. . .	Bg6xf5
15	Nh4xf5	e5xf4
16	Bc1xf4	Bd6-c5+

17	Bf4-e3	Bc5-f8
18	Qe2-f2!	Rd8-d7
19	Be3-c5!	Bf8xc5
20	Qf2xc5	Kc8-b8

White was treatening to invade by
21 Qc5-a7, and to follow it up with
22 Qa7-a8+, winning a Pawn and
breaking up the King's shelter of
Pawns.

The Pawn position is in White's
favour, and he plans to turn it to
account like this:

(a) to double Rooks on the King
Bishop file to induce the inevitable
advance . . . f7-f6,

(b) to exchange Queens and
Knights,

(c) to advance the King Knight
Pawn to g4 and g5, to eliminate
Black's Bishop Pawn, and thereby
create a passed Pawn on the King
file,

(d) then—well the rest is a matter
of endgame technique, which even
then Capablanca had at his finger
tips.

21	Rf1-f2	Nf6-e8

Anticipating White's treat of winning a Pawn by 22 Ra1-f1 followed
by 23 Nf5xg7, Black regroups his
pieces.

22	Ra1-f1	f7-f6

Sooner or later this move had to be
made, in view of the pressure on
the Pawn.

Black had no time for
22 . . . Qe6xa2, as after 23 Nf5-e7
Rg8-h8 24 Rf2xf7 lets the enemy
into the camp.

23	b2-b3	Ne8-d6

24　Rf2-f4　　Nd6xf5

Black hastens his own doom by this and the following exchange, but chess players often seem hypnotized and go knowingly into hopeless lines of play.

23　Qc5xf5　　Qe6xf5

26　Rf4xf5　　Rg8-e8

Ending 10

Position after 26 . . . Rg8-e8

Janowsky

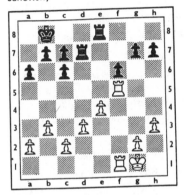

Capablanca to move

White's continuing initiative has left him with certain advantages: his Rook, strongly posted at f5, enjoys freedom of movement, and exerts great pressure on f6, the critical point in the position; his King can move quickly to e3, where it can support an advance by the Queen Pawn, and later on the King Pawn.

In contrast, Black is hampered by Rooks that are restricted to defence, and by the doubled Pawns on the c-file. These cannot be easily dissolved, as the preparatory . . . b7-b6 would be parried by b3-b4, restraining the advance of the Bishop Pawn.

Capablanca plans to create a passed Pawn on the King file, with which he expects to win.

To do this he must

(a) prevent Black's Queen-side Pawns from advancing,

(b) bring his King to e3,

(c) effect an exchange of Black's f-Pawn by means of g2-g4 and g4-g5,

(d) advance the Queen Pawn, and then the King Pawn, to acquire a passed Pawn.

27　g2-g4!

The first step in the process. The Pawn is to push on to g5 when the time is ripe, to attack f6, the key square in the position.

27　. . .　　b7-b6

28　b3-b4!

Squashes any attempt to undouble the Pawns.

28　. . .　　Kb8-b7

29　Kg1-f2　　b6-b5

Black intends 30 . . . Kb7-b6, followed by 31 . . . a6-a5 and 32 . . . a5xb4. This would give him an open file for his Rook, and a chance for counter-play.

White, however, nips that idea in the bud.

30　a2-a4!　　Rd7-d4

No good comes of 30 . . . b5xa4, which leaves Black's Q-side Pawns split up and isolated, while the Pawn he has gained cannot be maintained after 31 Rf1-a1.

31	Rf1-b1	Re8-e5
32	Kf2-e3	Rd4-d7

If 32 . . . Re5xf5 33 g4xf5 Rd4-d7
34 d3-d4, and White has a winning
position.

33   a4-a5!

This fixes Black's Pawns on the
Queen side, and lets White devote
his energies to the other side of the
board.

33	. . .	Re5-e6
34	Rb1-f1	Rd7-e7
35	g4-g5	f6xg5

Defending the Pawn instead by the
meek 35 . . . Re7-f7 succumbs to
36 d3-d4, 37 Rf1-f4, and 38 e4-e5.

36   Rf5xg5

Capablanca says at this point that
his chances of winning are excellent.
He cites these advantages:

(a) he has a passed Pawn,

(b) his King is in an ideal position—
ready to assist the Pawns in their
march up the board, or if need be
to occupy the dominating square c5,
or if danger threatens, to shift to
the King side,

(c) he has a Rook commanding the
open Bishop file.

36	. . .	Re6-h6
37	Rg5-g3	Rh6-e6

Keeps the center Pawns from
moving.

38	h3-h4	g7-g6
39	Rg3-g5	

The object is to simplify the
position with 40 h4-h5 g6xh5

41 Rg5xh5. White could then
double his Rooks against the isolated Pawn and win it, or keep
Black occupied with the thankless
task of defending it.

39	. . .	h7-h6

Or 39 . . . Re6-e5 40 Rf1-f8
Re7-e8 41 Rg5xe5 Re8xe5
42 Rf8-f4 with easy sailing for
White.

40	Rg5-g4	Re7-g7

Otherwise, White could force this
with 41 Rf1-f8, threatening
42 Rf8-g8.

But now the Pawns in the center
begin their advance.

41	d3-d4	Kb7-c8
42	Rf1-f8+	Kc8-b7

The King hurries back, not caring
for 42 . . . Kc8-d7, when 43 Rf8-a8
wins the Rook Pawn and clears the
road for another passed Pawn.

43	e4-e5	g6-g5
44	Ke3-e4	Re6-e7
45	h4xg5	h6xg5

Clearly, 45 . . . Rg7xg5 46 Rg4xg5
h6xg5 47 Rf8-g8 loses a Pawn without affording any relief.

46	Rf8-f5	Kb7-c8
47	Rg4xg5	Rg7-h7
48	Rg5-h5	Kc8-d7
49	Rh5xh7	Re7xh7
50	Rf5-f8	Rh7-h4+
51	Ke4-d3	Rh4-h3+
52	Kd3-d2	c6-c5

Desperation, but there is no hope in
52 . . . Rh3-h4 53 Kd2-c3 Rh4-h3+
54 Kc3-b2 Rh3-h4 55 c2-c3
Rh4-h2+ 56 Kb2-b3, and White is

free to attack the Rook Pawn and win it.

53	b4xc5	Rh3-a3
54	d4-d5	**Black Resigns**

If 54 . . . Ra3xa5 55 Rf8-f7+ Kd7-d8 56 c5-c6 b5-b4 57 Rf7-f8+

Kd8-e7 58 d5-d6+! c7xd6 (if 58 . . . Ke7xf8 59 d6xc7 wins) 59 c6-c7, and White wins.

'Capablanca's play was beyond reproach,' says Lasker, 'and he executed his plan in a very able manner.'

GAME 11

White H. Kline
Black J. R. Capablanca
New York, 1913

Irregular Opening

Some exquisite endgame play marks this little-known game of Capablanca's.

The scanty notes furnished by Euwe, Nimzowitsch, or Capablanca himself (in whose books the score of this game appears) do not indicate the beauties that are hidden beneath the surface of the play.

There is a tantalizing comment, though, by Capablanca after Black's 37th move, which reads, 'The student should, from now on, examine the ending move by move.

I did as instructed, and discovered (to my pleasure) that there was brilliance galore in the moves that were never made—in the ideas that gave meaning to the moves actually made!

1	d2-d4	Ng8-f6
2	Ng1-f3	d7-d6
3	c2-c3	

It's only White's third move, and we're out of the books.

| 3 | . . . | Nb8-d7 |

4	Bc1-f4	c7-c6
5	Qd1-c2	Qd8-c7
6	e2-e4	e7-e5

Black thereby establishes e5 as a strong point for a Pawn (one, it turns out, he maintains for the entire game).

7	Bf4-g3	Bf8-e7
8	Bf1-d3	0-0
9	Nb1-d2	Rf8-e8
10	0-0	Nf6-h5

The Bishop must be eliminated!

11	Nd2-c4	Be7-f6
12	Nc4-e3	Nd7-f8

The Knight is headed for an outpost station at f4.

| 13 | d4xe5 | |

In anticipation of a triple attack on his Queen Pawn by 13 . . . Nf8-e6, White hastens to make this exchange.

13	. . .	d6xe5
14	Bg3-h4	Qc7-e7

Nimzowitsch suggests instead
14 . . . Bc8-e6, followed by doubling Rooks on the Queen file, to
take advantage of the rather uncomfortable position of White's
Bishop at d3.

15	Bh4xf6	Qe7xf6
16	Nf3-e1	Nh5-f4
17	g2-g3	Nf4-h3+
18	Kg1-h1	h7-h5

Not at once 18 . . . g7-g5, as he
wants to retain control of the f5
square against an invasion by the
Knight.

| 19 | Ne3-g2 | g7-g5 |

'Now White will have to go back,'
says Capablanca, 'in order to post
his Knight at f5, and Black can use
the time to good advantage.'

20	f2-f3	Nf8-g6
21	Ng2-e3	h5-h4
22	g3-g4	

White missed a glorious chance,
according to Nimzowitsch, to win
the game by 22 Ne3-f5 h4xg3
23 h2xg3 Bc8xf5 24 e4xf5 Ng6-e7
25 Kh1-g2 Kg8-g7 26 Kg2xh3
Re8-h8+ 27 Kh3-g2 Qf6-h6
28 Kg2-f2 Qh6-h2+ 29 Ne1-g2
Rh8-h3 30 Kf2-e1 Rh3xg3
31 Ng2-e3, and Black's attack is
contained.

| 22 | . . . | Nh3-f4 |

'Now the Knight rejoices in his re-
discovered freedom, and Black,
after this doubtful excursion, which
could easily have ended fatally for
him, takes up the right line, play in
the Queen file, and pursues it with
complete mastery to victory.'

23	Rf1-f2	Nf4xd3
24	Ne1xd3	Bc8-e6
25	Ra1-d1	Re8-d8
26	b2-b3	Ng6-f4
27	Ne3-g2	Nf4xd3
28	Rd1xd3	Rd8xd3
29	Qc2xd3	

Ending 11

Position after 29 Qc2xd3

Capablanca to move

Kline

Material is even, and a positional
advantage for Black seems nebulous.
It is true that he can obtain control
of the Queen file, and that his
Bishop has more potential power
than White's Knight, but can Capablanca turn this slight superiority
into a win?

Watch the master magician create
something out of nothing!

| 29 | . . . | Ra8-d8 |

Drives the Queen off, and takes
command of the open file.

Nimzowitsch asks, 'Why not win a Pawn by 29 . . . Be6xg4?'

The answer is that there would follow 30 Ng2xh4 g5xh4 31 Rf2-g2, and the greedy Bishop is pinned.

30   Qd3-e2

If 30 Qd3-c2 instead (in order to follow with 31 Rf2-d2, to dispute possession of the open file) the continuation could be: 30 . . . h4-h3 31 Ng2-e3 Qf6-f4 32 Ne3-d1 (on 32 Qc2-c1 Qf4xe3 is decisive) 32 . . . Be6xg4 33 f3xg4 Rd8xd1+ 34 Qc2xd1 Qf4xf2, and White is helpless to avert mate.

Or if 30 Qd3-c2 h4-h3 31 Ng2-e1 Qf6-f4 (prevents 32 Rf2-d2, and threatens further invasion by 32 . . . Qf4-e3) 32 Rf2-e2 Be6xg4 33 f3xg4 Qf4-f1 mate.

30   . . .   h4-h3!

31   Ng2-e3   a7-a5

Capablanca turns his attention to the other side of the board, where he will try to create a passed Pawn by breaking up White's Queen-side.

32   Rf2-f1   a5-a4

33   c3-c4

An attempt to wrest control of the Queen file loses at least a Pawn, thus: 33 Rf1-d1 Rd8xd1+ (or the simple 33 . . . a4xb3 34 a2xb3 Be6xb3) 34 Qe2xd1 a4xb3 35 a2xb3 Be6xb3 and if 36 Qd1xb3 Qf6xf3+ followed by 37 . . . Qf3xe3+ wins easily.

Or if 33 b3xa4 Qf6-f4 34 Rf1-d1 Rd8xd1+ 35 Ne3xd1 Be6-c4! 36 Qe2-f2 (on 36 Qe2-e3, Qf4xe3 37 Nd1xe3 Bc4-e2 will remove a

couple of Pawns) 36 . . . Qf4-c1 37 Qf2-e1 (if 37 Qf2-g1, Bc4-e2 wins at once) 37 . . . Bc4-d3, and the threat of 38 . . . Bd3-c2 is insuperable.

33   . . .   Rd8-d4!

34   Ne3-c2   Rd4-d7

35   Nc2-e3   Qf6-d8

36   Rf1-d1   Rd7xd1+

37   Ne3xd1

Perhaps 37 Qe2xd1 would be better, with some intriguing possibilities: 37 Qe2xd1 Qd8-a5 38 b3xa4 Qa5-c3 39 Qd1-e2 Qc3-c1+ 40 Ne3-d1 (on 40 Ne3-f1, Be6xc4 would come quick as a wink) 40 . . . Be6xc4 41 Qe2-e1 Bc4-d3 42 Qe1-g1 (to meet 42 . . . Bd3-c2 with 43 Nd1-f2) 42 . . . Bd3-e2 43 Nd1-f2 Be2xf3 mate.

Or if 37 Qe2xd1 Qd8-a5 38 Qd1-e2 (definitely not 38 Qd1-d3 Qa5-e1+ 39 Ne3-f1 Qe1-f2 40 Nf1-e3 Qf2xf3+ 41 Kh1-g1 Kg8-h7, and White is helpless against the threat of 42 . . . Be6xg4 followed by 43 . . . Bg4-h5 and 44 . . . Bh5-g6) 38 . . . a4xb3 39 a2xb3 Qa5-c3, and Black wins a Pawn and the ending.

37   . . .   Qd8-d4!

Combines centralization with control of the Queen file.

38   Nd1-f2   b7-b5!

39   c4xb5   a4xb3

40   a2xb3

Of course not 40 b5xc6, when 40 . . . b3xa2 in reply will compel White to give up his Queen for a Pawn.

40   . . .   Be6xb3

With the powerful threat of 41 . . . Qd4-a1+, winning the Knight—as a start.

41   Nf2xh3

This is the position:

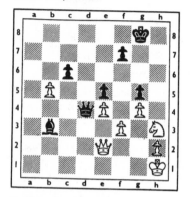

Position after 41 Nf2xh3

41   . . .   Bb3-d1

42   Qe2-f1

Or 42 Qe2-f2, with this delightful finish: 42 Qe2-f2 c6xb5 43 Qf2xd4 e5xd4 44 Nh3-f2 Bd1-e2, and White cannot head off the Pawn, as 45 e4-e5 (to clear a square for the Knight) fails after 45 . . . b5-b4 46 Nf2-e4 Be2xf3+, and Black wins the Knight.

42   . . .   c6xb5

43   Kh1-g2   b5-b4

44	Qf1-b5	b4-b3
45	Qb5-e8+	Kg8-g7
46	Qe8-e7	b3-b2

'The forward march of the Pawn,' says Capablanca himself, 'is irresistible.'

47   Nh3xg5

No better is coming behind the Pawn by 47 Qe7-b7, when 47 . . . Be1xf3+ 48 Kg2xf3, Qd4-d3+ assures the Queening of the Pawn.

Nor can White seek salvation in a perpetual check, as after 47 Qe7xg5+ Kg7-f8 48 Qg5-h6+ Kf8-e7 49 Qh6-g5+ Ke7-d7 50 Qg5-f5+ Kd7-c6 51.Qf5-c8+ Kc6-b5 52 Qc8-b7+ Kb5-a4 53 Qb7-a6+ Ka4-b4 54 Qa6-b7+ Kb4-a3 55 Qb7-a6+ Bd1-a4 56 Qa6-b7 Qd4-b4, and White can resign.

47	. . .	Bd1-b3
48	Ng5xf7	Bb3xf7
49	Qe7-g5+	Kg7-f8
50	Qg5-h6+	Kf8-e7
51	Qh6-g5+	Ke7-e8
52	**White Resigns**	

The play is pretty enough to be an endgame study.

GAME 12

White J. H. Stapfer
Black J. R. Capablanca
New York, 1913

Slav Defence
Capablanca seizes the initiative early in the game, and obtains the makings of a King-side attack.

An offer of a Pawn (which the

opponent eagerly accepts) suddenly transforms the situation. The King-side attack has disappeared, and is replaced by an endgame where Black has all the pressure.

The play from then on illustrates simply and clearly the power that a Rook exerts on the seventh rank absolute—Nimzowitsch's felicitous term for this desirable situation.

1	c2-c4	Ng8-f6
2	Nb1-c3	c7-c6
3	Ng1-f3	d7-d5
4	e2-e3	e7-e6
5	d2-d4	Nb8-d7
6	c4xd5	

There is no need to release the tension in the center, and free Black's Queen Bishop so soon.

A better course was 6 Nf3-e5, and if then 6 . . . d5xc4 7 Ne5xc4 followed by 8 f2-f3 and 9 e3-e4, building up a good Pawn center.

Or the simple 6 Bf1-d3, after which 6 . . . d5xc4 leads to the wilds of the Meran variation, while quiet development leaves Black with a cramped game.

6	. . .	e6xd5
7	Bf1-d3	Bf8-d6
8	0-0	0-0
9	Bc1-d2	Rf8-e8
10	Qd1-c2	Qd8-e7
11	Ra1-e1	Nf6-e4!
12	Bd2-c1	

White's pieces are throttled by a terrible Knight which he dare not remove, as 12 Nc3xe4 d5xe4 costs a piece, while 12 Bd3xe4 d5xe4 13 Nf3-e5 Nd7xe5 14 d4xe5

Qe7xe5 loses more than a Pawn.

12	. . .	Nd7-f6
13	h2-h3	

This Pawn advance, meant to prevent 13 . . . Bc8-g4 or 13 . . . Nf6-g4, furnishes Black with a target for attack.

13	. . .	g7-g5!

Naturellement! The idea is to follow with 14 . . . g5-g4, breaking up the King-side.

14	Bd3xe4	d5xe4
15	Nf3-h2	

Of course not 15 Nf3xg5 h7-h6, and the poor Knight is all dressed up, with no place to go.

15	. . .	g5-g4
16	Nc3-e2	

White loses quickly after 16 h3-h4 by 16 . . . g4-g3 17 f2xg3 Bd6xg3 18 Re1-d1 Qe7-d6, and Black wins the Knight at h2, which may not move and cannot be further protected.

16	. . .	g4xh3
17	g2-g3	

Obviously if 17 g2xh3 Bc8xh3 wins the exchange.

17	. . .	h7-h5
18	Kg1-h1	Kg8-h8
19	Rf1-g1	Re8-g8
20	b2-b3	Nf6-d5
21	Ne2-f4	

Guards the square d3 against intrusion by 21 . . . Nd5-b4 followed by 22 . . . Nb4-d3.

21	. . .	Bc8-g4
22	Bc1-d2	Bd6xf4

23	e3xf4	Ra8-e8
24	Bd2-e3	Nd5-b4
25	Qc2-d2	Re8-d8
26	Re1-a1	

Protects the Rook Pawn so that he can play 27 Qd2-c3, though that accomplishes little.

Truth to tell, it is hard to suggest anything constructive, as White's position is lifeless.

26	...	c6-c5
27	Qd2-c3	Nb4-d5
28	Qc3xc5	

Stapfer snatches at the Pawn (which one must never do against Capablanca!) and comes to grief.

Ending 12

Position after 28 Qc3xc5

Capablanca to move

Stapfer

Black has sacrificed a Pawn with his last move, for the sake of being able to penetrate the seventh rank with his Rook, after a couple of preliminary exchanges.

He relies on the strength of the Rook on the seventh, combined with the pressure of his Bishop and Rook Pawn on the critical white squares.

28	...	Qe7xc5
29	d4xc5	Nd5xe3
30	f2xe3	Rd8-d2
31	Nh2xg4	

Practically forced, if White is to breathe at all. The enemy Rook cannot be driven off by 31 Nh2-f1, as 31 ... Bg4-f3+ in reply would be fatal.

Meanwhile, Black threatens a playful finish by 31 ... Rg8-d8 followed by 32 ... Rd3xh2+ 33 Kh1xh2 Rd8-d2+ 34 Kh2-h1 Bg4-f3+ 35 Rg1-g2 Rd2xg2 36 Ra1-f1 Rg2-d2+ 37 Kh1-g1 h3-h2 mate.

31	...	h5xg4
32	Rg1-d1	Rg8-d8
33	Rd1xd2	Rd8xd2
34	b3-b4	a7-a6
35	Ra1-b1	

White must activate his Rook, or wait for Black's King to wander over to his Pawns by way of c4 and d3, and pick them off at his leisure.

White's King can no nothing to help out, i.e., if 35 Kh1-g1 Kh8-g7 36 Kg1-f1 h3-h2 37 Kf1-e1 Rd2-g2, and mate comes next move.

35	...	Rd2xa2
36	b4-b5	a6xb5
37	Rb1xb5	Ra2-c2
38	Rb5xb7	Kh8-g7
39	Rb7-e7	Rc2xc5
40	Re7xe4	Rc4-c1+

A well-known finesse for posting the Rook on the seventh rank, *and keeping the move.*

41	Kh1-h2	Rc1-c2+
42	Kh2-h1	Rc2-g2
43	Re4-e5	f7-f6

Eliminates the possibility of the Rook getting behind the Knight Pawn.

| 44 | Re5-c5 | Rg2xg3 |

45	e3-e4	Rg3-e3
46	Rc5-c4	g4-g3
47	**White Resigns**	

After 47 Rc4-c1 to stop mate, 47 . . . Re3xe4 ends the last shred of resistance.

An ending played with an economy of style that makes it look easy—the hallmark of Capablanca.

GAME 13

White J. R. Capablanca
Black A. Kupchik
Havana, 1913

Four Knights Game
Although successful with this opening early in his career, Capablanca abandoned it after a heart-breaking loss to Tarrasch in the great St. Petersburg Tournament of 1914.

Kupchik takes a line played by Jaffe against Capablanca in an earlier round—but the wily Cuban had discovered an improvement for White in the meantime, and found a ready victim in Kupchik.

1	e2-e4	e7-e5
2	Ng1-f3	Nb8-c6
3	Nb1-c3	Ng8-f6
4	Bf1-b5	Bf8-b4

The merits of 4 . . . Nc6-d4, Rubinstein's fighting defence, were unknown to most American masters. They made no effort to keep up with the play of their contemporaries, to say nothing of being familiar with the literature of chess.

| 5 | 0-0 | 0-0 |
| 6 | Bb5xc6 | b7xc6 |

The safer recapture is by 6 . . . d7xc6, after which 7 Nf3xe5 poses no danger, as Black equalizes by 7 . . . Rf8-e8 8 Ne5-d3 Bb4xc3 9 d2xc3 Nf6xe4.

| 7 | Nf3xe5 | Qd8-e8 |

'Follows in Jaffe's footsteps,' says Capablanca, 'though this move, as demonstrated here, is bad. Better defences were 7 . . . Rf8-e8, or 7 . . . Bb4xc3.'

The move, however, was not new. It was played by Vidmar against Alekhine at Carlsbad in 1911. Alekhine uncorked a beautiful series of surprise moves that bowled the worthy Doctor over. This is what followed: 8 Ne5-g4 Nf6xe4 9 Ng4-h6+ Kg8-h8 10 Rf1-e1

d7-d5 11 d2-d3 Qe8-e5 12 d3xe4
d5-d4 13 a2-a3 d4xc3 14 a3xb4
c3xb2 15 Nh6xf7+ Kh8-g8
16 Ra1-b1! (what a move!) Rf8xf7
17 Bc1xb2 Qe5-g5 18 Qd1-d3, and
Alekhine eventually won a brilliant
game.

8   Ne5-d3!

Simple and powerful—the Capablanca style. It is doubtful that
Capablanca would have ventured
on so wild-looking a King-side
attack as did Alekhine, even if he
were familiar with the Alekhine-
Vidmar game.

Both Capablanca and Alekhine
were geniuses, but their techniques
differed from each other as Bach's
differed from Beethoven's.

It is we who are fortunate
enough to enjoy their wondrous
though different creations.

Coming back to the game, it is
worthy of note that Capablanca
says of his last move, 'This is the
correct move, after which Black is
lost.'

It is significant that a great
master can foresee that a game is
lost at a point where ordinary
mortals (such as you or I) view it
as being in the opening stages.

8   ...   Bb4xc3

9   d2xc3   Qe8xe4

Obviously, 9 . . . Nf6xe4 is fatal
after 10 Rf1-e1 followed by
11 f2-f3.

10   Rf1-e1   Qe4-h4

11   Qd1-f3   Bc8-a6

12   Bc1-f4   Ra8-c8

13   Bf4-e5   Ba6xd3

Necessary, in view of the threat of
14 Be5xf6 followed by 15 Nd3-c5,
winning a couple of Pawns.

14   c2xd3

'A stronger reply was 24 Be5xf6,'
says Capablanca, 'but Black has a
bad game in either case.'

14   ...   Qh4-g4

15   Be5xf6   Qg4xf3

16   g2xf3   g7xf6

Capablanca has managed to leave
himself with the more active Rooks,
and three Pawn islands (as he so
aptly named them) against four of
his opponent's.

Ending 13

Position after 16 . . . g7xf6

Kupchik

Capablanca to move

White's positional advantage consists
of his control of the open King file,
the greater mobility of his pieces,
and the superior Pawn position.

Capablanca plans to attack the
isolated a-Pawn, and tie Black's

pieces down to its defence. After an exchange of Rooks (inevitable, sooner or later) the remaining Rook can switch from one side of the board to the other, presenting problems to the defender, which may turn out to be insuperable.

17	Re1-e4	Rf8-e8
18	Ra1-e1	Re8-e6
19	Re1-e3	Rc8-e8
20	Kg1-f1	Kg8-f8

Black brings his King to the centre, in conformance with general endgame principles.

More aggressive measures would be dangerous, viz., 20 . . . f6-f5 21 Re4-d4 Re6xe3 22 f2xe3 Re8xe3 23 Kf1-f2 Re3-e7 24 Rd4-a4, followed by 25 Ra4xa7, when suddenly White has a passed Pawn and probable win.

| 21 | Kf1-e2 | Kf8-e7 |
| 22 | Re4-a4! | |

Forces one of Black's Rooks into a passive position.

| 22 | . . . | Re8-a8 |
| 23 | Ra4-a5! | |

And this fine move gains control of the fifth rank stopping either of the doubled Pawns from moving forward to the fourth rank.

| 23 | . . . | d7-d5 |

The Queen Pawn advances (the only Pawn daring to do so) but at the cost of weakening the Queen Bishop Pawn.

| 24 | c3-c4! | Ke7-d6 |

Practically forced, as 24 . . . d5xc4 25 d3xc4 leaves all six of Black's remaining Pawns doubled or iso-

lated, and consequently weak.

As for advancing the Queen Pawn, Capablanca says of that, 'If 24 . . . d5-d4 25 Re3-e4 Ke7-d6 26 b2-b4! Re6-e5 27 Ra5-a6 and Black's game is hopeless.'

| 25 | c4-c5+ | |

Fixes the Bishop Pawns.

| 25 | . . . | Kd6-d7 |
| 26 | d3-d4 | f6-f5 |

Ready to swing his Rook over to h6 to get some counterplay, but Capablanca, always on the *qui vive*, removes the Rook from the scene.

| 27 | Re3xe6 | f7xe6 |

Undoubles his Pawns, thereby getting something out of the mess.

| 28 | f3-f4 | |

Stifles the King Pawn completely, and clears a way for the Rook to swing over to the King side.

| 28 | . . . | Kd7-c8 |

Clearly in order to guard the Rook Pawn, and release the Rook for active duty.

| 29 | Ke2-d2 | Kc8-b7 |

Black misses a drawing chance by 29 . . . Ra8-b8, when 30 b2-b3 in reply blocks the third rank for White's Rook, while if 30 Kd2-c2 Rb8-b4 31 Kc2-c3 Rb4-c4+ 32 Kc3-d3 Rc4-b4 makes it difficult for White to make progress.

| 30 | Ra5-a3 | Ra8-g8 |
| 31 | Ra3-h3 | Rg8-g7 |

Once again the Rook assumes a passive position.

In Rook endings, the Rook, *win-or-lose*, must be active.

Black should play Rg8-g1, where

he might threaten (or at least frighten) some of the Pawns.

32	Kd2-e2	Kb7-a6
33	Rh3-h6	Rg7-e7
34	Ke2-d3	

Black is in semi-*zugzwang*. Only his King can move without losing a Pawn.

| 34 | ... | Ka6-b7 |

The King is on his way to d7, to relieve the Rook of guard duty.

35	h2-h4	Kb7-c8
36	Rh6-h5	Kc8-d7
37	Rh5-g5	

Seizes control of the open file before Black can do so.

| 37 | ... | Re7-f7 |
| 38 | Kd3-c3 | Kd7-c8 |

Black prepares against a possible invasion by White's King at a6.

39	Kc3-b4	Rf7-f6
40	Kb4-a5	Kc8-b7
41	a2-a4	a7-a6
42	h4-h5	Rf6-h6
43	b2-b4	Rh6-f6

This is the situation:

Position after 43 ... Rh6-f6

| 44 | b4-b5 | |

Capablanca himself calls this a weak move, which gives Black a fighting chance.

'In this ending,' he says, 'as is often the case with most players, White plays the best moves whenever the situation is difficult and requires careful handling, but once his position seems to be overwhelming he relaxes his efforts, and the result is nothing to be proud of. The right move was 44 Rg5-g7.'

Analysis shows this probable continuation: 44 Rg5-g7 Rf6-h6 45 b4-b5 a6xb5 46 a4xb5 c6xb5 (or 46 ... Rh6xh5 47 b5-b6) 47 Ka5xb5 Rh6xh5 48 c5-c6+ Kb7-b8 49 Kb5-a6 and mate next move.

I am confident (says Chernev) that 44 b4-b5 would have been marked as the winning move by all other annotators, had not Capablanca himself said that the move was weak, and should have been replaced by 44 Rg5-g7.

| 44 | ... | a6xb5 |
| 45 | a4xb5 | Rf6-f8! |

At last! Black wakes up to the fact that *the Rook must be aggressive in the endgame!*

46	Rg5-g7	Rf8-a8+
47	Ka5-b4	c6xb5
48	Kb4xb5	Ra8-a2
49	c5-c6+	Kb7-b8
50	Rg7xh7	Ra2-b2
51	Kb5-a5	Rb2-a2+
52	Ka5-b4	Ra2xf2
53	Rh7-e7	Rf2xf4

Natural enough, but it loses. The

last drawing chance (if any) was offered by 53 . . . Rf2-b2+ 54 Kb4-c3 Rb2-h2 55 Re7xe6 Kb8-a7 56 h5-h6 Ka7-b6.

54	h5-h6!	Rf4xd4+
55	Kb4-b5	Rd4-d1
56	h6-h7	Rd1-b1+
57	Kb5-c5	Rb1-c1+
58	Kc5-d4	Rc1-d1+
59	Kd4-e5	Rd1-e1+
60	Ke5-f6	Re1-h1
61	Re7-e8+	Kb8-a7
62	h7-h8(Q)	Rh1xh8
63	Re8xh8	Ka7-b6
64	Kf6xe6	Kb6xc6
65	Ke6xf5	Kc6-c5
66	Kf5-e5	c7-c6
67	Rh8-h6	Kc5-b5

68	Ke5-d4	**Black Resigns**

Hooper in his *Practical Chess Endgames* sums it up well, when he says, 'A characteristic of this kind of endgame is the switching of the attack from wing to wing. This is not a random thing. The broad pattern of this game is that White first draws Black's King and Rook over to defend the Queen side; Black's King side is then less well-defended; so White switches his attack to the King side; in trying to defend himself there too, Black becomes disorganized; White finishes with a two-pronged attack on both wings. Altogether White made use of the third, fourth, fifth, sixth, seventh, and eighth ranks, and of the a-, e-, g-, and h-files.'

GAME 14

White J. R. Capablanca
Black F. P. Beynon
New York, 1913

Sicilian Defence
Capablanca handles the opening in thoroughly modern style, and keeps his opponent busy warding off threats on both sides of the board.

The ending is particularly interesting, studded as it is with unexpected stabbing Pawn moves.

1	e2-e4	c7-c5

Even so far back as 1851, when the First International Chess Tournament took place at London, players have resorted to the Sicilian Defence, to avoid the complexities of the Ruy López. (Today the Sicilian Defence, with its myriads of variations and nests of subvariations, has a whole literature of its own.)

2	Ng1-f3	Nb8-c6
3	d2-d4	c5xd4
4	Nf3xd4	Ng8-f6
5	Nb1-c3	d7-d6

Here 5 . . . g7-g6 is premature, as
after 6 Nd4xc6 b7xc6 7 e4-e5 the
Knight must return home.

6	Bf1-e2	g7-g6
7	0-0	Bc8-d7
8	Bc1-e3	Bf8-g7
9	h2-h3	0-0
10	Qd1-d2	a7-a6

A good move, as it prevents
11 Nd4-b5, and prepares for
Queen-side counterplay by
11 . . . b7-b5, 12 . . . Nc6-a5,
13 . . . Qd8-c7 and 14 . . . Na5-c4,
the attack on the c-file being
compensation to Black for his
otherwise cramped position.

11   Ra1-d1

The immediate 11 Be3-h6 (to get
rid of Black's strongest minor
piece) would be an error, as after
11 . . . Nc6xd4 12 Bh6xg7
Nd4xe2+ 13 Qd2xe2 Kg8xg7,
Black wins a piece.

| 11 | . . . | Qd8-c7 |
| 12 | Nd4-b3 | Ra8-d8 |

More to the point was
12 . . . Ra8-c8, followed by
13 . . . Nc6-a5 and 14 . . . Na5-c4,
to gain control of c4 (and perhaps
enforce an exchange of Knight for
Bishop).

13	Be3-h6	Bd7-c8
14	Bh6xg7	Kg8xg7
15	Qd2-e3	e7-e5
16	f2-f4	Bc8-e6
17	Nc3-d5	Be6xd5

The exchange is forced, the consequences of a Queen move being
disastrous. For example, if

17 . . . Qc7-d7 18 Nd5xf6 Kg7xf6
19 Rd1xd6! Qd7xd6 20 f4xe5+,
and Black must either play
20 . . . Kf6xe5 and be mated by
21 Qe3-f4+, or move his King and
allow the impudent Pawn to take
his Queen.

Or if 17 . . . Qc7-c8 18 Nd5xf6
Kg7xf6 19 f4xe5+ Kf6-e7
20 e5xd6+ Rd8xd6 21 Qe3-c5
Rf8-d8 22 e4-e5 and Black must
give up his Knight.

| 18 | e4xd5 | Nc6-e7 |

Much better is the aggressive
18 . . . Nc6-b4, with a double
attack on the d-Pawn by the
Knights, and a double attack on the
c-Pawn by Queen and Knight.

The line that seems best for
White is this: 19 f4xe5 d6xe5
20 d5-d6! Rd8xd6 21 Qe3xe5
Rf8-d8 (or 21 . . . Rd6-c6
22 Qe5xc7 Rc6xc7 23 c2-c3, with
honours even) 22 Nb3-d4, and the
annoying threat of 23 Nd4-e6+ is
hard to meet (to say nothing of
23 Rf1xf6, or 23 g2-g4 and 24 g4-g5).

19	c2-c4	Ne7-f5
20	Qe3-f3	e5-e4
21	Qf3-c3	

Pins the Knight and menaces
22 g2-g4 and 23 g4-g5, winning
the unfortunate creature.

| 21 | . . . | Qc7-b6+ |
| 22 | Nb3-d4 | |

This Knight, though pinned, is
dangerous.

| 22 | . . . | Rd8-c8 |
| 23 | Kg1-h1 | Nf5xd4 |

Safest, as otherwise this might
occur: 24 g2-g4 Nf5-e7 25 g4-g5

Nf6-d7 (or to h5) 26 Nd4-f5+
Kg7-g8 27 Nf5-h6 mate.

24	Rd1xd4	Kg7-g8
25	f4-f5	Rc8-e8
26	b2-b4	Qb6-c7
27	Qc3-g3	Qc7-e7
28	f5xg6	f7xg6
29	c4-c5!	

The birth of a passed Pawn!

29	. . .	d6xc5
30	d5-d6	Qe7-e5

Ending 14

Position after 30 . . . Qe7-e5

Beynon

Capablanca to move

Capablanca is a Pawn behind—for
the moment. After he recovers it,
material will be even.

Positionally, White may enjoy a
slight advantage, as his passed Pawn
has only two steps to take to
become a Queen, while Black's
King Pawn has three. The road is
heavily guarded though, and Capablanca's problem is to dispose of
the powerful blockaders.

31	Qg3xe5	Re8xe5
32	b4xc5	Nf6-d7

On 32 . . . Re5xc5, the reply
33 Rf1xf6 Rf8xf6 34 d6-d7 wins a
piece.

After Black's actual move, it
would seem that White can make
no progress, and is bound to lose
the Bishop Pawn.

So it would seem but watch!

33	Be2xa6!	b7xa6

Some pretty play follows
33 . . . Rf8xf1+ 34 Ba6xf1 Re5xc5
(if 34 . . . Nd7xc5 35 d6-d7 wins a
piece for White) 35 Rd4xe4, thus:

(a) 35 . . . Rc5-d5 (to attack the
Pawn) 36 Bf1-c4 pinning the Rook.

(b) 35 . . . Rc5-c6 (to attack the
Pawn) 36 Re4-e8+ Kg8-f7
37 Re8-e7+, and White wins a
piece.

(c) 35 . . . Nd7-f6 36 Re5-e8+!
Kg8-f7 (on 36 . . . Nf6xe8 37 d6-d7
wins nicely) 37 Re8-e7+ Kf7-f8
38 Rd7xb7, and White has won a
second Pawn.

34	Rf1xf8+	Kg8xf8

Clearly, this offers more hope than
34 . . . Nd7xf8 35 c5-c6 Re5-c5
36 d6-d7 Nf8-e6 37 Rd4xe4
Ne6-d8 (on 37 . . . Rc5xc6
38 Re4xe6 wins) 38 Re4-e8+
Kg8-f7 39 Re8xd8 Rc5xc6
40 Rd8-f8+, and White wins.

35	c5-c6

Threatens to take the Knight, and
then move on to become a Queen.

35	. . .	Kf8-e8
36	c6-c7	Re5-c5

Does this head off the Pawn?

37	Rd4xe4+	Ke8-f8
38	Re4-e7	Nd7-f6
39	d6-d7	Nf6xd7

What else is there? If 39 . . . Rc5xc7
40 d7-d8(Q)+ forces mate, or if
39 . . . Kf8xe7 40 d7-d8(Q)+ wins

at once.

40	Re7xd7	Black Resigns

As the threat of 41 Rd7-d8+
followed by Queening the Pawn
cannot be met.

A scherzo by Capablanca who
went through this tournament with
a score of 13 wins, no draws, no
losses.

GAME 15

White O. Duras
Black J. R. Capablanca
New York, 1913

Queen's Gambit Accepted
Capablanca turns out one of his
most famous Rook-and-Pawn endings in this game against Duras.

The play is instructive enough
(though not wearisomely so) to have
found its way into practically every
book on endgame play.

Very attractive is the way
Black's Pawns, escorted by their
King, march irresistibly up the
board to victory, sweeping away all
obstacles in their path.

1	d2-d4	d7-d5
2	Ng1-f3	Ng8-f6
3	c2-c4	e7-e6

The Queens' Gambit Declined . . .

4	Nb1-c3	d5xc4

. . . but now accepted.

5	e2-e3	a7-a6
6	Bf1xc4	b7-b5
7	Bc4-d3	Bc8-b7

8	a2-a4	

A good alternative was 8 Qd1-c2,
preparing to advance the King
Pawn.

8	. . .	b5-b4
9	Nc3-b1	

Worth more than a passing glance
was 9 Nc3-a2 in order to deploy the
Knight (after 10 Bc1-d2) to b3 (by
way of c1) where it would occupy a
strong, unassailable position.

A fine example of this strategic
placement of the Knight occurs in
the Alekhine–Tarrasch game at
Hastings in 1922.

9	. . .	c7-c5
10	0-0	Nb8-c6
11	d4xc5	

With this White gives up the center,
fearing perhaps that his opponent
might capture first, leaving him
with an isolated Pawn.

11	...	Bf8xc5
12	Qd1-e2	Qd8-d5
13	Rf1-d1	Qd5-h5
14	Nb1-d2	Nc6-a5!

An exclamation mark for this move, which prevents White's Knight from reaching b3.

To my mind, the strategy of preventing a good move being made is as brilliant as the flashy sacrifice of a piece.

15	Nd2-f1	

So the Knight must change its itinerary.

15	...	0-0
16	Nf1-g3	Qh5-g4
17	e3-e4	Na5-b3
18	Ra1-b1	Rf8-d8

An impetuous attacker would have moved 18 . . . h7-h5, when the reply 19 h2-h3 (to stop the further advance 19 . . . h5-h4) would have failed, on account of 19 . . . Qg4xg3, snapping off a Knight whose protection was illusory.

Capablanca is in no hurry, but brings another piece into play.

19	Bc1-e3	

A temporary sacrifice of a Pawn, which leads to a wholesale clearance of material, the return of the Pawn, and good prospects of a draw.

19	...	Nf6xe4
20	Bd3-c2	Bc5xe3
21	Qe2xe3	

Carefully avoiding 21 Bc2xb3, the penalty for which being

21 . . . Be3xf2+ 22 Kg1-h1 (or to f1) Bf2xg3, and the impudent Bishop is immune to capture, on pain of loss of the Queen.

21	...	Nb3-c5
22	h2-h3	Qg4-g6
23	Ng3xe4	Rd8xd1+
24	Rb1xd1	Bb7xe4
25	Bc2xe4	Nc5xe4
26	Qe3-d4	

Regains the Pawn by the threat of mate in two.

26	...	h7-h6
27	Qd4xb4	Ne4-f6
28	Qb4-b7	Qg6-e4
29	Qb7xe4	Nf6xe4
30	b2-b4	

Unfortunate, as with 30 Rd1-d4, White has a fairly easy game.

30	...	Ne4-c3

The Knight pounces on Rook and Pawn like a hawk.

31	Rd1-d3	

To his consternation, White discovers that he cannot save the Pawn, as 31 Rd1-a1 Ra8-b8 32 Ra1-a3 Nc3-d5 wins the b-Pawn.

31	...	Nc3xa4
32	Rd3-a3	Na4-b6
33	Nf3-e5	Kg8-f8
34	Ne5-d3	Nb6-d5
35	Ra3-a4	Ra8-b8
36	Ra4xa6	Nd5xb4
37	Nd3xb4	Rb8xb4
38	Ra6-a7	

Ending 15

Position after 38 Ra6-a7

Capablanca to move

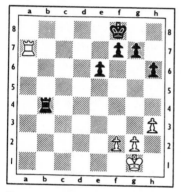

Duras

Capablanca is a Pawn ahead, but Rook endings are notoriously difficult to win even with an extra Pawn, and especially so when all the Pawns are on one side of the board.

Capablanca's plan is to turn his King Pawn into a passed Pawn, or split up his opponent's Pawns—or both!

In the course of this, he will try to advance his Pawns up the board, accompanied by the King.

| 38 | ... | h6-h5 |
| 39 | g2-g3 | h5-h4! |

Prevents White from playing 40 h3-h4. The preliminary 39 . . . g7-g5 is thwarted by 40 Ra7-a5 f7-f6 41 Ra5-a7, cutting off the King.

| 40 | g3xh4 | |

Better than this, which splits up his Pawns, might have been 40 g3-g4

followed by 41 Kg1-g2.

40	...	Rb4xh4
41	Kg1-g2	e6-e5
42	Kg2-g3	Rh4-d4

This is best, though it allows 43 h3-h4 in reply.

| 43 | Ra7-a5 | f7-f6 |
| 44 | Ra5-a7 | Kf8-g8 |

The King must take the long way round to get into the game.

45	Ra7-b7	Kg8-h7
46	Rb7-a7	Kh7-g6
47	Ra7-e7	Rd4-d3+
48	Kg3-g2	

The King must retreat. Alternatives are:

(a) 48 Kg3-h4 Rd3-f3, and Black wins a Pawn,

(b) 48 Kg3-g4 f6-f5+ 49 Kg4-h4 Kg6-f6 50 Re7-a7 g7-g5+, and mate next move.

(c) 48 f2-f3 Kg6-f5 49 Re7xg7 e5-e4 50 h3-h4 Rd3xf3+, and Black's two connected passed Pawns assure the win.

| 48 | ... | Rd3-d5 |

Protects the e-Pawn, enabling the f-Pawn to advance.

49	Kg2-g3	f6-f5
50	Re7-a7	Rd5-d3+
51	Kg3-g2	e5-e4
52	Ra7-a4	Kg6-g5

Black gains more territory.

| 53 | Ra4-a5 | g7-g6 |

The march of the little Pawns is slow but inexorable.

| 54 | Ra5-b5 | Kg5-f4 |

55	Rb5-a5	Rd3-d2
56	Ra5-a4	

Holds back the King Pawn—for the time being!

56	...	g6-g5
57	Ra4-b4	Kf4-e5

Renews the threat of 58 . . . e4-e3, striking again at the pinned Pawn.

58	Rb4-b5+	Rd2-d5
59	Rb5-b8	

Exchanging Rooks is out of the question, as a pure Pawn ending would present no problems.

59	...	f5-f4
60	Rb8-g8	Ke5-d4

Black could play for a mating combination by 60 . . . Rd5-d2 61 Rg8xg5+ Ke5-f6 62 Rg5-g4 Kf6-f5 63 Kg2-f1 f4-f3 64 Kf1-e1 Rd2-e2+ 65 Ke1-f1 Re2-a2 66 Kf1-e1 Ra2-a1+ 67 Ke1-d2 Ra1-f1 68 Kd2-e3 Rf1-e1+ 69 Ke3-d4 Re1-e2 70 Rg4-g8 (ready to meet 70 . . . Re2xf2 with 71 Rg8-f8+, regaining the Pawn) Re2-d2+ 71 Kd4-e3 Rd2-d3 mate.

But why go in for complications when there is a clearer road to the goal?

61 Kg2-f1

This is to prevent further entry by 61 . . . Kd4-d3 and 62 . . . Kd3-e2.

61 ... Kd4-d3

Black in turn keeps White's King out of the square e2.

62 Rg8-a8 e4-e3!

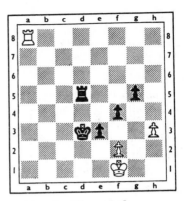

Position after 62 . . . e4-e3

This begins the final phase, with Black posing threats of mate or Pawn promotion.

63 Ra8-a3+

If 63 f2xe3 Kd3xe3 64 Ra8-a3+ (on 64 Ra8-e8+ Ke3-f3 followed by 65 . . . Kf3-g3 wins) 64 . . . Rd5-d3 65 Ra3-a2 f4-f3! (definitely not 65 . . . Rd3-d1+ 66 Kf1-g2 Rd1-d2+ 67 Ra2xd2 Ke3xd2 68 Kf2-f3 and draws by playing 69 h3-h4 next move) 66 Ra2-a1 Rd3-d4 followed by 67 . . . Ke3-f4 and 68 . . . Kf4-g3, and Black wins.

White might have drawn here, according to Levenfisch and Smyslov, by 63 Ra8-e8 Kd3-d2 64 Re8-e7 Rd5-d3 65 Re7-e5 Kd2-d1 66 Re5-e8 e3xf2 67 Re8-e5 Kd1-d2 68 Kf1xf2! (but not 68 Re5xg5, because of 68 . . . Kd2-e3 and Black wins!).

63	...	Kd3-e4
64	f2xe3	f4-f3!

The point of Black's 62 . . . e4-e3! move, and far superior to the anticipated 64 . . . f4xe3, which offers White drawing chances by 65 Ra3-a8

Rd5-f5+ 66 Kf1-e2 Rf5-f2+
67 Ke2-e1 Ke4-f3 68 Ra8-f8+
Kf3-g3 69 Rf8-e8! Rf2-f3
70 Ke1-e2.

65   Kf1-g1

A nice point is that White's King
must be confined to the first rank,
or risk sudden death, thus:
65 Kf1-f2 Rd5-d2+ 66 Kf2-g3
Rd2-g2 mate!

65   ...   Rd5-d3

66   Ra3-a8

There is no relief in 66 Ra3-a5
Ke4xe3 67 Ra5-e5+ Ke3-f4
68 Re5-a5 g5-g4! 69 Ra5-a4+ (or
69 h3xg4 Kf4-g3 70 Ra5-a1
Rd3-d2 71 g4-g5 Rd2-g2+
72 Kg1-f1 Rg2-h2 73 Kf1-g1
f3-f2+ 74 Kg1-f1 Rh2-h1+, and
wins) 69 . . . Kf4-e3 70 Ra3-a1
g4-g3, and Black wins.

Nor does an exchange of Rooks
offer comfort: if 66 Ra3xd3 Ke4xd3
67 Kg1-f2 Kd3-e4 68 Kf2-f1
Ke4xe3 69 Kf1-g1 f3-f2+ (or the
brutal 69 . . . Ke3-e2) 70 Ke1-f1
Ke3-f3 71 h3-h4 g5-g4 72 h4-h5
g4-g3 73 h5-h6 g3-g2 mate.

66   ...   Ke4xe3

67   Ra8-e8+   Ke3-f4

68   Re8-g8   Rd3-d1+

69   Kg1-f2   Rd1-d2+

70   Kf2-f1

On 70 Kf2-g1, Black finishes brilliantly with 70 . . . g5-g4! (letting
White capture with check!)
71 Rg8xg4+ (of course not
71 h3xg4 Kf4-g3, and mate next)
71 . . . Kf4-e3 72 Rg4-g8 Rd2-d1+
73 Kg1-h2 f3-f2 74 Rg8-e8+
Ke3-d2 75 Re8-d8+ Kd2-c2
76 Rd8xd1 Kc2xd1 77 Kh2-g2
Kd1-e2, and wins.

70   ...   Rd2-h2

71   Kf1-g1

On 71 Rg8-h8 Kf4-g3 adds a mate
threat to White's troubles.

71   ...   Rh2xh3

72   Rg8-g7   g5-g4

73   Rg7-g8   Kf4-g3

74   White Resigns

Duras has had enough, and does not
care to see this: 74 Rg8-f8 f3-f2+
75 Rf8xf2 (or 75 Kg1-f1 Rh3-h1+
76 Kf1-e2 Rh1-e1+ and the Pawn
becomes a Queen) 75 . . . Rh3-h1+
76 Kg1xh1 Kg3xf2, and the last
Pawn strolls up the board to the
coronation.

A well-played ending that merits
careful study.

GAME 16

White J. R. Capablanca
Black R. Teichmann
Berlin, 1913

Queen's Gambit Declined
Capablanca was justifiably proud of
winning this ending, which, as he
says, 'has the merit of having been
played against one of the best

players in the world.'

It is noteworthy that Teich-mann's possession of the two Bishops caused Capablanca no dis-may, as he soon stripped them of their powers.

One was disposed of by an ex-change, while the other was render-ed impotent by the flock of Pawns in its path hampering its move-ments.

1	d2-d4	d7-d5
2	Ng1-f3	Ng8-f6
3	c2-c4	e7-e6
4	Bc1-g5	Bf8-e7
5	Nb1-c3	Nb8-d7
6	e2-e3	0-0
7	Ra1-c1	b7-b6
8	c4xd5	e6xd5
9	Bf1-b5	

An innovation of Capablanca's, the aim being to exert pressure on the Queen-side, in particular on the hanging Pawns resulting from an eventual . . . c7-c5.

This is stronger than the old move 9 Bf1-d3, made with an eye to a King-side attack.

9	. . .	Bc8-b7
10	0-0	

Capablanca was above playing to win by a trap. But for ordinary mortals who have no such com-punctions, the Pittsburgh Trap is subtle, effective and painless—the victim scarcely realizing he is in it until it is too late. It goes this way: 10 Nf3-e5 a7-a6 11 Bb5-c6 Bb7xc6 12 Ne5xc6 Qd8-e8 13 Nc6xe7+ Qe8xe7 14 Nc3xd5 Qe7-e4

15 Nd5xf6+ g7xf6 16 Bg5-h6 Qe4xg2 17 Qd1-f3! (this move always comes as a shock) 17 . . . Qg2xf3 18 Rh1-g1+ Kg8-h8 19 Bh6-g7+ Kh8-g8 20 Bg7xf6+, and White mates next move.

10	. . .	a7-a6
11	Bb5-a4	Ra8-c8
12	Qd1-e2	c7-c5
13	d4xc5	Nd7xc5

Black is left with an isolated Pawn, a weakness that leads to his loss. It was a choice of evils though, as capturing with the Pawn instead would have left him with hanging Pawns in the centre.

14	Rf1-d1	Nc5xa4

Black snaps at the opportunity to exchange his Knight and be left with the two Bishops, believing that they will increase his chances in the coming endgame.

Capablanca, looking further ahead into the position, sees that he can blunt the power of the Bishops and render them harmless.

15	Nc3xa4	b6-b5
16	Rc1xc8	Qd8xc8
17	Na4-c3	Qc8-c4

Black's object is to exchange Queens and increase the effectiveness of his Bishops, as the surplus pieces dis-appear from the board. He fails to realize that his inactive Queen Bishop cannot come into play easily, being tied down to the defence of the Queen Pawn.

18	Nf3-d4	

Blockades the isolated Pawn—the usual recipe for such cases.

18 ... Qc4xe2

19 Nc3xe2

'Notice the co-ordination of the Knights,' says Capablanca. 'They are maneuvered chain-like, so to speak, in order to maintain one of them either at d4 or ready to go there.'

Hooper and Brandreth in *The Unknown Capablanca* make this perceptive observation, 'It is possible that Black already has a lost game. That such judgments were harder to make then than now shows how technique has since advanced; and much of the pioneer work was done by Capablanca.'

Ending 16

Position after 19 Nc3xe2

Teichmann to move

Capablanca

It may not be evident that White has the superior position, but consider this:

White's Knight, admirably posted at d4, is a mobile (and there-fore ideal) blockader of the isolated Queen Pawn. In the event of its exchange, the other Knight is prepared to spring up and take its place at d4.

White's Bishop has a grip on the enemy Knight, and this pressure is not easily shaken off.

In contrast, Black's Knight may not move; his King Bishop is tied down to defending the Knight, and his Queen Bishop is restricted in its movements by the many Pawns occupying squares of the same colour.

Capablanca's plan is to exploit these circumstances by increasing the pressure, and thus forcing Black to give up a Pawn or two to obtain a measure of freedom.

19 ... Rf8-c8

If 19 ... g7-g6 to prevent the Knight from coming in at f5, there follows 20 Rd1-c1 Rf8-c8 21 Rc1xc8+ Bb7xc8 22 Nd4-c6 Kg8-f8 23 Ne2-f4 Bc8-b7 24 Nc6xe7 Kf8xe7 25 f2-f3 and White's threat to bring his King over to e5 to win the pinned Knight would be decisive.

It is true that Black can save his Knight by playing ... h7-h6 giving up a Pawn, but that amounts to losing the game in a different way.

20 Nd4-f5! Kg8-f8

The only defence. On 20 ... Be7-f8 21 Bg5xf6 g7xf6 leaves Black's King-side Pawns miserably placed. Or if 20 ... Be7-d8 21 Nf5-d6 Rc8-c7 22 Nd6xb7 Rc7xb7 23 Bg5xf6 Bd8xf6 24 Rd1xd5 Rb7-c7 25 Rd5-d2, and White has an extra Pawn, as Capablanca shows.

21	Nf5xe7	Kf8xe7
22	Ne2-d4	g7-g6

Practically forced, to avoid these evil consequences: 23 Nd4-f5+ Ke7-f8 24 Bg5xf6 g7xf6 25 Nf5-d6 Rc8-c7 26 Nd6xb7 Rc7xb7 27 Rd1xd5, and Black has lost a Pawn, and has had his King-side Pawn position shattered.

23 f2-f3!

White threatens (after due preparation) a King wandering to e5, by way of f2, g3 and f4, to attack the unfortunate Knight again and remove it from circulation.

23 ... h7-h6

Black gives up a Pawn to shake off the troublesome pin.

24	Bg5xh6	Nf6-d7

25 h2-h4!

Starts the King-side majority of Pawns rolling. Capablanca intends to follow up with g2-g4 and h4-h5, to create an outside passed Pawn.

25 ... Nd7-c5

If instead, the Rook swings over to the King-side by 25 ... Rc8-h8, the reply is not 26 Bh6-g5+, which is met by 26 ... f7-f6, but 26 Bh6-f4, and the Pawn is immune to capture.

26 Bh6-f4 Nc5-e6

Black seizes his best drawing chance—to exchange Knights and remain with Bishops of opposite colour.

27 Nd4xe6 Ke7xe6

On 27 ... f7xe6 28 Bf4-e5 dominates the center and the black squares, with a winning position

for White.

The text leaves a theoretical draw, but Capablanca is death on theoretical draws.

28 Rd1-d2 Rc8-h8

A thrust at the Rook Pawn which Capablanca parries easily—by paying no attention to it!

This is the position:

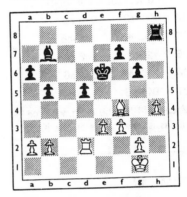

Position after 28 ... Rc8-h8

29 Rd2-c2 Rh8-c8

On 29 ... Rh8xh4, White can regain his Pawn with advantage by 30 Rc2-c7 Bb7-a8 31 Rc7-a7 Ba8-c6 32 Ra7xa6, or leave his Rook stationed permanently at c7, where it hangs like the Sword of Damocles over the Black King's head.

30 Rc2xc8 Bb7xc8

31 Kg1-f2!

The King is on his way to d4, from which square he can penetrate further into Black's position by way of e5 or c5, with fatal effect.

31 ... d5-d4

The King's march must be stopped even at the cost of another Pawn.

(For didn't Paulsen draw against Morphy in their fourth round game at New York in 1857 in an ending with Bishops of opposite colours, though he was two Pawns down and could have been three?).

32	e3xd4	Ke6-d5

Black's Pawn sacrifice has allowed his King and Bishop more freedom, which offers some consolation.

33	Kf2-e3	Bc8-e6
34	Ke3-d3	Kd5-c6
35	a2-a3	Be6-c4+
36	Kd3-e3	Bc4-e6
37	Bf4-h6	

Vacates f4 for the King, whence he can assist the Pawns on the King-side. The Bishop meanwhile is to be deployed to g7, where it protects the Queen Pawn as well as the Knight Pawn behind it.

37	. . .	Kc6-d5
38	Bh6-g7!	**Black Resigns**

Teichmann is convinced, foreseeing this possible sequel: 38 . . . Be6-f5 39 Ke3-f4 (threatens 40 h4-h5) Bf5-d3 40 Kf4-g5 Kd5-e6 41 g2-g4 Bd3-c2 42 f3-f4 Bc2-d3 43 f4-f5+ g6xf5 44 g4xf5+ Bd3xf5 (otherwise the Rook Pawn moves on unhindered) 45 d4-d5+, and White wins the Bishop and the game.

There is subtlety and elegance in this finely-played ending.

GAME 17

White Capablanca
Black Salwe and allies
Exhibition Game, Lodz, 1913

Ruy López

I have never ceased to wonder at Capablanca's mysterious faculty for deciding almost at sight that he had a won game, though the game might still be in its opening stages. It calls to mind Fine's comment, 'What others could not see in a month's study, he saw at a glance.'

Asked for his opinion of the position at the 18th move of this game, he replied without hesitation, 'Black is lost; White's King Pawn will win the game.'

'And so it happened,' Capablanca says, 'to the great surprise of all present.'

1	e2-e4	e7-e5
2	Ng1-f3	Nb8-c6
3	Bf1-b5	a7-a6
4	Bb5-a4	Ng8-f6
5	0-0	Nf6xe4

Black obtains active play for his pieces, at the risk of weakening his Pawn structure.

6	d2-d4	b7-b5
7	Ba4-b3	d7-d5
8	d4xe5	Bc8-e6
9	c2-c3	Bf8-e7
10	Nb1-d2	

In order to remove the strongly-posted Knight at e4, or drive it off.

| 10 | ... | Ne4-c5 |

This is not as safe as castling, as Capablanca demonstrated in his game against Chajes at New York in 1915.

| 11 | Bb3-c2 | Be6-g4 |

Chajes tried 11 . . . d5-d4 at this point, believing Black's game to be superior, but he was quickly dis-illusioned, the next few moves being: 12 Nd2-e4 d4xc3 13 Ne4xc5 Be7xc5 14 Bc2-e4 Qd8-d7 15 b2xc3 Ra8-d8 16 Qd1xd7+ Be6xd7 17 Rf1-d1 Nc6-e7 (if 17 . . . 0-0 18 Bc1-e3! Bc5xe3 19 Rd1xd7! Rd8xd7 20 Be4xc6, and White will emerge with two pieces for a Rook and Pawn) 18 Nf3-d4 h7-h6 19 Nd4-b3 Bc5-b6 20 Bc1-a3, and White's beautifully-placed Bishops soon won a Pawn, and thereafter the game.

12	h2-h3	Bg4-h5
13	Rf1-e1	Bh5-g6
14	Nf3-d4	Nc6xd4

Practically forced, as after 14 . . . Qd8-d7 15 f2-f4 is hard to meet.

| 15 | c3xd4 | Nc5-e6 |
| 16 | Nd2-b3 | Be7-g5 |

Black would have liked to dispute the center with 16 . . . c7-c5, but after 17 d4xc5 his Queen Pawn, now isolated, would be difficult, yea impossible, to defend, and would eventually fall.

| 17 | g2-g3 | Bg5xc1 |
| 18 | Ra1xc1 | 0-0 |

The diagram shows the position at the point where Capablanca stated that he had a won game:

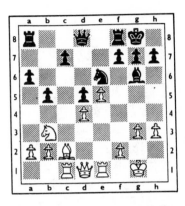

Position after 18 . . . 0-0

| 19 | f2-f4 | |

The threat of winning a piece by 20 f4-f5 forces another exchange.

19	...	Bg6xc2
20	Rc1xc2	g7-g6
21	Nb3-c5!	

Gets a strong grip on the position. The Knight can be removed by exchange, only to be replaced by another piece.

21	...	Rf8-e8
22	Qd1-d3	Ne6xc5
23	Rc2xc5	Qd8-d7

Ending 17

Salwe and allies

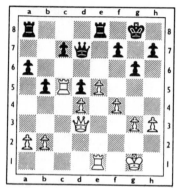

Capablanca to move

White's position is superior:

(a) he exerts pressure on the Queen Bishop file,

(b) his pieces are aggressively placed,

(c) he can switch the attack from one side to the other, while his opponent is restricted to patient defence.

Capablanca plans to combine threats against the backward Queen Bishop Pawn with threats of establishing a Pawn at f5. (This maneuvering against weaknesses on both sides of the board, by alternating the attack, was also demonstrated beautifully by Lasker at St. Petersburg in 1909, against Salwe, the same opponent.)

24	g3-g4	c7-c6
25	Re1-c1	Ra8-c8
26	Qd3-c3	Re8-e6

Black's heavy pieces closely guard the Queen Bishop Pawn, as its loss would be catastrophic.

The moment would seem to be ripe to advance by 27 f4-f5, but this would be premature, as after 27 . . . g6xf5 28 g4xf5 Re6-h6, two of White's Pawns are suddenly under attack.

27	Kg1-h2	Kg8-h8
28	Qc3-a3	Qd7-b7
29	Qa3-g3	f7-f5

This prevents the advance 30 f4-f5. White plans to renew the threat by compelling Black to play . . . f5xg4.

30 Qg3-f3

Threatens to win brilliantly by 31 Qf3xd5! c6xd5 32 Rc5xc8+ Re6-e8 (if 32 . . . Kh8-g7 33 Rc1-c7+ wins) 33 Rc8xe8+ Kh8-g7 34 Re8-c8 Qb7-b6 35 Rc1-c7+ Kg7-h6 36 g4-g5+ Kh6-h5 37 Rc7xh7 mate.

30	. . .	Qb7-d7
31	Kh2-g3	

Now 31 Qf3xd5 would fail after 31 . . . c6xd5 32 Rc5xc8+ Re6-e8.

31	. . .	Rc8-f8
32	Qf3-a3	Rf8-a8
33	Qa3-c3	Ra8-c8
34	Qc3-c2	Kh8-g8
35	Kg3-f3!	

White does not rush to win a Pawn, as after 35 g4xf5 g6xf5 36 Qc2xf5, there follows 36 . . . Re6-g6+, and White loses his Queen!

But now, as a result of Capablanca's clever maneuvering, Black cannot protect both his Bishop Pawns, and is forced to exchange

Pawns—to White's advantage.

35	...	f5xg4+
36	h3xg4	Qd7-f7

This is the situation:

Position after 36 ... Qd7-f7

'A careful examination of the position will reveal,' says Capablanca, 'that besides the advantage of position on White's part, the power of the Pawn at e5 is enormous, and that it is the commanding position of this Pawn, and the fact that it is free to advance, once all the pieces are exchanged, that constitutes the pivot of all White's maneuvers.'

37 Kf3-e3

Here too, 37 f4-f5 might be premature, and offer counter-chances, say by 37 ... g6xf5 38 g4xf5 Qf7-h5+ 39 Kf3-e3 Qh5-g5+ 40 Ke3-e2 Re6-h6, etc.

37	...	Rc8-f8

Not only stops 38 f4-f5, but actually threatens to take the Pawn!

38 Rc1-f1

Defends one Bishop Pawn and threatens to capture another.

38	...	Qf7-d7
39	Qc2-g2	

Not yet, not yet! If 39 f4-f5 g6xf5 40 g4xf5 Qd7-g7, and Black might still cause trouble in view of White's exposed King.

39	...	Qd7-e7

Ready to answer 40 f4-f5 with 40 ... Qe7-g5+, winning a Pawn after 41 Ke3-f2 g6xf5 42 g4xf5 Rf8xf5+ (but not 42 ... Qg5xg2+ 43 Kf2xg2 Re6-h6 44 f5-f6 Rf8-c8 45 e5-e6, and White wins).

40 Rf1-c1

More veering and tacking, to keep Black on his toes.

40	...	Re6-f6
41	Rc1-f1	Kg8-h8
42	Qg2-c2	Qe7-e8
43	Qc2-h2	Qe8-e7
44	Rf1-f3	Rf6-e6
45	Ke3-f2	a6-a5

At last all is in readiness. Capablanca has finally secured the position he wants.

46	f4-f5!	g6xf5
47	g4xf5	Qe7-g5!

Black seizes his chance to attack—an attack that might even lead to mate!

48 Qh2-f4!

Capablanca avoids capturing the Rook, as the continuation would be (after 48 f5xe6) 48 ... Qg5-d2+ 49 Kf2-g1 (if 49 Kf2-g3 Rf8-g8+ 50 Kg3-h3 Qd2-h6 mate) 49 ... Qd2-d1+ 50 Kg1-f2 Rf8xf3+ 51 Kf2-g2 Qd1-f1 mate.

48	...	Rf8xf5

Game 18

A reckless capture, but exchanging Queens instead leaves White with two connected passed Pawns, and an easy win.

49   Qf4xf5   Qg5-d2+

Whereas this offers some hope of a draw by perpetual check.

50   Kf2-f1   Re6-g6

51   Qf5-f8+   Rg6-g8

52   Qf8-f6+   Rg8-g7

53   Rf3-g3   Black Resigns

He can get in a few more checks, but after 53 . . . Qd2-d1+ 54 Kf1-g2 Qd1-e2+ 55 Qf6-f2 Qe2-e4+ 56 Qf2-f3 Rg7xg3+ 57 Kg2xg3 Qe4-g6+ 58 Kg3-f2, the checks have run out, and hope is gone.

Magnificent endgame play by Capablanca.

GAME 18

White A. Nimzowitsch
Black J. R. Capablanca
Exhibition Game, Riga, 1913

Giuoco Piano

From the placid atmosphere of a quiet opening, Capablanca stirs up a surprise wind. It blows most of the pieces away, leaving each side a Bishop and some Pawns.

Ordinarily an easy draw, the Bishops being of opposite colour, but Capablanca by skilful play threatens to create a passed Pawn on each side of the board. The problem of restraining both Pawns becomes insuperable, as Nimzowitsch's pieces find they cannot be in two places at the same time.

Capablanca rises to the heights in this ending, of which he himself said, 'It is one of the finest I ever played, and I have had very often the pleasure of hearing my opponent pay tribute to the skill displayed by me in winning it.'

1   e2-e4   e7-e5

2   Ng1-f3   Nb8-c6

3   Nb1-c3   Ng8-f6

4   Bf1-c4   Bf8-c5

5   d2-d3   d7-d6

6   Bc1-g5

Nimzowitsch plays the Canal Variation, which was 'invented' 16 years later at Carlsbad, and netted Canal a couple of points.

6   . . .   Bc8-e6

A good alternative is 6 . . . Nc6-a5, to do away with White's strong Bishop. If then the over-eager 7 Nc3-d5, the continuation 7 . . . Na5xc4 8 d3xc4 c7-c6 9 Nd5xf6+ g7xf6 10 Bg5-h4 Rh8-g8 gives Black the edge.

7   Bc4-b5   h7-h6

8   Bg5-h4   Bc5-b4

Intended to weaken the effects of 9 d3-d4.

9   d3-d4

Instead of this, Lasker suggests a rearrangement of forces by 9 Nf3-d2, 10 f2-f3 and 11 Bh4-f2, in preparation for building up the center later on.

9	...	Be6-d7
10	0-0	Bb4xc3!
11	b2xc3	g7-g5!

This and the next few moves seem dangerous, as Black's position is exposed and vulnerable to attack.

'The spectators,' (according to Capablanca) 'looked at one another when they saw the bold course I was pursuing, reckless on my part they thought and bound to bring disaster, especially after my next move 12 . . . Nf6xe4, when I had not castled and my King was in the center of the board.'

12	Bh4-g3	Nf6xe4
13	Bb5xc6	

Against 13 Qd1-d3, which maintains the pressure, Capablanca had prepared this defence: 13 . . . Ne4xg3 14 f2xg3 0-0 15 d4xe5 Nc6xe5 16 Nf3xe5 Bd7xb5 17 Qd3xb5 d6xe5 18 Qb5xe5 Rf8-e8 19 Qe5-f5 Qd8-e7 20 Ra1-e1 Qe7-f8.

13	...	Bd7xc6
14	d4xe5	d6xe5
15	Bg3xe5	

Better drawing chances were offered by 15 Nf3xe5 Qd8xd1 16 Ra1xd1 0-0 17 Ne5xc6 b7xc6, but Nimzo-witsch, confident that he had the better position, was playing for a win.

15	...	Qd8xd1
16	Ra1xd1	f7-f6!

This, together with 17 . . . Ke8-f7 next move, getting the King into active play, is what Capablanca had counted on when he played the risky-looking 11 . . . g7-g5 .

17	Be5-d4	

White does not care for 17 Be5xc7 Ne4xc3, when he must lose time protecting his a-Pawn

17	...	Ke8-f7
18	Nf3-d2	Rh8-e8

Capablanca must have seen far into the position to allow exchanges which reduce the number of pieces and allow White (on account of the Bishops of opposite colour) increased drawing chances.

19	f2-f3	Ne4xd2
20	Rd1xd2	Ra8-d8
21	g2-g4	

White tries to whip up an attack on the King-side to compensate for his weaknesses on the Queen-side.

Ending 18

Position after 21 g2-g4

Capablanca to move

Nimzowitsch

Capablanca's two Pawn-islands against his opponent's three offers him a slight positional advantage. This advantage is minimized by the presence on the board of Bishops of opposite colour, a circumstance which usually presages a draw.

With consummate mastery, Capablanca conjures up a fantastically long combination, wherein he blends a threat of creating a passed Pawn on one wing with threats of obtaining a Pawn majority on the other, and this synthesis proves too much for Nimzowitsch to handle.

| 21 | ... | Bc6-b5 |
| 22 | Rf1-b1 | Bb5-a6 |

With this threat: 23 ... c7-c5 24 Bd4-e3 Rd8xd2 25 Be3xd2 Re8-e2 26 Rb1-d1 Kf7-g6, and White will soon run out of decent moves.

| 23 | Rb1-d1 |

The plausible 23 Kg1-f2 fails after 23 ... c7-c5 24 Bd4-e3 Rd8xd2 25 Be3xd2 Re8-e2+, and White must part with his Bishop.

| 23 | ... | Re8-e2 |
| 24 | Rd2xe2 |

Otherwise Black might double Rooks on the King file.

| 24 | ... | Ba6xe2 |
| 25 | Rd1-e1 |

Other tries offer no hope: if 25 Rd1-d2, Be2xf3 26 h2-h3 c7-c5 27 Bd4-e3 Rd8xd2 28 Be3xd2 Bf3-d1 and Black's two extra Pawns should win. Or if 25 Rd1-b1, Be2xf3 26 Bd4xa7 b7-b6, and the Bishop is trapped.

| 25 | ... | Be2xf3 |
| 26 | Re1-f1 |

Ready to meet 26 ... Bf3xg4 with 27 Rf1xf6+ followed by 28 Rf6xh6, with an easy draw.

| 26 | ... | c7-c5! |
| 27 | Bd4xf6 |

Very attractive, but not the best. Strangely enough, Nimzowitsch had good chances of drawing by going into a Rook ending, instead of relying on the opposite-coloured Bishops, this way: 27 Rf1xf3 c5xd4 28 Rf3-d3 Rd8-c8 29 Rd3xd4 Rc8xc3 30 Rd4-d7+ Kf7-g6 31 Rd7xb7 Rc3-a3 32 c2-c4, eventually reaching an ending of two Pawns to three on the King-side.

27	...	Rd8-d1!
28	Bf6-e5	Rd1xf1+
29	Kg1xf1	Bf3xg4
30	a2-a4

White hopes to advance the Pawn to the fifth, where it could be protected by the Bishop, but Capablanca overcomes the plan in elegant style.

30	...	Kf7-e6
31	Be5-b8	

This is the position:

Position after 31 Be5-b8

31	...	a7-a5!

Much stronger than the timid 31 . . . a7-a6, as we shall see.

32	Kf1-e1

Against 32 Bb8-c7, Capablanca had prepared the following:
32 . . . b7-b5! 33 a4xb5 a5-a4 34 c3-c4 (the only way to stop the Pawn, as 34 Bc7-a5, to get to the long diagonal, is foiled by 34 . . . Ke6-d5, while 34 b5-b6 succumbs to 34 . . . Bg4-f3) 34 . . . a4-a3 35 Bc7-a5 a3-a2 36 Ba5-c3 Ke6-d6! followed by 37 . . . Bg4-e6, when two Pawns will fall.

32	...	Ke6-d5!
33	Ke1-d2	

There is nothing to be gained by winning the Rook Pawn, as after 33 Bb8-c7 Kd5-c6 34 Bc7xa5 b7-b6, and the Bishop is caught.

33	...	Bg4-d7
34	Bb8-c7	Kd5-c6
35	Bc7-d8	b7-b6
36	c3-c4	Kc6-b7
37	Kd2-c3	Bd7xa4

An important gain, as Black now has a passed Pawn on the a-file.

38	Kc3-b2	Ba4-d7
39	Kb2-b3	Bd7-e6
40	Kb3-c3	a5-a4
41	Kc3-d3	Kb7-c6
42	Kd3-c3	g5-g4
43	Bd8-h4	h6-h5

White must not only keep an eye on Black's a-Pawn, but must also guard against his opponent's acquiring a passed Pawn on the King-side.

44	Bh4-g3	a4-a3
45	Kc3-b3	

This is the situation:

Position after 45 Kc3-b3

| 45 | ... | Be6xc4+! |

Sparkling play! White must not take the Bishop, as the sequel (after 46 Kb3xc4) would be: 46 . . . a3-a2 47 Bg3-e5 h5-h4 48 Kc4-b3 g4-g3! 49 h2xg3 (or 49 Kb3xa2 g3-g2) h4-h3 50 g3-g4 h3-h2, and though both Pawns are *en prise*, only one may be captured next move while the other Pawn Queens!

46	Kb3xa3	b6-b5
47	c2-c3	Kc6-d5
48	Bg3-f2	Bc4-e2

Vacates c4, a good square for the King.

49	Ka3-b3	Be2-d1+
50	Kb3-b2	Kd5-c4
51	Kb2-c1	Bd1-f3
52	Kc1-d2	b5-b4
53	c3xb4	c5xb4

Black has lost his passed Pawn on the Rook file, but one has sprung up on the Knight file in its place.

54	Bf2-h4	Bf3-e4
55	Bh4-f6	Be4-g6
56	Bf6-h4	b4-b3
57	Bh4-f6	

If instead 57 Kd2-c1 to head off the Pawn, the continuation is 57 . . . Kc4-d3 58 Kc1-b2 Bg6-f7 59 Bh4-g5 Kd3-e2 60 Bg5-f6

Ke2-f3 61 Bf6-h4 Kf3-g2 62 Bh4-g3 h5-h4 63 Bg3-e5 g4-g3 64 h2xg3 h4xg3, and White must give up his Bishop for the Pawn, after which Black's King comes back to b4 and a3, and helps the Pawn become a Queen.

| 57 | ... | h5-h4! |

The impudent Pawn is immune to capture as 58 Bf6xh4 loses instantly by 58 . . . b3-b2.

| 58 | Kd2-e3 | g4-g3! |
| 59 | h2xg3 | |

If 59 Ke3-f3 to approach the Pawns, 59 . . . Bg6-e4+ banishes the King from the neighbourhood.

| 59 | ... | h4-h3 |
| 60 | Ke3-f2 | Bg6-f5 |

A necessary precaution to prevent the Knight Pawn from advancing without loss.

61	g3-g4	Bf5xg4
62	Kf2-g3	Kc4-d3
63	White Resigns	

The King moves to c2, winning the Bishop for the Pawn, and then marches over to the King-side, and forces the last Pawn to the queening square.

A magnificent display, one of the finest of Capablanca's many fine endings.

GAME 19

White H. Fahndrich A. Kaufmann
Black J. R. Capablanca R. Réti
Consultation Game, Vienna, 1914

French Defence
One move by Capablanca was enough to give Réti a whole lesson in modern chess technique. It was an insight offered by a touch of genius.

So startled was Réti by Capablanca's refusal *even to look at* a move that developed a piece, seized an open file, and gained a tempo by driving the Queen off the file, that he was moved to say 'With this game began a revolution in my conviction as to the wisdom of the old principle, according to which in the opening every move should develop another piece. I studied Capablanca's games and recognized that contrary to all the masters of that period, he had for some time ceased to adhere to that principle.'

The ending is notable for the nonchalant way in which Capablanca gives away Pawns to centralize his King and activate his Rook.

Fascinating how Capablanca summarily dispatches the enemy Rook to the sidelines, where it remains helpless and out of play, while the rest of White's position is brought to a state of near-*zugzwang*.

1	e2-e4	e7-e6
2	d2-d4	d7-d5
3	Nb1-c3	Ng8-f6
4	e4xd5	e6xd5
5	Bf1-d3	c7-c5

A risky-looking move, as it isolates the Queen Pawn, but Black wants to take the initiative.

6	d4xc5	Bf8xc5
7	Ng1-f3	0-0
8	0-0	Nb8-c6
9	Bc1-g5	Bc8-e6
10	Nc3-e2	

Rather than this time-wasting move, White should play 10 Qd1-d2, uniting his Rooks.

10	...	h7-h6
11	Bg5-h4	Be6-g4
12	Ne2-c3	

The Knight returns, having discovered to his sorrow that 12 Ne2-g3 (or 12 Ne2-f4) loses a piece by 12 ... g7-g5.

12	...	Nc6-d4
13	Bd3-e2	Nd4xe2+
14	Qd1xe2	

At this point, as Réti tells it, 'A position was arrived at in which the opportunity presented itself to develop a hitherto undeveloped piece and indeed with an attack. The move 14 ... Rf8-e8 would have had that effect and was in accordance with the principles prevailing when I grew up and which corresponded with Morphy's principles (for he would without considering have chosen that move)'.

'To my great astonishment *Capa-*

blanca would not even consider the move at all. Finally he discovered the following maneuver by which he forced a deterioration of White's Pawn position and thereby later on his defeat.'

14	...	Bc5-d4!!
15	Qe2-d3	Bd4xc3
16	Qd3xc3	Nf6-e4!
17	Qc3-d4	g7-g5
18	Nf3-e5	

White is evidently playing to win, as the alternative 18 Bh4-g3 Bg4xf3 19 g2xf3 Qd8-f6 probably leads to a draw.

| 18 | ... | Bg4-f5 |
| 19 | f2-f3 | |

Here too 19 Bh4-g3 might have been played, when this continuation 19 . . . Ne4xg3 20 f2xg3 Bf5xc2 21 Ne5-g4 f7-f5 22 Ng4-e3 Bc2-e4 23 Ra1-d1 Qd8-b6! 24 Ne3xd5 Be4xd5 25 Qd4xb6 a7xb6 26 Rd1xd5 Ra8xa2 leaves Black with just a bit of an advantage.

| 19 | ... | g5xh4 |
| 20 | f3xe4 | Bf5xe4 |

White may have been quite pleased with the situation. At the cost of a mere Pawn he has saddled Black with four sad-looking isolated Pawns, while he (White) has an open file for his Rook, and his Queen dominates the center.

He is soon disillusioned, though, as Black's Bishop is now beautifully centralized, safe from any fear of being dislodged by Pawns. As for the Pawns—one of them serves to break up White's King-side, while

the other three survive to the end of the game, co-operating efficiently to confine the enemy forces.

| 21 | Rf1-f2 | |

The attractive-looking 21 Ne5-g4 is met by 21 . . . f7-f5, when 22 Ng4xh6+ Kg8-h7 followed (after 23 Qd4-d2) by 23 . . . Qd8-b6+ ends the Knight's career.

| 21 | ... | h4-h3! |

Drives a wedge into the opponent's position. The Pawn can be taken, of course, but that means letting Black have a passed Pawn on the f-file.

| 22 | Ra1-e1 | f7-f5 |
| 23 | g2xh3 | Qd8-f6 |

This certainly looks strong enough, but Capablanca, always objective, says that the right move was 23 . . . Kg8-h7, as White could now probably draw by 24 Re1xe4 d5xe4 25 Rf2-g2+ Kg8-h8 26 Rg2-g6 Rf8-g8 27 Ne5-f7+ Kh8-h7 28 Qd4xf6 Rg8xg6+ 29 Nf7-g5+ Rg6xg5+ 30 Kg1-f2 (a beautiful line of play, which shows that Capablanca could create brilliant combinations as well as any other great tactician).

24	Ne5-f3	Kg8-h7
25	Qd4xf6	Rf8xf6
26	Re1-e3	

The stage is set for an ending which Capablanca conducts with impeccable technique.

Ending 19

Position after 26 Re1-e3

Capablanca and Réti to move

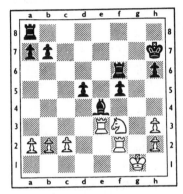

Fahndrich and Kaufmann

Capablanca plans to threaten the Queen-side Pawns. Their advance will not only render them more susceptible to attack, but will hamper the movements of White's Rooks along the files. The second part of the plan is to effect a Pawn breakthrough on the Queen-side, so that a Rook may reach the 8th rank. Add to this the power of the King (which Capablanca will central-ize) and there should be enough pressure generated to force the opponent to capitulate.

26	...	Rf6-b6!
27	b2-b3	

An instinctive reaction, but it weakens the Queen Bishop Pawn.

Lasker's suggestion of 27 Re3-b3 to exchange a pair of Rooks offers drawing chances.

27	...	Ra8-c8

This attack on the Bishop Pawn will tie two pieces down to its defence.

28	Nf3-d4	Rb6-f6
29	Rf2-f4	Kh7-g6
30	c2-c3	Kg6-g5
31	Nd4-e2	

On 31 Rf4-f1, f5-f4 drives the other Rook off and wins the Bishop Pawn.

31	...	Rf6-a6!

This will force a2-a4 (after White gets in a preliminary, harmless check); then Black can effect a breakthrough by . . . b7-b5.

32	h3-h4+	Kg5-f6
33	a2-a4	b7-b5!

A fine sacrifice, by means of which a road is cleared for Black's Rooks to swoop down to the seventh and eighth ranks to get at the King him-self.

34	a4xb5	Ra6-a1+
35	Rf4-f1	

The least of the evils, as disaster could strike after 35 Kg1-f2 by 35 . . . Kf6-e5 (threatens 36 . . . Ra1-a2 followed by 37 . . . Ra2xe2+ 38 Kf2xe2 Ke5xf4) 36 Kf2-g3 Rc8-g8+ 37 Kg3-h3 (on 37 Kg3-f2 Rg8-g2 is mate) 37 . . . Be4-g2 mate!

35	...	Ra1xf1+
36	Kg1xf1	Kf6-e5

Black is closing in.

37	Ne2-d4	

With a vague hope of stirring up trouble by 38 Nd4-c6+

Ending 19

This is the situation:

Position after 37 Ne2-d4

37	...	f5-f4
38	Re3-h3	

A miserable spot for a self-respecting Rook, but another move, say 38 Re3-e1, forfeits the Bishop Pawn, and White's position falls apart.

The White allies had an interesting alternative (which they no doubt considered) in this line: 38 Nd4-c6+ Rc8xc6 39 Re3xe4+ (or 39 b5xc6 f4xe3 40 c6-c7 Be4-f5, with an easy win for Black) 39 ... d5xe4 40 b5xc6 Ke5-d6 41 b3-b4 Kd6xc6 42 c3-c4 Kc6-b6 43 Kf1-e2 a7-a5 44 c4-c5+ Kb6-b5, and Black wins.

38	...	Rc8-g8

Black's palpable threat of winning a Rook by 39 ... Be4-g2+ is incidental to the real purpose of his move, which is to gain control of the seventh rank with his Rook.

39	Kf1-e1	Rg8-g1+
40	Ke1-e2	Rg1-g2+
41	Ke2-f1	Rg2-b2

Renewing the threat of 42 Be4-g2+ gains another move for Black.

42	Kf1-e1	h6-h5

White is in semi-*zugzwang*: if

(a) 43 Nd4-c6+ Ke5-f5 followed by 44 ... Kf5-g4 wins the unhappy Rook,

(b) 43 Ke1-f1 Be4-g2+ wins the Rook,

(c) 43 b3-b4 leaves the Pawns immobilized.

43	Ke1-d1	

A sorry state of affairs when the King is the only active piece.

43	...	Be4-f5
44	Nd4xf5	Ke5xf5
45	c3-c4	

The alternative 45 Rh3-d3 is hopeless, as Capablanca shows, the continuation being 45 ... Kf5-e4 46 Rd3-d4+ Ke4-e3 47 Rd4xd5 f4-f3 48 Rd5-e5+ Ke3-f4 49 Re5-e7 f3-f2 50 Re7-f7+, and Black will eventually have to give up his Rook for the Pawn.

45	...	Kf5-e4
46	Rh3-c3	

On 46 c4xd5 f4-f3 47 d5-d6 f3-f2 wins at once.

46	...	f4-f3
47	Kd1-e1	d5-d4
48	**White Resigns**	

If 48 Rc3-c1 Ra2xh2 49 c4-c5 Ke4-e3 50 Ke1-d1 d4-d3, and mate follows next move.

Triumph of the little Pawns!

A great Capablanca ending, artistic in its iron precision.

GAME 20

White J. R. Capablanca
Black B. Villegas
Exhibition Game, Buenos Aires,
1914

Queen's Gambit Declined
In the good old days, masters such as Morphy and Anderssen gave away Queens, Rooks, Knights, and Bishops with a lavish hand. These sacrifices were usually unexpected, and their acceptance led to vicious attacks terminating in mate. Defensive play was little known, and its practice considered cowardly. In fact the French Defence was called 'King's Pawn one sneak'.

Later, when defence became sophisticated (especially with Steinitz, who made it an art) brilliancies were few and far between, and Queen sacrifices appeared as often in the notes as in the actual game.

Take as example this beautiful specimen by Capablanca. There is a Queen sacrifice in the midgame, but it is not made in order to finish the game in a blaze of glory. The Queen is offered almost nonchalantly (so far as Capablanca is concerned, it is a routine move!) in order to gain a positional advantage.

And it does gain a positional advantage, whether the Queen is captured or not!

1	d2-d4	d7-d5
2	Ng1-f3	Ng8-f6
3	e2-e3	

This may not be so energetic as 3 c2-c4 or 3 Bc1-g5, but White still has the option of developing the

Queen Bishop at b2, and the other at d3.

| 3 | ... | c7-c6 |

Black too is content with modest development, refraining from the aggressive 3 . . . c7-c5.

| 4 | Bf1-d3 | Bc8-g4 |
| 5 | c2-c4! | |

The usual recipe in Queen Pawn openings: attack on the center Pawn, opening of the Queen Bishop file for the heavy pieces, and clearance of a diagonal for the Queen.

| 5 | ... | e7-e6 |
| 6 | Nb1-d2 | |

White defends the King Knight with a minor piece, relieving the Queen of that duty.

| 6 | ... | Nb8-d7 |
| 7 | 0-0 | Bf8-e7 |

Cautious development. Braver souls would venture on 7 . . . e6-e5, attempting to have a say in the center.

| 8 | Qd1-c2 | Bg4-h5 |

Having failed to make anything of the pin, Black decides to exchange his lacklustre Bishop for the more aggressive one of White's.

| 9 | b2-b3 | Bh5-g6 |
| 10 | Bc1-b2 | |

Capablanca continues calmly about

about

the business of getting all his pieces into play.

10	. . .	Bg6xd3
11	Qc2xd3	0-0
12	Ra1-e1	

The Rook's presence on the King file will add power to the coming advance of the King Pawn—a necessary step in gaining more mobility for the pieces.

12	. . .	Qd8-c7
13	e3-e4!	

As a result of Black's loss of time with the Queen Bishop, Capablanca now has some initiative. The text leads to exchanges which make White's Queen Rook a formidable attacking weapon.

13	. . .	d5xe4

Otherwise Black must live in constant dread of e4xd5 or e4-e5, either of which moves White will play at his own convenience.

14	Nd2xe4	Nf6xe4
15	Re1xe4!	Be7-f6

Institutes a pretty threat to simplify by 16 . . . Nd7-c5 17 d4xc5 Bf6xb2, and Black has obtained a respectable game.

16	Qd3-e3!	c6-c5

Black relies on this move to eliminate White's d-Pawn, after which the squares e5 and c5 will be available to his Knight.

But the move is brilliantly refuted by Capablanca, who never misses a trick.

17	Nf3-e5!	c5xd4

Black continues on his merry way, anticipating this natural sequence

of events: 18 Bb2xd4 Bf6xe5 19 Bd4xe5 Nd7xe5 20 Re4xe5 Rf8-d8, and his command of the Queen file gives him an excellent position.

18	Ne5xd7!	

A bolt from the blue!

18	. . .	Qc7xd7

Black discovers that accepting the offer of a Queen loses by this delightful combination: 18 . . . d4xe3 19 Nd7xf6+ Kg8-h8 (if 19 . . . g7xf6 20 Re4-g4+ Kg8-h8 21 Bb2xf6 mate) 20 Re4-h4 (threatens 21 Rh4xh7 mate) 20 . . . h7-h6 21 Rh4xh6+! g7xh6 22 Nf6-d5+ Kh8-g8 23 Nd5xc7 and White has two pieces for a Rook.

19	Bb2xd4	Bf6xd4

More or less forced, as White had another arrow in his quiver, and was aiming at ending the King's career by 20 Bd4xf6 g7xf6 21 Re4-g4+ Kg8-h8 22 Qe3-h6 Rf8-g8 23 Qh6xf6+ Rg8-g7 24 Qf6xg7 mate.

20	Re4xd4	Qd7-c7

Ending 20

Position after 20 . . . Qd7-c7

Villegas

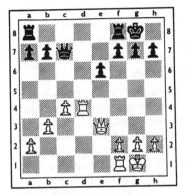

Capablanca to move

White's positional advantage consists in having three Pawns to two on the Queen-side, and in his control (albeit temporary) of the open Queen file.

Capablanca's plan is admirable in its simplicity: acquire a passed Pawn (by virtue of the Pawn majority on the Queen-side), push it up the board, and turn it into a Queen.

21 Rf1-d1

Strengthens White's grip on the file, and threatens to seize the seventh rank.

21 . . . Rf8-d8

Black must oppose Rooks immediately or be crushed (especially since White might triple heavy pieces on the Queen file).

22 b3-b4!

Now that the position is simplified, White can proceed to turn his Queen-side majority of Pawns into a passed Pawn! An exchange of Pawns will convert the three to two majority into two to one, a further exchange will simplify that into one to nothing—and that one a passed Pawn!

Capablanca of course does not fall into the catchpenny trap 22 Rd4xd8+ Ra8xd8 23 Rd1xd8+ Qc7xd8 24 Qe3xa7 Qd8-d1 mate.

22 . . . Rd8xd4

Black must exchange, or remain passive and await his fate.

23 Qe3xd4

The Queen recaptures maintaining White's pressure on the file.

23 . . . b7-b6

Either this, or 23 . . . a7-a6 is necessary, to release the Rook from guard duty.

24 g2-g3

Creates a flight-square for the King. In Queen-and-Rook endings, it is important to watch out for surprise checks (often with mate attached) on the last rank.

24 . . . Ra8-c8

25 Rd1-c1

The Rook belongs behind the passed Pawn (or in this case, the potential passed Pawn).

The Rook protects the Pawn now, and will continue to do so along every step of its way up the board.

25 . . . Rc8-d8

Now that he has the opportunity Black attacks the Queen, dislodges her from the file, and seizes it for himself.

26 Qd4-e3!

A modest move, but a beautiful one! The Queen keeps in touch with the Rook, prevents the adverse Rook from swooping down to the seventh rank, and exerts her strong influence over the strategic square c5, the next stop for the Bishop Pawn.

It may seem strange to see Capablanca give up control of the Queen file when he had so tight a grip on it, but it is the mark of a great master to know when to relinquish one advantage for the sake of securing another.

26 ... Kg8-f8

The King decides to render whatever help be can, by moving closer to the center.

27 c4-c5

Every step forward is an important gain for the candidate.

27 ... b6xc5

Anticipating 28 b4xc5 in reply, when 28 ... Qc7-c6 would stop the Pawn dead in its tracks.

A diagram would be *à propos*:

Position after 27 ... b6xc5

28 Qe3-e4!

The brilliant touch! Capablanca prevents the aforementioned blockade by the enemy Queen at c6, and sets the stage for 29 b4xc5 followed by the further advance of the Pawn to c6.

28 ... Rd8-d5

Protects the Bishop Pawn once again—or so it seems!

29 b4xc5

Capablanca sticks to his original concept, that of acquiring a passed Pawn and promoting it to a Queen.

He is not swayed by the prospect of picking up a couple of Pawns with 29 Qe4xh7 followed by 30 Qh7-h8+ and 31 Qh8xg7, though that would leave him with a passed Pawn on the King Rook file.

29 ... g7-g6

Clearly, 29 ... Rd5xc5 would be met (quick as a flash) by 30 Qe4-b4, pinning and winning the impetuous Rook.

30 c5-c6

One more step nearer the goal!

30 ... Kf8-g7

The King has second thoughts about moving towards the center, as he might suffer this misadventure: 30 ... Kf8-e7 31 Qe4-h4+ Ke7-d6 32 Qh4-b4+ Kd6-e5 33 Qb4-f4 mate!

31 a2-a4!

A clever preparatory move! On 31 Qe4-b4 immediately, followed by 32 Qb4-b7, the sequel would be 32 ... Qc7xb7 33 c6xb7, and 33 ... Rd5-b5 brings the Pawn to a dead stop.

But after the text move
(31 a2-a4!) the Rook could not
move to the b5 square!

31 ... Rd5-d6

Now the Pawn seems to be held
under lock and key. But Capablanca smashes the heavy blockade
with one powerful blow!

32 Qe4-e5+ f7-f6
33 Qe5xd6! Qc7xd6

34 c6-c7 Black Resigns

The Pawn becomes a Queen next
move, leaving White a Rook ahead
and an easy win.

Capablanca's clear-cut play in
this ending calls to mind a comment
by Sir George Thomas, 'Against
Alekhine you never knew what to
expect; against Capablanca you
knew what to expect, but you
couldn't prevent it!'

GAME 21

White Ed. Lasker
Black J. R. Capablanca
New York, 1915

Queen's Gambit Declined
Capablanca can win a piece for
three Pawns early in the game.
Characteristically he prefers instead
to simplify the position (to his advantage of course). A series of
exchanges sweeps the pieces off the
board leaving his opponent with a
Knight stranded at the side while
he (Capablanca) has a Bishop
proudly occupying the center.

Relinquishing one advantage to
secure another, Capablanca forces a
final exchange of pieces to leave a
pure Pawn ending. As usual, Capablanca manages to have only two
islands of Pawns against three of
Lasker's, and he brings about the
win in a delightfully instructive
way.

Edward Lasker thought so
highly of the play in this game as
to devote twelve pages on it in his

classic book *Chess and Checkers:
The Way to Mastership.*

1 d2-d4 d7-d5
2 Ng1-f3 Ng8-f6
3 c2-c4 e7-e6
4 Nb1-c3 Nb8-d7
5 Bc1-g5 Bf8-b4

The usual move is 5 ... Bf8-e7, but
Capablanca experiments with a
more aggressive reply.

6 e2-e3

I like this note in *Schachblätter*:
'Much stronger is 6 c4xd5 e6xd5
7 Qd1-a4, and Black's American
bluff is entirely exploded.'

A plausible continuation of the
bluff would be 7 ... c7-c5 8 d4xc5
Bb4xc3+ 9 b2xc3 0-0 10 c5-c6
Qd8-c7!, and Black has a good
game.

6 ... c7-c5

Already threatening 7 . . . Qd8-a5
(double attack on the pinned
Knight) followed by 8 . . . Nf6-e4
(triple attack on the poor creature).

7 Bf1-d3

The natural 7 Qd1-c2 is countered
by 7 . . . Qd8-a5 8 c4xd5 Nf6xd5
9 Ra1-c1 Qa5xa2, and Black has
stolen a Pawn.

7 . . .   Qd8-a5

8 Qd1-b3

Edward Lasker himself thinks that
he should have castled. 'It is true,'
he says, 'that Black can then win a
Pawn by taking twice at c3; however in doing so he would retard his
development and White is bound to
obtain a strong attack by getting all
his pieces quickly into action, while
Black's Queen is separated from the
rest of her troops.'

8 . . .   Nf6-e4

Capablanca could have won a piece
for three Pawns by 8 . . . b7-b5
9 c4xb5 c5-c4 10 Bd3xc4 d5xc4
11 Qb3xc4 Bc8-b7, but as
Schachblätter (redeeming itself)
says, 'The Cuban adopts a more
subtle way of winning. His conduct
of the game from now on displays
exquisite accuracy.'

9 0-0

White is running short of good
moves. Disaster follows 9 Bd3xe4,
by 9 . . . d5xe4 10 Nf3-e5 (if
10 Nf3-d2, c5xd4 wins a piece)
10 . . . f7-f6 11 Ne5xd7 Bc8xd7
12 Bg5-f4 Bd7-a4, and White loses
his Queen.

9 . . .   Ne4xg5

This is preferable to winning the

Pawn at c3 by 9 . . . Ne4xc3, as
White will afterwards either regain
his Pawn, or obtain attacking
chances.

10 Nf3xg5   c5xd4

With the transparent threat (after
11 e3xd4) of continuing with
11 . . . d5xc4 winning the exposed
Knight.

11 Nc3-b5   Nd7-c5

12 Qb3-c2

'There's small choice in rotten
apples,' as Shakespeare succinctly
observed.

If instead 12 Nb5-d6+ Ke8-e7
13 Qb3-c2 Nc5xd3 14 Nd6xf7
Rh8-f8, and Black wins two pieces
for a Rook. Or if 12 Nb5-d6+
Ke8-e7 13 Qb3-c2 Nc5xd3
14 Nd6xc8+ Ra8xc8 15 Qc2xd3
d5xc4, and again the poor Knight
at g5 falls victim.

12 . . .   Nc5xd3

13 Qc2xd3   a7-a6

14 Nb5xd4   d5xc4

15 Qd3xc4   Bc8-d7

Once again Black threatens to win
the unprotected Knight by driving
the Queen away from the Bishop at
b4 (which she is attacking) thus:
16 . . . Ra8-c8 17 Qc4-b3 Bd7-a4
18 Qb3-d3 Qa5xg5.

16 Nd4-b3

Perhaps 16 Ng5-e4 was better, but
White wants to eliminate one of the
Bishops.

16 . . .   Qa5xg5

17 Qc4xb4   Bd7-c6

18 e3-e4   a6-a5

19 Qb4-d2

White offers to exchange Queens, as the alternative 19 Qb4-e1 loses a Pawn by 19 . . . Qg5-e5 20 f2-f3 Qe5xb2, and White dare not reply 21 Nb3xa5 on pain of losing his Knight by 21 . . . Qb2-b6+.

Ending 21

Position after 19 Qb4-d2

Capablanca to move

Ed. Lasker

Capablanca has managed to retain the initiative.

He plans to exchange Queens and be left with a Bishop (which he prefers) to his opponent's Knight. The Knight is to be driven to the side of the board and then forced into an exchange which will saddle White with a couple of isolated Pawns.

This might in itself not be fatal, but for the fact that Capablanca's King (even after castling Queen-side) will be closer to the theater of action, and in a dominating enough position to force a decision.

| 19 . . . | Qg5xd2 |
| 20 Nb3xd2 | 0-0-0 |

Gains a tempo by the attack on the Knight.

21 Nd2-c4

If 21 Rf1-d1 Rd8-d4 (threatens to double Rooks) 22 Nd2-b3 Rd4xd1+ 23 Ra1xd1 Bc6xe4 24 Nb3xa5 Be4-d5, with a similar ending to that which occurred in the actual game.

21 . . .	Bc6xe4
22 Rf1-c1	Kc8-b8
23 f2-f3	

Edward Lasker himself criticizes this move, 'as it drives the Bishop where it wants to go,' but if 23 Nc4xa5 at once, then after 23 . . . Be4-d5 24 Na5-c4 Bd5xc4 25 Rc1xc4 Rd8-d2, and Black has all the play.

| 23 . . . | Be4-d5 |
| 24 Nc4xa5 | Rd8-c8! |

An excellent move; it offers White various ways to get an inferior ending!

If 25 Rc1xc8+ Rh8xc8, and Black threatens 26 . . . Rc8-c2, as well as 26 . . . b7-b6 27 Na5-b3 Bd5xb3 28 a2xb3, and White has been left with a wretched pair of doubled Pawns.

If 25 Na5-b3 Bd5xb3 26 a2xb3 Rc8xc1+ 27 Ra1xc1 Rh8-d8 28 Rc1-c2 Rd8-d3, and the hapless Knight Pawn is not long for this world.

25 b2-b3	Rc8xc1+
26 Ra1xc1	Rh8-c8
27 Rc1xc8+	

This leads to a hopeless Pawn ending, as Capablanca will force an exchange of Knight for Bishop which will result in White's Pawns being split up and isolated.

White might have done better to go into a Rook ending a Pawn down, thus: 27 Rc1-d1 b7-b6 28 Na5-c4 Bd5xc4 29 b3xc4 Rc8xc4 30 Rd1-d2, with theoretical drawing chances.

But Lasker may not have taken into consideration the fact that Capablanca would exchange his beautifully-placed Bishop for a Knight almost completely out of play. Perhaps he also failed to realize that Capablanca was not one to hold on stubbornly to whatever advantage he had, but would cheerfully exchange one advantage for another.

27	. . .	Kb8xc8
28	Kg1-f2	Kc8-c7!!

A simple move, but a beautiful one strategically. Note its superiority to the natural one of 28 . . . b7-b6, driving the Knight off. After the reply 29 Na5-c4, there follows 29 . . . Bd5xc4 30 b3xc4 Kc8-c7 31 Kf2-e3 Kc7-c6 32 Ke3-d4, and Black's King cannot reach c5.

Contrast this position of Black's King with the following: 28 . . . Kc8-c7 29 Kf2-e3 Kc7-b6 30 Na5-c4 Bd5xc4 31 b3xc4 Kb6-c5, and Black's King is in a dominating position.

It is such unobtrusive touches of genius that make it exciting to watch the great strategists in action, and to play over and analyze their games.

Now let us look behind the scenes! Why did Capablanca not play 28 . . . b7-b6, which drives the Knight off, forces its exchange, and leaves White with a couple of isolated Pawns? Wouldn't that be good enough to win?

Perhaps, but the King move does it more efficiently, by enabling the King to reach the square c5, where it dominates the position, *without loss of time*. In short, Capablanca was following his own rule of making the King a powerful piece in the ending.

What makes it most impressive, though, is the fact that Capablanca is not content with making a good move, but finds a better one (if there is one) that realizes the same objective, but does it more efficiently.

That is the mark of a great master. That is Capablanca!

29	Kf2-e3	Kc7-b6
30	Na5-c4+	Bd5xc4
31	b3xc4	Kb6-c5

Capablanca now has the position he wants, the one he visualized when he exchanged Queens (or perhaps even before that!).

32	Ke3-d3	e6-e5

Now that White's King is tied down to the defence of the Queen Bishop Pawn, Capablanca is free to go about the business of acquiring a passed Pawn on the King-side, where he has a majority of Pawns. Sooner or later, White will run out of waiting moves.

This is how the board looks:

Position after 32 ... e6-e5

33 g2-g4

This is meant to hinder 33 ... f7-f5.
On 33 a2-a3 instead (to prevent
... Kc5-b4 at some stage) the play
could run like this: 33 ... f7-f5
34 g2-g4 g7-g6 35 h2-h3 h7-h6
36 h3-h4 h6-h5 37 g4-g5 b7-b6!
38 Kd3-c3 e5-e4 39 f3-f4 e4-e3
(the idea is to force White go go
after the e-Pawn, which will enable
Black to gobble up the c-Pawn, and
then go after the a-Pawn) 40 Kc3-d3
e3-e2 41 Kd3xe2 Kc5xc4
42 Ke2-e3 b6-b5, and the rest is
elementary. Black captures the
a-Pawn and wins.

33	...	f7-f6
34	h2-h4	g7-g6
35	Kd3-e4	

If 35 Kd3-c3 f6-f5 36 Kc3-d3
Kc5-b4, and White must soon part
with a Pawn.

35 ...   Kc5-d6

Black could win as well with
35 ... Kc5xc4 36 g4-g5 f6xg5,
but this is simpler, as it allows no
hint of counter-play.

36 f3-f4

On 36 h4-h5 Kd6-e6 followed by
37 ... f6-f5+ forces the King back,
after which Black returns to the
Queen-side, winning easily, while
36 Ke4-d3 succumbs to
36 ... f6-f5 followed by
37 ... Kd6-c5.

36	...	e5xf4
37	Ke4xf4	Kd6-c5
38	h4-h5	Kc5xc4
39	Kf4-e4	b7-b5
40	a2-a3	Kc4-b3
41	White Resigns	

Impeccable play, and a delightful
lesson in the fine art of conducting
a King-and-Pawn ending.

GAME 22

White J. R. Capablanca
Black R. T. Black
New York, 1916

Ruy López
Capablanca gives a brilliant display
of his tactical powers.

He evolves an unusual combination beginning with a Pawn

sacrifice, that allows the enemy Queen the freedom of the board. It ends when, by a series of problem-like moves he captures the fleet-footed Queen.

In the endgame Capablanca's advantage in material of a Queen for his opponent's Rook, Knight, and Pawn is enough to win the game—theoretically. But winning a theoretically won game is not an automatic process.

Capablanca's relentless procedure is a valuable lesson in the technique of finishing, and an intellectual treat as well.

1	e2-e4	e7-e5
2	Ng1-f3	Nb8-c6
3	Bf1-b5	a7-a6
4	Bb5-a4	Ng8-f6
5	0-0	Bf8-e7
6	Rf1-e1	d7-d6
7	c2-c3	0-0
8	d2-d4	b7-b5
9	Ba4-c2	Bc8-g4
10	d4-d5!	Nc6-b8

The Knight goes home, ready to start life over again by developing at d7. The alternative 10 . . . Nc6-a5 11 Nb1-d2 c7-c6 12 d5xc6 Na5xc6 13 Nd2-f1 is not appetizing.

11	h2-h3	Bg4-h5

From this square the Bishop will be driven back to g6, where it is out of play, but bringing the Bishop back home by 11 . . . Bg4-c8 does not appeal to Black (the player of Black).

12	Nb1-d2	Nb8-d7
13	Nd2-f1	

Standard operating procedure: the Knight is to emerge at g3, where it will exert pressure on (and perhaps occupy) the square f5, a key square in most forms of the Ruy López.

13	. . .	Rf8-e8
14	g2-g4	Bh5-g6
15	Nf1-g3	h7-h6

Secures a flight-square for the Bishop in the event of a threat to exchange it by 16 Ng3-h4.

16	a2-a4	

A sudden shift to the other wing, to keep Black on his toes.

16	. . .	Nf6-h7
17	Qd1-e2	Ra8-b8
18	a4xb5	a6xb5

Black seems to have some prospects of getting some counter-play by 19 . . . b5-b4, which would secure his Queen-side Pawn position against attack, and also provide a good square for his Queen Knight at c5.

19	b2-b4	

But Capablanca squelches that possibility!

19	. . .	Qd8-c8
20	Bc2-d3	

The beginning of an attack which will range over the entire board, and give Black no time to breathe.

20	. . .	c7-c6
21	d5xc6	Qc8xc6

This is the position:

Position after 21 ... Qc8xc6

22   Ra1-a5!

This brilliant offer of the Queen-side Pawns in order to trap the Queen on an open board is rather like the one that characterized (and illuminated) the beautiful Capablanca–Vidmar game at London in 1922.

The theme may be somewhat similar, but the execution differs enough to make both combinations outstanding.

22   ...   Qc6xc3

23   Bd3xb5

This is more economical (and therefore more artistic) than 23 Bc1-d2, driving the Queen back to c7, as the Queen must return there in any event.

23   ...   Qc3-c7

Of course not the greedy 23 ... Qc3xb4, as the reply 24 Bc1-d2 attacking the Queen allows Black no time to save his Queen Knight from capture.

24   Bc1-e3   Re8-d8

25   Re1-c1

The Rook seizes the open file, gaining a tempo by the attack on the Queen.

25   ...   Qc7-b7

26   Bb5-c6

Capablanca continues his combination to win the Queen, though he had a good alternative in 26 Bb5xd7 Qb7xd7 (but not 26 ... Rd8xd7 27 Ra5-a7) 27 b4-b5, and White has an excellent game.

26   ...   Qb7xb4

27   Ra5-a4   Qb4-b3

This is forced, as 27 ... Qb4-b2 loses a piece by 28 Qe2xb2 Rb8xb2 29 Ra4-a7 (Rook to the seventh—so often the magic move that wins!) 29 ... Nh7-f6 30 Bc6xd7 Rd8xd7 (if 30 ... Nf6xd7 31 Rc1-c7 does the trick) 31 Ra7xd7 Nf6xd7 32 Rc1-c7, and the Knight (or the Bishop behind the Knight) must fall.

28   Ra4-a7!

Here too, Rook to the seventh is the magic move in the combination.

28   ...   Nh7-f8

29   Nf3-d2   Qb3-b2

Though 17 squares are open to the Queen, she can find no safe refuge.

Fleeing to the King-side would allow this sequel: 29 ... Qb3-e6 30 Bc6-d5 Qe6-f6 31 Nd2-f3 (threatens 32 g4-g5 h6xg5 33 Be3xg5 winning the Queen) 31 ... Bg6-h7 (if 31 ... Nf8-h7 32 Rc1-c7 wins a piece) 32 g4-g5 Qf6-g6 33 Nf3-h4, and White wins the Queen.

30   Qe2-d1   Be7-g5

The best move at Black's command.

31	Rc1-c2	Bg5xe3

The Queen cannot escape, the reply to 31 . . . Qb2-b4 being 32 Ra7-a4, and the Queen is surrounded and caught.

32	Rc2xb2	Be3xa7
33	Rb2xb8	Nd7xb8

Awkward, but 33 . . . Rd8xb8 loses a piece after 34 Qd1-a4.

34	Bc6-d5	Nf8-e6
35	Ng3-e2	Nb8-d7
36	Qd1-a4	Ba7-b8
37	Qa4-a2	Nd7-c5
38	f2-f3	Kg8-f8
39	Nd2-c4	Kf8-e7

Blissfully unaware of what Destiny has in store for him, the King goes forward to meet his fate.

40	Nc4-a5	Ke7-f6

And now moves on, into a mating net.

41	Na5-c6	Rd8-c8
42	h3-h4	Bb8-c7

Ending 22

Position after 42 . . . Bb8-c7

Black

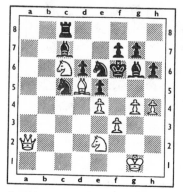

Capablanca to move

White has an advantage in material and in position.

Black's King is stalemated and susceptible to sudden mate, while his King-side pieces are threatened by menacing Pawns.

What is White's problem? Shouldn't the win be fairly easy?

Perhaps, but it is Capablanca's quick and efficient method of procedure that provides a valuable study in endgame technique. The latter part of the ending, showing the Queen driving the enemy pieces into a corner, is rare in actual play, and particularly interesting.

43	f3-f4

The first move in a ten-move combination, which sweeps away a dozen pieces and Pawns from the board!

White poses two threats now of winning a piece: one is by 44 f4-f5 attacking Knight and Bishop, while the other is 44 g4-g5+ h6xg5 45 h4xg5+, forcing Black to give up his Knight for two Pawns.

43	...	Bg6xe4

Capturing the Bishop Pawn instead allows a sparkling finish, 43 ... Ne6xf4 44 Ne2xf4 e5xf4 45 Qa2-a1 mate—a picturesque mate from afar!

44	g4-g5+	h6xg5
45	h4xg5+	Ne6xg5

There is no choice, as 45 ... Kf6-g6 (or to f5) loses a whole Rook by 46 Nc6-e7+

46	f4xg5+	Kf6xg5
47	Bd5xe4	Nc5xe4
48	Qa2xf7	Bc7-b6+

This wins a piece, but only *pour le moment.*

49	Kg1-g2	Rc8xc6
50	Qf7xg7+	Kg5-h5

Best, though it loses a Knight. If 50 ... Kg5-f5 instead, 51 Qg7-d7+ wins a Rook, and then another piece!

51	Qg7-h7+	Kh5-g5
52	Qh7xe4	Rc6-c7

Black might have resigned gracefully here, but as he did not, we do get an interesting lesson in finishing off an opponent who insists on fighting on to the bitter end.

53 Ne2-g3

With this in mind: 54 Qe4-f5+ Kg5-h6 (on 54 ... Kg5-h4 55 Qf5-h5 is mate) 55 Qf5-f6+ Kh6-h7 56 Ng3-f5 followed by 57 Nf5-e7 (cutting off the Rook

from the King's aid) and the threat of mate in two will force Black to give up his Rook for the Knight.

53	...	Kg5-f6

Moving to the other side offers no relief: 53 ... Kg5-h6 54 Qe4-g4, and the threat of winning by 55 Ng3-f5+ Kh6-h7 56 Nf5-e7 Rc7xe7 57 Qg4-h4+ followed by Qh4xe7 cannot be obviated; the Rook cannot come to the aid of the King, as (after 53 ... Kg5-h6 54 Qe4-g4):

(a) 54 ... Rc7-h7 55 Ng3-f5 is mate,

(b) 54 ... Rc7-g7 55 Qg4-h5 is mate,

(c) 54 ... Rc7-f7 55 Ng3-f5+ Kh6-h7 56 Qg4-h5+ Kh7-g8 57 Nf5-h6+ wins the Rook.

54	Qe4-d5	Bb6-c5

Necessary, as 54 ... Kf6-e7 allows 55 Ng3-f5+ winning the Queen Pawn.

55 Ng3-e4+

This is the position:

Position after 55 Ng3-e4+

If Black now plays 55 . . . Kf6-f5, the reply is not the prosaic 56 Ne4xd6+, but the imaginative 56 Kg2-f3, with the pretty possibility of mating by 57 Qd5-g8 and 58 Qg8-g4.

Then if 56 . . . Rc7-g7, there comes 57 Qd5-a8, and the threat is 58 Qa8-f8+ Kf5-g6 59 Qf8-f6+ Kg6-h7 60 Ne4-g5+ Kh7-h8 (on 60 . . . Kh7-g8 61 Qf8-d8 is mate) 61 Qf6-f8+ Rg7-g8 62 Qf8-h6 mate.

If (in reply to 57 Qd5-a8) 57 . . . Rg7-f7 58 Qa8-e8 Kf5-g6+ 59 Kf3-g4 (threatens 60 Ne4-g5 winning the Rook) 59 . . . Kg6-g7 (on 59 . . . Bc5-e3 60 Ne4xd6 wins the Rook) 60 Ne4xc5 d6xc5 61 Qe8xe5+ followed by 62 Qe5xc5, and the rest is easy.

On 55 . . . Kf6-f5 56 Kg2-f3 Kf5-g6, there is a problem-like finish as follows: 57 Qd5-g8+ Rc7-g7 (if 57 . . . Kg6-h6 58 Qg8-g5+ Kh6-h7 59 Ne4-f6+ Kh7-h8 60 Qg5-g8 mate) 58 Qg8-e6+ Kg6-h7 (or 58 . . . Kg6-h5 59 Qe6-f5+ Kh5-h6 60 Qf5-f6+ Rg7-g6—here if 60 . . . Kh6-h7 61 Ne4-g5+ wins easily—61 Qf6-h8 mate) 59 Ne4-f6+ (are you still with me?) 59 . . . Kh7-g6 (if 59 . . . Kh7-h6 60 Nf6-e8+ Rg7-g6 61 Qe6-h3+ Kh6-g5 62 Qh3-g4+ Kg5-h6 63 Qg4-h4 mate) 60 Nf6-e8+ Kg6-h7 61 Ne8xg7 Kh7xg7 62 Kf3-g4 Bc5-b4 63 Kg4-h5 Bb4-c5 64 Qe6-e7+ Kg7-g8 65 Kh5-g6, and White mates next move.

55 . . . Kf6-e7

56 Kg2-f3 Ke7-d7

The position is tricky. The Rook, for example, hasn't a single plausible move. If

(a) 56 . . . Rc7-d7 57 Ne4xc5 d6xc5 58 Qd5xe5+ followed by 59 Qe5xc5 wins,

(b) 56 . . . Rc7-a7 57 Ne4xc5 d6xc5 58 Qd5xc5+ wins the Rook,

(c) 56 . . . Rc7-c8 57 Qd5-b7+ Ke7-d8 58 Ne4-g5!, with the irresistible threat of 59 Ng5-e6+ winning the Rook.

57 Kf3-g4 Rc7-c6

58 Qd5-f7+ Kd7-c8

Black is driven to the wall. Quick loss follows 58 . . . Kd7-d8, when the threat by 59 Ne4-f6 of mate at d7 forces 59 . . . Kd8-c8 (or 59 . . . Rc6-c7 60 Qf7-e8 mate) and 60 Qf7-d7+ wins the Rook.

59 Ne4-f6 Rc6-c7

Of no avail is 59 . . . Rc6-b6 when 60 Nf6-d5 threatens mate on the move. If then 60 . . . Rb6-c6 (of course not 60 . . . Rb6-b7 Qf7-e8 mate) 61 Qf7-e8+ Kc8-b7 62 Qe8-d7+, and White wins a whole Rook.

60 Qf7-e8+ Kc8-b7

61 Nf6-d5 Rc7-c8

62 Qe8-b5+ Kb7-a7

63 Nd5-e7 Black Resigns

Any Rook move is followed by 64 Ne7-c6+, forcing Black to give up the exchange or be mated.

A midgame and ending quite out of the ordinary.

GAME 23

White J. R. Capablanca
Black D. Janowsky
New York, 1916

Slav Defence

Janowsky gets quite a good game from the opening, and his initiative persists even after a dubious offer of the exchange.

A hasty advance in the center, which should have been preceded by the prophylactic 25 . . . g6-g5, gives Capablanca an opportunity (which he seizes at once) to free his King-side position and take over the direction of the game.

In the absorbing ending that follows, Capablanca has a Bishop and two Pawns against a Bishop and Pawn. The task of conducting his passed Pawn to the queening square is delicate, and requires exquisite timing, as the opposing Bishop threatens to sacrifice itself for the Pawn and force a draw.

Needless to say, Capablanca displays his usual deadly accuracy in an ending that is a valuable contribution to the theory of Bishop-and-Pawn endings.

1	d2-d4	Ng8-f6
2	Ng1-f3	d7-d5
3	c2-c4	c7-c6
4	Nb1-c3	d5xc4
5	e2-e3	Bc8-g4

You will search the opening books in vain for this move of Janowsky's. Janowsky was never Pawn-hungry, or he would have tried to hold on to the extra Pawn by 5 . . . b7-b5.

6	Bf1xc4	e7-e6

7	h2-h3	Bg4-h5
8	0-0	Bf8-e7
9	Qd1-b3	Qd8-b6

If instead 9 . . . Bh5xf3 10 g2xf3, and White's two Bishops compensate him for the broken-up Pawn position on the King-side.

10	Nf3-e5	Nb8-d7
11	Qb3xb6	a7xb6

The exchange of Queens is favourable to Black, as he now has an open file for his Rooks.

12	Ne5xd7	Ke8xd7
13	Bc1-d2	b6-b5
14	Bc4-d3	Bh5-g6
15	Bd3xg6	h7xg6

Janowsky has emerged from the opening with the better game. His Rooks are in possession of two open files, and his minor pieces have more scope than Capablanca's.

16	Rf1-c1	Ra8-a6
17	a2-a3	Rh8-a8

Threatens to win a Pawn by 18 . . . b5-b4—a four-fold attack on the Rook Pawn.

18	Nc3-a2	Nf6-d5
19	Ra1-b1	f7-f5
20	Kg1-f1	Ra6-a4

Black has a strong alternative in 20 . . . Ra6-b6 followed by 21 . . . b5-b4, but Janowsky has a bolder course in mind.

21 Na2-c3 Ra4-c4

Janowsky goes in for the sacrifice of the exchange, confident that it will yield him an advantage in position.

He should have been content with 21 . . . Nd5xc3 22 Bd2xc3 b5-b4, with excellent endgame prospects.

But again it's a matter of temperament. Janowsky would rather stir up complications in the midgame than play a long, hard endgame.

22	b2-b3	Rc4xc3
23	Bd2xc3	Ra8xa3
24	Bc3-e1	Be7-f6
25	Kf1-e2	e6-e5

This advance is premature, as it is important after 26 d4xe5 Bf6xe5 to prevent 27 f2-f4 dislodging the centrally-placed Bishop.

The preparatory move 25 . . . g6-g5 was in order.

Ending 23

Position after 25 . . . e6-e5

Janowsky

Capablanca to move

Capablanca is ahead in material, as he has a Rook for a Knight and a-Pawn. This advantage is offset by Black's superior position. His Rook is headed for the seventh rank, along which it might cause some trouble; his Knight stands like a rock in the center; and his Bishop occupies a strong post.

Capablanca plans to restrain the adverse Queen-side Pawns, get rid of the powerful Knight, and advance the Pawns on the King-side where he has the majority of Pawns.

| 26 | d4xe5 | Bf6xe5 |
| 27 | f2-f4! | Be5-d6 |

On 27 . . . Be5-f6, there might follow 28 g2-g4 with the threat of evicting the Bishop from the long diagonal by 29 g4-g5

| 28 | Be1-c3 | Ra3-a2+ |
| 29 | Ke2-f3 | Bd6-c5 |

Instead of meekly defending his g-Pawn by 29 . . . Bd6-f8, Janowsky (as usual) tries for a little counter-attack. He visualizes the following: 30 Bc3xg7 Bc5xe3 31 Rc1-d1 (rescues the Rook from attack, and threatens 32 Rd1xd5+ c6xd5 33 Kf3xe3) 31 . . . Ra2-f2+ 32 Kf3-g3 Rf2xf4, and Black has picked up a Pawn.

30   Rc1-d1

Now of course the capture of 30 . . . Bc5xe3 fails after 31 Rd1xd5+.

30	. . .	Kd7-e6
31	Rd1-d3	Bc5-f8
32	Bc3-e5	

Now it is Capablanca's Bishop that is centrally located and in possession of the long diagonal.

32   . . .   b5-b4

Black tries to start his Queen-side majority of Pawns rolling . . .

33   Rb1-c1   g6-g5

. . . but hesitates to continue with 33 . . . c6-c5, as that would remove a strong support from the Knight.

34   g2-g4

Threatens to win a couple of Pawns by 35 g4xf5+ Ke6-f7 (on 35 . . . Ke6xf5 36 e3-e4+ wins the Knight) 36 f4xg5.

34	. . .	g7-g6
35	e3-e4	f5xe4+
36	Kf3xe4	Ra2-e2+
37	Ke4-f3	Re2-h2
38	Kf3-g3	Rh2-e2
39	h3-h4	g5xh4+
40	Kg3xh4	Bf8-e7+

41	Kh4-g3	g6-g5

Black plays to undermine the Bishop.

42	Kg3-f3	Re2-h2
43	Rc1-e1	

Not with any threat of discovering on the King, but of discovering an attack on the Rook by 44 f4-f5+.

43	. . .	Rh2-h3+
44	Kf3-e4	Rh3-h4
45	f4xg5!	Be7xg5

Janowsky carefully avoids 45 . . . Rh4xg4+ when 46 Ke4-f3 forces the Rook to move to a black square and into a discovered attack by the Bishop.

46	Ke4-f3	Rh4-h3+
47	Be5-g3+	Ke6-d7
48	Kf3-g2	Rh3-h7

This is the picture on the board:

Position after 48 . . . Rh3-h7

49	Re1-e5	Bg5-f6
50	Re5xd5+	

The Knight must be destroyed!

50	. . .	c6xd5

51	Rd3xd5+	Kd7-e8

Nothing is to be gained by coming towards the center: if 51 . . . Kd7-e6 52 Rd5-d6+ Ke6-f7 (the King must retreat) 53 Rd6-b6, and the King must lose another move to save the Pawn at b7.

52	Rd5-b5	Rh7-d7

If 52 . . . Bf6-c3 53 Bg3-d6 does the trick.

53	Rb5xb4	Ke8-f7
54	Rb4-b6	Bf6-d4

This leads to an exchange of Rooks, but leaving them on the board means passive resistance, with no chance of counter-play.

55	Rb6-d6	Rd7xd6
56	Bg3xd6	Kf7-g6
57	Kg2-f3	Bd4-f6
58	Bd6-f4	Kg6-f7
59	Kf3-e4	Kf7-e6

Both Kings are now centralized (and probably breathing defiance at each other).

60	Bf4-e3	Bf6-e7
61	g4-g5	Be7-d8
62	Ke4-f4	Bd8-c7+
63	Kf4-g4	Bc7-e5
64	Kg4-h5	Ke6-f7

He must prevent this: 65 Kh5-g6 Be5-c3 66 Kg6-h7 Ke6-f7 67 g5-g6+ Kf7-f8 68 Be3-c5+ Kf8-e8 69 g6-g7, and Black must give up his Bishop for the Pawn.

65	Kh5-h6	Kf7-g8
66	Be3-b6	Be5-c3
67	Kh6-g6	Bc3-d2
68	Kg6-f6	Bd2-c3+

69	Kf6-e6	Bc3-d2
70	g5-g6	Bd2-c3

Against 70 . . . Kg8-g7, the play would go thus: 71 Ke6-f5 Bd2-c3 72 Bb6-c7 (threatens to win by 73 Bc7-e5+) 72 . . . Bc3-e1 73 Bc7-e5+ Kg7-g8 (but not 73 . . . Kg7-h6, when 74 Kf5-f6 followed by 75 Kf6-f7 wins), and White resumes operations on the Queen-side now that his King Knight Pawn is safe from harm.

71	Ke6-d5	Bc3-d2

Attacking the Pawn is fatal, as after 71 . . . Kg8-g7 72 Bb6-d4+ Bc3xd4 73 Kd5xd4 Kg7xg6 74 Kd4-c5 Kg6-f6 75 b3-b4 Kf6-e5 (on 75 . . . Kf6-e7 76 Kc5-b6 wins easily) 76 b4-b5 (but not 76 Kc5-b6 Ke5-d4 77 b4-b5 Kd4-c4, and Black draws) 76 . . . Ke5-e6 77 Kc5-b6 and White wins.

72	Bb6-d4	b7-b5
73	Kd5-e4	b5-b4
74	Bd4-e3	Bd2-c3

Clearly, 74 . . . Bd2xe3 75 Ke4xe3 Kg8-g7 76 Ke3-d4 Kg7xg6 77 Kd4-c4 Kg6-f7 78 Kc4xb4 Kf7-e7 79 Kb4-c5 Ke7-d7 80 Kc5-b6 is a win for White, as the King on the sixth in front of the Pawn on the same file is always a win, with or without the move.

75	Ke4-d3	Bc3-e1
76	Be3-d2	Be1-f2
77	Kd3-e4	Bf2-c5
78	Ke4-d5	

Attacks the Bishop with gain of tempo.

78	. . .	Bc5-e7

79	Kd5-c4	Kg8-g7
80	Bd2xb4	Be7-d8
81	Bb4-c3+	Kg7xg6
82	b3-b4	Kg6-f5
83	Kc4-d5	

The position at this point:

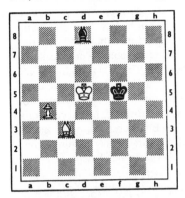

Position after 83 Kc4-d5

Janowsky analyzing the position (mentally of course) came to the conclusion that Capablanca had a clear-cut win by the following line of play: 83 . . . Bd8-c7 84 Bc3-d4 Bc7-d8 85 Bd4-c5 Bd8-c7 86 Bc5-d6 Bc7-d8 87 Kd5-c6 Kf5-e6 88 b4-b5 Bd8-a5 89 Bd6-c7 Ba5-d2 90 b5-b6 Bd2-e3 91 b6-b7

Be3-a7 92 Kc6-b5 Ke6-d7 93 Kb5-a6, and White wins.

The conviction that his game was hopeless prompted his decision, which was . . .

83 . . . Black Resigns

Many years later, Chéron and Averbach demonstrated that Black still had a draw at the point when he resigned, by a remarkable line of play (which Janowsky could hardly be blamed for missing) to wit: 83 . . . Kf5-f4! 84 Bc3-d4 (if 84 Bc3-e5+ Kf4-e3 85 b4-b5 Ke3-d3 86 Kd5-c6 Kd3-c4) 84 . . . Kf4-f3! 85 b4-b5 (if 85 Bd4-c5, Kf3-e2! 86 Kd5-c6 Ke2-d3 87 Kc6-d7 Bd8-g5 88 b4-b5 Kd3-c4) 85 . . . Kf3-e2! 86 Kd5-c6 Ke2-d3 87 Bd4-b6 Bd8-g5 88 Kc6-b7 Kd3-c4 89 Kb7-a6 Kc4-b3! (but not 89 . . . Kc4-b4, when 90 Bb6-a5+ Kb4-a4 91 b5-b6 and White wins) 90 Bb6-f2 Bg5-d8 91 Bf2-e1 Kb3-a4, and the King arrives just in time to force the draw.

A difficult line of play to foresee, especially since it involved such an extraordinary idea as maneuvering the King *behind* the passed Pawn!

GAME 24

White D. Janowsky
Black J. R. Capablanca
New York, 1916

Slav Defence
Capablanca shows his consummate mastery of all styles of play in this game.

The subtle strategy initiated by his 10th move could have been a profound concept of Lasker's.

The powerful restraining moves by the Pawns are worthy of a Philidor.

The switch attack from one side of the board to the other is reminiscent of a Bogolyubov attack.

The sacrifice of a Pawn on the Queen-side in order to win a piece on the King-side is in the style of a Spielmann.

The mate threat on an open board in the endgame might have been the inspiration for the finish of the Nimzowitsch-Bernstein game at Carlsbad in 1923.

The whole game might have been a breath-taking brilliancy of Alekhine's except that it was played by Capablanca!

1	d2-d4	Ng8-f6
2	Ng1-f3	d7-d5
3	c2-c4	c7-c6
4	Nb1-c3	Bc8-f5
5	Qd1-b3	

A stronger continuation is 5 c4xd5 c6xd5 6 Qd1-b3, practically forcing the Bishop to return home.

5	...	Qd8-b6
6	Qb3xb6	a7xb6
7	c4xd5	Nf6xd5
8	Nc3xd5	c6xd5

Janowsky was no doubt pleased at having saddled his opponent with doubled and isolated Pawns on the b-file, but the position is deceptive. Black has two fine open files for his Rooks to disport in—and as for the Pawns, Capablanca has a plan to turn this weakness into strength.

| 9 | e2-e3 | Nb8-c6 |
| 10 | Bc1-d2 | Bf5-d7!! |

What a move! This undeveloping of the Bishop is as subtle a piece of strategy as you will ever see on a chessboard! The idea is this: Capablanca intends to continue by . . . Nc6-a5, . . . b6-b5, and . . . Na5-c4. The Knight would then occupy an important outpost and be strongly supported by Pawns. It could not be left there dominating the entire neighborhood, and removing it would be practically compulsory. The recapture by . . . b5xc4 would undouble the Pawns, and leave Black with the advantage of the two Bishops. In the consequent play, Black could bring a great deal of pressure to bear on his opponent's Queen-side Pawns.

| 11 | Bf1-e2 | |

Had Janowsky suspected the profundity of Capablanca's concept, he would not have played a routine developing move, but stationed his Bishop at b5 instead, rendering it difficult to carry out the plan.

| 11 | ... | e7-e6 |

Locking in the Bishop is unimportant, as the Bishop, destined for great deeds, will come to life later.

| 12 | 0-0 | Bf8-d6 |
| 13 | Rf1-c1 | Ke8-e7! |

Capablanca prepares for the ending (even at this early stage) by bringing his King to the center, instead of castling.

| 14 | Bd2-c3 | Rh8-c8 |
| 15 | a2-a3 | |

This frees the Queen Rook from the task of defending the Rook Pawn, but it creates a hole at b3, an organic weakness which is irremediable.

A better course was 15 Nf3-d2, waiting (like Mr Micawber) for something to turn up, or the energetic 15 Nf3-e5, doing something about it.

15 ... Nc6-a5!

The Knight, in accordance with the plan, is headed for c4.

White can prevent this by playing 16 Bc3xa5, but he is not anxious to straighten out Black's Pawns, and as well to leave Black with the two Bishops.

(Meanwhile Black, *en passant,* is threatening 16 ... Na5-b3, winning the exchange).

16 Nf3-d2 f7-f5!

Capablanca of course will not permit White to free himself by 17 e3-e4, and obtain counter-play.

Great players do not let their opponents make good moves.

17 g2-g3 b6-b5!

18 f2-f3

Janowsky misses his last chance to prevent the Knight from coming in at c4, by removing it from circulation, but he was loth to part with one of his beloved Bishops.

18 ... Na5-c4!

Capablanca has realized the first part of his plan, which was to post the Knight in a commanding position.

Janowsky is fully aware that the Knight *must* be removed, but how?

19 Be2xc4

Janowsky would rather have captured with his Knight, but after

19 ... b5xc4 in reply, his Bishop would be badly hemmed in, and the prospect of advancing his King Pawn rendered impossible for a long time to come.

After the text move, his Knight supports the advance, which is imperative if his pieces are to get any freedom of movement.

19 ... b5xc4

20 e3-e4 Ke7-f7

Clears a flight-square for the Bishop in the event of an attack on it by 21 e4-e5.

21 e4-e5

This is the sort of move that many players find irresistible, but it violates the tenets of position play, as it cuts down the scope of White's Bishop.

The beautiful central square e5 should be reserved for a piece, and Janowsky should have striven for that possibility by playing instead 21 e4xd5 e6xd5 22 f3-f4 followed by 23 Nd2-f3 and 24 Nf3-e5. Black could then only remove the strongly-posted Knight at the cost of giving up his dark-squared Bishop for it.

21 ... Bd6-e7

22 f3-f4

If White's object was to place all his pieces and Pawns on black squares, he has succeeded in that ambition!

Ending 24

Position after 22 f3-f4

Capablanca to move

Janowsky

Black's positional advantage is two-fold:

(a) he has two Bishops against his opponent's Knight and bad Bishop (one whose movements are restricted by the many Pawns occupying squares of the same colour), and

(b) he has the possibility of opening up lines on both side of the board for his Rooks.

Capablanca plans to force a breakthrough on the Queen-side with his b-Pawn, and one on the King-side with his g-Pawn. These two Pawns will be the spearheads of an attack that will enable his Bishops and Rooks to penetrate the enemy position.

What makes this strategy particularly attractive is the sudden shifting of the attack from one side to the other—and back again, and again, and again! It would be amusing, if tournament chess were not so serious an affair where life-time reputations are at stake in every game.

| 22 | ... | b7-b5 |

Clearly with the intention of advancing to b4 at the right time.

White can prevent this advance and get rid of his bad Bishop as well, but at the cost of a Pawn, like this: 23 Bc3-b4 Be7xb4 24 a3xb4 Ra8-a4 25 Ra1xa4 b5xa4, and the coming 26 ... Rc8-b8 will win a Pawn.

| 23 | Kg1-f2 | Ra8-a4 |
| 24 | Kf2-e3 | Rc8-a8 |

Threatens to win the Bishop by 25 ... b5-b4.

| 25 | Ra1-b1 | h7-h6 |

So ... Capablanca turns his attention to the other side of the board, obviously intending to push the Knight Pawn, as the start of an attack on the King-side.

| 26 | Nd2-f3 | |

White might have fared better with 26 h2-h4, then if 26 ... g7-g5 27 h4xg5 h6xg5 28 Nd2-f3 g5-g4 29 Nf3-g5+ Be7xg5 (on 29 ... Kg6 30 Rc1-h1) 30 f4xg5 Kf7-g6 31 Rc1-h1!

| 26 | ... | g7-g5 |
| 27 | Nf3-e1 | |

A strange-looking move, but the Knight hopes to exert more influence at g2 than at f3.

| 27 | ... | Ra8-g8 |
| 28 | Ke3-f3 | |

White should have continued with 28 Ne1-g2, ready to meet

28 . . . g5xf4 with 29 Ng2xf4, and
the Knight stands on a good square.

28   ...   g5xf4

29   g3xf4   Ra4-a8

The Rook returns to home base,
ready to swing over to the King-side,
and the attack on the g-file.

30   Ne1-g2   Rg8-g4

31   Rc1-g1   Ra8-g8

Signals the beginning of Janowsky's
troubles. His Knight is pinned and
may not move without loss of his
King Rook, and his King Rook may
not move without loss of his Knight!

But how does Capablanca add to
the pressure on White's position?
How does he enlist the services of
the light-squared Bishop now standing idly at d7?

We'll see in a moment. Meanwhile . . . its's Janowsky who is on
the move!

32   Bc3-e1

An ingenious idea! He plans to
rescue the Knight, who is threatened by the march of the Rook Pawn,
this way: 32 . . . h6-h5 33 Be1-f2
(to protect the Rook) 33 . . . h5-h4
34 h2-h3 Rg4-g7 35 Ng2-e3, and
he can breathe again.

But Capablanca is ready for this
contingency, and forces Janowsky
to direct his attention to the other
wing.

32   ...   b5-b4!

Brilliant play! Capablanca gives
away a Pawn to clear a path for the
Queen Bishop. The Bishop intends
to whirl around the board by way
of a4, stopping at c2 to attack the
Rook (if it hasn't been frightened

away) and finally come to a stop at
e4, where a check to the King will
strike at the Knight behind the
King.

33   a3xb4

The alternative is 33 Be1xb4
Be7xb4 34 a3xb4, and Black can
then pursue the attack by
34 . . . h6-h5, with threats against
the pinned Knight, or play
34 . . . Rg8-b8, regaining the Pawn
immediately with advantage.

33   ...   Bd7-a4

34   Rb1-a1

On 34 Rb1-c1 (to stop the intended
34 . . . Ba4-c2) then Black continues
effectively with 34 . . . Rg4xf4+
35 Kf3xf4 Be7-g5+ 36 Kf4-f3
Bg5xc1, and remains with a winning
position.

34   ...   Ba4-c2

35   Be1-g3

Janowsky has adroitly managed to
relieve the pin on the Knight, but
Capablanca, in compliance with
Pillsbury's epigram, 'So set up your
attacks that when the fire is out, it
isn't out!', throws another log on
the fire.

35   ...   Bc2-e4+

36   Kf3-f2   h6-h5

37   Ra1-a7

White tries to work up some kind
of counter-attack, since 37 Ng2-e3
offers no hope after 37 . . . h5-h4
38 Ne3xg4 h4xg3+ followed by
39 . . . f5xg4, and Black will have
won two pieces for a Rook.

37   ...   Be4xg2!

A clever exchange by the great

master of the art of exchanging.

No matter how White retakes, his Bishop will be pinned!

38   Rg1xg2   h5-h4

Sad, but true. The noble Bishop that rescued the Knight from a pin is now itself victim of a pin.

39   Bg3xh4

Makes the best of the situation. Instead of losing a whole Bishop, Janowsky gets by with loss of the exchange.

39   . . .   Rg4xg2+

Of course not the hasty 39 . . . Rg4xh4, as the reply 40 Rg2xg8 would come like a shot.

40   Kf2-f3   Rg2xh2

41   Bh4xe7

No better is 41 Ra7xe7+ Kf7-f8 42 Bh4-f6 Rg8-h8, and the threat of instant mate forces 43 Bf6xh8 Kf8xe7, and the rest is child's play.

41   . . .   Rh2-h3+

Drives the King back a rank.

42   Kf3-f2   Rh3-b3

The threat of discovered check

poses no danger to Black, as all of Capablanca's pieces and Pawns stand on white squares.

43   Be7-g5+

Shuts out the Rook at g8 temporarily, but there are many roads to checkmate.

43   . . .   Kf7-g6

44   Ra7-e7   Rb3xb2+

45   Kf2-f3   Rg8-a8

Threatens instant mate—which can be delayed only with spite checks.

46   Re7xe6+   Kg6-h7

Never in a million years would Capablanca fall into 46 . . . Kg6-h5 47 Re6-h6 mate.

47   White Resigns

After 47 Re6-h6+ Kh7-g7 48 Kf3-g3 there follows 48 . . . Ra8-a3+ 49 Kg3-h4 Rb2-h2 mate.

Magnificent play throughout marks a game of the highest order—definitely one of the greatest masterpieces in the entire literature of chess.

GAME 25

White F. J. Marshall
Black J. R. Capablanca
New York, 1918

Queen's Gambit Declined
Capablanca's conduct of the game is truly impressive. It is as fine an illustration of *The Power of Position Play* as you will ever see.

Early in the game Capablanca gives up a Pawn in order to maneuver his opponent into a state of *zugzwang.*

I am always intrigued by the mysterious power exerted by

zugzwang, whereby several pieces of one player hold an equal or even greater number of his opponent's pieces in so tight a grip that no piece or Pawn can move without incurring loss.

Such is the efficacy of Capablanca's strategy in this game as to keep Marshall's pieces completely in a bind. A Knight that is under attack must stay where it is, while neither of the Rooks protecting the Knight dare move away from the file it occupies. The King—well, the King by himself can do very little. All that is left to Marshall are some feeble moves by his Pawns. When these die out, Marshall tries out a swindle or two. The swindles come to nothing, and Marshall must turn down his King in surrender.

1	d2-d4	d7-d5
2	Ng1-f3	Ng8-f6
3	c2-c4	e7-e6
4	Nb1-c3	Nb8-d7
5	Bc1-g5	Bf8-e7
6	e2-e3	0-0
7	Ra1-c1	c7-c6

It took quite a while after the history-making game between Pillsbury and Tarrasch at Hastings in 1895 for the masters to discover the superiority of 7 . . . c7-c6 to 7 . . . b7-b6. In the meantime Pillsbury kept on slaughtering the innocents who stuck to the latter move.

| 8 | Qd1-c2 | d5xc4 |
| 9 | Bf1xc4 | Nf6-d5 |

This move, made popular by Capablanca, frees Black's rather crowded game by bringing about some exchanges.

| 10 | Bg5xe7 | Qd8xe7 |
| 11 | 0-0 | Nd5xc3 |

But not at once 11 . . . b7-b6, which Vidmar tried against Capablanca at London in 1922. He was smashed by 12 Nc3xd5 c6xd5 (if 12 . . . e6xd5 13 Bc4-d3 wins a Pawn) 13 Bc4-d3 h7-h6 14 Qc2-c7 Qe7-b4 15 a2-a3!, and Black's Queen sortie led to loss, Vidmar having discovered to his horror that 15 . . . Qb4xb2 would be followed by 16 Rc1-b1 Qb2xa3 17 Bd3-b5 Qa3-e7 (or 17 . . . Nd7-f6 18 Rb1-a1 Qa3-b4 19 Rf1-b1, and White wins the Queen) 18 Bb5-c6 Ra8-b8 19 Nf3-e5 Qe7-d8 20 Qc7xa7 Nd7xe5 21 d4xe5, and White wins a piece, as Capablanca demonstrated.

| 12 | Qc2xc3 | b7-b6 |

'This is the key,' says Capablanca, 'to this system of defence. Having simplified the game considerably by a series of exchanges, Black will now develop his Queen Bishop along the long diagonal without having created any apparent weakness. The proper development of the Queen Bishop is Black's greatest problem in the Queen's Gambit.'

| 13 | e3-e4 |

An excellent alternative is 13 Qc3-d3, which Bogolyubov used to good effect in his game against Tarrasch at Hastings in 1922, enabling him to win the shortest game of the tournament by means of a Knight fork which he described as a 'family check'.

The continuation was
13 . . . Rf8-d8 (inferior to
13 . . . c6-c5, which led to a draw
between Alekhine and Capablanca
at London in 1922) 14 Qd3-e2
c6-c5 15 Bc4-b5 c5xd4
16 Nf3xd4 Bc8-b7 17 Rc1-c7
Ra8-b8 18 Rf1-d1 Bb7-d5
19 Nd4-c6!, and White wins a
piece.

| 13 | . . . | Bc8-b7 |
| 14 | Rf1-e1 | Rf8-d8 |

Black plans to continue with
15 . . . Nd7-f6, 16 . . . Ra8-c8 and
17 . . . c6-c5, the freeing key move
in such positions.

15   d4-d5

Marshall does not wait for things
to happen to him—so he attacks!
The immediate threat is 16 d5xe6
f7xe6, and Black is left with an
isolated King Pawn.

15   . . .   Nd7-c5!

Much stronger than the modest
15 . . . Nd7-f8, which Capablanca
had tried in an earlier round against
Kostics.

  Black now threatens to win a
Pawn by 16 . . . c6xd5 17 e4xd5
Bb7xd5, or to shatter White's
center by 16 . . . Nc5xe4
17 Re1xe4 c6xd5 18 Re4-g4
f7-f5, and Black regains his piece.

| 16 | d5xe6 | Nc5xe6 |
| 17 | Bc4xe6 | Qe7xe6 |

Capablanca thought that his attack
on the Rook Pawn would cause
White to lose a move defending the
Pawn, whereupon he could play
18 . . . c6-c5 with the superior
game.
  But he was disillusioned, as

Marshall had quite a little surprise
for him.

18   Nf3-d4!

Ending 25

Position after 18 Nf3-d4!

Capablanca to move

Marshall

Capablanca, whose Queen is attacked, is faced with a problem. He
may not play 18 . . . Qe6xa2, as
19 Rc1-a1 in reply wins his Queen.
Nor may his Queen move to e7, as
his c-Pawn is loose. Finally, if
18 . . . Qe6-d7 (to protect the
Pawn) he faces the fury of a
Marshall attack, beginning with
19 Nd4-f5 f7-f6 20 Qc3-g3
(threatens 21 Rc1-d1 Qd7-f7
22 Nf5-h6+ winning the Queen)
.20 . . . Kg8-h8 21 Rc1-d1 Qd7-f7
22 h2-h4, with a powerful game
for White.

18   . . .   Qe6-e5!

A brilliant move, this sacrifice of a
Pawn. It is not evident at first

sight what advantage will accrue in return for the Pawn, as Queens will be exchanged, and little material left with which to work up an attack.

But it must have been clear to Capablanca, who had looked deeply into the position and foreseen the various possibilities.

19 Nd4xc6   Qe5xc3

20 Rc1xc3   Rd8-d2!

'The powerful position of the Black Rook at d2,' says Capablanca, fully compensates Black for the Pawn minus.'

Marshall should now play for a draw, according to Capablanca, who suggests this line: 21 Nc6-e7+ Kg8-f8 22 Rc3-c7 Ra8-e8 22 Rc7xb7 (best—not 23 Ne7-g6+ f7xg6 24 Rc7xb7 Re8xe4) 23 . . .Re8xe7 24 Rb7-b8+ Re7-e8 25 Rb8xe8+ Kf8xe8, and White should be able to draw, *even though he is a Pawn ahead.*

21 Re1-b1

Marshall forgets that he is Marshall, and plays a surprisingly meek defensive move. At this stage, Rooks are supposed to be out in the open, picking up stray Pawns—or at least terrorizing them.

21 . . .   Ra8-e8

This demonstration against the center is the prelude to an attack on the King himself.

22 e4-e5

This is preferable to 22 f2-f3 f7-f5 23 e4xf5 Re8-e2, and the doubled Rooks are enough to frighten a man to death.

22 . . .   g7-g5!

Masterly play! At one stroke Capablanca prevents White from supporting the King Pawn by 23 f2-f4, provides a flight-square for his King against mate threats on the last rank, and threatens to win a Pawn by 23 . . . Bb7xc6 24 Rc3xc6 Re8xe5.

23 h2-h4

Marshall, alert to the danger, is willing to return the extra Pawn, if he can thereby disrupt Black's Kingside Pawn position.

23 . . .   g5xh4

24 Rb1-e1

Rather than await a slow death, Marshall decides to get his Rook back into active play, even at the cost of losing his Queen-side Pawns.

On 24 f2-f4 instead, the sequel might be: 24 . . . h4-h3 (better than 24 . . . Re8-e6 25 Rb1-c1, followed by 26 f4-f5) 25 g2-g3 (or 25 g2xh3 Kg8-h8!) 25 . . . h3-h2+ 26 Kg1-h1 Re8-c8 27 Rb1-c1 Kg8-f8 28 f4-f5 Kf8-e8 29 e5-e6 (to prevent 29 . . . Ke8-d7, attacking the Knight with three pieces) 29 . . . f7xe6 30 f5xe6 Rd2-d6, and Black wins the helpless piece.

24 . . .   Re8-e6!

Capablanca is never petty! Instead of picking up innocent Pawns, he goes after big game.

The attack on the Knight gains a tempo for the Rook, which is on the way over to g6, to take aim at the enemy King.

25 Re1-c1

The Knight may not budge! If for example 25 Nc6xa7 Re6-g6 26 g2-g3 h4-h3 (threatens mate in three by 27 ... h3-h2+ 28 Kg1xh2 Rg6-h6+ 29 Kh2-g1 Rh6-h1 mate) 27 Kg1-h2 Rd2xf2+ 28 Kh2xh3 Bb7-d5! 29 g3-g4 Rf2-g2 30 Kh3-h4 Rg6xg4+ 31 Kh4-h3 Bd5-e6, and mate follows quickly.

25 ...   Kg8-g7

Not at once 25 ... Re6-g6, as the reply 26 Nc6-e7+ wins the exchange for White.

26 b2-b4

Intending of course to defend the Knight by 27 b4-b5, and release the Rooks for active duty.

26 ...   b6-b5

Puts an end to that little notion!

27 a2-a3   Re6-g6

This is the situation:

Position after 27 ... Re6-g6

Marshall is running short of moves! If he tries 28 Nc6xa7 Rg6xg2+ 29 Kg1-f1 Rg2xf2+ wins quickly, or if he plays 28 Rc3-c5 (the only move by either Rook which does not lose the Knight) the reply

28 ... h4-h3, striking again at the Knight Pawn, is decisive. Or finally, if 28 f2-f3 (to interfere with the pressure of the Bishop) 28 ... Rg6xg2+ leads to quick mate.

28 Kg1-f1   Rd2-a2!

29 Kf1-g1   h4-h3

The isolated doubled Pawn, usually a weakling, suddenly becomes ferocious!

30 g2-g3   a7-a6

A quiet little waiting move, which brings the opponent to a state of *zugzwang.* It is reminiscent of the famous 25 ... h7-h6 move by Nimzowitsch in his game against Samisch (*The Golden Dozen,* p. 8) which produced the same startling effect.

In both cases the opponent is tied up, but obliged to move by the rules of the game—and any move results in loss of some kind.

31 e5-e6   Rg6xe6

32 g3-g4

The Knight still may not move. For example, if 32 Nc6-d8 (or 32 Nc6-d4) there is a mate in three by 32 ... h3-h2+ 33 Kg1xh2 Re6-h6+ 34 Kh2-g1 Rh6-h1 mate.

32 ...   Re6-h6

33 f2-f3

Marshall tries to close the Bishop's diagonal, but in doing so he exposes himself to other dangers. Had he played 33 g4-g5 instead, some pretty play would have followed: 33 ... h3-h2+ 34 Kg1-h1 (if 34 Kg1-g2 h2-h1(Q)+ 35 Rc1xh1 Bb7xc6+ 36 Rc3xc6 Rh6xc6,

and Black is a Rook ahead)
34 . . .Rh6xc6 35 Rc3xc6 Ra2xf2
36 a3-a4 (trying for stalemate)
36 . . . b5xa4 37 b4-b5 a6xb5
38 g5-g6 h7xg6 39 Rc1-c2 Rf2-f6,
and White can go home.

33 . . .   Rh6-d6

This is superior to the obvious
33 . . . h3-h2+.

34   Nc6-e7   Rd6-d2

Doubled Rooks on the seventh
rank—a dream position!

35   Ne7-f5+

For Marshall, there is always a
flicker of hope in the most desperate position, and against the most
implacable opponent.

The hasty reply 35 . . . Kg7-f8
loses by 36 Rc3-c8+ and mate in
two more moves.

35   . . .   Kg7-f6
36   Nf5-h4   Kf6-g5

The Knight must be evicted to
make a Rook check at g2 possible.

37   Nh4-f5   Rd2-g2+
38   Kg1-f1

On 38 Kg1-h1 instead, there is a
mate in three, beginning with
38 . . . Rg2-h2+.

38   . . .   h3-h2
39   f3-f4+

The last despairing gasp! If Black
replies 39 . . . Kg5-f6 40 Rc3-c6+
forces mate.

39   . . .   Kg5xf4
40   White Resigns

'An ending worth very careful
study,' says Capablanca.

Napier put it succinctly, when he
commented, 'The curious focus of
Capablanca's forces, in maximum
utility, charms and amazes.'

GAME 26

White J. R. Capablanca
Black B. Kostics
First Match Game, Havana, 1919

Petroff Defence
There are interesting aspects of
Capablanca's style in this little
known masterpiece.

I won't dwell on his infinite
patience in exploiting a minute
advantage, or his clever use of
zwischenzug, or his fine handling of
a Rook ending.

What particularly impresses me
is his indifference to Pawn forma-
tions that would be regarded with
horror by most masters. It was not
the ragged look of the Pawns that
counted with Capablanca, but the
effect they exerted on his opponents's position.

Thus at the 44th move of this
game, Capablanca forces an exchange of Knights that leaves him
with an isolated Rook Pawn, and

doubled, isolated Pawns on the Bishop file.

To make up for this, one of his doubled Pawns gets a grip on the critical squares e6 and g6, a grip that turns out to have a decisive effect on the game.

The point is that Capablanca's plans are based on positional considerations, and moves that do not fit in with these plans amount to waste of valuable time.

1	e2-e4	e7-e5
2	Ng1-f3	Ng8-f6
3	Nf3xe5	d7-d6
4	Ne5-f3	Nf6xe4
5	Qd1-e2	

Introduced by Morphy (at the age of 13!) in his first encounter with a master (Lowenthal) and played successfully in the games Capablanca-Marshall and Lasker-Marshall at St. Petersburg in 1914, this move is stronger than 5 d2-d4 or 5 Nb1-c3.

It leads to an exchange of Queens and a simplified position, but Capablanca's opponents never had an easy time of it in a simplified position.

5	. . .	Qd8-e7
6	d2-d3	Ne4-f6
7	Bc1-g5	Qe7xe2+

Marshall tried 7 . . . Bc8-e6 in both St. Petersburg games, but to no avail, as he lost both times.

It would be dangerous for Black to pursue the symmetry, as this could happen: 7 . . . Bc8-g4 8 Bg5xf6 Bg4xf3 9 Qe2xe7+ Bf8xe7 10 Bf6xe7, and White has won a piece.

| 8 | Bf1xe2 | Bf8-e7 |
| 9 | Nb1-c3 | Bc8-d7 |

Either this or 9 . . . c7-c6 is necessary, to prevent 10 Nc3-b5.

| 10 | 0-0 | |

Quite good, though Lasker won a fine game with 10 0-0-0 against Teichmann at Cambridge Springs in 1904.

10	. . .	0-0
11	Rf1-e1	Nb8-c6
12	d3-d4	Rf8-e8

Primarily to dispute control of the e-file, this also takes into account the threat of 13 Be2-b5 and 14 d4-d5, which might be annoying.

13	Be2-b5	a7-a6
14	Bb5-a4	b7-b5
15	Ba4-b3	Nc6-a4
16	Re1-e3	c7-c6
17	Ra1-e1	

Applies more pressure, which Black cannot alleviate by exchange, as after 17 . . . Be7-d8 18 Bg5xf6 Bd8xf6 19 Nc3-e4 Bf6-e7 20 Ne4-c5 d6xc5 21 Re3xe7, and White will win a Pawn.

| 17 | . . . | Kg8-f8 |
| 18 | Bg5-f4 | |

Now the threat of winning a Pawn by 19 Re3xe7 Re8xe7 20 Bf4xd6 will force the Queen Knight to retreat.

| 18 | . . . | Na4-b7 |
| 19 | h2-h3 | |

Prepares a flight-square for the Bishop against the threat of its being exchanged by 19 . . . Nf6-h5, and a flight-square for the King against a threat of check on the back rank.

The last seems a remote possibility—until it suddenly happens!

19	...	h7-h6
20	Bf4-h2	Be7-d8
21	Re3xe8+	Bd7xe8
22	a2-a4	

Having gained undisputed possession of the open King file, White turns to other matters, such as opening the position for his better-developed pieces.

22	...	c6-c5
23	Nc3-e4	

To this Black may not reply 23 . . . c5-c4, as Ne4xd6 wins an important center Pawn, while 23 . . . Bd8-e7 succumbs to 24 d4xc5 d6xc5 25 Ne4xf6 Be7xf6 (or 25 . . . g7xf6 26 Bb3-d5 Ra8-a7 27 Bh2-b8 Ra7-a8 28 Bb8-f4 Ra8-a7 29 Bf4xh6+, and everything falls) 26 Bb3-d5 Ra8-a7 27 Bh2-b8 Ra7-a8 28 Bb8-d6+ Nb7xd6 29 Bd5xa8, and White has won the exchange.

23	...	Nf6xe4

Expecting 24 Re1xe4 in reply, when 24 . . . c5-c4 shuts in the Bishop and improves his chances, but Capablanca, anticipating this possibility, throws a monkeywrench into the machinery by interposing a *zwischenzug.*

24	Bb3-d5!	Ra8-a7
25	Bd5xe4	Bd8-e7

The Queen Pawn was in danger of loss.

26	a4xb5	a6xb5
27	d4xc5	d6xc5
28	Bh2-b8	Ra7-a8
29	Bb8-g3	Ra8-a7
30	Bg3-b8	Ra7-a8
31	Bb8-g3	

The repetition of moves is not a tacit offer of a draw, but to gain time on the clock.

31	...	Ra8-a7
32	Nf3-e5	

Threatens to remove an enemy Bishop by 33 Ne5-c6, leaving White with the advantage of the two Bishops.

32	...	Nb7-d8
33	b2-b3	Nd8-e6
34	Be4-d5	

Black must now guard against loss of a Pawn by 35 Ne5xf7 followed by 36 Bd5xe6.

34	...	Ne6-d4
35	c2-c3	Nd4-f5
36	Bg3-h2	b5-b4
37	g2-g4	Nf5-d6

The Knight's caracoling has taken him from b7 to d6 in five moves, whereas (a cynic might observe) he might have done the trip in one step.

38	c3-c4	Ra7-a3
39	Re1-e3	

Protects the Pawn and threatens 40 Bd5-c6 followed by 41 Bc6xe8, winning some material, e.g., if 41 . . . Kf8xe8 in reply (on 41 . . . Nd6xe8 42 Ne5-d7+ wins a piece) 42 Ne5-c6 Nd6-c8 43 Nc6xe7

Nc8xe7 44 Bh2-d6 Ra3-a7
45 Bd6xc5, after which White
exchanges all the pieces and wins
with his extra Pawn.

39	...	Nd6-c8
40	Bd5-b7	Nc8-a7
41	Bb7-d5	f7-f6

An instinctive thrust against the
importunate Knight, but it creates
holes which are later exploited by
White.

| 42 | Ne5-f3 | Na7-c6 |

Ending 26

Position after 42 ... Na7-c6

Kostics

Capablanca to move

Material is even, and Capablanca's
positional advantage, if any, is
minute. His Rook, bearing down on
a center file, is more aggressively
placed than Black's whose role
seems to be a defensive one.

Capablanca's plan for the coming
endgame is in line with his own

advice, 'The handling of the King
becomes of paramount importance once the endgame stage is
reached.'

After an exchange of Knights,
to reduce the danger of attack, the
King will march up the board to
take a hand in the struggle.

The King is to be a fighting
piece!

| 43 | Nf3-h4 |

The Knight is on its way to f5,
whence it can threaten 45 Nf5xe7
(but of course not 45 Bd5xc6
Be8xc6 46 Nf5xe7, when
46 ... Ra3-a1+ is an unpleasant
surprise) 45 ... Nc6xe7 46 Bh2-d6
Ra3-a7 47 Re3xe7 Ra7xe7
48 Bd6xc5 Be8-g6 49 Bc5xb4
Kf8-e8 50 Bb4xe7 and wins—the
mixture as before.

43	...	Nc6-d4
44	Nh4-f5!	Nd4xf5
45	g4xf5	

White's Pawns are doubled on the
King Bishop file, but it is of small
moment in view of the pressure
exerted by the foremost Pawn,
which cramps Black's game considerably.

45	...	Be8-d7
46	Bd5-e4	Ra3-a6
47	Re3-d3	Bd7-c6
48	Be4xc6	Ra6xc6
49	Kg1-g2	

The King starts out along a white-
squared highway, his ultimate des-
tination being g6. Notice how
Capablanca's advantage has increased
in the last half-dozen moves. His
Bishop, for example, has more

potential power than Black's, the
latter being hampered by Pawns (all
five of them!) occupying squares of
the same colour as does the Bishop.

As Jenö Kapu puts it in *Die Welt-
meister des Schachspiels*, 'White has
the better Bishop, the better Rook,
and the better King.'

49	...	Rc6-a6
50	Kg2-f3	Ra6-a2
51	Bh2-g3	Kf8-e8

A better fight might have been put
up by 51 . . . Ra2-a7, guarding his
second rank against invasion, followed by 52 . . . Kf8-f7 and
53 . . . g7-g6, to do away with the
annoying Pawn at f5.

52	Bg3-f4	Ra2-a3
53	Bf4-e3	

The Bishop is now beautifully
centralized; it attacks two Pawns
while protecting its own Bishop
Pawn.

53	...	Ra3-a1
54	Kf3-g4	Ra1-a7
55	Kg4-h5	

The King goes on his merry way.

55	...	Ke8-f7

'In chess, as in life,' says Tartakover,
'the right perception often comes
too late.'

Black has set up a tight defence,
and it's hard to see how White will
break through, but Capablanca (like
love) will find a way!

56	Rd3-d5	Ra7-a3

The natural defence 56 . . . Ra7-c7
allows 57 h3-h4 Be7-f8 58 Rd5-d8
Bf8-e7 59 Rd8-a8, and White dominates the situation.

57	Rd5-d7	Kf7-e8

Of course not 57 . . . Ra3xb3
58 Be3xc5, and White wins a
piece.

58	Rd7-d3	Ke8-f7
59	h3-h4	Ra3-a7
60	Rd3-d5	Ra7-a5
61	Rd5-d7	Kf7-e8
62	Rd7-d3	Ke8-f7

The King returns, as he must not
allow 63 Kh5-g6, which could be
fatal.

This is how things look:

Position after 62 . . . Ke8-f7

63	Rd3-d5!	

'Señor Capablanca has composed a
Zugzwang Symphony,' says the en-
thusiastic Tartakover.

If now 63 . . . Kf7-e8 64 Kh5-g6
wins easily, or if 63 . . . Be7-f8
64 Rd5-d7+ Bf8-e7 (or
64 . . . Kf7-e8 65 Rd7-b7 followed
by 66 Kh5-g6) 65 Rd7-c7!, and
Black's King must give way, as a
Rook move loses a piece after
66 Be3xc5.

63	...	Ra5-a3

64	Be3xc5	Be7xc5
65	Rd5xc5	Ra3xb3
66	Rc5-c7+	Kf7-f8
67	Kh5-g6	Rb3-f3

The forces are equal in number, but the aggressive position of White's King and Rook makes the win 'a matter of technique', and of this Capablanca has a considerable supply.

68	Rc7-f7+	Kf8-e8
69	Rf7xg7	Rf3-f4
70	h4-h5	Rf4xc4

Black can play to promote his Knight Pawn and switch to a Queen ending with 70 . . . Rf4-g4+ 71 Kg6xf6 Rg4xg7 72 Kf6xg7 b4-b3 73 f5-f6 b3-b2 74 f6-f7+ Ke8-d7 75 f7-f8(Q) b2-b1(Q), but after 76 c4-c5, the win for White offers no problems.

71	Kg6xh6	Ke8-f8

Black tries to get closer to the passed Pawn.

72	Rg7-b7	Rc4-g4

On 72 . . . Kf8-g8 instead, there comes 73 f2-f3 (to prevent being disturbed by a Rook check after Kh6-g6) and White follows with 74 Kh6-g6, Kg8-f8 (mate was

threatened) 75 h5-h6, and Black can call it a day.

73	f2-f3!	Rg4-g5

The Rook must abandon the Pawn, as after 73 . . . Rg4-f4 74 Kh6-g6 is fatal.

74	Rb7xb4	Kf8-f7
75	Rb4-g4!	

A subtle maneuver which forces the release of White's King.

75	. . .	Rg5xf5
76	f3-f4	Rf5-a5
77	Rg4-g7+	Kf7-f8
78	Rg7-b7	f6-f5
79	Kh6-g6	Ra5-a6+
80	Kg6xf5	Ra6-a5+
81	Kf5-g4	Ra5-a6
82	Kg4-g5	Ra6-c6
83	f4-f5	Kf8-g8
84	f5-f6	Rc6-c1
85	Rb7-g7+	Kg8-f8
86	h5-h6	Black Resigns

It is endings such as this one that inspired Reuben Fine to say in *The World's Great Chess Games,* 'The ending was Capablanca's forte; it is here that the passion for clarity is most frequently reflected.'

GAME 27

White B. Kostics
Black J. R. Capablanca
Fourth Match Game, Havana, 1,919

Queen's Pawn Opening
Capablanca's midgame strategy has a family resemblance to that in his game against Janowsky (Game 24).

After allowing his Pawns to be

doubled on the Queen Knight file, Capablanca maneuvers his Queen Knight over to c4, where its forced removal opens new vistas for his Rooks.

His sudden shifting of the attack from one side of the board to the other throws Kostics off balance, and he finds himself drawn into an uncomfortable pin. In trying to escape from the pin, Kostics chooses a move that seems to be forced, only to discover that he has been lured into a lost endgame.

The ending, an unusual one, leaves Kostics altogether helpless against the threat of a decisive entry by Capablanca's King into his paralyzed Queen-side position.

1	d2-d4	Ng8-f6
2	Ng1-f3	e7-e6
3	Bc1-g5	

This abandonment of the b-Pawn is premature, and is no improvement on the customary 3 c2-c4.

3	...	c7-c5

The right response—attack on the center Pawn, as well as creating the possibility of continuing with ... Qd8-b6, with an attack on two Pawns.

4	e2-e3	Nb8-c6
5	c2-c3	Qd8-b6
6	Qd1-b3	d7-d5
7	Nb1-d2	Bc8-d7
8	Bf1-e2	c5xd4

At first glance unattractive, as it lets White reply 9 e3xd4 with a favourable Pawn position. But the recapture, as Capablanca foresees, leaves a slight weakness at f4, which

he will exploit in the course of the game.

9	e3xd4	

'Had Kostics looked deeper into the position,' says Bogolyubov, 'he would have continued instead with 9 Qb3xb6 a7xb6 10 Nf3xd4! (threatens to invade by 10 Nd4-b5) 10 ... Nc6xd4 11 e3xd4!.

'After Kostics misses the opportunity to rid the board of Black's Queen Knight, it swings over to c4, where its forced capture straightens out Black's Pawn position on the Queen-side.'

9	...	Bf8-d6
10	0-0	h7-h6!

This will compel the eventual exchange of the Bishop for a Knight, as the Bishop does not have the square f4 available for its escape.

11	Bg5-h4	Nf6-h5
12	Qb3xb6	a7xb6
13	Rf1-e1	g7-g5
14	Bh4-g3	

This enables Black to exchange and obtain what Pollock away back in 1894 called 'the two-Bishop racket'.

Attempting to avoid the exchange by 14 Nf3-e5 instead would have this sequel: 14 ... Bd6xe5 15 d4xe5 (on 15 Be2xh5 Be5-f4 wins a piece) 15 ... Nh5-f4 16 Bh4-g3 Nc6xe5, and Black has won a Pawn.

14	...	Nh5xg3
15	h2xg3	f7-f6
16	g3-g4	

Kostics is anxious to prevent further

expansion by 16 . . . h6-h5.

16	...	Ke8-f7
17	Nf3-h2	Nc6-a5
18	Nh2-f1	

But not 18 c3-c4, when
18 . . . Bd6-b4 will cost White his
c-Pawn.

18	...	b6-b5
19	a2-a3	

Stops Black from undoubling his
Pawns by 19 . . . b5-b4, but creates
a hole at his b3 square—a weakness
which will prove fatal.

But how could Kostics have foreseen this in a position that looks as
peaceful as a Constable landscape?

19	...	Na5-c4
20	Nd2xc4	

Sooner or later this Knight, which
interferes with the free movement
of White's pieces, would have to be
done away with.

20	...	b5xc4
21	Nf1-e3	

The Knight does not seem to have
any future at this square, but if it
emerged at g3, in order to reach h5,
the reply 21 . . . Bd6xg3 would
leave White (after the recapture)
with tripled Pawns.

21	...	Ra8-a6
22	g2-g3	Ra6-b6
23	Ra1-a2	

Awkward-looking and reminiscent
of a similar Rook move made by
Paulsen against Morphy in the New
York 1857 First American Chess
Tournament, which gave Morphy
the opportunity to execute his first
brilliancy against a master player.

The alternative 23 Ra1-b1 was
less attractive, as Black could swing
his Bishop over in a couple of moves
to g6 and dispossess the Rook.

23	...	Rh8-a8
24	Be2-f3	Ra8-a5
25	Kg1-g2	Ra5-b5
26	Re1-e2	Bd7-e8
27	Re2-d2	Kf7-g7
28	Bf3-d1	Be8-g6

Black's pieces are well-placed, his
threat of winning the Queen Knight
Pawn by 29 . . . Bg6-b1 being
merely incidental to the general
strategy, which will be devoted to
tying White up so that he cannot
stir.

29	Bd1-a4	Rb5-a5
30	Ba4-c2	

Ending 27

Position after 30 Ba4-c2

Capablanca to move

Kostics

Black's advantage, the aggressive

position of his pieces, is a minimal one.

Capablanca manages to combine threats on the Queen-side with an attack on the King-side, to keep his opponent busy. When the time is ripe for a *coup de maître*, he cleverly sacrifices a precious passed Pawn to bring the enemy camp into a state of *zugzwang*.

Capablanca's final threat of having his King wander calmly over to the Queen-side to decide the issue, causes Kostics, whose game is all tied up, to panic and lose a piece.

30	...	Bg6xc2
31	Rd2xc2	Kg7-g6

Prepares for the break, sooner or later, by ... h6-h5 or ... f6-f5.

32	Rc2-e2	Ra5-b5
33	Ne3-d1	

This defence of the Pawn with a minor piece releases the Queen Rook from guard duty.

33	...	Bd6-f8
34	Ra2-a1	h6-h5
35	f2-f3	

Black supports his g-Pawn (even at the cost of retaining a doubled Pawn) rather than play 35 g4xh5+, which would facilitate Black's Pawn advance by ... f6-f5.

35	...	h5xg4
36	f3xg4	f6-f5!

He goes there anyway!

37	g4xf5+	

White exchanges with the hope of getting play for his Rook on the open file. But Black benefits too,

as his Rook can swing over to the King-side to support the Bishop Pawn, the spearhead in the attack.

37	...	e6xf5
38	Ra1-c1	Rb6-f6

Capablanca's two Pawns to one on the King-side presage his obtaining a passed Pawn on that wing. On the other side of the board his three Pawns have no trouble containing the four of his opponent's.

39	Rc1-c2	Bf8-d6
40	Re2-e8	

'Beginning of the attack,' Tarrasch used to say.

40	...	Kg6-f7
41	Re8-e1	

And 'End of the attack.'

41	...	f5-f4

Keep your eye on this Pawn!

42	g3-g4	f4-f3+

Otherwise White blockades this Pawn by 43 Kg2-f3, followed if necessary by 44 Nd1-f2.

43	Kg2-f2	

This is the picture on the board:

Position after 43 Kg2-f2

43 ... Rf6-h6!

A brilliant sacrifice of a valuable Pawn!

44 Kf2xf3

White must take the Pawn, or run into difficulties. The situation abounds in interesting play, for example:

(a) 44 Rc2-d2 (to avoid loss of the Rook by 44 . . . Rh6-h2+) 44 . . . Rh6-h2+ 45 Kf2-e3 Bd6-f4+, and the Rook falls;

(b) 44 Rc2-c1 Bd6-f4 45 Rc1-b1 Rh6-h3 (threatens 46 . . . Bf4-g3+ 47 Kf2-f1 Rh3-h1 mate) 46 Re1-g1 Rb5-b6 47 Nd1-e3 Rb6-e6 48 Rb1-e1 (on 48 Ne3-d1 Re6-e2+ 49 Kf2-f1 Rh3-h2 followed by 50 . . . Bf4-d2 ends the struggle) 48 . . . Rh3-h2+ 49 Kf2xf3 (on 49 Kf2-f1, f3-f2 is a pretty Pawn fork winning a Rook) 49 . . . Bf4xe3 50 Re1xe3 Rh2-h3+ 51 Rg1-g3 Re6xe3+ 52 Kf3xe3 Rh3xg3+, wins a Rook and the game;

(c) 44 Rc2-c1 Bd6-f4 45 Nd1-e3 Rb5xb2+ 46 Ne3-c2 (the best of a bad lot, as 46 Kf2xf3 is penalized by 46 . . . Rh6-h3 mate, as is 46 Kf2-f1 by 46 . . . Rh6-h1, while 46 Kf2-g1 succumbs to 46 . . . Bf4xe3+ 47 Re1xe3 Rb2-g2+ and mate next, and finally 46 Rc1-c2 loses a Rook after 46 . . . Bf4xe3+) 46 . . . Bf4xc1 47 Re1xc1 Rh6-h2+, and Black winds up a Rook ahead.

44 ... Rh6-h3+

45 Kf3-e2

Other moves lose the Rook, but this lets White interpose the Knight in response to a check.

45 ... Rh3-h2+

46 Nd1-f2 Bd6-g3

Capablanca immediately applies more pressure to the pin.

47 Re1-f1

This natural move, which preserves the Queen Knight Pawn against loss, after an exchange of pieces—loses!

The saving move, according to Selesniev, was 47 Ke2-f1! (giving up the Queen Knight Pawn) after which the play might go thus: 47 . . . Rh2xf2+ 48 Rc2xf2+ Bg3xf2 49 Kf1xf2 Rb5xb2+ 50 Re1-e2 Rb2-b3 (exchanging Rooks leads to a draw) 51 Re2-e5 Rb3xc3 52 Re5xd5 Rc3xa3 53 Rd5-c5, and White draws easily.

47 ... Rb5-b6

48 Ke2-f3 Bg3-h4

49 Kf3-e2 Rb6-f6

50 Ke2-e3

There is no breaking loose from the pin, as all of White's pieces are needed to defend the Knight.

50 ... b7-b5!

51 Rc2-d2

White is in the frustrating situation of being a Pawn ahead, but helpless to benefit by it, as he cannot disentangle his pieces.

51 ... Kf7-e7

Capablanca's intention, if White continues to make waiting moves, is to march his King down to a4, exchange all the pieces at f2, and then win by . . . Kb3 followed by removing the all-important Queen Knight Pawn.

52   b2-b4

Desperation! If Black does not capture *en passant* . . .

52   . . .   c4xb3 *en passant*

. . . but he does!

53   Nf2-d3

The last dying effort! Perhaps

Capablanca may falter, and capture the wrong Rook.

53   . . .   Rh2xd2

54   White Resigns

Kostics does not wait for 54 Rf1xf6 Rd2xd3+ 55 Ke3xd3 Ke7xf6 56 Kd3-d2 Bh4-e1+ 57 Kd2-d3 b3-b2 48 Kd3-c2 Be1xc3 and wins.

GAME 28

White J. R. Capablanca
Black F. D. Yates
Hastings, 1919

Ruy López

Early in the game, Capablanca sacrifices material for position. He gives up a Rook for a Bishop and Pawn, in order to attain mastery of the white squares.

Thanks to his beautifully centralized pieces, Capablanca is able to snip off Pawns almost at will and to acquire two passed Pawns in the middle of the board.

Yates fights back (as he always does) but Capablanca, inexorable as Fate itself, will not be denied the victory.

The whole game, from 1 e2-e4 to 61 Bf5-e4, is a positional masterpiece on a grand scale.

1	e2-e4	e7-e5
2	Ng1-f3	Nb8-c6
3	Bf1-b5	a7-a6
4	Bb5-a4	Ng8-f6
5	0-0	Bf8-e7
6	Rf1-e1	b7-b5

7	Ba4-b3	d7-d6
8	c2-c3	Nc6-a5
9	Bb3-c2	c7-c5
10	d2-d4	Qd8-c7
11	Nb1-d2	Bc8-g4

The safer procedure was 11 . . . c5xd4 12 c3xd4 Na5-c6, to bring the Knight back towards the center, but Yates, well-versed in the intricacies of the Ruy, tries an experiment.

12	d4-d5	g7-g5

Dangerous play, as it weakens the square f5, and breaks up his Kingside Pawn position, thus rendering castling on that side (for practical purposes) impossible.

Such risky-looking attempts at attack could hardly succeed against a Capablanca.

13	Nd2-f1	h7-h6
14	Nf1-g3	Ra8-d8

Having begun operations on the
King-side, Black should have continued in attacking vein there by
14 . . . Nf6-h5.

15   a2-a4!   b5-b4

This prevents White from opening
up the a-file by 16 a4xb5, but
relinquishes control of c4, another
important white square, which
Capablanca will appropriate for
his own fell designs.

16	c3xb4	c5xb4
17	Bc2-d3	Bg4-c8
18	Bc1-e3	Nf6-g4
19	Ra1-c1	Qc7-b8
20	Be3-d2	Qb8-b6
21	Qd1-e2	

Begins an attractive positional combination, which Capablanca preferred to the stolid, unimaginative protection of the f-Pawn by 21 Re1-e2.

Capablanca saw that he would
have to sacrifice the exchange as a
result of his 21 Qd1-e2 move, but
he relied on getting adequate compensation in the strong placing of
his pieces.

21	. . .	Na5-b3
22	Rc1-c6	Qb6-a5
23	Bd3xa6!	Bc8-d7
24	Ba6-b5!	Bd7xc6
25	Bb5xc6+	Ke8-f8
26	Qe2-c4	

'Going after the Queen Knight
Pawn,' says a contemporary writer,
'which is so weak that its fall can
only be a question of time.'

The Pawn *does* seem marked for
doom. Strangely enough—well,
we'll see later!

26	. . .	Nb3xd2
27	Nf3xd2	Qa5-a7
28	Qc4-e2	h6-h5
29	Ng3-f5	Be7-f6
30	Nd2-c4	Qa7-c5
31	b2-b3	Ng4-h6
32	Nf5xh6	Rh8xh6
33	Qe2-e3!	Rd8-c8

Ending 28

Position after 33 . . . Rd8-c8

Yates

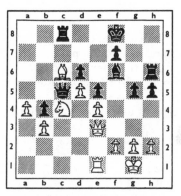

Capablanca to move

Capablanca's superior position, and
the potential power of his passed
Pawn more than compensate him
for the loss (by sacrifice) of the
exchange.

Black's pieces are awkwardly
placed and after the inevitable
exchange of Queens, they will
have trouble defending the weak
Pawns.

Capablanca begins by forcing the
Queens off the board.

34   Re1-c1!

Threatens to win a Pawn by
35 Nc4xe5 Qc5xe3 36 Ne5-d7+,
and 37 f2xe3. There seems to be no
way for Black to prevent loss of a
Pawn. For example if

(a) 34 . . . Kf8-e7 35 Nc4-b6
Qc5xe3 36 Nb6xc8+, wins the
exchange,

(b) 34 . . . Kf8-g7 35 Qe3xc5
d6xc5 36 Nc4-d6 followed by
37 Nd6-f5+ wins the exchange,

(c) 34 . . . Kf8-g8 35 Qe3xc5
d6xc5 36 Nc4-d6 Rc8-d8
37 Nd6-f5 followed by 38 Rc1xc5
wins a Pawn,

(d) 34 . . . Qc5xe3 35 Nc4xe3
Bf6-d8 36 Rc1-c4 Bd8-a5
37 Ne3-c2 Rc8-b8 38 Bc6-b5, and
White wins the b-Pawn.

34   . . .   Bf6-d8

35   Qe3xc5   d6xc5

36   Nc4xe5

One Pawn falls, and the other (at
c5) cannot be saved. If
36 . . . Bd8-e7 37 Ne5-d7+ does
the trick.

36   . . .   Kf8-e7

37   Rc1xc5   f7-f5

This does more harm than good, but
good moves are scarce.

38   Rc5-c4   Bd8-a5

If 38 . . . f5xe4 39 Rc4xe4, and
the b-Pawn cannot be saved. There
is a threat of winning the Rook by
discovered check, and if
39 . . . Ke7-f6 (to attack the
Knight and tie the Rook down to
its defence) 40 Ne5-d7+ followed
by 41 Re4xb4 removes the Pawn,

while 39 . . . Ke7-d6 allows
40 Ne5-f7+, which is even worse.

39   Bc6-b5!

Practically forces the exchange of
Rooks, as after 39 . . . Rc8-a8
40 Ne5-c6+ Ke7-f7 (but not
40 . . . Ke7-d6 41 Nc6xa5 Ra8xa5
42 Rc4-c6+ winning a Rook)
41 e4-e5, and the rest is easy sailing.

39   . . .   Rc8xc4

40   Ne5xc4

The Knight recaptures with an
attack on the Bishop—a gain of
tempo which enables White to
secure two connected passed Pawns
in the center.

40   . . .   Ba5-c7

41   e4-e5

The threat of 42 d5-d6+ forces the
Bishop to lose another move.

41   . . .   Bc7-b8

42   Nc5-e3

Attacks and wins another Pawn—
again with gain of tempo, as the
Pawn will be captured either with
check or with an attack on the
Rook.

42   . . .   Rh6-h7

43   Ne3xf5+   Ke7-f7

44   e5-e6+   Kf7-f6

45   e6-e7   Rh7xe7

An unfortunate necessity, as the
Pawn had to be halted.

46   Nf5xe7   Kf6xe7

47   g2-g3   Bb8-c7

48   Kg1-g2   Ke7-d6

49   Bb5-e8

White's next few moves are devoted

to simplifying the position on the King-side.

49	...	h5-h4
50	Be8-f7	Kd6-e5
51	Kg2-h3	Bc7-d8
52	Kh3-g4	h4xg3
53	f2xg3	Ke5-f6
54	Bf7-e6	Kf6-g6
55	d5-d6	Kg6-f6
56	Be6-f5	Bd8-b6
57	d6-d7	Bb6-d8
58	h2-h4	g5xh4
59	g3xh4	Bd8-c7
60	h4-h5	Kf6-g7

| 61 | Bf5-e4 | **Black Resigns** |

The rest is easy enough. If 61 ... Kg7-h6 62 Kg4-f5 Bc7-d8 (or 62 ... Kh6xh5 63 Kf5-f6 Bc7-d8+ 64 Kf6-f7, and Black will have to give up his Bishop for the Queen Pawn) 63 Kf5-e6 Kh6-g7 64 h5-h6+ Kg7-f8 65 h6-h7 Kf8-g7 66 h7-h8(Q)+ Kg7xh8 67 Ke6-f7, and White wins.

Strange that Black's Queen Knight Pawn, whose demise was predicted at the 26th move, was the only one of Black's eight Pawns to survive!

GAME 29

White W. Winter
Black J. R. Capablanca
Hastings, 1919

Four Knights Game
Right from the very beginning, Capablanca creates an amusing situation rarely seen in actual play. He shuts an enemy Bishop out of the game—renders it *hors de combat*—so it cannot take any part in the subsequent action.

This amounts to his being a piece ahead, but the game still needs winning. And the smooth, efficient way in which Capablanca does so is worthy of our attention and admiration.

1	e2-e4	e7-e5
2	Ng1-f3	Nb8-c6
3	Nb1-c3	Ng8-f6
4	Bf1-b5	Bf8-b4

Simple and strong. The Rubinstein line 4 ... Nc6-d4 is at least equally good, and introduces wild complications into an opening that is often tame and symmetrical.

While Capablanca had no trouble handling wild complications, he never went out of his way to introduce them.

| 5 | 0-0 | 0-0 |
| 6 | Bb5xc6 | |

The customary play is 6 d2-d3 d7-d6 7 Bc1-g5 with strong pressure, continued imitation of White's moves being fatal, thus:
7 ... Bc8-g4 8 Nc3-d5 Nc6-d4 9 Nd5xb4 Nd4xb5 10 Nb4-d5

Nb5-d4 11 Qd1-d2 Qd8-d7
12 Bg5xf6 Bg4xf3 13 Nd5-e7+
Kg8-h8 14 Bf6xg7+, and mate
follows in two more moves.

6 ...   **d7xc6**

7 d2-d3   **Bb4-d6**

8 Bc1-g5

The proper strategy, indicated by
Capablanca, was to play 8 h2-h3,
followed in due time by g2-g4, and
then the posting of the Queen
Knight at f5 by way of e2 and g3.
After an eventual f2-f4, White can
launch an attack on the King.

8 ...   **h7-h6**

9 Bg5-h4   **c6-c5!**

A deceptively strong move! It
creates a strong point at d4, meanwhile preventing White from
advancing his d-Pawn.

The fact that it relinquishes control of d5 misleads Winter completely, who must have thought that he
had caught Capablanca napping.

So he leaped in with . . .

10 Nc3-d5

'White falls into the trap,' says
Capablanca. 'Only lack of experience can account for this move.
White should have considered that a
player of my experience and
strength could never have allowed
such a move if it were good.'

This might seem like a conceited
remark, except for the fact that
Capablanca was not conceited. He
knew his own strength, and did not
believe in false modesty.

Nothing can detract from the
fact that Capablanca's comment
contains a great deal of practical
wisdom.

10 ...   **g7-g5!**

11 Nd5xf6+

The tempting 11 Nf3xg5 costs
White a piece after the reply
11 . . . Nf6xd5. If White still persists and tries for counter-play by
12 Qd1-h5, the continuation
12 . . . h6xg5 13 Bh4xg5 Bd6-e7
14 Bg5-h6 Nd5-f4, ends the demonstration.

11 ...   **Qd8xf6**

12 Bh4-g3   **Bc8-g4**

This completes the blockade of the
King's wing, which Capablanca had
planned.

White's Bishop can come into
active play in the game only at
great cost in material.

13 h2-h3

Ending 29

Position after 13 h2-h3

Capablanca to move

Winter

Capablanca's plan, like all truly
great schemes, is simple in essence.

Being for practical purposes a Bishop ahead, he will reduce the number of pieces on the board, and then transfer the action to the Queen-side. There he will effect a breakthrough with his Pawns in order to acquire a passed Pawn.

The passed Pawn should cost the life of one of the enemy Rooks.

13	. . .	Bg4xf3
14	Qd1xf3	Qf6xf3
15	g2xf3	f7-f6

Adds a link to the chain of Pawns imprisoning White's Bishop.

Black's Bishop is also hemmed in, but the condition is only temporary.

| 16 | Kg1-g2 | |

White might have offered more resistance with this continuation: 16 c2-c3 Ra8-d8 17 Rf1-d1 Rd8-d7 18 Rd1-d2 Rf8-d8 19 Ra1-e1 Kg8-f7 20 d3-d4 e5xd4 21 c3xd4 Bd6xg3 22 f2xg3 Rd7xd4, though Black should still win the ending.

16	. . .	a7-a5
17	a2-a4	Kg8-f7
18	Rf1-h1	Kf7-e6
19	h3-h4	Rf8-b8!!

I love this move! It seems almost contemptuous of any efforts White might make to whip up an attack on the King-side. Apparently nothing on that side even interests Black at this time!

| 20 | h4xg5 | h6xg5 |
| 21 | b2-b3 | |

No relief is offered in 21 c2-c4, when Black will force open the b-file by 21 . . . c7-c6 and 22 b7-b5.

21	. . .	c7-c6
22	Ra1-a2	b7-b5
23	Rh1-a1	c5-c4!

This offer of a Pawn is perfectly safe, as Black can always get the Pawn back by . . . Rb8-b4.

| 24 | a4xb5 | c4xb3 |
| 25 | c2xb3 | |

This looks meek, but the impetuous 25 Ra2xa5 loses on the spot by 25 . . . Ra8xa5 26 Ra1xa5 b3-b2, and the Pawn promotes to a Queen next move.

| 25 | . . . | Rb8xb5 |
| 26 | Ra2-a4 | |

On 26 Ra1-b1, a5-a4 followed by 27 . . . a4-a3 and 28 . . . Ra8-b8 is decisive.

26	. . .	Rb5xb3
27	d3-d4	Rb3-b5
28	Ra4-c4	Rb5-b4
29	Rc4xc6	

Or 29 Rc4xb4 Bd6xb4 30 d4xe5 f6xe5 31 Ra1-c1 c6-c5, and the rest plays itself.

| 29 | . . . | Rb4xd4 |
| 30 | White Resigns | |

The rest could go like this: 30 Rc6-c2 a5-a4 31 Rc2-a2 a4-a3 32 Kg2-f1 Ra8-b8 33 Kf1-e2 Rb8-b2+ 34 Ra2xb2 a3xb2 35 Ra1-b1 Bd6-a3 (protects the key Pawn) 36 Ke2-e3 Rd4-c4 37 Ke3-d2 Rc4-c1, and Black wins.

'White falls into error on his 10th move, after which his position crumbles away before the logical strategy of the Cuban master' (*The Chess Amateur*).

GAME 30

White J. R. Capablanca
Black A. G. Condé
Hastings, 1919

Ruy López

Condé, like many other masters, has been lulled into a false sense of security, by what seemed to be smooth sailing.

In a Pawn ending, the players have reached an impasse, where Capablanca's King dare not penetrate enemy territory, and Condé's King (by the laws of chess) may not do so.

It is Capablanca who effects a remarkable breakthrough by a surprise sacrifice of a Pawn on one side of the board, followed by some exchanges of Pawns on the other.

Suddenly, and seemingly out of thin air, two passed Pawns make their appearance—far enough apart from each other to make it impossible for one King alone to hold both of them back.

1	e2-e4	e7-e5
2	Ng1-f3	Nb8-c6
3	Bf1-b5	a7-a6
4	Bb5-a4	Ng8-f6
5	0-0	d7-d6

This delayed form of the Steinitz Defence makes for an interesting change from the routine lines, such as 5 . . . Nf6xe4—the Open Game, where Black plays for counterattack—or 5 . . . Bf8-e7, the Strong Point (or Tchigorin) line, where Black's object is to maintain the point e5.

6	Ba4xc6+

Though most authorities do not recommend the exchange of a strong Bishop for a Knight, Capablanca, who never sought guidance from the books, but followed his own instincts and judgment, selects the move which maintains the initiative.

6	. . .	b7xc6
7	d2-d4	

Again hits the nail on the head. Less vigorous measures allow Black to work up a counter-attack, thus: 7 Nb1-c3 Bc8-g4 8 d2-d3 Bf8-e7 9 Nc3-e2 Qd8-c8 10 Ne2-g3 h7-h5, and Black has the edge.

7	. . .	e5xd4

Gives up the center, but what else is there? If:

(a) 7 . . . Nf6xe4 8 Qd1-e2 f7-f5 9 d4xe5 d6-d5 10 Rf1-d1 c6-c5 11 c2-c4! c7-c6 (but not 11 . . . d5-d4 12 b2-b4 followed by 13 Bc1-b2) 12 Nb1-c3 Bf8-e7, and White has the better game.

(b) 7 . . . Bc8-g4 8 d4xe5 Nf6xe4 9 e5xd6 Bf8xd6 10 Qd1-e2! f7-f5 11 Nb1-d2 0-0 12 Nd2xe4 f5xe4 13 Qe2-c4+, and again White's game is preferable.

8	Nf3xd4	Bc8-d7
9	Nb1-c3	

A good aggressive alternative is 9 Qd1-f3, with the threat of 10 e4-e5.

9	. . .	Bf8-e7

10	Bc1-g5	0-0
11	Qd1-d3	Rf8-e8
12	Rf1-e1	h7-h6
13	Bg5-h4	c6-c5
14	Nd4-f5	

Knights posted at this square are rarely permitted to live long, but in giving up their lives they dispose of potentially-powerful Bishops.

14	...	Bd7xf5
15	e4xf5	

In this case, Capablanca secures another advantage—the advanced Pawn acts as a wedge in the enemy position.

15	...	Qd8-d7
16	h2-h3	a6-a5
17	Re1-e3	Nf6-h7
18	Bh4xe7	Re8xe7
19	Re3xe7	Qd7xe7
20	Nc3-d5	Qe7-d7
21	Ra1-e1	Ra8-e8
22	Re1xe8+	Qd7xe8
23	Qd3-e3	Qe8-d7

Ending 30

Position after 23 . . . Qe8-d7

Condé

Capablanca to move

White's Pawn structure, consisting of two Pawn islands (as Capablanca called them) against the three of his opponent's, offer him a positional advantage.

In order to reap the most benefit from this circumstance, the position must be simplified, preferably to a Pawn ending.

Capablanca begins by forcing an exchange of Queens.

24 Qe3-e7! Qd7xe7

Black has no reasonable alternative as 24 . . . Qd7xf5 loses the Queen by 25 Qe7-e8+ Nh7-f8 26 Nd5-e7+, while 24 . . . Qd7-a4 is even worse, the sequel being 25 Qe7-d8+ Nh7-f8 26 Nd5-e7+ Kg8-h7 27 Qd8xf8 h6-h5 28 Qf8-g8+ Kh7-h6 29 Qg8-h8+ Kh6-g5 30 Qh8xg7+ Kg5-f4 31 Qg7-g3+ Kf4-e4 32 Qg3-e3 mate.

25 Nd5xe7+ Kg8-f8

26	Ne7-d5	Kf8-e8

Rather than lose his Rook Pawn, allowing White a passed Pawn on that file, Condé decides to give up the Bishop Pawn at once, and get his King into play. Against 26 . . . c7-c6, White could continue with 27 Nd5-b6 (threatening to win a Pawn by 28 Nb6-c4) 27 . . . Kf8-e7 (on 27 . . . d6-d5 28 Nb6-d7+ wins a Pawn) 28 Nb6-c4 a5-a4 29 Nc4-b6 and the Rook Pawn is lost.

27	Nd5xc7+	Ke8-d7
28	Nc7-d5	Kd7-c6
29	c2-c4	Nh7-f6

Black offers an exchange of Knights, hoping thereby to build up an impregnable Pawn position. This seems preferable to 29 . . . Nh7-g5, when 30 f2-f3 leaves the Knight without a future.

30	Nd5xf6	g7xf6
31	a2-a4!	

A subtle preparatory move, whose purport will be evident later.

31	. . .	d6-d5
32	b2-b3!	d5-d4

Strange that Black, who has the passed Pawn, is the one who loses!

33	f2-f4	

This shuts the enemy King out, confining his activities to the first three ranks.

33	. . .	Kc6-d6
34	g2-g4	Kd6-e7
35	Kg1-f2	Ke7-d6
36	Kf2-f3	Kd6-e7

It is not yet clear how White will force anything, as his King may not stray too far from the passed Pawn.

Despite this obstacle in his path, Capablanca manages to create within a few moves two passed Pawns, one on each side of the board.

37	Kf3-e4	Ke7-d6
38	h3-h4	Kd6-d7

This is the situation:

Position after 38 . . . Kd6-d7

39	b3-b4!	

A surprise breakthrough!

39	. . .	a5xb4

The Pawn must be captured, and this way of taking it is clearly better than 39 . . . c5xb4, and 40 Ke4xd4 in reply leaves Black without any counter-play, as his passed Pawn poses no threat.

Black on the other hand would have to worry about White's passed Pawn, as well as the possibility of his acquiring another one by g4-g5 and g5-g6.

40	a4-a5	Kd7-c7
41	g4-g5	f6xg5
42	f4xg5	h6xg5
43	h4xg5	b4-b3

44	Ke4-d3	Kc7-d7
45	g5-g6	f7xg6
46	f5xg6	**Black Resigns**

Black's King cannot be in two places

at the same time to head off the passed Pawns: contrariwise, White's King has no such problem, as he can cope with the passed Pawns that are so close to each other.

GAME 31

White J. R. Capablanca
Black T. Germann, D. Miller, and
W. Skillcorn
Simultaneous, London, 1920

Queen's Gambit Declined
This is a typical Capablanca game in that its outward appearance of classic simplicity conceals inner workings of fiendish ingenuity.

Capablanca fashions a win from slender material. He obtains a minute advantage in the opening, and with a fine sense of continuity carries it through to the midgame and then into the ending.

In that stage, his King is closer to the center than that of his opponent, and his Rook is the more active one. This may not seem to be much, but it is enough for Capablanca, who fixes his sights on a Pawn, surrounds it, and then removes it from the board.

Once he is a Pawn ahead, and the road cleared for the advance of a passed Pawn, the rest is child's play for Capablanca, though the finishing touch—the luring away of a pursuing Rook—deserves mention.

All this is done smoothly and effortlessly, as though Capablanca were demonstrating a composed ending whose terms were 'White to play and win.'

1	d2-d4	d7-d5
2	c2-c4	e7-e6
3	Ng1-f3	Ng8-f6
4	Bc1-g5	Nb8-d7
5	e2-e3	Bf8-e7
6	Nb1-c3	a7-a6

Black aims at getting active counterplay by continuing with 7 . . . d5xc4 8 Bf1xc4 b7-b5 9 Bc4-d3 c7-c5.

7	Qd1-c2	0-0
8	Ra1-c1	

White prepares to assume control of the Bishop file, which is bound to become an open file with the exchange of the center Pawns.

8	. . .	d5xc4
9	Bf1xc4	b7-b5
10	Bc4-d3	Bc8-b7
11	a2-a4!	

This attack weakens Black's Pawn structure on the Queen-side, and makes it difficult for him to get in the freeing move . . . c7-c5.

11	. . .	b5-b4

12   Bg5xf6!

This is much better than 12 Nc3-e4
Nf6xe4 13 Bg5xe7 Qd8xe7
14 Bd3xe4 Bb7xe4 15 Qc2xe4
c7-c5, and Black has survived the
opening perils.

12   . . .   Nd7xf6

13   Nc3-e4

Now the tactical threat of winning
a Pawn by 14 Ne4xf6+ Be7xf6
15 Bd3xh7+, or the strategic one of
securing a powerful grip on the
position by 14 Ne4-c5, forces more
exchanges.

13   . . .   Bb7xe4

14   Bd3xe4   Nf6xe4

Again forced, as after
14 . . . Ra8-b8, the retreat
15 Be4-d3 wins a Pawn.

   Or if 14 . . . Ra8-a7 (to save the
Bishop Pawn) 15 Nf3-e5 Nf6xe4
16 Ne5-c6 Qd8-a8 (what else is
there, with everything *en prise*?)
17 Nc6xe7+ Kg8-h8 18 Ne7-c6,
and White wins the exchange.

15   Qc2xe4   c7-c5

No matter what the consequences,
Black must advance this Pawn. Any
delay allows White to play
16 Qe4-c6, with unremitting pressure.

16   d4xc5   Qd8-a5

17   b2-b3!

Capablanca stays clear of such transparent traps as 17 Qe4-c2 Ra8-c8
18 c5-c6 b4-b3+ 19 Qc2-d2 Be7-b4,
and White must interpose his Rook
and lose the exchange.

   The text move avoids complications, and leads to a slightly
superior ending.

17   . . .   Be7xc5

18   Nf3-g5

The threat of instant mate is
incidental to the real purpose of
this move and the next, which is to
compel Black to weaken the Pawn
structure of his King-side.

   Eagle-eyed connoisseurs of
master play will no doubt note
that the position at this point is
almost identical with that which
occurred in the famous Capablanca-
Schroeder game, played at New
York in 1916 (*The Golden Dozen*,
p. 301).

   They continue in completely
different vein, though, so that
Capablanca has the distinction of
having produced two masterpieces
from the same midgame position.

18   . . .   g7-g6

19   Qe4-h4   h7-h5

20   Ng5-e4

The plausible attempt to break up
the King-side by a Pawn attack is
met by: 20 g2-g4 Bc5-e7 (pins the
Knight) 21 f2-f4 Be7xg5 (and
removes it) 22 f4xg5 h5xg4
23 Qh4xg4 Qa5-d5!, and Black has
wrested the initiative.

20   . . .   Rf8-c8

21   Qh4-g5!

Protects the King Pawn, and attacks
the Bishop a third time. This will
force an exchange of Queens, and a
simplifying of the position to
White's advantage.

21   . . .   Bc5-b6

22   Qg5xa5   Bb6xa5

If 22 . . . Rc8xc1+ 23 Ke1-d2

Bb6xa5 24 Rh1xc1, and White is
in undisputed control of the c-file.

Ending 31

Position after 22 . . . Bb6xa5

Allies

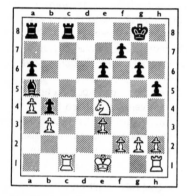

Capablanca to move

White's only advantage for the coming endgame is the position of his
King, which is centralized and ready
to take part in the action.

Capablanca's plan involves seizing
control of the c-file, with a view to
attacking the vulnerable a-Pawn.
With its fall, the way would be
clear for the advance of his own
a-Pawn.

23   Ke1-e2!

There are always threats against
exposed (unprotected) pieces in
innocent-looking positions. The
stranded Bishop in this case is a
likely candidate for abduction.

One possibility (were it White's
move) is this: 24 Ne4-d6 Rc8-d8
(to control one of the open files)

25 Nd6-b7 (attacks Rook and
Bishop) 25 . . . Rd8-d5 26 e3-e4
(attacks the defender of the Bishop)
26 . . . Rd5-e5 27 f2-f4 Re5xe4+
28 Ke2-f3, and White wins a piece.

23	...	Ba5-d8
24	Ne4-d6	Rc8-c7
25	Rc1-c4	Rc7-d7

Yields the Bishop file, in preference to this possibility:
35 . . . Rc7xc4 26 Nd6xc4 Kg8-f8
27 Rh1-d1 Kf8-e7 28 f2-f4, and
White has all the play.

26	Nd6-e4	Bd8-e7
27	Rh1-d1	

Naturally, Capablanca does not
snap at the Pawn by 27 Rc4xb4,
when 27 . . . f7-f5 (but not
27 . . . Be7xb4 28 Ne4-f6+ regaining the Rook) winning a piece for
Black is the penalty.

27	...	Rd7xd1

On 27 . . . Ra8-d8 28 Rd1xd7
Rd8xd7 29 Rc4xb4 wins a Pawn
for White, as 29 . . . f7-f5 is countered by 30 Rb4-b8+.

28	Ke2xd1	Ra8-d8+
29	Kd1-e2	Rd8-d5
30	Rc4-c6	a6-a5

If Black defends the Pawn by
30 . . . Rd5-a5 (a sad spot for a
Rook) the reply 31 Ne4-d2 followed by 32 Nd2-c4 dislodges the
Rook and wins the Pawn.

This is the position:

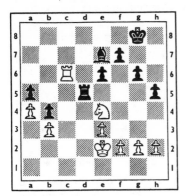

Position after 30 . . . a6-a5

White now has a fixed target in the
a-Pawn. He can attack the Pawn
with Rook and Knight, and Black
can defend it with Rook and
Bishop.

So far—honours even. But if
one of the defending pieces is
driven off, why then the Pawn can
be captured.

31	Ne4-d2	Kg8-g7
32	Nd2-c4	Be7-d8
33	e3-e4	Rd5-d4

The Rook must abandon the
fourth rank and the defence of the
Pawn. If the Rook moves to g5,
stubbornly refusing to leave the
rank, then 34 g2-g3 threatens
Black with the loss of a whole
Rook by 35 f2-f4 Rg5-g4
36 Ke2-f3 followed by 37 h2-h3.

| 34 | f2-f3 | Rd4-d7 |
| 35 | Rc6-a6 | Kg7-f6 |

On 35 . . . Rd7-c7, White would
hardly be lured into hastily capturing the Pawn by 36 Ra6xa5,
when there would follow

36 . . . Rc7xc4 37 Ra5-a8
Rc4-d4, nor by 36 Nc4xa5, when
36 . . . Rc7-c3 37 Na5-c6
Bd8-c7 offers Black counterplay.

White's response on
35 Rd7-c7 would simply be
36 Ra6-a8!, and the Pawn falls next
move.

| 36 | Nc4xa5 | Bd8xa5 |

Black exchanges, as a Rook ending
offers drawing chances, even with a
Pawn minus.

| 37 | Ra6xa5 | Rd7-d4 |

Protecting the Knight Pawn by
37 . . . Rd7-b7 succumbs to
38 Ra5-b5 Rb7xb5 39 a4xb5
Kf6-e5 40 Ke2-d3 followed by
41 Kd3-c4, and another Pawn bites
the dust.

| 38 | Ra5-b5 | e6-e5 |

On 38 . . . Kf6-e7 39 Ke2-e3 dislodges the Rook and wins the
Knight Pawn.

| 39 | a4-a5 | Kf6-e6 |
| 40 | a5-a6 | Rd4-d6 |

Or 40 . . . Rd4-d7 (to head off the
Pawn) 41 Rb5-b6+ Ke6-e7
42 Rb6-b7 Ke7-d8 43 Rb7xd7+,
and the Pawn will promote to a
Queen.

| 41 | a6-a7 | |

How to stop the Pawn? Since
41 . . . Rd6-d8 is circumvented by
42 Rb5-b8, Black's only feasible
try is to get the Rook behind the
Pawn, and stop its mad rush to the
last square.

| 41 | . . . | Rd6-a6 |

But Capablanca has an elegant reply
to that move!

42   Rb5-b6+!   Black Resigns

A fine example of beautifully precise endgame play.

GAME 32

White Em. Lasker
Black J. R. Capablanca
Tenth Match Game, Havana, 1921

Queen's Gambit Declined

Capablanca's play is a model of clarity and logic in a game that is rich in beautiful, instructive situations.

After some simplification (brought on by Lasker!) Capablanca assumes the offensive, posts his pieces on strikingly effective squares, and drives Lasker's forces further and further back. After nonchalantly disregarding a trap set by the wily Lasker, Capablanca wins a Pawn and thereafter the game in an ending characterized by extraordinary precision and beauty.

Lasker commented, with admirable objectivity, that Capablanca's play from the 24th move on was enchanting.

1	d2-d4	d7-d5
2	c2-c4	e7-e6
3	Nb1-c3	Ng8-f6
4	Bc1-g5	Bf8-e7
5	e2-e3	0-0
6	Ng1-f3	Nb8-d7
7	Qd1-c2	c7-c5!

Energetic, and a better way for Black to free his game than the cautious 7 . . . c7-c6 or the passive 7 . . . b7-b6.

8	Ra1-d1	Qd8-a5

This, together with the opening of the c-file by . . . c5xd4, is the beginning of interesting counterplay on the Queen-side.

9	Bf1-d3	

Threatens to steal a Pawn by 10 Bd3xh7+ Nf6xh7 11 Bg5xe7.

9	. . .	h7-h6
10	Bg5-h4	c5xd4

Foltys tried 10 . . . Nd7-b6 11 c4xd5 c5xd4 at Podebrad, but Alekhine pounced on him with 12 d5-d6 Be7xd6 13 Bh4xf6 g7xf6 Nf3xd4, wrecking Black's Pawn position on the King-side.

11	e3xd4	

Better than 11 Nf3xd4 Nd7-e5, and Black's opening difficulties vanish.

11	. . .	d5xc4
12	Bd3xc4	Nd7-b6
13	Bc4-b3	Bc8-d7

Black's game is a bit cramped, though he has no organic weaknesses. In compensation, he has a fixed target in White's isolated Queen Pawn, at which he can aim his shafts.

14 0-0 Ra8-c8

Better than 14 . . . Bd7-c6, which
Capablanca tried against Stahlberg
at Moscow in 1935, with near-fatal
results.

15 Nf3-e5

An over-eager attacking move, no-
where near as strong as 15 Qc2-e2,
the move that Lasker underrated
(or missed).

The point is that 15 Qc2-e2 unpins the Queen Knight, prevents
Black from playing the powerful
15 . . . Bd7-b5, and threatens to
eliminate the isolated Queen Pawn
by advancing 16 d4-d5.

It also sets a little trap (though
the chances of snaring Capablanca
in it were mighty slim) in this
continuation: 15 . . . Nb6-d5
16 Nf3-e5 Bd7-c6 17 f2-f4
Nd5xc3 18 b2xc3 Qa5xc3
19 Bh4-e1, and the Queen is
caught.

15 . . . Bd7-b5

Although this move turned out to
be effective, and was highly
praised by the critics, it was depre-
cated by Capablanca himself, who
thought that a better course was
15 . . . Bd7-c6 followed by
16 . . . Bc6-d5.

16 Rf1-e1 Nb6-d5

17 Bb3xd5

Breyer proposed the illogical-look-
ing 17 Bh4xf6 as offering White
winning chances, but Bogolyubov's
analysis showed that Black had a
draw in all variations, and vindi-
cated Capablanca's claim of never
having been in a losing position in
his match with Lasker.

17 . . . Nf6xd5

18 Bh4xe7 Nd5xe7

19 Qc2-b3 Bb5-c6

Better than 19 . . . Bb5-a6, when
White can simplify by 20 Ne5-d7
Rf8-d8 21 Nd7-c5 b7-b6
22 Nc5xa6 Qa5xa6 23 d4-d5.

20 Ne5xc6 b7xc6

The exchange has left Black with
two isolated Pawns, but they are
less susceptible to attack than the
one isolated Pawn of White's.

21 Re1-e5

If 21 Nc3-a4 Rf8-d8 (threatens
22 . . . Rd8xd4) 22 Re1-e5
Rd8-d5, with the better game for
Black.

21 . . . Qa5-b6

22 Qb3-c2

Exchanging Queens would eliminate Black's Pawn weaknesses, while
intensifying White's.

22 . . . Rf8-d8

This is the position:

Position after 22 . . . Rf8-d8

23 Nc3-e2

Lasker decides that having the

Knight watch over the tender Queen Pawn is safer than abandoning it by 23 Nc3-a4, after which Black has the pleasant choice of attacking it in full force, either by 23 . . . Qb6-b8 24 Re5-c5 Rd8-d6 followed by 25 . . . Rc8-d8, 26 . . . Qb8-b7, and 27 . . . Qb7-d7 (Bogolyubov).

| 23 | . . . | Rd8-d5 |
| 24 | Re5xd5 | |

This has been called the losing move, but it does block a frontal attack on the Pawn (after the reply 24 . . . c6xd5).

The alternative 24 Re5-e3, suggested by Lasker himself, is hardly preferable, the sequel being 24 . . . Ne7-f5 25 Re3-b3 Qb6-d8 26 Rb3-b4 Qd8-d7, and Black threatens 27 . . . e6-e5, or 27 . . . Rc8-d8.

| 24 | . . . | c6xd5 |

This is how Capablanca sees the situation: 'Black has consolidated the position. He holds the open file, his pieces are very well placed, and the only weak point—the isolated Queen Rook Pawn—cannot be attacked because of the general situation of the pieces. The question is, how can Black get the benefit of all this? From now on the student will do well to study every move carefully up to the end. It is one of Black's best efforts in his whole career, and that against one of the strongest players the World has ever seen.'

| 25 | Qc2-d2 | |

Ending 32

Position after 25 Qc2-d2

Capablanca to move

Lasker

Black has the initiative, as his Rook dominates the c-file, and his pieces are poised for attack.

In contrast, White is tied down to the defence of the d-Pawn and the b-Pawn.

Capablanca plans to induce a weakening of the adverse Queen-side Pawn position. This will furnish him with objects of attack, and further limit the mobility of White's pieces.

| 25 | . . . | Ne7-f5 |

This attack on a Pawn that is projected by three pieces has an ulterior object—to prevent White from disputing control of the c-file.

If White tries to do so, he removes one piece from the Queen Pawn's protection, and an exchange of Rooks removes another piece, thus: 26 Rd1-c1 Rc8xc1+ 27 Qd2xc1 (or 27 Ne2xc1), and 27 . . . Nf5xd4 wins a Pawn for

Black. (Simple enough, like all secrets of magic when the magician takes you behind the scenes.)

26   b2-b3

This frees the Queen from the defence of the b-Pawn, and also serves to prevent further invasion of his position by 26 . . . Rc8-c4.

26   . . .   h6-h5

This secures the Knight against being dislodged by 27 g2-g4.

27   h2-h3

Lasker's attempt to enforce 27 g2-g4 is weak, and fails in its object.

More opportunity for resistance was offered by 27 Ne2-g3, when there might follow 27 . . . Nf5xg3 28 h2xg3 Qb6-c7 29 Kg1-f1 Qc7-c2 30 f2-f3, though Black still stands better, owing to his grip on the c-file.

27   . . .   h5-h4!

Excellent! Not only does this render 28 Ne2-g3 impossible, but it provides against 28 g2-g4, when 28 . . . h4xg3 *en passant* 29 f2xg3 leaves White's King-side in a weakened state.

28   Qd2-d3   Rc8-c6

This move secures the square a6 against invasion by White's Queen after Black plays . . . Qb6-b4.

29   Kg1-f1   g7-g6

30   Qd3-b1

'Instead of this much-too-passive maneuver,' says Tartakover, 'there came 30 Qd3-d2 into consideration.'

I am sure that Lasker did consider this move, but abandoned it

in view of the reply 30 . . . Qb6-c7 with the powerful threat of 31 . . . Rc6-c2. White could not counter this with 31 Rd1-c1 on pain of losing the d-Pawn (31 . . . Rc6xc1+ 32 Ne2xc1 Nf5xd4).

30   . . .   Qb6-b4!

Pentrates further into the enemy camp.

31   Kf1-g1

This was Lasker's sealed move—a quiet waiting move, as White is curiously unable to take any active measures.

31   . . .   a7-a5!

'Again a fine piece of strategy,' says Winter. 'Black will now force another weak, isolated Pawn on the Queen's wing. From now on to the end Capablanca's play is a model.'

32   Qb1-b2   a5-a4

33   Qb2-d2

Offers to exchange Queens, to relieve the pressure. Other moves fail, thus:

(a) 33 Rd1-d2 a4-a3, and the Queen is forced to abandon the Rook,

(b) 33 Rd1-b1 a4-a3 (thrusts the Queen into a cul-de-sac) 34 Qb2-a1 Rc6-c2, and White is in a bad way.

33   . . .   Qb4xd2

34   Rd1xd2   a4xb3

35   a2xb3   Rc6-b6

36   Rd2-d3

Best, as 36 Rd2-b2 loses a Pawn after 36 . . . Rb6-b4 in reply.

But now the Rook is tied to the defence of *two* weak, isolated

Pawns.

36 ...   Rb6-a6!

The proper strategy. The Rook is to get behind the white Pawns.

37 g2-g4

White gives his King some *lebensraum*. Any effort to improve the position of his Rook fails, as after 37 Rd3-d2 there comes 37 ... Ra6-a1+ 38 Kg1-h2 Ra1-b1 39 Rd2-d3 Rb1-b2, and Black wins a Pawn, as the Knight must give way.

37 ...   h4xg3 *en passant*

38 f2xg3   Ra6-a2

39 Ne2-c3   Ra2-c2

Threatens 40 ... Nf5xd4, and if 41 Nc3xd5 in reply, then 41 ... Nd4-e2+ wins a piece.

40 Nc3-d1   Nf5-e7!

The Knight has fulfilled its purpose at f5, and now switches over to the Queen-side to aid in the attack on the isolated Pawns.

41 Nd1-e3

If 41 b3-b4 instead, the Rook works its way behind the Pawn by 41 ... Rc2-c1 followed by 42 ... Rc1-b1, and wins it.

41 ...   Rc2-c1+

42 Kg1-f2   Ne7-c6

43 Ne3-d1

This is the position:

Position after 43 Ne3-d1

With this move Lasker sets up an insidious trap to catch Capablanca, if he (Capa) tries to win a piece by a clever combination. This is the plot: 43 ... Nc6-b4 44 Rd3-d2 Rc1-b1, 45 Nd1-b2 Rb1xb2 46 Rd2xb2 Nb4-d3+ 47 Kf2-e2 Nd3xb2 48 Ke2-d2, and White wins the Knight, which has no escape square, after which the game should be drawn.

43 ...   Rc1-b1

But Capablanca does not pursue a will-o'-the-wisp; he continues on his chosen course.

44 Kf2-e2

This looks like an error, but the Pawn is lost in any event, 45 Kf2-e3 yielding to 45 ... Nc6-b4, and White's Rook must abandon Pawn or Knight.

44 ...   Rb1xb3!

45 Ke2-e3

Clearly, if 45 Rd3xb3, Nc6xd4+ recovers the Rook with two Pawns as net profit.

45 ...   Rb3-b4

Capablanca could exchange Rooks and go into a Knight ending, but decides to keep the Rooks on the board, his Rook having more mobility than White's.

46 Nd1-c3   Nc6-e7

Threatens to win the Pawn by 47 ... Ne7-f5+, driving the King away.

47 Nc3-e2

The Knight does yeoman service, not only protecting the unhappy Queen Pawn a third time, but guarding the Knight Pawn as well.

47	...	Ne7-f5+
48	Ke3-f2	g6-g5
49	g3-g4	Nf5-d6
50	Ne2-g1	Nd6-e4+
51	Kf2-f1	Rb4-b1+
52	Kf1-g2	Rb1-b2+
53	Kg2-f1	

The King must step carefully to avoid such perils as 53 Kg2-h1 Ne4-f2+ followed by 54 ... Nf2xd3, or 53 Kg2-f3 Rb2-f2+ 54 Kf3-e3 f7-f5 (threatens instant mate) 55 Rd3-d1 (if 55 Rd3-a3 f5-f4+ 56 Ke3-d3 Rf2-d2 mate) 55 ... f5-f4+ 56 Ke3-d3 Rf2-a2, and if White moves his Rook to avoid its loss by 57 ... Ne4-f2+, there follows 57 ... Ra2-d2 mate.

53	...	Rb2-f2+
54	Kf1-e1	Rf2-a2
55	Ke1-f1	Kg8-g7

Having immobilized his opponent with the last few moves, Black

brings his King into play, to help in securing a passed Pawn.

56	Rd3-e3	Kg7-g6
57	Re3-d3	f7-f6

Intending to follow with ... e6-e5 —when the time is ripe.

58	Rd3-e3	Kg6-f7
59	Re3-d3	Kf7-e7
60	Rd3-e3	Ke7-d6
61	Re3-d3	Ra2-f2+
62	Kf1-e1	Rf2-g2
63	Ke1-f1	Rg2-a2
64	Rd3-e3	e6-e5!

The time is ripe! Capablanca now obtains a passed Pawn with this, his sealed move 'unquestionably the best way to win'.

65 Re3-d3

If 65 Ng1-f3 Ne4-d2+, exchanging Knights, wins. Against 65 Ng1-e2, Capablanca planned this little combination: 65 ... Ne4-d2+ 66 Kf1-f2 e5-e4 67 Re3-c3 Nd2-f3 (threatens 68 ... Nf3xd4) 68 Kf2-e3 Nf3-e1 (threatens 69 ... Ne1-c2+ winning the d-Pawn) 69 Ke3-f2 Ne1-g2 70 Kf2xg2 Ra2xe2+ 71 Kg1-f1 Re2-d2, and the d-Pawn falls.

65 ...   e5xd4

66 Rd3xd4

If 66 Ng1-e2, Ra2-d2 67 Rd3xd4 (or 67 Rd3xd2 Ne4xd2+ followed by 68 ... Nd2-b3 wins) 67 ... Ne4-g3+ 68 Kf1-f2 Rd2xe2+ 69 Kf2xg3 Kd6-c5, and Black wins easily.

66	...	Kd6-c5
67	Rd4-d1	d5-d4

68 Rd1-c1+ Kc5-d5

69 White Resigns

This finish (if Lasker were skeptical) could be 69 Rc1-d1 Ne4-g3+ 70 Kf1-e1 Ra2-g2 winning the Knight, which dare not move away, as mate at e2 would be the penalty.

'An ending of rare precision and beauty' (Tartakover).

'A fine example of Capablanca's perfect technique which gave Lasker no opportunity of producing any of his characteristic complications' (Winter).

'This is the finest win of the match, and probably took away from Dr. Lasker his last real hope of winning or drawing the match' (Capablanca).

GAME 33

White J. S. Morrison
Black J. R. Capablanca
London, 1922

Queen's Indian Defence
This is a game that is thoroughly absorbing from start to finish.

An indication of Capablanca's mood as he embarked on a series of exciting combinations can be gathered from the remark he made to Tartakover after making his 16th move, 'I think I'll play to the gallery.'

The complications extend through the midgame and into the ending, and evoked this comment from Euwe and Prins in their book *Das Schachphänomen 'Capablanca'*. 'The combination that ruins White's Pawn position and seals his fate very much justifies its being included in this book (in the chapter *Une Petite Combinaison*). The whole game in fact must be ranked as one of Capablanca's all-time finest.'

1 d2-d4 Ng8-f6

2 Ng1-f3 e7-e6

3 e2-e3 b7-b6

4 Bf1-d3 Bc8-b7

5 0-0

Instead of this hurried spiriting away of the King, there was more point to 5 Nb1-d2, which develops a piece and prevents Black from posting his Knight at e4.

5 ... Bf8-e7

6 b2-b3 0-0

7 Bc1-b2

This method of development goes back to the days of Zukertort (who did pretty well with it).

7 ... Nf6-e4

8 c2-c4 f7-f5

9 Nb1-c3 Qd8-e8

Capablanca begins a King-side attack, the usual recipe in a Dutch Defence sort of formation.

10 Qd1-c2 Ne4xc3

11	Bb2xc3	Qe8-h5
12	Qc2-e2	Nb8-a6

Hyper-modern strategy to tempt White to advance his Pawns—and weaken them!

13	c4-c5	

White gains time (seemingly) by attacking the Knight and forcing its retreat. In reality, it will benefit Black, who will be enabled to anchor his Knight strongly at d5, that square having been cleared by the Pawn's advance.

13	...	Na6-b8
14	b3-b4	Be7-f6
15	Ra1-c1	Nb8-c6
16	e3-e4	

Quite plausible, as after 16 . . . f5xe4 17 Bd3xe4 White has visions of continuing either with 18 b4-b5 and 19 c5-c6, or 18 Rf1-d1 and 19 d4-d5, with a good game.

16	...	Nc6-e7!

Again a subtle move by the Knight, tempting White to advance his King Pawn.

17	e4-e5	

White leaps at the chance to simplify the position on the King-side, and be left undisturbed to operate on the Queen-side.

But he reckons without his host, as the novelists used to say.

17	...	Ne7-d5!

Capablanca offers his Bishop, having these possibilities in mind:

(a) 18 e5xf6 Nd5-f4 19 Qe2-e3 Nf4xg2 20 Qe3-g5 (of course 20 Kg1xg2 loses at once by

20 . . . Qh5-g4+ 21 Kg2-h1 Bb7xf3+, and White must give up his Queen) 20 . . . Qh5xg5 21 Nf3xg5 Ng2-f4 22 f6xg7 (if 22 f6-f7+ Rf8xf7 23 Ng5xf7 Nf4-h3 mate) 22 . . . Rf8-f6 and Black wins,

(b) 18 e5xf6 Nd5-f4 19 Qe2-d1 Nf4xg2! (better than 19 . . . Bb7xf3 20 Qd1xf3 Qh5xf3 21 g2xf3 Nf4xd3) 20 Nf3-e5 Qh5-h3 (threatens to mate or win the Queen by 21 . . . Ng2-e3) 21 Qd1-d2 g7xf6 22 f2-f3 Ng2-h4 23 Ne5-c4 (ruin follows 23 Ne5xd7 Rf8-f7) 23 . . . Kg8-f7, and Black's attack prevails easily (Tartakover).

18	Bc3-d2	Bf6-e7
19	Nf3-e1	Qh5-f7
20	f2-f4	Ra8-b8

A quiet, unassuming move that most players would not even think of in a week, yet a master would spot its hidden potential in a flash.

(Keep your eye on this Rook!)

21	Bd3-c4	b6xc5
22	b4xc5	h7-h6
23	Ne1-c2	g7-g5
24	Rc1-b1	g5xf4
25	Rb1-b3	

Threatens 26 Rf1-b1, pinning and winning the Bishop.

25	...	Bb7-c6
26	Bd2xf4	Nd5xf4
27	Rf1xf4	Kg8-h7

This is the position:

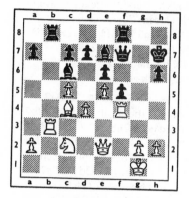

Position after 27 . . . Kg8-h7

Alekhine called this move a blunder, while Maroczy in the Book of the Tournament said that White could win a Pawn here with a winning position.

Euwe and Prins, however, dissent from this view, and suggest that Capablanca's move be graced with an exclamation mark. An objective analysis shows that after the suggested 28 Rf4xf5 there would follow 28 . . . Qf7-g7 (not of course 28 . . . Qf7xf5 29 Bc4-d3 winning the Queen) 29 Rb3xb8 Rf8xb8 30 Rf5-f1 Rb8-g8, and Black should succeed in the attack, aided and abetted as it is by the power of the two Bishops.

No better (after 28 Rf4xf5 Qf7-g7) is 29 Rf5xf8 Rb8xf8, and again control of the Bishop file combined with the threat of . . . Be7-h4 should help decide the game for Black.

28 Nc2-e3   Be7-g5!

Tempts White to proceed with what seems to be a winning combination.

But Capablanca (as usual) has

looked further ahead into the complications than his opponent!

29 Rf4xf5   Bg5xe3+

30 Qe2xe3

On 30 Rb3xe3 Qf7xf5 31 Bc4-d3 pinning the Queen, the surprise check 31 . . . Rb8-b1+! breaks the pin and wins.

30 . . .   Qf7-g6!

Threatens mate on the move while still attacking the Rook—three times!

31 Rf5-f2   Bc6xg2!

Surprise number two! Should White play 32 Rf2xg2, he gets knocked out by 32 . . . Qg6-b1+! 33 Rb3xb1 Rb8xb1+, and mate in two. A splendid resource!

32 Rb3xb8

White loses his head; there was more fight in 32 Qe3-g3 Bg2-e4 33 Bc4-d3 Be4xd3 34 Rf2xf8 Rb8xf8 35 Rb3xd3 Qg6-e4, though it still was not easy.

32 . . .   Bg2-e4+

33 Qe3-g3   Rf8xb8

34 Qg3xg6+   Kh7xg6

35 Rf2-f6+

This offers more resistance than 35 Bc4-b3 (to block the file) 35 . . . Rb8-b4 36 Rf2-d2 (White is now reduced to passive defence) 36 . . . a7-a5 37 Kg1-f2 a5-a4 38 Bb3-d1 a4-a3 (threatens 39 . . . Rb4-b2 followed by 40 . . . Be4-b1, and the removal of a highly important Pawn) 39 Bd1-b3 Rb4xb3! 40 a2xb3 Be4-b1, and Black wins, as his passed Pawn can only be stopped at the cost of a Rook.

Ending 33

Capablanca to move

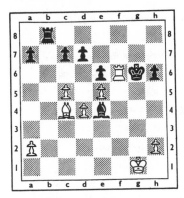

Morrison

Capablanca's advantage in this ending lies in the dominating position of his Rook. It has good prospects of an attack on the d-Pawn, either by ... Rb8-b4, or by moving to the seventh rank, and getting behind the Pawn.

The d-Pawn is the support of White's Pawn position—one might say it's the support of his entire position. Should it fall, White's whole game will fall apart.

Meanwhile—Black is in check!

35 . . .   Kg6-g7

The attractive 35 ... Kg6-g5 is countered by 36 Kg1-f2, when an attempt to win the d-Pawn by 36 ... Rb8-b4 fails after 37 h2-h4+ Kg5-h5 (or to g4) 38 Bc4-e2+, and White has all the play.

36 Rf6-f4

The Rook prudently retreats, rather than risk being shut in by

36 ... Be4-f5.

36 . . .   Be4-f5

37 Rf4-f3   Rb8-b1+

Not at once 37 ... Rb8-b4, as 38 Rf3-c3 holds the position.

The text move gives White an opportunity to go wrong.

38 Kg1-f2

But not 38 Rf3-f1 Rb1-b2 39 Rf1-f2 Rb2-b4 40 Bc4-b3 (the Rook, having been lured to the second rank, may not now move to c2 to protect the Bishop) 40 ... Rb4xd4, and Black has won a valuable Pawn.

38 . . .   Rb1-b2+

39 Kf2-g3   Rb2-d2

Fixes on White's weakness, and relegates White's Rook to passive defence.

40 Rf3-f4   a7-a5

41 h2-h4

Frees his King from the task of protecting the Pawn.

While the attempt instead to get behind the Queen Pawn and win it by 41 Bc4-a6 and 42 Ba6-c8, would be defeated by 41 ... Kg7-f7 and 42 ... Kf7-e7, Black must not now play 41 ... Kg7-f7 of his own accord, as the reply 42 Rf4xf5+ would come as a terrible shock.

41 . . .   c7-c6

Puts an end to any thoughts White might have entertained of breaking through by d4-d5.

42 Kg3-f3   a5-a4

43 Kf3-e3   Rd2-c2

44 Bc4-a6   Rc2xa2

Black is willing to exchange his

Queen Pawn for White's Queen Rook Pawn, as he acquires thereby a passed Pawn. Defending instead by 44 . . . Kg7-f7 allows White time to repel the invading Rook by 45 Rf4-f2.

45	Ba6-c8	Ra2-a3+
46	Ke3-e2	Ra3-c3
47	Bc8xd7	a4-a3
48	d4-d5	

White prefers to die fighting, rather than defend by 48 Rf4-f1, which would lose slowly but surely.

And of course 48 Bd7xc6 loses on the spot by 48 . . . a3-a2 49 Rf4-f1 Bf5-b1, and the Pawn promotes.

48	. . .	c6xd5
49	c5-c6	Kg7-f7
50	Rf4-a4	

White's only chance to head off the Pawn is to have the Rook get be-

hind it.

| 50 | . . . | Kf7-e7 |
| 51 | Ra4-a8 | d5-d4 |

But *this* passed Pawn could cause some trouble!

| 52 | Ra8-e8+ | Ke7-f7 |
| 53 | Re8-a8 | Bf5-e4 |

Paralyzes the menacing Pawn.

54	Ra8-a7	Rc3-c2+
55	Ke2-e1	a3-a2
56	K-1-d1	d4-d3
57	Bd7-c8+	Kf7-g6
58	White Resigns	

There is no way to avoid 58 . . . Be4-f3+ followed by 59 . . . d3-d2+, and the queening of the Pawn with check.

Beautifully played throughout, this is one of the unknown masterpieces of chess literature.

GAME 34

White J. R. Capablanca
Black E. D. Bogolyubov
London, 1922

Ruy López
The first encounter between the newly-crowned World Champion Capablanca and Bogolyubov, one of the leading representatives of the Hyper-modern School, results in a great fighting game.

The game bristles with moves that are characteristic of Capablanca's style—moves that are simple, yet unexpected!

Some of the fascinating highlights of the game are:

(a) Capablanca's readiness to accept a miserable Pawn formation, confident in the power of the Pawns to burst their bonds,

(b) Capablanca's refusal to lose time trying to hold on to his two Bishops,

(c) Capablanca's shutting out of action one of his opponent's valuable Bishops (as he did in the Winter-Capablanca game of 1919: see Game 29),

(d) Capablanca's conduct of an exciting ending, featuring a race to queen a Pawn.

All in all, as you can gather, the game is a magnificent one.

1	e2-e4	e7-e5
2	Ng1-f3	Nb8-c6
3	Bf1-b5	a7-a6
4	Bb5-a4	Ng8-f6
5	0-0	Bf8-e7
6	Rf1-e1	b7-b5
7	Ba4-b3	d7-d6
8	c2-c3	0-0

The usual line is 8 ... Nc6-a5 9 Bb3-c2 c7-c5 10 d2-d4 Qd8-c7, but Bogolyubov is intent on another procedure. This will involve a series of tortuous Knight moves, all for the sake of getting rid of White's light-squared Bishop.

9   d2-d4

White had two good alternatives here in the quiet 9 d2-d3, and in the conservative 9 h2-h3, which prevents the Knight being pinned, with the consequent pressure on White's center.

9   ...   e5xd4

This seems illogical, as it gives up the center, and also enables White (after the recapture 10 c3xd4) to develop his Knight at c3, but there is method to Bogolyubov's madness. He expects to obtain adequate compensation by effecting weaknesses

in White's position.

10	c3xd4	Bc8-g4
11	Bc1-e3	

Good enough, though Lasker won a fine game against Bogolyubov a year later with this continuation: 11 Nb1-c3 Nc6-a5 12 Bb3-c2 c7-c5 13 d4xc5 d6xc5 14 e4-e5! Qd8xd1 15 Re1xd1 Nf6-d7 16 h2-h3! Bg4-e6 (but not 16 ... Bg4xf3 17 Rd1xd7, and White wins a piece) 17 Nc3-d5! Be6xd5 18 Rd1xd5, and Lasker won the ending.

11	...	Nc6-a5
12	Bb3-c2	Na5-c4
13	Be3-c1	

Capablanca is not hidebound by convention, but is quick to embrace hyper-modern ideas. The Bishop's loss of time in returning home will be made up for by his next move 14 b2-b3, which forces the enemy Knight to retreat, after which the Bishop can begin a new career at b2.

13	...	c7-c5
14	b2-b3	Nc4-a5
15	Bc1-b2	

This is simpler and more energetic than attempting to preserve his light-squared Bishop by 15 Nb1-d2 Na5-c6 16 h2-h3 Bg4-h5 17 g2-g4 Bh5-g6 18 d4-d5 Nc6-b4 19 Bc2-b1 a6-a5 20 a2-a3 Nb4-a6 21 Bc1-b2.

15	...	Na5-c6
16	d4-d5	Nc6-b4
17	Nb1-d2	Nb4xc2

Bogoyubov has now accomplished what he set out to do, when he

played the anti-positional
9 . . . e5xd4:

(a) he has disposed of White's light-squared Bishop (though it took the Knight seven moves to do so),

(b) he has induced the advance of White's d-Pawn, with a consequent weakening of the e-Pawn,

(c) he has acquired a majority of Pawns on the Queen-side.

To offset these advantages, White has acquired some of his own:

(a) his remaining Bishop is beautifully posted on a long diagonal,

(b) he exerts pressure on the center,

(c) he has good prospects of breaking up Black's Pawn cluster by a2-a4 at the first available opportunity.

18   Qd1xc2   Rf8-e8

More to the point was 18 . . . Nf6-d7 followed by 19 . . . Be7-f6, to dispute control of the long diagonal.

19   Qc2-d3

Protecting the King Knight by the Queen will relieve the other Knight of that duty, and enable it to take active part in the game by swinging over to g3 by way of f1.

Capablanca himself suggested 19 a2-a4 as more precise, in order to keep Black occupied on the Queen-side, especially as the advance 19 . . . b5-b4 would provide a good square at c4 for the Knight.

19   . . .   h7-h6

Apparently either a waiting move, or to provide a hiding spot for the Bishop against an effort to

exchange it. On 19 . . . Nf6-d7 instead (which Capablanca said was better) he may have feared this continuation, suggested by Tartakover: 20 e4-e5 Bg4xf3 21 Nd2xf3 d6xe5 22 Nf3xe5 Nd7xe5 23 Bb2xe5 Be7-d6 24 Be5xd6 Qd8xd6 25 Ra1-d1, and the passed Pawn offers White practical winning chances.

20   Nd2-f1   Nf6-d7

21   h2-h3   Bg4-h5

Black should be content to play 21 . . . Bg4xf3 22 Qd3xf3 Be7-f6 with fair chances, but he is reluctant to part with one of his Bishops, as their combined power can often be terribly strong. So he keeps his Bishops!

But Capablanca meets their potential threats by imprisoning one of them, and putting it out of the action.

Despite this (going a bit ahead with our story) Bogolyubov is able to conjure up all sorts of dangerous threats on the Queen-side, which take all of Capablanca's skill to parry.

22   Nf3-d2   Be7-f6

Bogolyubov offers an exchange, having apparently decided that White's one Bishop, commanding the long diagonal, was as strong as both of his Bishops. So the Bishop must be liquidated!

23   Bb2xf6   Qd8xf6

24   a2-a4   c5-c4!

A fighting move, as ingenious as it is energetic. At one stroke Bogolyubov clears a good square (c5) for his Knight, obtains a passed Pawn, and secures an open file (the b-file) for his Rook!

25   b3xc4

This is the position:

Position after 25 b3xc4

25   ...   Nd7-c5

26   Qd3-e3   b5xa4

Suddenly Bogolyubov has a protected passed Pawn!

27   f2-f4

Embodies two threats: one of 28 f4-f5, cutting off the Bishop, and then winning it by 29 g2-g4, and the other of 28 e4-e5, undermining the support of the Knight.

27   ...   Qf6-e7

28   g2-g4

Not at once 28 f4-f5, to which the reply might be 28 ... f7-f6, providing a better flight-square for the Bishop than h7, and also strengthening the square e5 to Black's advantage.

28   ...   Bh5-g6

29   f4-f5   Bg6-h7

The Bishop is now relegated to the sidelines, so that White is in effect

a piece ahead. White's Pawn formation may be the worst ever (as Capablanca puts it) but an extra piece to play with can cover a lot of sins.

30   Nf1-g3   Qe7-e5

The Queen takes command of the center, incidentally squashing any attempt to advance the King Pawn.

31   Kg1-g2   Ra8-b8

32   Ra1-b1   f7-f6

This move has good and bad points: the good points being that it provides the King with entry to the center in the coming ending, makes possible the Bishop's return to the game by way of g8, and renders it more difficult for White to advance his King Pawn after the departure of the Queen from e5. The chief drawback to the move is that it weakens the square e6, whereon White might plant a Knight with mighty strong effect.

33   Nd2-f3

The time has come to dislodge the Black pieces from their strongholds.

33   ...   Rb8-b2+

34   Rb1xb2   Qe5xb2+

35   Re1-e2   Qb2-b3

Ending 34

Position after 35 ... Qb2-b3

Bogolyubov

Capablanca to move

At first glance, Black seems to have a bit of advantage for the endgame. His Queen, Rook, and Knight are placed aggressively, and enjoy more mobility than do White's pieces, which stand in defensive positions. Black has a trump too in his passed Pawn, which becomes more dangerous with every step forward it takes.

In White's favour though, is the fact that the enemy Bishop is shut out of the game, which is the equivalent of putting White a piece ahead.

Ergo, if White is a piece ahead, he must seize the initiative in order to reap the benefit of this extra force.

White's Pawn formation may not be a thing of beauty, but despite this handicap, Capablanca, displaying his own brand of endgame magic, manages to come up with two connected passed Pawns in the

center.

Remarkable!

36   Nf3-d4!

A brilliant offer of a Pawn, which Bogolyubov does not dare accept!

After 36 ... Qb3xc4, the strongest line for White is not Capablanca's recommendation 37 Re2-c2, as that allows Black to put up a fight by 37 ... Qc4xd5 38 Nd4-e6 Re8xe6! 39 f5xe6 Qd5xe6, with three Pawns for the exchange, but 37 Nd4-e6 at once, after which 37 ... Re8-b8 38 Ne6xc5 d6xc5 39 Re2-d2 Rb8-b3 40 Qe3-f2 probably wins for White.

36   ...   Qb3xe3

37   Re2xe3   Re8-b8

Black's Queen-side looks menacing!

In view of this, Capablanca must set about the task of transforming his Queen Pawn at all cost into a passed Pawn.

38	Re3-c3	Kg8-f7
39	Kg2-f3	Rb8-b2
40	Ng3-e2	Bh7-g8
41	Nd4-e6!	

Offers Black some unattractive choices. If:

(a) 41 ... Nc5xe6 42 d5xe6+, with an easy win for White, as Black's Bishop will be buried alive,

(b) 41 ... Nc5xe4 42 Kf3xe4 Rb2xe2+ 43 Ke4-d4 Re2-d2+ 44 Rc3-d3 Rd2-a2 45 c4-c5, and White wins.

41   ...   Nc5-b3

42   c4-c5!

White's Pawns begin to burst their

chains. What follows is a race between the passed Pawns.

42	...	d6xc5
43	Ne6xc5	Nb3-d2+
44	Kf3-f2	

This is less complicated than
44 Kf3-e3, when this might occur:
44 ... a4-a3 45 d5-d6 (of course
not 45 Rc3xa3 Nd2-c4+, and the
Rook goes) 45 ... a3-a2 (on
45 ... Kf7-e8 46 Ne2-d4 follows
with the threat of 47 d6-d7+ and
48 Nd4-c6+) 46 Nc5-e6 (threatens
mate in two) 46 ... Rb2-b7
47 Ne6-d8+ Kf7-f8 48 Nd8xb7
a2-a1(Q) 49 Rc3-c8+ Kf8-f7
50 Rc8-c7+ Kf7-f8 51 d6-d7, and
White wins.

So Capablanca pursues the
course he envisioned earlier.

Meanwhile, this is how things
look after his actual move:

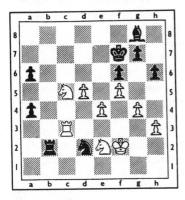

Position after 44 Kf3-f2

44	...	Kf7-e7

Capablanca says that Black might
have tried 44 ... Nd2-b1
45 Nc5xa4 Nb1xc3 46 Na4xb2
Nc3xe4+ 47 Kf2-e3 Ne4-d6, with
good chances to draw.

45	Kf2-e1!	Nd2-b1
46	Rc3-d3	

'With this move, White assures his
victory in the finish of a game
which has been extremely difficult'
(Capablanca).

46	...	a4-a3
47	d5-d6+	Ke7-d8
48	Ne2-d4!	

Now the threat of 49 Nd4-c6+
followed by 50 d6-d7+ forces
Black's next move.

48	...	Rb2-b6
49	Nd4-e6+	Bg8xe6

'At last the Bishop comes out,' says
Capablanca, 'but only as a stepping-
stone for White's Pawns.'

50	f5xe6	

The ugly duckling of a Pawn formation, pictured earlier, has been transformed into a beautiful swan.

50	...	Rb6-b8
51	e6-e7+	Kd8-e8
52	Nc5xa6!	**Black Resigns**

Bogolyubov does not wait for the
dénouement: 52 ... a3-a2
53 Na6xb8 a2-a1(Q) 54 d6-d7+
Ke8xe7 55 d7-d8(Q)+ Ke7-f7
56 Qd8-d5+ Kf7-f8 57 Qd5-c5+
Kf8-e8 58 Qc5-h5+ Ke8-e7
59 Nb8-c6+ Ke7-f8 60 Rd3-d8
mate.

An ending marked by superb
position and combination play.

GAME 35

White H. E. Atkins
Black J. R. Capablanca
London, 1922

Caro-Kann Defence
In this little-known masterpiece of Capablanca's, the World Champion heads for the ending almost from the first few moves. The whole game, in fact, might be considered one long endgame—and a magnificent one it is!

With infinite patience that overlooks no detail as unimportant, Capablanca's pieces slowly and methodically infiltrate into the enemy territory, and take possession of every good square in sight.

Capablanca is inexorable, as usual, and the air of inevitability that permeates this game is perhaps the most fascinating aspect of his style.

| 1 | e2-e4 | c7-c6 |
| 2 | d2-d4 | d7-d5 |

Capablanca adopted the Caro-Kann early in his career, and it stood him in good stead. He used it about a dozen times in tournament play, and never lost a game with it!

3 e4-e5

Unlike the cramping Pawn chain in the French Defence, this formation does not restrict the activity of Black's Queen Bishop.

| 3 | ... | Bc8-f5 |
| 4 | Bf1-d3 | |

White hastens to get rid of his good Bishop, a strategic error repeated by Nimzowitsch in his famous 1927 encounter against Capablanca (see

Game 42).

There are so many other good moves! White can go in for the complications arising from 4 c2-c4, when 4 ... d5xc4 could lead to 5 Bf1xc4 e7-e6 6 Nb1-c3 Nb8-d7 7 Ng1-e2! Ng8-e7 8 0-0 Nd7-b6 9 Bc4-b3 Qd8-d7 10 a2-a4! a7-a5 11 Ne2-g3, as in the Tal-Golombek game played at Munich in 1958.

A simple conservative course is 4 Ng1-e2 e7-e6 5 Ne2-g3, avoiding an early exchange of Bishops.

There is also the daring, original 4 h2-h4, introduced by Tal, which is not as wild-looking as might first appear. To begin with, it prevents the normal development of Black's King-side pieces by 4 ... e7-e6, which costs a piece after 5 g2-g4 Bf5-e4 6 f2-f3 Be4-g6 7 h4-h5, and the Bishop is trapped.

Instead of 4 ... e7-e6, in the game Tal-Bagirov, as well as in the game Tal-Pachmann at Bled in 1961, Black played 4 ... h7-h6, and the continuation was: 5 g2-g4 Bf5-d7 (forced, as after 5 ... Bf5-h7 6 e5-e6! f7xe6 7 Bf1-d3 Bh7xd3 8 Qd1xd3, White has the advantage) 6 h4-h5 c6-c5 7 c2-c3 e7-e6 8 f2-f4, and White has the better position, though he has made eight Pawn moves in the opening, and has not developed a single piece.

'However,' say Levy and Keene in *How to Play the Opening in Chess*, 'Tal's way is not to be recommended to lesser mortals (or perhaps not even to Tal). For White's somewhat unwarranted Pawn avalanche must surely carry with it the seeds of its own destruction if Black plays carefully.'

| 4 | ... | Bf5xd3 |
| 5 | Qd1xd3 | e7-e6 |

Black has the advantage of the French without the disadvantages. After . . . c6-c5 (striking at the base of the Pawn chain) he will have at least equality.

| 6 | Ng1-e2 | Qd8-b6 |
| 7 | 0-0 | Qb6-a6 |

An exchange of Queens would suit Capablanca, his opponent being weak on the white squares, and his Bishop restricted by the Pawn chain.

| 8 | Qd3-d1 | |

Rather than retreat, White should either exchange Queens or play 8 Qd3-e3.

8	...	c6-c5
9	c2-c3	Nb8-c6
10	Nb1-d2	

Preferable to this meek development, which meant being gradually crushed to death positionally, was the aggressive 10 f2-f4. But Atkins may have overlooked the effect of Capablanca's next two moves.

| 10 | ... | c5xd4 |
| 11 | c3xd4 | Qa6-d3! |

This is reminiscent of Morphy's paralyzing 12 . . . Qd8-d3! move, which must have come as a similar shock to Paulsen in their famous New York 1857 tournament en-

counter.

The immediate threat of winning a Pawn by 12 . . . Nc6xd4 forces the exchange of Queens.

12	Nd2-b3	Qd3xd1+
13	Rf1xd1	Ng8-e7
14	Bc1-d2	

Ending 35

Position after 14 Bc1-d2

Capablanca to move

Atkins

Offhand, there seems to be little to choose between the two positions, but Black's pieces do have more freedom, and his King is closer to the center.

Capablanca intends to prevent White's pieces from occupying good squares, bring his own King into active play, and seize control of the c-file with his Rooks. It is the domination of this file which will enable his pieces to penetrate into the vitals of the enemy territory, especially on the Queen-side.

| 14 | ... | a7-a5! |

This prevents any intrusion by White's Knight at a5.

| 15 | Ra1-c1 | b7-b6 |

While this keeps the Knight out of c5.

| 16 | a2-a4 |

White's fear of permitting 16 . . . a5-a4 (driving his Knight away) results in a weakening of his b4 square, and saddles him with two Pawns vulnerable to attack, the d-Pawn and the a-Pawn.

| 16 | ... | Ke8-d7 |
| 17 | Ne2-c3 | Nc6-a7 |

This inhibits 18 Nc3-b5, as the resulting exchange of Knights would greatly favour Black; after 18 . . . Na7xb5 19 a4xb5, the play might proceed with 19 . . . a5-a4 20 Nb3-a1 Ne7-f5, followed by 21 . . . a4-a3.

18	Kg1-f1	Ne7-c6
19	Kf1-e2	Ra8-c8
20	Bd2-e1	Bf8-e7
21	Nc3-b1	f7-f5
22	e5xf6 *en passant*

Atkins may have hoped to give his Bishop more mobility, but the recapture exposes his Queen Pawn to direct attack by another piece.

22	...	Be7xf6
23	Be1-c3	Nc6-b4
24	Bc3-d2

White was faced with a difficult decision. Exchanging pieces would rid him of the ineffectual Bishop,

but his pieces could not then make use of the focal point c3, and the life of his a-Pawn would be further endangered.

| 24 | ... | Na7-c6 |
| 25 | Bd2-e3 | Nb4-a2! |

Capablanca continues to make things uncomfortable for his opponent. This move, controlling c1, renders it impossible for White to double Rooks on the file and oppose Black's domination of it.

| 26 | Rc1-c2 |

'White continues to lose ground,' says Maroczy in the tournament book, 'Mr. Atkins must have been in time pressure.'

But what else could Mr. Atkins have played?

| 26 | ... | Rc8-c7 |
| 27 | Nb1-a3 |

The attempt to drive off Black's annoying Knight by 27 Nb1-c3 fails after 27 . . . Nc6-b4 28 Rc2-d2 Na2xc3 29 b2xc3 Rc7xc3, and Black has won a Pawn.

| 27 | ... | Rh8-c8 |

Forestalls any such ambitious move as 28 Na3-b5, when 28 . . . Nc6xd4+ wins a Pawn against any of the four ways of capturing the Knight.

| 28 | Rc2-d2 | Nc6-a7 |

Once again hinders White from playing 29 Na3-b5.

29	Rd2-d3	Na2-b4
30	Rd3-d2	Rc7-c6
31	Rd1-b1	Bf6-e7

Black aims to eliminate White's Knight at a3, in order to be able to establish a Rook on the seventh rank.

32	Rb1-a1	Be7-d6
33	h2-h3	Rc6-c7
34	Ra1-d1	Nb4-a2!
35	Rd1-a1	

The Knight (at a3) must stay put,
as 35 Na3-b1 would lead to
35 . . . Bd6-b4 36 Rd2-d3 Rc7-c2+,
and a Pawn comes off.

35	. . .	Bd6xa3
36	Ra1xa2	

Naturally, if 36 b2xa3 instead,
36 . . . Na2-c3+ wins an innocent
Rook Pawn.

36	. . .	Ba3-b4
37	Rd2-d1	Rc7-c4
38	Rd1-c1	

This frustrates Black's attempts to
post a Rook on the seventh rank,
but he finds a new way to revive
the attack.

38	. . .	Na7-c6!

Threatens to win a Pawn by
39 . . . Nc6xd4+.

39	Rc1xc4	d5xc4
40	Nb3-d2	Bb4xd2!

A shrewd exchange; Black's remaining Knight will prove to be superior
to the opposing Bishop, which is
tied down to the defence of the
Queen Pawn.

41	Ke2xd2	

The diagram shows the position, as
the last act begins:

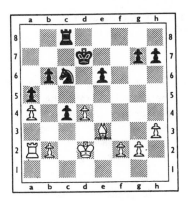

Position after 41 Ke2xd2

41	. . .	Kd7-d6
42	Kd2-c3	Kd6-d5
43	Ra2-a1	g7-g6
44	f2-f3	Rc8-b8

Prepares to open the b-file, enabling his Rook to take an active part
in the game.

45	Ra1-a3	b6-b5
46	a4xb5	Rb8xb5
47	Be3-f2	Nc6-b4!

Cuts down White's options: if
48 Bf2-e3 (to avoid 48 . . . Nb4-d3,
attacking two units) 48 . . . Nb4-d3
49 Ra3-a2 Rb5-b3+ 50 Kc3-d2 (on
50 Kc3-c2, Nb3-b4+ is fatal)
50 . . . Rb3xb2+, and Black wins a
Pawn and the game.

48	b2-b3	c4xb3
49	Kc3xb3	

Or 49 Ra3xb3 Nb4-a2+ 50 Kc3-b2
Rb5xb3+ 51 Kb2xb3 Na2-c1+
52 Kb3-a4 Nc1-d3 53 Bf2-e3
Nd3-e1, and the rest plays itself.

49	. . .	Nb4-c6+
50	Kb3-c3	

Of course not the suicidal
50 Kb3-a4, when 50 . . . Rb5-b4
mates neatly.

50   . . .   Rb5-b1

This sort of move, getting behind
the lines, usually presages the
bringing down of the curtain, but
Atkins puts up a hard fight, and
makes Capablanca extend himself
to achieve the victory.

51   Ra3-a4   Rb1-c1+!

A powerful check which gains more
ground for Black. If

(a) 52 Kc3-b2 Rc1-f1 53 Bf2-e3
(on 53 Bf2-g3, Rf1-g1 will remove
some Pawns) 53 . . . Rf1-e1
(threatens 54 . . . Re1-e2+)
54 Be3-d2 Re1-e2 55 Kb2-c1
Re2xg2 56 Bd2xa5 Nc6xd4 should
suffice,

(b) 52 Kc3-d3 Nc6-b4+ 53 Kd3-e3
Rc1-c3+ 54 Ke3-d2 Rc3-c2+
55 Kd2-e3 Kd5-c4! wins, for if
56 Ra4xa5 Nb4-d5+ 57 Ke3-e4
Rc2-e2+, and mate next move,
while other moves allow
57 . . . Kc4-b5, which unpins the
Knight for the check at d5, attacks
the Rook, and threatens to move
on with the Pawn when the Rook
retreats.

52   Kc3-d2   Rc1-c4

53   Ra4-a1

Clearly, 53 Ra4xc4 Kd5xc4 offers
no hope, as Black captures the d-
Pawn next move, leaving him a
Pawn ahead—an outside passed
Pawn at that!

53   . . .   a5-a4

54   Ra1-a2   Nc6-a7!

Reculer pour mieux sauter, as they
say in Paris.

55   Ra2-a1   Na7-b5

56   Ra1-b1   Kd5-c6

Capablanca prefers to keep up the
pressure rather than win the Queen
Pawn, at the expense of allowing an
exchange of a sturdy Knight for a
Bishop that is practically useless.

57   Kd2-d3

This is the position:

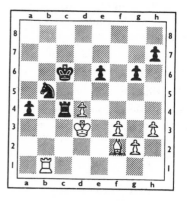

Position after 57 Kd2-d3

57   . . .   Rc4-c3+

58   Kd3-d2   Rc3-b3!

Every move a picture!

59   Rb1-c1+

Exchanging Rooks is hopeless, the
play going like this: 59 Rb1xb3
a4xb3 60 Kd2-d3 b3-b2!
61 Kd3-c2 Nb5-c3! 62 Kc2xb2
Nc3-d1+ followed by 63 . . . Nd1xf2
(yes, the Knight can escape).
     Or if 59 Rb1xb3 a4xb3
60 Kd2-c1 Kc6-d5 61 Kc1-b2
Nb5xd4 62 Bf2xd4 Kd5xd4

63 Kb2xb3 Kd4-e3, and the King
waltzes in and removes the Pawns.

59	...	Kc6-b7
60	Rc1-c2	a4-a3
61	Bf2-g3	

Desperation, but he was threatened
with being the victim of this piquant
finish: 61 ... Rb3-b2 62 Rc2xb2
a3xb2 63 Kd2-c2 Nb5-c3!
64 Kc2xb2 Nc3-d1+, and the unfortunate Bishop meets his end (as
in the note following White's 59th
move).

61	...	Nb5xd4
62	Rc2-c7+	Kb7-b6
63	Rc7-c4	Kb6-b5
64	Rc4-c8	

Obviously 64 Rc4xd4 loses instantly by 64 ... a3-a2.

64	...	Nd4-c6
65	Rc8-a8	Rb3-b2+
66	Kd2-e3	

If 66 Kd2-c3 Rb2xg2 followed by
67 ... a3-a2 and 68 ... Nc6-a5,
cutting off the Rook, will force the
queening of the Pawn.

66	...	Rb2xg2
67	Bg3-f2	Nc6-b4
68	White Resigns	

If 68 Ra8xa3 Nb4-c2+ wins the
Rook, or if 68 Bf2-h4 g6-g5
69 Bh4-f2 a3-a2 (threatens
70 a2-a1(Q) Ra8xa1 71 Nb4-c2+)
70 Ke3-e2 Rg2xf2+ 71 Ke2xf2
Nb4-a6, and Black wins.

An absorbing ending, every step
of the way.

GAME 36

White J. R. Capablanca
Black S. G. Tartakover
New York, 1924

Dutch Defence
Search the annals of chess from the
days of Philidor to the reign of
Karpov, and you will find no ending equal to this for demonstrating
the power of a Rook on the seventh
rank. It packs in more solid instruction (of the most pleasurable kind,
I hasten to add) than the thousand
Rook-and-Pawn endings that Capablanca is said to have studied in
his youth.

Alekhine, in *The Book of the*
New York International Chess
Tournament of 1924, pays tribute
to his great rival's skill with these
words, 'A really pleasurable game
on the part of the Champion, and a
fine example of his machine-like
precision and superior technique.
White sacrifices material in order
to obtain the classical position with
King on f6, Pawn on g6, and Rook
on h7. Although Dr. Tartakover
was two Pawns ahead, he could not

stem the tide. The Pawns tumble like ripe apples.'

1	d2-d4	f7-f5
2	Ng1-f3	e7-e6
3	c2-c4	Ng8-f6
4	Bc1-g5	Bf8-e7
5	Nb1-c3	0-0
6	e2-e3	b7-b6
7	Bf1-d3	Bc8-b7
8	0-0	Qd8-e8

Black evidently intends to attack on the King-side by 9 . . . Qe8-h5 and 10 . . . Nf6-g4—customary strategy in the Dutch Defence.

9	Qd1-e2!	Nf6-e4

Forcibly prevents 10 e3-e4, and effects some welcome exchanges.

10	Bg5xe7	Ne4xc3
11	b2xc3	Qe8xe7

The exchanges have left White with a weakness in the form of a doubled Pawn on the Bishop file. As consolation, though, Capablanca has an open Knight file available to his Rooks, of which they make clever use.

12	a2-a4!	

A witty preventive move! It stops an unwelcome intrusion by 12 . . . Qe7-a3, and also prepares to meet 12 . . . Nb8-c6 with 13 Rf1-b1, and if then 13 . . . Nc6-a5, 14 c4-c5 undoubles the Pawns by force as 14 . . . b6xc5 15 Rb1-b5 is to White's advantage.

12	. . .	Bb7xf3

It seems illogical to give up a long-range Bishop for a less-active Knight, but Tartakover wanted to

avoid the variation given above. He trusted his remaining Knight to prove more effective than Capablanca's Bishop—but it is the Bishop that turns out to be the superior piece!

13	Qe2xf3	Nb8-c6
14	Rf1-b1	Ra8-e8

Instead of this routine move, Black might have tried the energetic 14 . . . g7-g5, with a view to counter-attack.

15	Qf3-h3!	

Stops Black from freeing himself by 15 . . . e6-e5, as 16 Bd3xf5 wins a Pawn—as a start. If then 16 . . . Re8-d8, to prevent loss of the exchange by 17 Bf5xd7, then 17 Qh3xh7+ Kg8-f7 18 Qh7-h5+ Kf7-g8 19 Bf5-h7+, and mate in two.

15	. . .	Rf8-f6

Here too 15 . . . g7-g5 offered better chances of counter-attack.

16	f2-f4!	

Gets a firm grip on the square e5, retraining Black's King Pawn for a long time.

16	. . .	Nc6-a5
17	Qh3-f3	

The Queen returns to f3, to dominate the long diagonal.

17	. . .	d7-d6
18	Rb1-e1	

There being no more future for the Rook on the b-file, it returns to the center to support the break by 19 e3-e4, with an advantageous opening of the lines for White.

18	. . .	Qe7-d7

Black delays the advance of his e-Pawn, as this possible continuation does not attract him: 18 . . . e6-e5 19 e3-e4 e5xd4 20 e4-e5 Rf6-f7 21 c3xd4 Na5-b3 22 e5xd6 Qe7xe1+ 23 Ra1xe1 Re8xe1+ 24 Kg1-f2, Re1-e8 25 Qf3-c6, and White has good winning chances.

19   e3-e4!

White opens the position to give his pieces more scope.

This is how the board looks:

Position after 19 e3-e4!

19	. . .	f5xe4
20	Qf3xe4	g7-g6
21	g2-g3	

White makes suitable preparation for the advance of his King Rook Pawn.

21	. . .	Kg8-f8
22	Kg1-g2	Rf6-f7

Tartakover thought he might have done better with this line of play, which he pointed out after the game: 22 . . . Qd7-c6 23 Qe4xc6 Na5xc6 24 c4-c5 (threatens to win the exchange by 25 Bd3-b5)

24 . . . Re8-e7, whereby the Knight returns to the theater of action.

23   h2-h4   d6-d5

This leads to an exchange of Queens, leaving White with a tiny advantage—but a tiny advantage is all that Capablanca wants!

There was an alternative, but not an appealing one in 23 . . . Na5xc4 24 Bd3xc4 d6-d5 25 Bc4xd5 Qd7xd5 26 a4-a5, and the Queen Rook will soon have the a-file available to him.

24   c4xd5   e6xd5

25   Qe4xe8+

Capablanca is happy to reduce it to an ending, as he has a Bishop (which he prefers) to a Knight (which is stranded on the sidelines).

25	. . .	Qd7xe8
26	Re1xe8+	Kf8xe8

Ending 36

Position after 26 . . . Kf8xe8

Tartakover

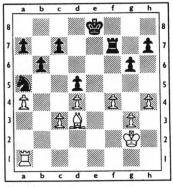

Capablanca to move

White's positional advantage consists in having more space for his pieces, and in possessing a centralized Bishop opposing a Knight that is temporarily out of play.

It is true that Capablanca has a weak c-Pawn, and it will be interesting to see how he defends it against capture. (Or will he?)

Capablanca plans to activate his Rook (that has done nothing but watch the game quietly from a corner) by swinging it over to the h-file, from where it may reach the all-important seventh rank.

27   h4-h5!

Yes, for - ward   on   the foe,

27   ...   Rf7-f6

The Rook sets out for the weakling, in preference to playing
27 . . . g6xh5, after which there would come 28 Ra1-h1 Ke8-f8
29 Rh1xh5, and White not only picks up the d-Pawn or the h-Pawn next move, but has set free his f-Pawn.

28   h5xg6   h7xg6

29   Ra1-h1

The Rook seizes the open file, aiming to zoom up to the seventh rank.

Black is helpless to prevent the invasion. If:

(a) 29 . . . Ke8-e7 30 Rh1-h7+ Rf6-f7 31 Bd3xg6 wins a Pawn,

(b) 29 . . . Rf6-f7 30 Bd3xg6 pins

the Rook,

(c) 29 . . . Rf6-c6 (to counter-attack) 30 Bd3-b5 pins the Rook.

What a Bishop!

29   ...   Ke8-f8

30   Rh1-h7

The seventh rank, the ideal location for a Rook!

The Rook is in position to attack any Pawn that has not yet moved, or to get behind any Pawn that has moved, and threaten it with capture.

More than that, the Rook is in possession of the *7th rank absolute,* which, says Nimzowitsch, means that the Rook confines the enemy King to the eighth rank. (One can see that the great masters were conversant with the Nimzowitsch theories long before he defined and published them.)

30   ...   Rf6-c6

31   g3-g4!

This is much stronger than the tempting 31 Rh7-d7, after which there would follow, not
31 . . . Rc6xc3 32 Bd3xg6, but
31 . . . Na5-c4! This would hold the position, 32 Bd3xc4 being met by 32 . . . Rc6xc4, while
32 Rd7xd5 runs into a deadly Knight fork.

31   ...   Na5-c4

The Knight must get back into the game, lest Black be minus the services of a piece.

Black naturally refrains from capturing the Bishop Pawn, as the reply
32 Bd3xg6 secures two connected passed Pawns for White.

32 g4-g5

Nails down the opposing Knight Pawn, and sets it up as a target for attack by 33 Rh7-h6 Kf8-g7 34 f4-f5.

32 ... Nc4-e3+

It is useless to throw a block in the Bishop's path by 32 . . . Nc4-d2 33 Rh7-h6 Nd2-e4, as 34 c3-c4 will pry it open.

33 Kg2-f3

This shows the highly interesting state of affairs:

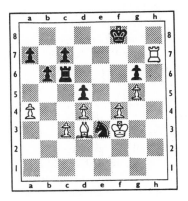

Position after 33 Kg2-f3

33 ... Ne3-f5

The consequences of 33 . . . Ne3-d1 were, as Tartakover indicated, 34 Rh7-h6 Kf8-g7 35 f4-f5 Nd1xc3 36 Kf3-f4! Nc3-e4 37 Bd3xe4 d5xe4 38 f5-f6+ Rc6xf6+ 39 g5xf6+ Kg7xh6 40 Kf4xe4 Kh6-h7 41 Ke4-d5! Kh7-g8 42 Kd5-c6 g6-g5 43 Kc6xc7 g5-g4 44 d4-d5 g4-g3 45 d5-d6 g3-g2 46 d6-d7 g2-g1(Q) 47 d7-d8(Q)+ Kg8-h7 48 Qd8-e7+ Kh7-h6

49 Qe7-g7+ Qg1xg7 50 f6xg7 Kh6xg7 51 Kc7-b7 Kg7-f7 52 Kb7xa7 Kf7-e7 53 Ka7xb6 Ke7-d7 54 Kb6-b7, and White wins.

Tartakover's analysis convinced him that Capablanca would experience no trouble in finding the winning moves, though it involved being a Pawn down, and queening a move later than his opponent, so he changed his mind and played the text move (33 . . . Ne3-f5).

34 Bd3xf5 g6xf5

Now comes as brilliant a move as ever was played in a Rook-and-Pawn ending, a move that Capablanca must have visualized long before reaching this position.

In a simplified ending, where Pawns are worth their weight in gold, Capablanca gives away two of them! Furthermore, he lets Black capture them with check!

35 Kf3-g3!

The King starts out for the square f6, an ideal position for assisting the Rook in mating threats and for helping the Pawn promote to a Queen (to say nothing of wreaking havoc among the neighboring Pawns).

35 ... Rc6xc3+

36 Kg3-h4 Rc3-f3

Black is intent on snatching up any Pawn that isn't nailed down.

An attempt to exchange Rooks instead would follow this course: 36 . . . Rc3-c1 37 Kh4-h5 Rc1-h1+ 38 Kh5-g6 Rh1xh7 39 Kg6xh7 c7-c5 40 g5-g6, and the Pawn cannot be headed off.

37   g5-g6!

Once again Capablanca lets the Rook capture a Pawn with check!

In return, his King will advance closer to the magic-square f6.

37   ...   Rf3xf4+

38   Kh4-g5

Attacks the Rook, and thereby gains a tempo.

Black is now two Pawns ahead, yet all is not well. He must guard against losing his Rook (or perhaps even suffer mate) which could be the consequence of picking up another Pawn, thus: 38 . . . Rf4xd4 39 Kg5-f6 Kf8-g8 (on 39 . . . Kf8-e8 40 Rh7-h8+ Ke8-d7 41 g6-g7, and Black must give up his Rook for the Pawn) 40 Rh7-d7, and White mates next move.

38   ...   Rf4-e4

This is the situation:

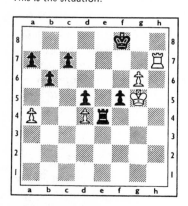

Position after 38 . . . Rf4-e4

39   Kg5-f6!

Note that White disdained the capture of the f-Pawn. Now it acts as a buffer against annoying checks.

The King is beautifully placed

to support the passed Pawn, and incidentally to frighten Black with threats of mate.

39   ...   Kf8-g8

40   Rh7-g7+   Kg8-h8

41   Rg7xc7

Captures a Pawn, and faces Black with three dire threats, to wit:

(a) mate on the last rank,

(b) promotion of the Knight Pawn,

(c) loss of all his Pawns.

41   ...   Re4-e8

42   Kf6xf5

Simple and strong; the energetic 42 Kf6-f7 would not yet have been decisive after 42 . . . Re8-d8 43 g6-g7+ Kh8-h7, and Black continues either with 44 . . . Rd8-g8 or 44 . . . f5-f4.

42   ...   Re8-e4

Black despairs of saving his a-Pawn, which would be lost after 42 . . . a7-a6 43 Rc7-a7 b6-b5 44 a4-a5, while the attempt to do so by 42 . . . Re8-a8 could lead to this pretty finish: 43 Kf5-e6 Ra8-g8 44 Rc7-h7 mate!

43   Kf5-f6!

Once again his threat of mate will give White time to collect a Pawn or two.

43   ...   Re4-f4+

44   Kf6-e5   Rf4-g4

45   g6-g7+   Kh8-g8

Black dare not take the Pawn, the sad consequences being; 45 . . . Rg4xg7 46 Rc7xg7 Kh8xg7 47 Ke5xd5 Kg7-f7 48 Kd5-d6 Kf7-e8 49 Kd6-c7 Ke8-e7

50 d4-d5, and the Pawn cannot be stopped.

| 46 | Rc7xa7 | Rg4-g1 |
| 47 | Ke5xd5 | |

For the two Pawns White sacrificed he has regained four!

47	...	Rg1-c1
48	Kd5-d6	Rc1-c2
49	d4-d5	Rc2-c1
50	Ra7-c7	Rc1-a1
51	Kd6-c6	Ra1xa4
52	d5-d6	Black Resigns

The continuation (for anyone still skeptical) would be 52 . . . Ra4-d4 53 d6-d7 Rd4-c4+ (of course if 53 . . . Kg8xg7 54 d7-d8(Q)+ wins) 54 Kc6-b7 Rc4-d4 55 Kb7-c8, and the Pawn becomes a Queen next move.

Capablanca's clear-cut methodical play is so easy to understand that the whole ending is a marvellous piece of instruction, and a thing of beauty.

'A most impressive ending, surely one of the greatest Rook-and-Pawn finishes of all time' (Em. Lasker).

GAME 37

White J. R. Capablanca
Black F. D. Yates
New York, 1924

King's Indian Defence
In the beginning—there is freshness and orginality in the way Capablanca induces little weaknesses in Yates's position.

In the midgame—there is the beauty of logic in the superb technique with which Capablanca exploits these weaknesses.

In the endgame—there is imagination and genuine artistry in Capablanca's remarkable concept of winning a Pawn by having a Knight circle about it like a hawk, and then swoop down to capture it.

Call it inspiration, or call it genius, it is a game which shows Capablanca at the height of his powers—a masterpiece of precision and beauty.

1	d2-d4	Ng8-f6
2	Ng1-f3	g7-g6
3	Nb1-c3	

Most masters interpolate 3 c2-c4, but this time Capablanca prefers simple, sound development of the pieces to building up a Pawn center. It may not be the sharpest way of dealing with these new-fangled defences, but it has its good points.

| 3 | ... | d7-d5 |

Evidently Yates wants to prevent 4 e2-e4, but the spirit of the fianchetto suggests 3 . . . d7-d6, with the idea of attacking the center later by . . . c7-c5, thereby increasing the power of the Bishop (at g7).

4	Bc1-f4	Bf8-g7
5	e2-e3	0-0
6	h2-h3	

'Not exactly necessary,' says Alekhine.

Nevertheless it is an excellent move, preventing as it does a good development of the Bishop by 6 . . . Bc8-g4, and providing as well a retreat for his own Bishop at h2, in the event of an attempt to exchange it by 6 . . . Nf6-h5.

| 6 | . . . | c7-c5 |

A plausible attempt to attack the center, and free his game as well.

It is stopped by Capablanca in a highly original manner.

| 7 | d4xc5! | |

'At first blush this makes a strange impression,' says Alekhine in the Tournament Book, 'but it is based on a profound concept of the position. White may permit his only Pawn to disappear from the center, inasmuch as he commands it efficiently with his pieces.'

| 7 | . . . | Qd8-a5 |

This looks strong, as it threatens 8 . . . Nf6-e4 with a triple attack on the pinned Knight.

But Capablanca disposes of the threat in a twinkling.

| 8 | Nf3-d2! | |

Though termed by Alekhine 'an unpleasant defensive maneuver, forced by the threat of 8 . . . Nf6-e4', this is a fine prophylactic move.

If now 8 . . . Nf6-e4 9 Nc3xe4 d5xe4 10 c2-c3, and White remains a Pawn ahead.

| 8 | . . . | Qa5xc5 |

| 9 | Nd2-b3 | Qc5-b6 |
| 10 | Bf4-e5! | |

Institutes two threats. The obvious one is 11 Be5xf6 followed by 12 Nc3xd5, winning the d-Pawn. Black's defence of the Pawn by 10 . . . e7-e6 will hem in his Queen Bishop.

The subtle threat—well, we'll come to that in a moment.

| 10 | . . . | e7-e6 |

Bitter necessity, but the alternative 10 . . . Bc8-e6 11 Be5-d4 Qb6-c6 12 Nb3-c5 is none too pleasing.

| 11 | Nc3-b5! | |

Now the threats against the Rook by 12 Nb5-c7, and against the Rook Pawn by 12 Be5-d4 force Black's rejoinder.

| 11 | . . . | Nf6-e8 |
| 12 | Be5xg7 | Ne8xg7 |

Thus was carried out the subtle object of White's 10th move Bf4-e5!, the forced exchange of Black's fianchettoed Bishop, the chief guardian of his black squares. As a consequence, these squares are weakened, and susceptible to attack, or occupation by White's pieces.

| 13 | h3-h4! | |

This is not a wild attempt to play for checkmate.

White's threat, though, of opening the h-file by h4-h5 (after suitable preparation) will induce Black to counter by . . . h7-h5 or . . . f7-f5.

This advance of another Pawn to a white square will further weaken his black squares.

| 13 | . . . | a7-a6 |

14	Nb5-c3	Nb8-c6
15	Bf1-d3	f7-f5

Yates evidently feared something like this: 16 h4-h5 Ng7xh5 17 Rh1xh5 g6xh5 18 Bd3xh7+ Kg8-g7 (if 18 . . . Kg8xh7 19 Qd1xh5+ Kh7-g8 20 Qh5-g5+ Kg8-h8 21 0-0-0, and mate follows) 19 Qd1xh5 Rf8-h8 20 Qh5-g5+ Kg7-f8 21 Qg5-h6+ Kf8-e7 22 0-0-0, and the King is exposed to many threats, one of them being 23 Rd1xd5. While he might survive, it is not a position to Yates's liking.

The move he plays though, is anti-positional, as it imprisons the Bishop behind a chain of Pawns, all occupying white squares, and further accentuates the weakness of his black squares.

16 Qd1-d2!

A triple-action move! It prevents any counter-demonstration by 16 . . . f5-f4, guards against a Queen check in the event he plays Nc3-a4 and Na4-c5, and clears the way for Queen-side castling.

16	. . .	Nc6-e5
17	Bd3-e2	Ne5-c4

There was more resistance in 17 . . . Bc8-d7 18 Qd2-d4 Qb6-c7 19 Qd4-f4 Ra8-c8 20 h4-h5 Ne5-c4 21 Nc3-d1 Qc7-d8, and Black follows with 22 . . . Qd8-f6 or 22 . . . g6-g5, though it would take the defensive genius of a Steinitz or a Lasker to uncover this line of play over the board.

18 Be2xc4!

Well played! It is not evident at this point that it is White who will control the d-file after the exchange of pieces, nor that the capturing Pawn will be vulnerable at c4, though it will have a stout defender in the b-Pawn.

18	. . .	d5xc4
19	Qd2-d4	Qb6-c7
20	Qd4-c5!	

White is confident that the exchange of Queens will leave the recapturing Knight out of play for a short time only.

20	. . .	Qc7xc5
21	Nb3xc5	

Ending 37

Position after 21 Nb3xc5

Yates to move

Capablanca

Black is at a disadvantage in this position.

His Knight is sadly situated at g7, and his Bishop is hampered by the many Pawns (all seven of them!) standing on squares of the same color, while the weaknesses of his black squares may bring him grief.

A win for White though, will not be easy. It will take meticulous play, combined with a beautiful tactical device known to problemists as *The Knight Wheel* to bring in a Pawn as the first fruit of victory.

21	...	b7-b6

Black must dislodge the annoying Knight if his Bishop is to come into play.

22	Nc5-a4	Ra8-b8
23	0-0-0	

Threatens 24 Rd1-d6, the prevention of which accounts for Black's next two moves.

23	...	b6-b5
24	Na4-c5	Rb8-b6
25	a2-a4!	

Very good indeed! White intends to break up the chain of Pawns on the Queen-side, and create targets for his Knights.

25	...	Ng7-h5

Black tries to improve his position, *faute de mieux*.

He does not care for 25 ... b5-b4 26 Nc3-e2, nor does 25 ... Rb6-c6 look inviting, a plausible continuation being 26 Nc5-d7 Bc8xd7 (any move of the King Rook costs the exchange) 27 Rd1xd7 b5-b4 28 Nc3-e2 Rf8-f7 29 Rh1-d1 Rc6-c7 30 Rd7xc7 Rf7xc7 31 Rd1-d6 a6-a5 32 Ne2-d4 e6-e5 33 Nd4-c6, and White wins a Pawn.

26	b2-b3

Now 26 Nc5-d7 does not have the same impact, as Black defends

cleverly by 26 ... Bc8xd7 27 Rd1xd7 Rf8-f7 28 Rh1-d1 Nh5-f6, and banishes White's Rook from the seventh rank.

26	...	c4xb3

Practically forced, White's threat being 27 a4-a5 Rb6-c6 28 b3-b4, and the Knight stands like a rock.

27	c2xb3	b5xa4
28	Nc3xa4	Rb6-c6
29	Kc1-b2	Nh5-f6
30	Rd1-d2	a6-a5

At last a Pawn moves to a black square!

This relieves the Bishop of the task of defending it, and also allows the Bishop some elbow-room.

Black advanced the Pawn as he feared its loss by 31 Rh1-d1 followed by 32 Rd2-d6, and as Alekhine points out, 'It was not easily to be foreseen at this point in just what manner White could capture it.'

31	Rh1-d1	Nf6-d5

Just in time to keep the Rook out!

32	g2-g3

A little precaution against counterplay by 32 ... f5-f4.

32	...	Rf8-f7
33	Nc5-d3!	

The Knight is headed for c4, where it can attack the isolated Rook Pawn.

33	...	Rf7-b7
34	Nd3-e5	Rc6-c7
35	Rd2-d4	

Of course not 35 Ne5-c4 at once, as the Knight would be snapped off

35	...	Kg8-g7
36	e3-e4!	f5xe4
37	Rd4xe4	

The exchange of Pawns has saddled Black with another weakness, the isolated e-Pawn, to add to his troubles.

37	...	Rb7-b5

Hoping to double Rooks on the b-file.

38	Re4-c4	

But he isn't given time to do so, as 38 . . . Rc7-b7 would leave the Bishop *en prise*.

38	...	Rc7xc4
39	Ne5xc4	Bc8-d7

The Bishop finally makes an entrance after waiting in the wings for 38 moves.

This is the position:

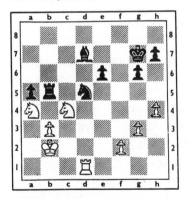

Position after 39 . . . Bc8-d7

Capablanca's Knight (at a4) now takes five moves to circle about like a hawk, and then swoops down on Yates's a-Pawn!

This beautiful, original way of

winning a Pawn had never before occurred in actual play.

40	Na4-c3	

White attacks the Rook, and does so four times in succession.

The poor Rook tries to evade the Knight, while still keeping in touch with the a-Pawn.

40	...	Rb5-c5

Forced, as 40 . . . Nd5xc3 41 Rd1xd7+ loses a piece for Black.

41	Nc3-e4	Rc5-b5
42	Ne4-d6	Rb5-c5
43	Nd6-b7	Rc5-c7

No better is 43 . . . Rc5-b5, as the Pawn is now attacked by both Knights.

44	Nb7xa5	

Being a Pawn ahead usually means that the rest is a matter of technique, but Capablanca's technique in converting an advantage in material into a win is always a priceless lesson in endgame play.

Yates puts up his customary hard fight, hoping that he can bring the position to a stage where his opponent will remain with only two Knights against his King, and be unable to enforce mate.

44	...	Bd7-b5
45	Nc4-d6	Bb5-d7

The Bishop must stay on the diagonal leading to e8 to prevent a Knight fork, and 45 . . . Bb5-c6 fails after 46 Rd1-c1 Nd5-e7 47 Nd6-e8+, and White wins the exchange.

46	Na5-c4	Rc7-a7
47	Nd6-e4	h7-h6

48	f2-f4

This stifles Black's attempt to simplify by 48 . . . g6-g5.

48	. . .	Bd7-e8
49	Nc4-e5	Ra7-a8
50	Rd1-c1	Be8-f7
51	Rc1-c6	

Though nothing is threatened, White exerts pressure on the position.

Notice that Capablanca makes no effort to advance the passed Pawn, until adequate preparations have been made for its safety.

51	. . .	Bf7-g8
52	Ne4-c5	

This seems to let Black's King into the game, but if 52 . . . Kg7-f6 53 Ne5-g4+ will force the King to abandon either the h-Pawn or the e-Pawn.

52	. . .	Ra8-e8

Necessary to save the e-Pawn, but it restricts the Rook to a closed file.

53	Rc6-a6	Re8-e7
54	Kb2-a3	Bg8-f7
55	b3-b4	Nd5-c7

Black tries to whip up some sort of counter-attack, as passive resistance lets the Pawn march up the board to win.

This is the scene on the board:

Position after 55 . . . Nd5-c7

56	Ra6-c6	Nc7-b5+

Yielding to the impulse to drive the Rook off by 56 . . . Bf7-e8 would allow White to finish neatly by 57 Rc6xc7 Re7xc7 58 Nc5xe6+ Kg7-f6 59 Ne6xc7, and White has won a piece (and the removal of the Bishop next move leaves an elementary win).

57	Ka3-b2	Nb5-d4
58	Rc6-a6	Bf7-e8

Otherwise 59 Ne5-c6 would force an exchange of minor pieces and lighten White's task.

59	g3-g4	Kg7-f6
60	Nc5-e4+	Kf6-g7
61	Ne4-d6	

The Knights continue to gain ground, slowly but inexorably.

White's move involves a threat: 62 Nd6xe8+ Re7xe8 63 Ra6-a7+ and the King must abandon the Knight Pawn or suffer mate (after 63 . . . Kg7-f6 by 64 Ra7-f7+).

61	. . .	Be8-b5

| 62 | Ra6-a5 | Bb5-f1 |

Practically the only spot for the Bishop, other moves losing thus:

(a) 62 . . . Bb5-c6 63 Kb2-c3,

(b) 62 . . . Bb5-d7 63 Ra5-a7,

(c) 62 . . . Bb5-e8 63 Nd6xe8+, as in the previous note.

| 63 | Ra5-a8 | g6-g5 |

Black gives up a Pawn to avert the mate threatened by 64 Nd6-e8+ Kg7-h7 65 Ne8-f6+ Kh7-g7 66 Ra8-g8+ Kg7xf6 67 Rg8xg6 mate!

If instead 63 . . . Bf1-b5 (to prevent check at e8) the procedure would be 64 Kb2-c3 Nd4-e2+ 65 Kc3-d2 Ne2-d4 66 Kd2-e3 Nd4-c2+ 67 Ke3-e4, and White pauses for a reply.

| 64 | f4xg5 | h6xg5 |
| 65 | h4xg5! | |

And thereby renews the threat of finishing off with 66 Nd6-e8+ Kg7-h7 67 Ne8-f6+ Kh7-g7 68 Ra8-g8 mate.

| 65 | . . . | Bf1-g2 |

Parries the mate by attacking the Rook.

The Rook must stay on the eighth rank to enforce the mate, but where can it go? If 66 Ra8-b8 (or to d8) 66 . . . Nd4-c6 disposes of one of the troublesome Knights, while 66 Ra8-c8 is met by 66 . . . Bg2-b7, banishing the Rook.

| 66 | Ra8-e8! | Re7-c7 |

Or 66 . . . Re7xe8 67 Nd6xe8+ Kg7-f8 68 g5-g6 with a quick win.

| 67 | Re8-d8 | |

Clears e8 for the Knight.

67	. . .	Nd4-c6
68	Nd6-e8+	Kg7-f8
69	Ne8xc7+	Nc6xd8
70	Kb2-c3	Bg2-b7
71	Kc3-d4	Bb7-c8
72	g5-g6	Nd8-b7
73	Nc7-e8!	

A bit of cat-and-mouse stuff. If 73 . . . Kf8xe8 74 g6-g7 and finis.

73	. . .	Nb7-d8
74	b4-b5	Kf8-g8
75	g4-g5	Kg8-f8
76	g6-g7+	Kf8-g8
77	g5-g6	Black Resigns

Mate will follow by 78 Kd4-e3, 79 Ne5-g4, and 80 Ng4-h6. Capablanca's exploitation of a positional advantage was carried out with accuracy and artistry.

GAME 38

White J. R. Capablanca
Black Em. Lasker
New York, 1924

Slav Defence

Capablanca's defeat of Dr. Lasker in one of the most dramatic games ever played between masters of World Championship calibre kept the spectators breathless with suspense and excitement.

It was a gigantic struggle between Lasker, holder for 27 years of the title of World Champion, hero of a thousand battles, and the greatest fighter ever produced by the game of chess, and Capablanca, the new Champion of the World, whose incomparable technique and smooth crystal-clear style made chess look like an easy game and not a bitter struggle.

It was a notable victory for Capablanca, worthy of the contestants and the occasion, and earned him a prize for brilliant play.

It was the only game lost by Lasker, who was then at the height of his powers, as evidenced by his winning first prize in so strong a tournament. The competition included such outstanding masters (besides Capablanca) as Alekhine, Marshall, Réti, Bogolyubov, Tartakover, and Maroczy.

The ending, conducted by Capablanca with classical precision, is in keeping with this great game, and eminently worthy of the masters engaged in its intricacies, undoubtedly the two finest endgame players of all time.

1	d2-d4	Ng8-f6
2	c2-c4	c7-c6
3	Nb1-c3	d7-d5
4	c4xd5	

Capablanca tries this move, which Marshall had played against Lasker in a previous round. Marshall obtained a winning position, but lost his way in the complications: Lasker wriggled out of his grasp, eventually giving up his Queen to force a draw by stalemate, a rarity in actual play.

4	...	c6xd5
5	Ng1-f3	Nb8-c6
6	Bc1-f4	e7-e6

Out of the multitudes of moves worthy of consideration, such as 6 . . . Bc8-f5, 6 . . . Qd8-a5, 6 . . . Qd8-b6, or 6 . . . Nf6-e4, the text is the safest.

7	e2-e3	Bf8-e7

This leads to a full-bodied game, in keeping with Lasker's style, whereas 7 . . . Bf8-d6 allows an exchange of Bishops which not only simplifies the position, but leaves Black with the inferior Bishop.

8	Bf1-d3	0-0
9	0-0	Nf6-h5

Clearly aiming to eliminate one of the Bishops.

10	Bf4-e5!	

This will force a break in Black's

Pawn position on the King-side, whereas 10 Bf4-g3 Nh5xg3 11 h2xg3 allows Black to go undisturbed about his business on the other side of the board.

10 ...   f7-f5

This is an improvement on 10 ... Nc6xe5 11 Nf3xe5 Nh5-f6 12 f2-f4 g7-g6 13 Qd1-f3, which enabled Marshall to whip up an irresistible King-side attack against Janowsky in their 1905 match.

Still better though, is 10 ... f7-f6, forcing the Bishop back to g3, the wild 11 Nf3-g5 being met by 11 ... Qd8-e8 12 Ng5xh7 (if 12 Bd3xh7+ Kg8-h8 13 Qd1-b1 f6-f5, and the gates are closed for the impetuous Bishop) 12 ... f6xe5 13 Nh7xf8 Be7xf8 14 Nc3-b5, Qe8-f7, and White has no attack to compensate him for the material so rashly given up.

11 Ra1-c1   Nh5-f6

The Knight returns, looking to anchor itself at e4, a strongly supported outpost.

12 Be5xf6

Man proposes, but Capablanca disposes!

12 ...   g7xf6

The best of the three ways to recapture, as 12 ... Rf8xf6 is met by 13 Nf3-e5, while 12 ... Be7xf6 allows 13 Nc3-a4 followed by 14 Na4-c5 with great pressure on the c-file, and the circumambient territory.

Capturing with the Pawn assures Black of control of the e5 square, and keeps any would-be intruders at bay.

13 Nf3-h4

The purpose could be to bring the King Rook into active play by 14 f2-f4 and 15 Rf1-f3, or to start a bayonet attack (*à la* Alekhine) by 14 g2-g4.

13 ...   Kg8-h8

14 f2-f4   Rf8-g8

15 Rf1-f3   Bc8-d7

16 Rf3-h3

A veiled threat of 17 Qd1-h5, followed by 18 Nh4-g6+ and 19 Qh5xh7 mate.

16 ...   Bd7-e8

Which Lasker easily shrugs off!

17 a2-a3

Just a little precaution. If White plays 17 Qd1-c2 at once, with a view to a powerful irruption by 18 Nh4xf5, the reply 17 ... Nc6-b4 would remove a valuable Bishop.

17 ...   Rg8-g7!

Black is on the *qui vive.* Not only is this a good defensive move, guarding the vital h-Pawn, but it clears the way for an attacking maneuver by ... Be8-f7 and ... Qd8-g8.

This is how things look:

Position after 17 . . . Rg8-g7!

18   Rh3-g3   Rg7xg3
19   h2xg3

Capablanca does not mind the doubling of his Pawns. In return he has an open Rook file for the convenience of his pieces.

19   . . .   Ra8-c8
20   Kg1-f2

And acts on it accordingly! The King steps aside, so that the Rook can swing over to the open file.

20   . . .   Nc6-a5

The Knight is on his way to c4, where he can exert pressure on the Queen-side.

21   Qd1-f3   Na5-c4

If White should now play 22 Nc3-d1, to protect the b-Pawn, the continuation 22 . . . Nc4xb2 23 Rc1xc8 Nb2xd3+ wins two Pawns for Black.

22   Qf3-e2   Nc4-d6

If there is one strategical concept that is the secret of much of Lasker's success, it is his faith in the power of centralization.

A careful study of Lasker's games shows that Lasker never embarks on quixotic adventures, no matter how strong the temptation, but centralizes his pieces instead (where their strength for attack and defence is at the maximum) and awaits developments.

23   Rc1-h1   Nd6-e4+

This is premature, according to Alekhine, and should be played after White's thrust 24 g3-g4, as then the Queen could not reach g4 (after the exchange by 25 Bd3xe4 f5xe4).

The play could go like this: 24 g3-g4 Nd6-e4+ 25 Bd3xe4 f5xe4 26 f4-f5 Be8-f7 27 Nh4-g6+ Kh8-g7 28 Ng6-f4 Qd8-d7, and Black can hold the fort.

24   Bd3xe4   f5xe4

If 24 . . . d5xe4 25 g3-g4 f5xg4, and White has the pleasant choice of pursuing the attack by 26 f4-f5, or by 26 Qe2xg4 f6-f5 27 Nh4xf5.

25   Qe2-g4   f6-f5

Practically forced, as after 25 . . . Rc8-c6 26 f4-f5 e6xf5 27 Qg4xf5, White has good winning chances.

Ending 38

Position after 25 . . . f6-f5

Lasker

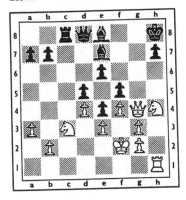

Capablanca to move

If White has any advantage in this position, it is not apparent to the naked eye. True, his Rook commands an open file leading to the King, but how to make use of it? If the Queen (which is attacked) moves to h3, the reply 26 . . . Be7xh4 27 Qh3xh4 (the capture by 27 g3xh4 closes the file) 27 . . . Qd8xh4 disposes of any danger to the King, while if White's first move is to retreat the Queen by 26 Qg4-e2, he loses a Pawn by 26 . . . Be7xa3 27 b2xa3 Rc8xc3.

Capablanca therefore evolves a plan, whereby he sacrifices a Knight for a couple of Pawns, *not for the sake of launching an attack, but to effect a transition to a favourable endgame.*

He visualizes, too, a change in the fortunes of his Pawns. Whereas they now seem to be condemned to inactivity, Capablanca's next few moves will make them spring to life, much as in the game against Bogolyubov at London in 1922 (see Game 34).

26	Nh4xf5!	e6xf5
27	Qg4xf5	h7-h5
28	g3-g4	

Considerably stronger than 28 Nc3xd5 (which allows Black at least a draw by 28 . . . Rc8-c2+ 29 Kf2-g1 Rc2-c1+, and an exchange of Rooks), this intensifies the attack, provides a flight-square for the King at g3, and maintains the option of capturing the d-Pawn. (A great deal for one little Pawn push to accomplish.)

28	. . .	Rc8-c6

The Rook takes up a good defensive post.

| 29 | g4-g5 | |

Even stronger was 29 Nc3xd5 (as indicated by Capablanca himself) with this continuation: 29 . . . Rc8-c2+ 30 Kf2-g3 h5-h4+ 31 Kg3-h3 Qd8-d6 32 Qf5-e5+ Qd6xe5 33 d4xe5 Be7-d8 34 Rh1-d1 Rc2xb2 35 e5-e6, and White wins.

Another line, analyzed in the Tournament Book, goes as follows: 29 Nc3xd5 Be7-h4+ 30 g2-g3! Rc8-c2+ 31 Kf2-g1 Rc2-c1+ 32 Kg1-g2 Rc1-c2+ 33 Kg2-h3 h5xg4+ 34 Kh3xg4! Be8-d7 35 Rh1xh4+ Qd8xh4+ (on 35 . . . Kh8-g8 36 Nd5-f6+ followed by 37 Qf5xd7 wins, while on 35 . . . Kh8-g7 36 Rh4-h7+ does likewise) 36 g3xh4 Bd7xf5+ 37 Kg4xf5 Rc2xb2 38 Kf5-e6! Kh8-g7 39 f4-f5 Kg7-f8 40 h4-h5 Rb2-a2

Ending 38

41 f5-f6 Ra2xa3 42 h5-h6 Ra3-a6+
43 Ke6-f5 Kf8-g8 44 Nd5-e7+ and
wins (after 44 . . . Kg8-f7 45 h6-h7
Ra6xf6+ 46 Kf5-g5 Kf7-g7
47 h7-h8(Q)+ compels the King to
abandon the Rook).

29   . . .   Kh8-g8

A more accurate defence (according
to both Alekhine and Capablanca)
was 29 . . . Rc6-d6, after which
30 g2-g4 Kh8-g8 31 g4xh5 Qd8-d7
32 Qf5xd7 Be8xd7, and Black's
Bishops could withstand the pressure of the passed Pawns.

30   Nc3xd5

White could have brought about the
foregoing variation by playing
30 g2-g4, but prefers to eliminate
one of the Bishops.

30   . . .   Be8-f7

31   Nd5xe7+   Qd8xe7

32   g2-g4   h5xg4

Lasker misses (or disdains) a drawing chance (according to the inde-
fatigable Alekhine) with this line:
32 . . . Rc6-c2+ 33 Kf2-g3 (but not
to f1 or g1, when 33 . . . Qe7-c7
subjects him to a mating attack by
. . . Rc2-c1+ and . . . Qc7-c2+)
33 . . . Rc2-e2 34 g5-g6 h5-h4+
35 Rh1xh4 Re2xe3+ 36 Kg3-g2
(of course not 36 Kg3-f2 Qe7xh4+
37 Kf2xe3 Qh4-e1 mate!—
beautiful!) 36 . . . Re3-e2+
37 Kg2-f1 Re2-e1+!, and Black
draws by perpetual check.

A picture of the position would seem to
be in order:

Position after 32 . . . h5xg4

33   Qf5-h7+   Kg8-f8

34   Rh1-h6   Bf7-g8

The exchange of Rooks seems safe
enough, a plausible continuation
being: 34 . . . Rc6xh6 35 Qh7xh6+
Kf8-g8 36 g5-g6 Bf7-b3 (but not
36 . . . Bf7-e6, when 37 g6-g7 wins
a piece for White, as the Queen
must capture the Pawn) 37 f4-f5
Qe7-c7!, and if 38 f5-f6,
38 . . . Qc7-c2+ 39 Kf2-g3 Qc2-c7+
40 Kg3-f2 (but not 40 Kg3xg4,
when 40 . . . Bb3-e6+ triggers a
mating attack) 40 . . . Qc7-c2+, and
White cannot escape the perpetual
check.

35   Qh7-f5+   Kf8-g7

If 35 . . . Kf8-e8 36 Rh6xc6 b7xc6
37 Qf5-c8+ wins a Pawn, while
35 . . . Bg8-f7 is unthinkable, the
penalty being a mate in two.

36   Rh6xc6   b7xc6

37   Kf2-g3

'A skilful King,' says Tartakover.
    This is definitely a better move

than 37 Qf5xg4, when 37 . . . c6-c5 offers good drawing chances. If then 38 f4-f5 Qe7-b7 is the reply, or if 38 d4xc5 Qe7xc5 39 f4-f5 Qc5-c2+ 40 Kf2-g3 Qc2-c8, and the open position should assure Black of saving the game.

37 . . .   Qe7-e6

This move leads to a lost endgame. Both Alekhine and Capablanca agree that Black might still have drawn by this line of play: 37 . . . Bg8-f7 38 Qf5xg4 (on 38 b2-b4, the reply is 38 . . . Qe7-e6, and the capture by 39 Kg3xg4 fails, as 39 . . . Bf7-h5+—a finesse possibly overlooked by Lasker—wins the Queen) 38 . . . c6-c5! 39 f4-f5 Qe7-d6+ 40 Qg4-f4 Qd6xf4+ 41 Kg3xf4 c5xd4 42 Kf4xe4 (or 42 e3xd4 Bf7-d5, and White's King is tied to the enemy King Pawn for ever after) 42 . . . d4xe3 43 Ke4xe3 Bf7-b3!, followed by 44 . . . a7-a5 and 45 . . . a5-a4.

38 Kg3xg4!

Lasker missed this move in his earlier calculations, whereas Capablanca must have anticipated this hidden resource when he played g3-g4 at his 28th move.

The rest may be a matter of technique, but it is conducted by the World Champion with his own touch of elegance (and of course deadly accuracy).

38 . . .   Qe6xf5+

Black must exchange, as an attempt to counter-attack, say by 38 . . . Qe6-c4, is brusquely defeated by 39 Qf5-f6+, and mate at h6.

39 Kg4xf5   Bg8-d5

Let's have another diagram:

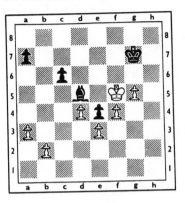

Position after 39 . . . Bg8-d5

40 b2-b4   a7-a6

41 Kf5-g4

Clearance for the Pawn's advance, and more accurate than 41 Kf5-e5 Kg7-g6 42 Ke5-d6 Kg6-f5 43 a3-a4, which should win eventually—but Capablanca never wastes a single move if he can help it.

41 . . .   Bd5-c4

42 f4-f5   Bc4-b3

43 Kg4-f4   Bb3-c2

44 Kf4-e5   Kg7-f7

45 a3-a4!   Kf7-g7

The Black Bishop can't dance at two weddings, not to mention three (Em. Lasker).

If 45 . . . Bc2xa4 46 Ke5xe4, and the three passed Pawns will be an irresistible force meeting a movable object.

46 d4-d5!

Capablanca is determined to secure one more passed Pawn, one way or another!

46 ...   **Bc2xa4**

or 46 ... c6xd5 47 Ke5xd5 Bc2xa4
48 Kd5xe4, followed by 49 Ke4-f4
and e3-e4, e4-e5, e5-e6, and Kf4-e5
with an easy win.

47   d5-d6   c6-c5

Necessary, if the Bishop is to stop
the Pawn.

48	b4xc5	Ba4-c6
49	Ke5-e6	a6-a5
50	f5-f6+	**Black Resigns**

GAME 39

White J. R. Capablanca
Black R. Réti
New York, 1924

French Defence

Capablanca was out for blood in
this game. If there was one man he
had to beat, it was Réti, for it was
Réti who had defeated him in
sensational style in the fifth round
of the tournament.

News of this upset had caused
great excitement, and word was
flashed to every corner of the world
that the mighty Capablanca had
lost a game—his first loss in eight
years!

In the opening and midgame of
this encounter, Capablanca could
make little impression, and create
no winning chances against Réti's
carefully-conducted defence.

But it was in the ending (Réti's
particular *métier* both as player and
composer of artistic endings) that
Capablanca fashioned a win out of
a position that looked for all the
world like an easy draw—an elegant
win out of pure air.

1   e2-e4   e7-e6

2   d2-d4   d7-d5

3   Nb1-c3

White has a great deal of choice at
this point:

(a) 3 e4xd5, Morphy's preference,

(b) 3 e4-e5, favoured by Steinitz
and Nimzowitsch,

(c) 3 Nb1-d2, the Tarrasch variation
(popular nowadays),

(d) 3 Nb1-c3, the Classical variation,
generally chosen by Capablanca.

The Knight comes into play
without blocking the Bishop's
development, protects the King
Pawn, and maintains the tension in
the center.

3   ...   Ng8-f6

4   Bc1-g5   Bf8-e7

5   e4-e5   Nf6-d7

6   Bg5xe7

I could not possibly imagine
Capablanca venturing on 6 h2-h4,
the Alekhine-Chatard attack, which
offers a Pawn for the sake of a

quick King-side attack.

A brilliant illustration of this is the Alekhine-Fahrni game, played at Mannheim in 1914, its first introduction in a Master Tournament.

6	...	Qd8xe7
7	Qd1-d2	

A strong move, though the theoreticians prefer 7 f2-f4, supporting the King Pawn, so that 7 . . . c7-c5 can be met by 8 d4xc5. This would enable White to use d4 as a base for his Knights.

7	...	0-0
8	f2-f4	c7-c5
9	Ng1-f3	Nb8-c6
10	d4xc5!	

Best, as castling allows counter-play by 10 . . . c5-c4.

10	...	Nd7xc5
11	Bf1-d3	f7-f6
12	e5xf6	Qe7xf6
13	g2-g3	Bc8-d7

Black misses an opportunity to equalize by 13 . . . Nc5xd3+ 14 Qd2xd3 Bc8-d7 15 0-0 Ra8-c8 16 Ra1-e1 Bd7-e8, as in the game (played many years later) Bhend-Christoffel, Zurich, 1961.

14	0-0	Nc5xd3
15	c2xd3	Bd7-e8
16	Rf1-e1	

Fixes his attention on the King Pawn, the only weakness in Black's position.

16	...	Be8-g6
17	Nc3-b5	

Either an oversight (strange as that might seem) or a transposition of moves.

The proper caper was 17 Nf3-e5, so that after 17 . . . Nc6xe5 18 Re1xe5, the square d4 is made available for the remaining Knight who can reach it by way of b5 or e2. It would be difficult for Black to get out of that bind.

17	...	e6-e5

Capablanca may have overlooked that 18 Nf3xe5 Nc6xe5 19 Re1xe5 loses a piece by 19 . . . Qf6-b6+.

18	Nb5-c3	d5-d4

'Useless finessing,' says Alekhine, who suggests instead 18 . . . e5xf4 19 Nc3xd5 Qf6-d6 20 Nd5xf4 Bg6xd3!, as depriving White of every hope of winning.

19	Nc3-e4	Bg6xe4
20	Re1xe4	e5xf4
21	Re4xf4	Qf6-d6
22	Ra1-e1	Rf8xf4
23	Qd2xf4	Qd6xf4

Réti simplifies at once—to his sorrow.

The safer line (though it was hard to foresee) was 23 . . . Qd6-d5 24 Qf4-e4 Ra8-d8! (but not 24 . . . Qd5xa2 25 Nf3-g5 g7-g6 26 Qe4-h4 h7-h5 27 Qh4-e4, and White wins, as after 27 . . . Kg8-g7 there follows 28 Re1-f1 (threatens 29 Rf1-f7+, and mate in two) 28 . . . Nc6-d8 (on 28 . . . Ra8-f8 29 Ng5-e6+ is decisive) 29 Qe4-e7+ Kg7-h6 30 Qe7-f8+ Kh6xg5 31 Qf8-f4 mate).

| 24 | g3xf4 | |

The difference is that the capturing Pawn will lend support to the Knight when it settles on e5.

24   ...   Kg8-f8

Clearly intending to follow up with 25 ... Ra8-e8, to dispute possession of the King file.

Ending 39

Position after 24 ... Kg8-f8

Réti

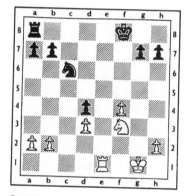

Capablanca to move

White's three isolated Pawns would seem to indicate that he has none the better of the position, except for the fact that they are immune from attack.

Capablanca, on the other hand, has a ready target in the adverse Queen Pawn whose defence will tie down Black's pieces, and give them no opportunity to become obstreperous.

His first move is evident enough ...

25   Re1-e4   Ra8-e8

Indirectly defends the Pawn, as 26 Nf3xd4 loses instantly by 26 ... Re8xe4 27 Nd4xc6 (if 27 d3xe4 Nc6xd4 wins a piece) 27 ... Re4-e2, while the exchange by 26 Re4xe8+ is pointless as it forfeits White's advantage in position.

Despite this, Alekhine disapproves of Black's last move, and recommends instead 25 ... Ra8-d8, and if 26 Nf3-g5 in reply, the simple 26 ... Kf8-g8 suffices.

26   Kg1-f2   h7-h6

'Also', says Alekhine, '26 ... Re8xe4 27 d3xe4 Nc6-b4 28 Nf3xd4 Nb4-d3+ (if 28 ... Nb4xa2 29 Nd4-c2 etc.) 28 Kf2-e3 Nd3xb2 30 Nd4-e6+ Kf8-g8! 31 Ke3-d4!, would have been more than questionable for Black. After the text move, Capablanca forces the win in an elegant manner.'

27   Nf3-e5

Now White threatens a winning simplification by 28 Ne5xc6 Re8xe4 29 d3xc4 b7xc6 30 b2-b4 (to isolate the Queen Pawn) 30 ... Kf8-e7 31 Kf2-e2 Ke7-d6 32 Ke2-d3 c6-c5 33 b4xc5+ Kd6xc5 34 f4-f5!, and Black runs out of moves, thus: 34 ... h6-h5 35 h2-h4 a7-a6 36 a2-a3 a6-a5 37 a3-a4 and it's all over.

27   ...   Nc6xe5

It was either this, or 27 ... Re8-d8, when 28 Ne5xc6 b7xc6 29 Re4-e5 (to restrain the Bishop Pawn) followed by 30 Kf2-f3 and 31 Kf3-e4, and a win for White is in sight.

28   f4xe5

And a passed Pawn appears on the scene!

28   ...   Kf8-f7

29   Kf2-f3

The King assumes a dominating position, intending eventually to reach the key square, e4.

Black, in contrast, is hampered by the passed Pawn, which requires his constant attention. ('The passed Pawn,' says Nimzowitsch, 'is a criminal, who should be kept under lock and key. Mild measures, such as police surveillance, are not sufficient.')

This is the position on the board:

Position after 29 Kf2-f3

29   ...   Re8-d8

What else was there against White's threats of 30 Kf3-f4, or 30 Re4-e1 followed by 31 Kf3-e4?

If 29 . . . g7-g5 30 Re4-e2 Kf7-e6 31 Kf3-e4 Re8-f8 (to prevent 31 Re2-f2 and Rf2-f6+) 32 Ke4xd4 Rf8-f4+ 33 Kd4-c5, and White wins easily enough.

Or if Black tries a King move, he

is driven back with loss of time, e.g., 29 . . . Kf7-g6 30 Re4-g4+ Kg6-f7 31 Rg4-f4+ Kf7-g6 (or 31 . . . Kf7-e6 32 Rf4xd4, and Black must not touch the King Pawn on pain of losing his Rook) 32 Kf3-e4 Re8-d8 33 e5-e6!, and Black is helpless against the multitude of threats following 34 Ke4-e5.

30   Re4-g4   g7-g5

31   h2-h4!

'White is in no hurry,' says Fine.

31   ...   Kf7-g6

32   h4xg5   h6xg5

Black has also acquired a passed Pawn—but it's a harmless little one.

33   Kf3-e4   Kg6-h5

34   Rg4-g1   Kh5-h4

35   e5-e6   g5-g4

36   e6-e7!

An artistic touch, in keeping with this fine ending, and more appropriate than the pedestrian 36 Ke4-e5 followed by 37 Ke5-f6.

36   ...   Black Resigns

The position at this point:

Position after 36 e6-e7!

Game 40

Réti, a composer of beautifully
subtle endgames, does not need
further demonstration, but gracefully concedes.

For us lesser mortals, though,
the continuation is appended:
36 . . . Rd8-e8 37 Ke4-f5! Re8xe7
(certainly not 37 . . . g4-g3, when
sudden death follows by 38 Rg1-h1
mate) 38 Rg1xg4+ Kh4-h5
39 Rg4xd4 Re7-e2 40 Rd4-b4!
b7-b6 41 d3-d4 Kh5-h6 42 d4-d5

Kh6-g7 43 Rb4-e4! (to enable
White's King to reach e6 and assist
the Pawn) 43 . . . Re3xb2
44 Kf5-e6 Rb2xa2 (on
44 . . . Kg7-f8 45 Ke6-d7 followed
by 46 Re4-f4+ will banish the King
from the vicinity of the Pawn)
45 d5-d6 a7-a5 46 Ke6-e7, and
White wins, as Black's Queen-side
Pawns are too far back to cause any
trouble.

A little jewel of an ending!

GAME 40

White J. R. Capablanca
Black W. P. Shipley
Simultaneous Display, Philadelphia,
1924

French Defence
Even in simultaneous play, where
he had only a few seconds to consider each move, Capablanca managed to turn out a goodly number
of masterpieces.

Personal friends were not spared,
nor those of high reputation in the
chess world.

In this game for example, Capablanca furnishes his lifetime friend
Walter Penn Shipley, 'The Dean of
American Chess for several generations', with an invaluable lesson in
the ancient and honorable art of
Pawn play.

1 e2-e4   e7-e6
2 d2-d4   d7-d5
3 Nb1-c3   Ng8-f6
4 Bc1-g5   Bf8-b4

The McCutcheon variation, a sharp

line of play whose drawback is that
the exchange of the King Bishop
leaves Black's King-side weakened.

5 e4xd5

Players who rejoice in either side
of the French can indulge themselves in the complexities attendant
on 5 e4-e5 h7-h6 6 Bg5-d2 Bb4xc3
7 b2xc3 Nf6-e4 8 Qd1-g4 Ke8-f8
9 h2-h4, and the double-edged
nature of the position would make
a computer despair.

5 . . .   Qd8xd5

6 Bg5xf6   Bb4xc3+

If 6 . . . g7xf6 (to hold on to the
two Bishops for a while) the continuation 7 Qd1-d2 Qd5-a5
8 Ng1-e2 Nb8-d7 9 Ne2-c1 Nd7-b6
10 Nc1-b3 Qa5-g5 11 a2-a3
Qg5xd2+ 12 Ke1xd2 Bb4-e7

13 Bf1-b5+ c7-c6 14 Bb5-d3
Bc8-d7 15 Nb3-c5 0-0-0
16 Nc5xd7 led to a complicated
midgame and an eventual win for
White in the game Capablanca-
Bogolyubov, New York, 1924.

Worthy of consideration though
(after 6 . . . 97xf6) is 7 Ng1-e2
Nb8-d7 8 a2-a3 Bb4xc3+ 9 Ne2xc3
Qd5-a5 10 Qd1-f3 c7-c6 11 0-0-0,
and Black has trouble extricating his
pieces, as occurred in the game
Vila-Mondragon at Siegen in 1970.

| 7 | b2xc3 | g7xf6 |

| 8 | Qd1-d2 | |

Introduced by Capablanca against
Alekhine at New York in 1924, this
move led to the better of the opening, and the gain of a Pawn, but
Alekhine managed to scrape through
with a draw.

| 8 | . . . | c7-c5 |

Suggested by Alekhine in his notes
to the game. There he played
8 . . . Nb8-d7, and came close to
disaster.

Shipley had a different reason
for playing 8 . . . c7-c5. He says,
'I played this move against the
Champion last March, and drew. I
do not know of any games in
which this move was played at this
stage of the game.'

(Shipley, incidentally, specialized
in the French Defence.)

| 9 | Ng1-f3 | |

Alekhine recommends 9 Qd2-e3 at
this point, but Capablanca goes his
own way—and gets a good game!

| 9 | . . . | Nb8-c6 |

| 10 | Qd2-e3 | |

Capablanca improves on his March
game with Shipley, where the play
went: 10 Qd2-f4 Ke8-e7 11 c3-c4
Qd5-d6 12 Qf4xd6+ Ke7xd6, with
a drawn result.

| 10 | . . . | c5xd4 |

| 11 | c3xd4 | Bc8-d7 |

| 12 | Bf1-d3 | Qd5-a5+ |

| 13 | Ke1-e2 | |

The King is perfectly safe here, and
beautifully placed for the ending
(which comes with frightening
rapidity).

| 13 | . . . | 0-0-0 |

| 14 | Rh1-b1 | e6-e5 |

'Don't simplify against Capablanca!,' I keep telling them at the
office.

| 15 | d4xe5 | Nc6xe5 |

| 16 | Nf3xe5 | Qa5xe5 |

| 17 | Qe3xe5 | f6xe5 |

Black must have been pleased at
having dissolved his doubled Pawn,
but his troubles have just begun, as
White's three remaining pieces
spring quickly to life.

Ending 40

Position after 17 . . . f6xe5

Shipley

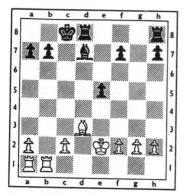

Capablanca to move

White has succeeded in maintaining the initiative, and the position is somewhat in his favor.

His King Rook attacks a Pawn near the enemy King, and this attack can be intensified by doubling Rooks on the Knight file.

Capablanca begins by striking at the vulnerable Pawn with his Bishop.

18   Bd3-e4   Bd7-c6

The only defence, as 18 . . . b7-b6 is met by 19 a2-a4 and 20 a4-a5, bringing all White's forces into play.

19   Be4xc6   b7xc6

Suddenly Black has two more isolated Pawns to worry about! He has four islands of Pawns against three of Capablanca's.

How does Capablanca always manage to have less Pawn islands than his opponents?

20 Rb1-b3!

Threatens to double Rooks and break into the seventh rank.

Black's next half-dozen moves are practically forced. He must offer to clear away all the Rooks, or suffer material loss quickly.

20   . . .   Kc8-c7

If 20 . . . Rd8-d7 21 Ra1-b1 Rh8-d8 22 Rb3-b8+ Kc8-c7 23 Rb1-b7+ Kc7-d6 24 Rb8xd8 Rd7xd8 25 Rb7xf7 Rd8-d7 26 Rf7xd7+, and the rest is a breeze, White being a Pawn ahead in a simple Pawn ending.

21   Ra1-b1   Rd8-b8

Here too, 21 . . . Kc7-d6 loses a Pawn, as after 22 Rb3-b7 Black dare not protect both his Pawns by 22 . . . Rd8-d7, for the reply 23 Rb1-d1+ would cost him a Rook.

22   Rb3xb8   Rh8xb8

23   Rb1xb8   Kc7xb8

The exchanges have forced Black's King one square further away from the center, and that could be dangerous, if not fatal.

24   Ke2-d3   Kb8-c7

25   Kd3-e4   Kc7-d6

This is the position:

Position after 25 ... Kc7-d6

Capablanca does not now bother to calculate the possibilities beginning with 26 Ke4-f5 Kd6-d5 27 Kf5-f6 c6-c5 28 Kf6-g7 Kd5-c4 29 Kg7xh7, with a view to queening his Rook Pawn (wherein both players Queen in ten moves), but instead plays to stifle any counter-chances, and bring his opponent into a state of *zugzwang*.

26   g2-g4!

This restrains the adverse King-side Pawns.

26   ...   Kd6-e6

This looks as though Black might just hold the position.

27   h2-h4   f7-f6

If instead 27 ... h7-h5 28 g4-g5 (certainly not 28 g4xh5 f7-f5+, and Black's situation brightens) 28 ... c6-c5 29 c2-c4 a7-a6 30 a2-a3 a6-a5 31 a3-a4 f7-f5+ 32 g5xf6 *en passant* Ke6xf6 33 f2-f4 (33 Ke4-d5 is also good enough to win) e5xf4 34 Ke4xf4 Kf6-g6 35 Kf4-e5 Kg6-h6 39 Ke5-f5 (or 36 Ke5-d5), and

White wins as he pleases.

28   f2-f4!

The key-move, which wins in all variations!

28   ...   e5xf4

Forced, as after 28 ... h7-h6 29 f4xe5 f6xe5 30 g4-g5 h6xg5 31 h4xg5, the outside passed Pawn wins easily for White.

29   Ke4xf4

Please note that the last *coup* left Black with four isolated Pawns.

29   ...   h7-h6

Forced, but it weakens the square g6, a circumstance of which White takes prompt advantage.

30   c2-c3!

This, and not 30 c2-c4, is the procedure for making Black's Queen-side pawns run out of moves.

30   ...   a7-a6

31   a2-a3   a6-a5

32   a3-a4   Ke6-e7

Or 32 ... c6-c5 33 c3-c4 Ke6-e7, and the same position occurs as in the game.

33   Kf4-f5   c6-c5

34   c3-c4   Black Resigns

After 34 ... Ke7-f7 35 h4-h5, Black's King will have to give way, and let White come in at e6 or g6, in either case winning a Pawn and the game.

Is chess really that easy?

As David Hooper and Dale Brandreth put it in their fine book *The Unknown Capablanca,* 'This is one of the many games won by

Capablanca, in which the end seems inevitable, not to say predestined, without his opponent's having made any apparent error.'

GAME 41

White J. R. Capablanca
Black M. Vidmar
New York, 1927

Ruy López

There is a crushing inevitability about Capablanca's play which makes it seem that the endgame begins with his very first move.

As early as the 15th move, Capablanca spies a weakness that he can pounce on in Vidmar's a-Pawn, which has been induced to advance two squares.

So, with all the pieces still on the board, Capablanca sacrifices a Knight (temporarily) in a combination to simplify the position and bring it to an ending.

His advantage is almost infinitesimal, but as Euwe says, 'Whether this advantage is decisive or not does not interest Capablanca. He simply wins the ending! That's why he is Capablanca!'

1	e2-e4	e7-e5
2	Ng1-f3	Nb8-c6
3	Bf1-b5	

White has only to make natural moves to get a strong position in the Ruy López opening—a good reason for its popularity.

3	. . .	a7-a6

This defence is very much favored, as it lets Black get his Queen-side Pawns rolling.

Equally good, and strongly recommended by Lasker, is straightforward development by 3 . . . Ng8-f6.

4	Bb5-a4	Ng8-f6
5	0-0	Bf8-e7

The Closed Defence (as distinguished from 5 . . . Nf6xe4, the Open Defence) aims at maintaining the Pawn at e5 as a strong point.

6	Rf1-e1	b7-b5
7	Ba4-b3	d7-d6
8	c2-c3	

A necessary precaution against the exchange of Knight for Bishop by 8 . . . Nc6-a5.

8	. . .	Nc6-a5
9	Bb3-c2	c7-c5
10	d2-d4	Qd8-c7
11	Nb1-d2	0-0

More aggressive is 11 . . . Bc8-g4, when the threat of winning the d-Pawn forces it to advance, locking up the position.

12	h2-h3	Na5-c6

This third attack on the d-Pawn will compel White to declare his intentions.

An interesting alternative is

12 ... Nf6-d7 followed by
13 ... Nd7-b6, bringing more
power to bear on the Queen-side.

13   d4-d5

Of course not 13 Nd2-f1 (heading
for e3) as 13 ... c5xd4 14 c3xd4
e5xd4 15 Nf3xd4 Nc6xd4
16 Qd1xd4 Qc7xc2, and Black wins
a piece.

13   ...   Nc6-d8

14   a2-a4!

A powerful thrust! It upsets the
balance of the Pawn position on the
Queen-side—to White's advantage.

14   ...   b5-b4

Yields the square c4 to the enemy
Knight, a circumstance that Capablanca will be sure to exploit.

The lesser evil was 14 ... Ra8-b8,
when 15 a4xb5 a6xb5 16 c3-c4! is
still in White's favor, one of the
benefits being his control of the
open a-file.

15   Nd2-c4!

A Knight for all seasons!
The Knight is in position to:

(a) settle down at b6, supported by
the a-Pawn,

(b) bear down on Black's center
Pawns,

(c) swing over to the King-side,
by way of e3.

15   ...   a6-a5

Vidmar is anxious to prevent
16 a4-a5, followed by 17 Nc4-b6.

According to Alekhine, this was
his best course, but he probably
had better chances with
15 ... Nd8-b7, when 16 a4-a5
Ra8-b8 17 Nc4-b6 is met by

17 ... Nb7xa5.
Now he falls victim to what
Capablanca called *'une petite com-
binaison'*.

This is how the board looks:

Position after 15 ... a6-a5

16   Nf3xe5!

A pretty offer, though it is just a
temporary loan.

16   ...   Bc8-a6

Of course if 16 ... d6xe5, the reply
17 d5-d6 wins the piece back at
once.

The text move prevents either
of White's Knights from moving,
but that's a minor inconvenience.

17   Bc2-b3   d6xe5

Black must capture, if he wants to
recover his Pawn.

18   d5-d6

A little move, but it accomplishes a
great deal. It will regain the piece,
open a diagonal for the light-
squared Bishop, and leave White
with the two Bishops for the better
ending.

18   ...   Be7xd6

19   Qd1xd6

Simpler than 19 Nc4xd6, when
19 . . . c5-c4 might introduce un-
necessary complications.

19   . . .   Qc7xd6

Forced, as the King Pawn was *en
prise.*

20   Nc4xd6   Nd8-b7
21   Nd6xb7   Ba6xb7

Ending 41

Position after 21 . . . Ba6xb7

Vidmar

Capablanca to move

White has a slight advantage in
position. He has the two Bishops,
and the prospect of an attack on
Black's Queen-side cluster of
Pawns. These, being fixed, are
particularly susceptible to attack.

White's weakness, if any, is his
e-Pawn, which needs further protection, but that can be remedied
easily enough.

22   c3xb4   c5xb4

Plausible enough, though it leaves
Black with a fixed, and consequently weak, a-Pawn.

Alekhine recommends the capture by 22 . . . a5xb4, but it is
none too appetizing. The continuation could be: 23 Bc1-e3 Nf6xe4
24 f2-f3 Ne4-f6 25 Be3xc5, and
the two menacing Bishops, to say
nothing of the passed a-Pawn, (and
the Pawn that White wins next
move), should assure the victory
for White.

23   f2-f3

Secures the e-Pawn, and clears a
path for the King's entrance into
the game.

23   . . .   Rf8-d8

Alekhine suggests instead
23 . . . Nf6-d7 24 Bc1-e3 Rf8-c8
25 Re1-d1 Rc8-c7 as tenable, but
if we continue with 26 Rd1-d6
Ra8-d8 27 Ra1-d1, the threat of
28 Be3-b6 winning a piece cannot
be adequately met.

24   Bc1-e3   h7-h6

'What for?' asks Alekhine.

Answering Alekhine's query, one
purpose of the move is to provide a
flight-square for the King, a measure
often necessary in endings with
Rooks on the board.

(Sudden mate on the last rank
has caught many an eminent
player.) As example:

If Black tries to oppose Rooks
instead by 24 . . . Ra8-a6 25 Re1-d1
Ra6-d6, then 26 Be3-b6 Rd6xd1+
27 Ra1xd1 Rd8-a8 28 Bb6xa5
wins a Pawn, as 28 . . . Pa8xa5
allows mate on the back rank.

25   Re1-d1   Bb7-c6

26	Ra1-c1	Bc6-e8
27	Kg1-f2	

The King moves closer to the center, in order to take an active part in the ending. Should there be a general exchange of pieces, his role increases in importance.

There is also a threat involved, the execution of which requires that the Bishop be protected, to wit: 28 Rd1xd8 Ra8xd8 29 Rc1-c5 Rd8-d3 30 Bb3-c2, and White will remove a Pawn or two.

27	...	Rd8xd1
28	Rc1xd1	Ra8-c8

Black's Rook now controls an open file, but strangely enough it has no decent point of entry.

This is the position:

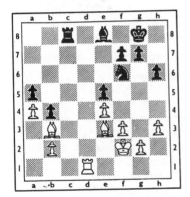

Position after 28 ... Ra8-c8

29 g2-g4!

With two noble thoughts: (1) to dislodge the Knight from his strong post by 30 h3-h4 next move, followed by 31 g4-g5, which would enable White's Rook to reach d5, and (2) to prevent Black's Knight from shifting over to f4 by way of h5.

29	...	Be8-d7

Good moves are getting scarce!

If 29 ... g7-g5, the reply 30 h3-h4 allows a convincing breakthrough. Or if 29 ... Nf6-d7 30 Rd1-d5 Rc8-a8 31 Rd5-b5!, after which 32 Bb3-d5 will dislodge the Rook from the a-file.

Alekhine's comment on Vidmar's move is, 'The last mistake, as 29 ... Kg8-f8 prolongs the agony.'

Not for long though, Monsieur Alekhine, as the consequences would be 30 Be3-b6 Nf6-d7 31 Bb6xa5 (the b-Pawn is now under threat of capture with check) 31 ... Nd7-c5 32 Ba5xb4 Kf8-g8 33 Bb4xc5 (of course not 33 Rd1-c1, to put pressure on the pin, as Nc5-d3+ would be an unpleasant surprise) 33 ... Rc8xc5 34 Rd1-d5, and White wins easily.

Or if 29 ... Kg8-f8 30 Be3-b6 Rc8-a8 31 Rd1-d8 Ra8-a6 32 Bb6-c5+ Kf8-g8 33 Bc5-e7, and White wins a piece.

30 Be3-b6

Finally! This move has been hanging in the air a long time.

30	...	Bd7-e6

The alternative is the meek 30 ... Rc8-a8, and that succumbs to 31 Bb6-c7 (simpler than 31 Rd1-c1 and 32 Rc1-c5) and Black's Rook cannot be in two places at once to guard the two Pawns under attack by the Bishop.

31	Bb3xe6	f7xe6

Nothing is to be gained by interposing 31 ... Rc8-c2+, as after 32 Kf2-e3 f7xe6 33 Rd1-d2, the

Rook must leave the premises.

32   Rd1-d8!

Clever simplification, after which Black's Knight will be no match for the fleet-footed Bishop.

32   ...   Rc8xd8

33   Bb6xd8   Nf6-d7

The Knight rushes towards the Queen-side to try to pick up a Pawn or two.

34   Bd8xa5   Nd7-c5

This is the state of affairs:

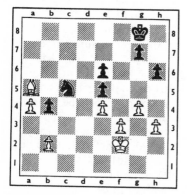

Position after 34 . . . Nd7-c5

35   b2-b3!

Capablanca finishes (as always) with cool elegance, and the accuracy for which he is famed.

Alekhine makes an interesting comment at this point. He says, 'In a clearly winning position, Capablanca always plays the most precise moves. Naturally, there was also a win by 35 Ba5xb4 Nc5xa4 36 b2-b3 Na4-b6 37 Bb4-d6 Nb6-d7 38 Kf2-e3, and this was easy enough.'

Alas and alack! Alekhine, who gives Capablanca none the best of it in his notes to the New York 1927 Tournament Book, commits several inaccuracies in annotating this game, and here he finishes with a dreadful howler.

After his suggested 35 . . . Ba5xb4, Black simply replies by 35 . . . Nc5-d3+ and wins the Bishop by a Knight fork!

35   ...   Nc5xb3

This Pawn is unimportant. It's the passed Pawn that counts!

36   Ba5xb4   Nb3-d4

37   a4-a5   Black Resigns

There could follow 37 . . . Nd4-b5 38 a5-a6 Nb5-c7 39 a6-a7 Kg8-f7 40 Bb4-d6 Nc7-a8 41 Bd6xe5, and Black cannot meet his opponent's threats of winning the Pawns on one side of the board, or the Knight on the other.

A clear-cut simple ending—as Capablanca plays it!

GAME 42

White A. Nimzowitsch
Black J. R. Capablanca
New York, 1927

Caro-Kann Defence

The various ways in which Capablanca defeated each of his opponents in the great New York International Chess Tournament of 1927 reveals fascinating facets of his style.

If there is perfection in opening play, it appears in Capablanca's second-round encounter with Nimzowitsch, where superior development enables him to launch a powerful King-side attack, complete with a Queen-sacrifice (in the notes) and a Rook-sacrifice (in the actual game).

In the fifth round, Capablanca offers Alekhine, his chief rival, no opportunities to indulge in delicious complexities, but smothers even a *soupçon* of attack before it gets started.

In the sixth round, Capablanca toys with Marshall in the ending, in a bit of cat-and-mouse play.

In the twelfth round, Capablanca disposes of Spielmann in classic style, in a game of such attractive elegance as to have it awarded the First Brilliancy Prize.

In the thirteenth round, Capablanca exploits a positional advantage so gradually against Vidmar, that his opponent hardly feels the pain of losing (see Game 41).

And then there is this beauty, where Nimzowitsch is systematically squeezed to death with the very weapons—Centralization, Control of the White Squares, and (most fearsome of all) *zugzwang*—whose powers he so admirably elucidates in his books.

It is a masterpiece, the best of its kind.

1	e2-e4	c7-c6
2	d2-d4	d7-d5
3	e4-e5	

This may not be so strong as 3 Nb1-c3, a developing move, but it suits Nimzowitsch's preference for close positions, and the thrusting of a wedge into the opponent's game.

3	...	Bc8-f5
4	Bf1-d3	

Nimzowitsch offers an exchange that results in weakening his white squares, removing as it does the chief defender of those squares.

A better way to develop his King-side was by 4 Ng1-e2 followed by 5 Ne2-g3

4	...	Bf5xd3
5	Qd1xd3	e7-e6
6	Nb1-c3	Qd8-b6
7	Ng1-e2	c6-c5

Strikes at the base of the Pawn chain (strategy recommended by Nimzowitsch himself) and clears a square for the Queen Knight.

8	d4xc5	Bf8xc5
9	0-0	

The attack by 9 Qd3-g3 Ng8-e7
10 Qg3xg7 is easily repulsed by
10 . . . Rh8-g8 11 Qg7xh7 Rg8xg2,
with advantage to Black.

9	. . .	Ng8-e7
10	Nc3-a4	Qb6-c6
11	Na4xc5	Qc6xc5
12	Bc1-e3	Qc5-c7
13	f2-f4	

Practically forced, but it limits
the scope of his Bishop, and accentuates the weakness of his white
squares.

13 . . . Ne7-f5

Capablanca seizes the opportunity
to plant a piece on a vital square.

   True, the Knight can be driven
off by 14 g2-g4, but at the risk of
exposing the King to attack.

14 c2-c3

Nimzowitsch may have wanted to
activate his Queen, now tied down
to the defence of the Bishop Pawn,
but his play is timid when it should
be aggressive, and aggressive (two
moves later) when it should be
timid.

   A better course (given the benefit
of hindsight) was 14 Ra1-c1!
Nb8-c6 15 Be3-f2 h7-h5 16 c2-c4
d5xc4 17 Qd3xc4 0-0 18 Rf1-d1.

14 . . . Nb8-c6

Capablanca has developed all his
pieces now, and is prepared to
castle on either side.

   Black can also postpone castling,
and in the event of a general exchange of pieces benefit by the fact
that his King is well placed in the
center for the ensuing endgame.

15	Ra1-d1	g7-g6

One would expect 15 . . . h7-h5, to
prevent the Knight being evicted from
its present strong position.

   But *Capablanca's play is flexible.*
He permits the Knight to be driven
off, as he is always ready to exchange one advantage for another.

16 g2-g4

While Alekhine graces this move
with two question marks, and calls
it 'an unbelievable maneuver for a
player of Nimzowitsch's class', the
line that he suggests—16 Be3-f2
h7-h5 17 Rd1-d2 followed by
18 Rf1-c1 and an eventual c3-c4—
is hardly inspired to invite confidence. Black's Knight would then
stand a tower of strength at f5
(supported if necessary by the
other Knight), while the only weak
square in Black's position, f6,
could not be approached by White.

16	. . .	Nf5xe3
17	Qd3xe3	

This is the situation:

Position after 17 Qd3xe3

17	. . .	h7-h5

18   g4-g5

Forced, as after 18 h2-h3 there
follows 18 . . . h5xg4 19 h3xg4
0-0-0, and Black's threats of
20 . . . Rh8-h4 or 20 . . . g6-g5
are decisive.

White's position on the King-
side is now full of holes, the consequence of his Pawns being too
far advanced.

18   . . .   0-0

Perhaps surprising, in view of the
weak black squares in the King-side
position. *But these are weaknesses
only if they can be exploited,* and
White has no means of obtaining
control of these squares.

19   Ne2-d4   Qc7-b6

20   Rf1-f2   Rf8-c8

21   a2-a3

'A new weakness,' says Alekhine,
though he admits that it can easily
be forced.

21   . . .   Rc8-c7

22   Rd1-d3   Nc6-a5

The Knight seems headed for a
strong post at c4, but as that would
block the action of his Rooks on
the file, Capablanca decides two
moves later to bring the Knight
back to greener pastures on the
King-side.

Meanwhile, the Knight's excursion might provoke a new weakness and Black can afford the loss
of a couple of moves if it doesn't.

23   Rf2-e2   Ra8-e8

Guards against a breakthrough by
24 f4-f5 e6xf5 25 e5-e6, and
White might become obstreperous.

Black must resist the

temptation (instead of the text
move) to win a Pawn by
23 . . . Na5-c4 24 Qe3-f2 Nc4xa3,
as White does not play 25 b2xa3
Qb6-b1+ losing his Rook for the
Knight, but turns the tables by
25 f4-f5 g6xf5 26 g5-g6 f7xg6
27 Rd3-g3 Na3-c4 38 Rg3xg6+
Kg8-f7 29 Qf2-g3, and White
wins.

24   Kg1-g2   Na5-c6!

The plot begins to reveal itself.
The Knight is on its way to f5,
there to force an exchange of
Knights.

Meanwhile, Black's Rooks will
occupy the c-file, one of them
settling down at c4, where it can
menace the Pawns along White's
fourth rank.

25   Re2-d2

Alekhine's comment on this move
is somewhat cryptic: 'Much better
practical drawing chances were
offered in this continuation:
25 Nd4xc6 Qb6xc6! 26 Rd3-d4
(but not 26 Qe3xa7 b7-b6
27 Qa7-a6 Re8-a8 etc.) whereby
the opponent is punished to a
certain extent for the inaccuracy
of his 22nd move. In any case,
with best play, he should still win.'

Question: how is he punished if
he still wins?

25   . . .   Re8-c8

26   Rd2-e2   Nc6-e7!

'This begins the final phase,' says
Alekhine, 'that Capablanca dispatches with accuracy. For students
it has a considerable didactic value,'
he adds grudgingly.

27   Re2-d2   Rc7-c4!

Initiates decisive action against
(strangely enough) the well-
protected (yes, over-protected!)
point at d4!

28   Qe3-h3

A cunning little move (though
Alekhine doesn't care for it) which
prevents 28 . . . Ne7-f5. The reply
29 Nd4xf5 would come instantly,
as the recapture would cost Black
either the d-Pawn or the h-Pawn.

28   . . .   Kg8-g7!

Black in turn prevents an irruption
by 29 f4-f5, as then 29 . . . g6xf5
30 Qh3xh5 Rc8-h8 would be to
Black's advantage.

29   Rd2-f2   a7-a5

30   Rf2-e2

Ending 42

Position after 30 Rf2-e2

Capablanca to move

Nimzowitsch

Capablanca has a positional advantage—barely discernible to the

naked eye.

He has a grip on the half-open
c-file, and the possibility of exploiting the weaknesses of his opponent's
white squares.

His plan is to use these squares
as stepping stones, to enable his
pieces to penetrate into the enemy
position. Once behind the lines,
these heavy pieces can gradually
squeeze the opponent into a state
of *zugzwang*—and submission.

30   . . .   Ne7-f5!

It is important to do away with
White's strongly-placed Knight in
order to make progress.

31   Nd4xf5+

On 31 Re2-d2 instead, the continuation 31 . . . Nf5xd4 32 Rd3xd4
(best) Rc4xd4 33 c3xd4 Rc8-c4
34 Qh3-e3 a5-a4, leaves Black with
two positional trumps—undisputed
control of the c-file, and a new
target for attack in White's weak
d-Pawn.

31   . . .   g6xf5

White had hoped to prevent this
way of recapture when he played
28 Qe3-h3, only to discover to his
dismay that 32 Qh3xh5 (the move
he depended on) succumbs to
32 . . . Rc8-h8 (now we see the
reason for 28 . . . Kg8-g7!)
33 Qh5-f3 Rh8-h4, winning in
every variation, thus:

(a) 34 Rd3-d4 Rh4-g4+ 35 Kg2-h1
Qb6xd4! 36 c3xd4 Rc4-c1+ and
quick mate,

(b) 34 Rd3-d4 Rh4-g4+ 35 Kg2-f2
Rc4xd4 36 c3xd4 Qb6xd4+
37 Qf3-e3 (*best*) Rg4xf4+ and wins,

(c) 34 Rd3-d4 Rh4-g4+ 35 Kg2-f1 Rc4xd4 36 c3xd4 Qb6xd4 37 Re2-f2 Qd4-c4+ 38 Qf3-e2 Qc4-c1+ 39 Qe2-e1 Rg4-g1+, and Black wins the Queen.

Black of course had no need to calculate this in detail. The pressure of the two Rooks (after 33 . . . Rh8-h4) on the f-Pawn would be enough to bring about the collapse of White's position.

32	Qh3-f3	Kg7-g6
33	Re2-d2	Rc4-e4!

Centralizes one Rook, and at the same time makes room for the other one to anchor itself at c4.

| 34 | Rd3-d4 | Rc8-c4 |

Doubles Rooks (and the pressure) on White's fourth rank.

Black's purpose, according to Capablanca, is to force a second exchange in order to work his Queen into White's position.

'Whether White exchanges the Rooks now or later,' he says, 'he always loses because of the fact that all the resulting Queen endings are lost for White, owing to the weak f-Pawn, and to the fact that the Black Queen can work her way into the open King's position of White.'

| 35 | Qf3-f2 | Qb6-b5! |

This is the position:

Position after 35 . . . Qb6-b5!

| 36 | Kg2-g3 |

More resistance was offered by 36 Rd4xc4 Qb5xc4 37 Rd2-d4 Qc4-b3, though it still left Black with much the better game.

| 36 | . . . | Rc4xd4 |
| 37 | c3xd4 | |

Clearly forced, as after 37 Rd2xd4, Re4-e2 comes in with irresistible effect.

| 37 | . . . | Qb5-c4 |

The Queen comes closer, this time taking possession of the only open file.

| 38 | Kg3-g2 |

White's difficulty is finding moves that do not abandon the two weaklings on his fourth rank.

If he tries 38 Qf2-g1, he may suffer this fate: 38 . . . h5-h4+ 39 Kg3xh4 (on 39 Kg3-f3, Qc4-b3+ wins the f-Pawn—as a start) 39 . . . Re4xf4+ 40 Kh4-h3 Qc4-b3+, and White must decide whether to lose his Queen by 41 Kh3-g2 Rf4-g4+, or by

41 Qg1-g3 Rf4-f3.

38 ... b7-b5

Before closing in on the foe, Capablanca eliminates any superfluous elements, strategy that is characteristic of his style.

39 Kg2-g1 b5-b4
40 a3xb4 a5xb4
41 Kg1-g2 Qc4-c1!

A paralyzing move, the first in a series that leave Nimzowitsch's pieces unable to stir without incurring loss.

42 Kg2-g3

About all that is left! A move by the Queen costs the Rook, while a move by the Rook forfeits the valuable f-Pawn (and the game, of course), while if 42 h2-h3 b4-b3 43 Kg2-h2 Re4-e1 44 Kh2-g2 Qc1-b1 45 Rd2-e2 Re1-c1 followed by 46 ... Rc1-c2 wins for Black.

White's King-move however, permits the Queen to make a problem-like move, and clears the way for further invasion by the Rook.

42 ... Qc1-h1!

43 Rd2-d3

If White tries to exchange Queens or Rooks, this is the consequence:

(a) 43 Rd2-e2 Re4xe2 44 Qf2xe2 Qh1-g1+, and wins the Queen Pawn.

(b) 43 Qf2-g2 Qh1xg2+ 44 Kg3xg2 (or 44 Rd2xg2 Re4xd4) 44 ... Re4xf4, and wins.

(c) 43 Qf2-f3 h5-h4+ 44 Kg3-f2 Qh1-e1+, and Black wins a Rook.

43 ... Re4-e1

And faces White with the threat of 44 ... Re1-f1 45 Qf2-e3 Rf1-g1+, and Black wins the Queen or forces mate.

44 Rd3-f3 Re1-d1

White is running short of moves in a position that is rapidly becoming untenable.

If 45 Kg3-h3 Rd1-d2 46 Qf2-g3 and 46 ... h5-h4 administers a fatal blow.

Or if 45 Rf3-b3 Qh1-e4 46 Rb3xb4 Rd1-d3+ 47 Kg3-h4, and 47 ... Rd3-f3 is conclusive.

Finally, if 45 h2-h3 Re1-g1+ 46 Kg3-h4 Rg1-g4 is checkmate.

45 b2-b3 Rd1-c1!

This is *Zugzwang* with a capital Z! As pretty and powerful in its effects as any *zugzwang* ever perpetrated by Nimzowitsch himself.

The proof: If

(a) 46 Kg3-h4 Rc1-c2 47 Qf2xc2 Qh1xf3 48 h2-h3 Qf3xf4 mate.

(b) 46 h2-h3 Rc1-g1+ 47 Kg3-h4 Rg1-g4 mate (pretty!).

(c) 46 Qf2-e2 Rc1-c2! 47 Qe2xc2 h5-h4+ 48 Kg3xh4 Qh1xf3 49 h2-h3 Qf3xf4 mate.

(d) 46 Qf2-d2 h5-h4+ 47 Kg3xh4 (or 47 Kg3-f2 Rc1-f1+ and mate next) 47 ... Qh1xf3, and Black mates in two.

46 Rf3-e3 Rc1-f1

This is the Rook's fourth move in a row, and this one is a killer!

There is no defence. If, for example, 47 Qf2-e2, there follows 47 ... Qh1-g1+ 48 Kg3-h3 Rf1-f2, and Black mates next move.

47   White Resigns

A magnificent game, it won a special prize for the best-played game of the tournament.

GAME 43

White J. R. Capablanca
Black A. Alekhine
World Championship, 29th Match Game, Buenos Aires, 1927

Cambridge Springs Defence
Capablanca won the third and seventh games of this match in blazing, combinative style—quite in the manner of his great rival, Alekhine.

But this game is pure, genuine, authentic Capablanca—the kind of game that only Capablanca could produce.

Capablanca applied pressure right from the start of the game. Alekhine was left with a lone, isolated Pawn on the Queen-side, and this Pawn fell on the 28th move. After a great deal of complex maneuvering, a position was reached where Alekhine had Bishop and three Pawns against Capablanca's Knight and four Pawns.

Capablanca was in his element, and handled the ending in his customary elegant style. His Knight dances about, preparing the way for the advance of his passed Pawn. Meanwhile, Alekhine's King is forced further and further back, until it can retreat no more.

Capablanca wins the ending as though he were demonstrating an endgame study.

It is as beautiful an ending as you will ever see, and richly deserves the adjective 'magnificent'.

1	d2-d4	d7-d5
2	c2-c4	e8-e6
3	Nb1-c3	Ng8-f6
4	Bc1-g5	Nb8-d7
5	e2-e3	c7-c6
6	Ng1-f3	Qd8-a5

Having been successful with the Cambridge Springs line in the 11th game of the match, Alekhine tries it again.

7	Nf3-d2	Bf8-b4
8	Qd1-c2	d5xc4
9	Bg5xf6	Nd7xf6
10	Nd2xc4	Qa5-c7
11	a2-a3	Bb4-e7

Black is willing to undergo the inconvenience of a slightly cramped position, for the sake of retaining the two Bishops.

12   g2-g3

In the 11th game, Capablanca developed the Bishop to f3 by way of e2. This might be a mite stronger, as the fianchettoed Bishop will not block the f-Pawn.

12 ...   0-0

On 12 . . . c6-c5 instead, the continuation 13 Bf1-g2 c5xd4
14 Nc3-b5, followed by 15 Nb5xd4 favours White.

13   Bf1-g2   Bc8-d7

14   b2-b4!

Prevents Black from freeing himself by 14 . . . c6-c5.

14   ...   b7-b6

An impatient attempt to obtain some counterplay by this and
15 . . . a7-a5, to break up White's Pawn position on the Queen-side.

Steinitzian defensive strategy was indicated here by
14 . . . Rf8-d8, 15 . . . Ra8-c8, and 16 . . . Bd7-e8.

15   0-0   a7-a5

'A surprising move for Alekhine to make,' says Winter.

Maybe surprising, but it offers White many chances to go wrong, thus: if

(a) 16 Ra1-b1 a5xb4 17 a3xb4, and Black controls the a-file,

(b) 16 Rf1-b1 a5xb4 17 a3xb4 Ra8xa1 18 Rb1xa1 Be7xb4, and Black has won a Pawn,

(c) 16 b4xa5 b6-b5 17 Nc4-b6 Ra8xa5, and White's remaining a-Pawn will not live long,

(d) 16 b4-b5 c6xb5! 17 Bg2xa8 Qc7xc4 18 Ba8-f3 b5-b4, and Black wins two pieces for a Rook.

Capablanca's reply is more than adequate, and changes the complexion of affairs.

16   Nc4-e5!

Avoids all tricks and traps with this move, which gains more control of the board, and threatens to win the c-Pawn by 17 Nc3-b5.

16   ...   a5xb4

17   a3xb4   Ra8xa1

Or 17 . . . Be7xb4 18 Nc3-b5 Qc7-d8 19 Bg2xc6 Ra8-c8 20 Rf1-c1, and White has much the better position.

18   Rf1xa1   Rf8-c8

Here too, 18 . . . Be7xb4 yields to 19 Nc3-b5, after which
19 . . . Qc7-d8 20 Bg2xc6 threatening 21 Ra1-a8 is not a pleasant prospect for Black.

This is the position:

Position after 18 . . . Rf8-c8

19   Ne5xd7

One may wonder why Capablanca exchanges a piece so beautifully posted as this Knight is, for a Bishop that has no mobility to speak of.

But two Bishops can become awfully dangerous, even when they seem to be doing nothing but quietly looking on.

19 ... Qc7xd7

Perhaps 19 . . . Nf6xd7 was better, to provide another defender for the b-Pawn (which needs all the friends it can get), but after 20 Qc2-b3 Black still has a hard game.

20 Nc3-a4! Qd7-d8

21 Qc2-b3 Nf6-d5

Black had two interesting alternatives:

(a) 21 . . . c6-c5 22 b4xc5 b6xc5 23 d4xc5 Be7xc5 24 Bg2-b7! Rc8-c7 25 Na4xc5 Rc7xc5 26 Ra1-a8, and White wins the Queen.

(b) 21 . . . b6-b5 22 Na4-c5 Be7xc5 23 b4xc5! Rc8-a8 24 Ra1xa8 Qd8xa8 25 Qb3xb5! c6xb5 26 Bg2xa8 b5-b4 27 Ba8-f3 b4-b3 28 Bf3-d1 b3-b2 29 Bd1-c2 Kg8-f8 30 e3-e4, and White wins.

22 b4-b5

A strong move which eventually wins a Pawn.

22 ... c6xb5

Or 22 . . . c6-c5 23 d4xc5 b6xc5 (on 23 . . . Be7xc5 24 Ra1-d1 wins a Pawn) 24 Ra1-d1 c5-c4 25 Qb3-c2, and White's passed Pawn, together with the annoying threat of 26 e3-e4, should assure him of the win.

23 Qb3xb5 Rc8-a8

The b-Pawn is doomed, and triply protecting it is of no avail. For example, if 23 . . . Rc8-b8 24 Bg2xd5 Qd8xd5 (on 24 . . . e6xd5 25 Na4-c3 wins the d-Pawn, after capturing which the

knight is ready to have the b-Pawn as dessert) 25 Qb5xd5 e6xd5 26 Ra1-b1 b6-b5 (or 26 . . . Be7-d8 27 Rb1-b5, and the d-Pawn falls) 27 Na4-c3 b5-b4 28 Nc3xd5, and White wins.

24 Ra1-c1

Carefully avoiding an attack on the Pawn by 24 Ra1-b1, when 24 . . . Ra8xa4! 25 Qb5xa4 Nd5-c3 regains the exchange and lets Black escape with a draw.

24 ... Ra8-a5

25 Qb5-c6 Be7-a3

26 Rc1-b1!

After which, Black must also avoid some traps!

If 26 . . . Ra5xa4 27 Qc6xa4 Nd5-c3 28 Qa4xa3 Nc3xb1 29 Qa3-b4, and the Knight's escape is cut off, with no help in sight.

Or if 26 . . . b6-b5 27 Rb1xb5 Ra5xa4 28 Rb5xd5 Qd8-a8 29 Qc6xa8+, and White is a Pawn up with good chances of scoring.

26 ... Ba3-f8

Renews the threat in a different form, e.g., 27 . . . Ra5xa4 28 Bg2xd5 Ra4-b4, and Black draws the game.

27 Bg2xd5 Ra5xd5

28 Na4xb6 Rd5-d6

Capablanca has won a Pawn, but the win is difficult, as all the Pawns are on one side of the board.

Ending 43

Position after 28 . . . Rd5-d6

Alekhine

Capablanca to move

White has managed to win a Pawn, but it will take patience and skilful maneuvering to reap the benefit of the extra material.

Capablanca's long-range plan is to post his pieces where they will be most effective, then at the most opportune time advance his center Pawns with a view to acquiring a passed Pawn on the d-file. This Pawn would then be escorted with the utmost care to the queening square.

| 29 | Qc6-b7 | h7-h5 |

How easy it is to go wrong in simple-looking positions!

For example, if 29 . . . Bf8-e7 30 Nb6-c8 Rd6-d7 31 Nc8xe7+ Rd7xe7 (on 31 . . . Qd8xe7 32 Qb7xd7! Qe7xd7 33 Rb1-b8+, and mate next) 32 Qb7xe7! Qd8xe7 33 Rb1-b8+ Qe7-f8 34 Rb8xf8+, and White wins the pure Pawn ending easily.

Black's last move provides the King with a flight-square, and assures his safety against threats of mate on the last rank.

30	Nb6-c4	Rd6-d7
31	Qb7-e4	Rd7-c7
32	Nc4-e5	Qd8-c8

Here too, the natural 32 . . . Bf8-e7 loses, this time by 33 Ne5-c6 Qd8-e8 (on 33 . . . Qd8-d5 34 Nc6xe7+ Rc7xe7 35 Rb1-b8+ followed by mate—did I say the King's safety was assured against threats of mate on the last rank?) 34 Rb1-b8! Rc7-c8 35 Rb8xc8 Qe8xc8 36 Nc6xe7+, and White wins Bishop, Queen, and game.

| 33 | Kg1-g2 | Bf8-d6 |
| 34 | Rb1-a1 | Rc7-b7 |

Alekhine sidesteps the plausible 34 . . . Qc8-b7 after which there comes 35 Ra1-a8+ Bd6-f8 36 Qe4xb7 Rc7xb7 37 Ra8-d8!, and the threat of winning the helpless Bishop will force Black to give up the exchange.

| 35 | Ne5-d3 | g7-g6 |
| 36 | Ra1-a6 | Bd6-f8 |

Safest, as protecting the Bishop by 36 . . . Rb7-d7 loses the Queen by 37 Ra6-a8, while 36 . . . Qc8-b8 loses a piece by the 'overworked Queen' theme: 37 Ra6xd6 Qb8xd6 38 Qe4xb7.

| 37 | Ra6-c6 | Rb7-c7 |

Black offers to exchange Rooks in lieu of undergoing other tribulations, such as:

(a) 37 . . . Qc8-a8 38 Rc6-c7

Rb7-a7 39 Qe4xa8 Ra7xa8
40 Nd3-e5, and White wins a Pawn,
or,

(b) 37 . . . Qc8-b8 38 Nd3-e5
(threatens 39 Ne5xg6 f7xg6
40 Qe4xe6+ Rb7-f7 41 Qe6xg6+,
and all Black's Pawns come off)
38 . . . Kg8-g7, and now not
39 Ne5xf7, nor 39 Ne5xg6, but
39 Rc6xe6 f7xe6 40 Qe4xg6+
Kg7-h8 41 Ne5-f7+ Rb7xf7
42 Qg6xf7, and Black can resign.

38   Rc6xc7   Qc8xc7

39   Nd3-e5

Threatens 40 Ne5xg6 f7xg6
41 Qe4xg6+, picking up three
Pawns for his Knight, and leaving
one weakling which is sure to be
won later.

39   . .   Bf8-g7

40   Qe4-a8+   Kg8-h7

41   Ne5-f3

Not only does this avoid an exchange of minor pieces which
would leave a Queen ending and a
probable draw, but it poses a new
threat, viz.: 42 Nf3-g5+ Kh7-h6
43 h2-h4 Bg7-f6 44 Qa8-g8
(intending 45 Qg8-h7 mate)
44 . . . Bf6xg5 45 Qg8-h8 mate.

41   . . .   Bg7-f6

42   Qa8-a6   Kh7-g7

43   Qa6-d3   Qc7-b7

44   e3-e4

With everything now in order,
White prepares to obtain a passed
Pawn on the d-file.

44   . . .   Qb7-c6

45   h2-h3   Qc6-c7

46   d4-d5   e6xd5

47   e4xd5   Qc7-c3!

This is the situation:

Position after 47 . . . Qc7-c3!

Alekhine offers to exchange Queens,
prompted by these considerations:

(a) an attempt to blockade the
passed Pawn by 47 . . . Bf6-e7
fails after 48 Nf3-d4 and 40 Nd4-b5.
Similarly, on 47 . . . Qc7-d6, White
can choose between 48 Qd3-c4
followed by 49 Qc4-c6, and
48 Nf3-d2 followed by 49 Nd2-e4,
dislodging the blockader;

(b) leaving Queens on the board
means guarding against a King-side
attack instituted by Queen and
Knight, as well as guarding against
the passed Pawn's advance;

(c) with Queens off the board, the
long-range Bishop would be more
than a match for the short-stepping
Knight. Added to this, the fact that
Capablanca favored the Bishop
over the Knight in similar types of
endings, may have influenced
Alekhine in making his decision.

In any case, it is a long-headed move, and is a fine illustration of Alekhine's genius for defence.

48 Qd3xc3

Capablanca does not avoid the exchange.

The Bishop may be the stronger piece in the ending, but *in endings where Capablanca has the Knight, the Knight is the stronger piece.*

48 ... Bf6xc3

The next part of White's plan is to maneuver his Knight over to c6, by way of d4, in order to keep Black's King from approaching the precious passed Pawn.

Before he can do that though, he must dislodge the Bishop—which explains his next two moves.

49 Kg2-f1 Kg7-f6

50 Kf1-e2 Bc3-b4

The Bishop is on its way over to c5, whence it can restrain the d-Pawn, and at the same time attack the f-Pawn, thereby tying the King down to its defence.

It is such use of the Bishop that supports the argument that the Bishop is superior to the Knight in most endings.

51 Nf3-d4 Bb4-c5

Obviously the King does not dare approach the Pawn by 52 ... Kf6-e7 or 52 ... Kf6-e5, on pain of a check by the Knight, lying in wait to pounce on both pieces.

52 Nd4-c6!

Dominates the proceedings! The King is kept at bay, away from the Pawn.

52 ... Kf6-f5

Black is not bereft of resources. If now 53 f2-f3, to stop 53 ... Kf5-e4, then 53 ... h5-h4! 54 g3-g4+ Kf5-f4 could be embarrassing.

53 Ke2-f3 Kf5-f6

54 g3-g4!

The only way to make progress, though an exchange of Pawns increases Black's drawing chances.

54 ... h5xg4+

55 h3xg4

This is the position:

Position after 55 h3xg4

55 ... Kf6-g5

The losing move, according to most critics, and Alekhine himself.

Such annotators and analysts as Becker, Panov, Euwe, Reinfeld, Golombek, Znosko-Borovsky, Gawlikowski, and Radulescu recommended 55 ... Bc5-d6 as drawing easily (some without submitting a shred of evidence to support the assertion).

Alekhine himself says that he could have drawn easily either with

55 . . . Bc5-d6 or 55 . . . Bc5-b6. He chose the text move as the simplest way to the draw, quite overlooking this pretty line: 55 . . . Kf6-g5 56 Nc6-e5 f7-f5 57 d5-d6! f5xg4+ 58 Kf3-g2! Kg5-f5 59 d6-d7 Bf5-b6 60 Ne5-c6 and wins.

If there is a draw after 55 . . . Bc5-d6, it is not easy! This is the continuation that would probably realize the win: 56 Kf3-e4 Kf6-g5 57 Nc6-e5 f7-f5+ 58 Ke4-d4 Kg5-f4 (but not 58 . . . Kg5-f6, when 59 g4-g5+ Kf6-g7 60 f2-f4 wins) 59 Ne5-f7 Bd6-a3 60 g4-g5! Kf4-f3 61 d5-d6 Ba3xd6 (if 61 . . . Kf3xf2 62 d6-d7 Ba3-e7 63 Kd4-d5 Kf2-g3 64 Kd5-e6, and the Pawn will Queen) 62 Nf7xd6 Kf3xf2 63 Nd6xf5 Kf2-f3 64 Kd4-e5 Kf3-g4 65 Ke5-f6 Kg4-h5 66 Nf5-e7 and White wins.

Now back to the game at Buenos Aires. It is White's 56th move in the 29th game for the Championship of the World.

56 Nc6-e5!

A powerful move, after which Black must lose his f-Pawn.

If, for example, 56 . . . f7-f5 57 d5-d6! f5xg4+ 58 Kf3-g2! (the move that Alekhine may have overlooked, probably counting only on 58 Kf3-e4 Bc5xd6 59 Ne5-f7+ Kg5-h4 60 Nf7xd6 g4-g3 and draws) 58 . . . Kg5-f5 59 d6-d7 Bc5-b6 60 Ne5-c6 and wins, as in the previous note.

Or if 56 . . . f7-f6 57 Ne5-f7+ Kg5-h4 58 d5-d6, and Black will have to give up his Bishop for the Pawn.

Finally, if 56 . . . Bc5-a3 57 d5-d6 Kg5-f6 58 d6-d7 Kf6-e7 59 Ne5xf7 Ke7xd7, and 60 Nf7-e5+ removes Black's last miserable Pawn.

A remarkable position!

Please note that in addition to the defences given, Black may not play 56 . . . Kg5-f6, nor 56 . . . Bc5-d6 on account of the resultant Knight fork.

Is the Knight really a stronger piece in the endgame than the Bishop?

56 . . . Bc5-d4

57 Ne5xf7+ Kg5-f6

58 Nf7-d8 Bd4-b6

The King may still not approach the Pawn, as after 58 . . . Kf6-e5 59 Nd8-c6+ Ke5xd5 60 Nc6xd4 Kd5xd4 61 Kf3-f4, the win is elementary.

59 Nd8-c6 Bb6-c5

How does Capablanca proceed now? If 60 Kf3-g3 Bc5-d6+ 61 f2-f4 g6-g5 wins a Pawn for Black, or if 60 Kf3-e2, Kf6-g5 61 f2-f3 Kg5-f4, and White makes no progress.

But Capablanca (being Capablanca) finds the master move that wins (which he must have foreseen long before).

60 Kf3-f4!!

Brilliant! With so little material on the board, Capablanca sacrifices a valuable Pawn!

60 . . . Bc5xf2

On 60 . . . g6-g5+ instead, White replies 61 Kf4-g3 followed by 62 f2-f3, setting up a barrier against an invasion by the enemy King. White is then free to bring

his King over to the Queen-side
and win the Bishop for his Queen
Pawn.

| 61 | g4-g5+ | Kf6-f7 |

Or 61 . . . Kf6-g7 62 d5-d6 Bf2-b6
63 d6-d7, and Black will have to
give up his Bishop.

| 62 | Nc6-e5+ | Kf7-e7 |

If 62 . . . Kf7-g7 63 d5-d6 Kg7-f8
64 Ne5xg6+ Kf8-e8 65 Kf4-e5 and
wins.

63	Ne5xg6+	Ke7-d6
64	Kf4-e4	Bf2-g3
65	Ng6-f4	Kd6-e7

66	Ke4-e5	Bg3-e1
67	d5-d6+	Ke7-d7
68	g5-g6	Be1-b4

The last hope. The hasty 69 g6-g7
allows 69 . . . Bb4-c3+ followed by
70 . . . Bc3xg7, drawing.

| 69 | Ke5-d5 | Kd7-e8 |
| 70 | d6-d7+ | **Black Resigns** |

A classic of endgame play, wherein
the Knight, directed by the pheno-
menal wizardry of Capablanca, gives
a virtuoso performance.

GAME 44

White J. Merenyi
Black J. R. Capablanca
Budapest, 1928

Sicilian Defence

In a quite original opening,
Capablanca prepares to fianchetto
his King Bishop at the second
move. Strangely enough, the
Bishop never does get to g7 in the
eighteen moves of its life.

Capablanca's King, sensing that
he is destined to have an important
role in the ending, starts out on his
journey as soon as the Queens have
disappeared from the board.

Faced with a decision at the
critical stage of the game, Capablanca cuts the Caissian Knot with
one swift stroke of his Rook, just
as Alexander of Macedon cut the
Gordian Knot with one swift
stroke of his sword.

1	e2-e4	c7-c5
2	Ng1-f3	g7-g6
3	c2-c3	d7-d5!

Black seizes the initiative—the
proper response to White's rather
timid third move.

4	Bf1-b5+	Bc8-d7
5	Bb5xd7+	Qd8xd7
6	e4xd5	Qd7xd5
7	d2-d4	c5xd4
8	Qd1xd4	Qd5xd4
9	Nf3xd4	e7-e5!

Capablanca establishes a Pawn in
the center. It is also the first step in
mobilizing his King-side majority
of Pawns, the side wherein he has

the advantage.

10 Nd4-b5

No doubt attractive, but the modest 10 Nd4-c2 followed by 11 Bc1-e3 and 12 0-0 was more to the point.

10 . . . Ke8-d7!

Merenyi may have expected 10 . . . Nb8-a6, a routine reply. Moving the King into the open at this early stage looks hazardous. If Merenyi thought so, he was grievously disappointed.

11 Ke1-e2 Kd7-c6!

'Alekhine's favourite weapon is the Queen,' says Znosko-Borovsky in *L'Echiquier*, 'swift and powerful, while the King, slow and weak, is the principal instrument in Capablanca's victory. Let us study for example, the games of the ex-Champion of the World during his stay in Europe. In most of these we find a great understanding of utilizing to the full the value of this piece in the endings.'

12 a2-a4 Nb8-d7

13 Bc1-e3 a7-a6

Not so much to frighten the Knight away (as 14 . . . a6xb5 is met by 15 a4xb5+) as to release the Rook that is now tied down to the Pawn's protection.

14 Rh1-d1 Ng8-f6

15 Nb1-d2 Ra8-d8

16 Nb5-a3 Nf6-d5

17 Nd2-c4 b7-b6

To prevent 18 Nc4-a5+, when White wins a piece—or more.

18 Rd1-d2 Bf8xa3!

Exchanging a powerful long-range Bishop for a Knight sitting on the sidelines may be surprising, but there is good reason for it, besides the obvious one that it prevents (or postpones) the doubling of White's Rooks on the Queen file.

19 Ra1xa3

If 19 Nc4xa3 (clearly 19 b2xa3 loses two Pawns by 19 . . . Nd5xc3+) 19 . . . Nd7-c5 (threatens 20 . . . Nc5-b3 winning the exchange as well as 20 . . . Nc5xa4) 20 Be3xc5 Nd5-f4+ 21 Ke2-e1 (or to e3) Nf4xg2+ 22 Ke1-e2 Ng2-f4+ 23 Ke2-e3 Rd8xd2 24 Ke3xd2 Rh8-d8+ 25 Kd2-e3 Kc6xc5 and Black wins.

19 . . . Rh8-e8

20 Nc4-d6

An ingenious attempt to get the Knight into more active play.

This is the situation

Position after 20 Nc4-d6

20 . . . Re8-e7

On 20 . . . Kc6xd6, the reply 21 c3-c4 regains the piece immediately.

21   c3-c4

But not at once 21 Nd6-e4, as then
21 . . . f7-f5 followed by
22 . . . f5-f4 traps the Bishop.

21	. . .	Nd5xe3
22	f2xe3	Nd7-c5
23	Nd6-e4	Rd8xd2+
24	Ne4xd2	

Ending 44

Position after 24 Ne4xd2

Capablanca to move

Merenyi

Here, as in so many of his endgames
Capablanca's advantage is almost
imperceptible. He does have a more
active Rook (White's being temporarily out of play), and his King
threatens to get to White's Queen-
side Pawns. But is that enough to
win?

The answer lies in one word—so
often the key word in the conduct
of an ending—*centralization*!

Capablanca bases his win on this
theme—*centralization*!

24   . . .   a6-a5!

It is important to forestall any
counterplay beginning with
25 b2-b4, an attack on the Knight.

25   Nd2-b1

The Knight is apparently heading
for c3, and a new start in life.

The alternative 25 Nd2-f3 does
not look promising, as after
25 . . . Nc5-a6 in reply, the threat
of 26 . . . Kc6-c5 is hard to meet.
White could not then move his King
to d3 (to protect the c-Pawn) nor
his Rook to d3 (to seize the open
file) as the Pawn fork 26 . . . e5-e4
would cost him a piece.

25   . . .   Re7-d7

Takes possession of the open file!
Black is now master of the situation.

26   Nb1-d2

White changes his mind, as the
sequel to 26 Nb1-c3 could be
Nc5-d3!, an attack on the b-Pawn.
This could not be met by
27 Ra3-b3, nor by 27 Ra3-a2, as
the Knight fork 27 . . . Nd3-c1+ in
response, wins the exchange.

Or if White plays 27 b2-b3,
Black replies 27 . . . Nd3-c1+
followed by 28 . . . Rd7-d3, and
something would have to give.

26   . . .   e5-e4!

Stifles a freeing attempt by
27 e3-e4, and sets up a support for
the Knight's entrance at d3.

27   Nd2-b3

The Knight has an eye on d4, a
fine spot from which it could not
be driven off. There it would inter-

fere with the Rook's pressure on the file, and prevent it from invading.

27	...	Nc5-d3
28	Nb3-d4+	Kc6-c5
29	b2-b3	

Here too, protecting the threatened Pawn by 29 Ra3-b3 or by 29 Ra3-a2 runs into a Knight fork 29 ... Nd3-c1+, impaling the Rook.

| 29 | ... | f7-f5 |
| 30 | Ra3-a1 | |

The Rook hastens to get back into play, everything apparently being securely protected.

But White is rudely awakened from this sweet dream of peace.

This is the position:

Position after 30 Ra3-a1

| 30 | ... | Rd7xd4! |

Destroys the centralized Knight, the key piece in White's defence!

Capablanca gives up Rook for Knight, in order to bring his King strongly into play.

In doing so, he follows his own advice, 'Time is of the utmost importance in the endgame. The fate of a game is often decided by a sacrifice which makes the Queening of a Pawn possible, or else by the fact that you are able to Queen one move ahead of your opponent.'

| 31 | e3xd4+ | Kc5xd4 |
| 32 | g2-g3 | |

Restrains the f-Pawn, but Capablanca will not long be denied.

| 32 | ... | g6-g5 |

Preparation for the advance of the Bishop Pawn, which would give him two connected passed Pawns.

| 33 | b3-b4 | |

Desperately trying to obtain some counterplay—to which attempt Capablanca pays no attention.

33	...	f5-f4
34	c4-c5	f4-f3+
35	Ke2-f1	e4-e3

Institutes a threat of winning by 36 ... e3-e2+ 37 Kf1-g1 f3-f2+ 38 Kg1-g2 e2-e1 (Q).

| 36 | Ra1-e1 | |

With the faint hope that his offer of a Rook for the Knight might divert Black.

| 36 | ... | b6xc5 |

Black merely goes about his business.

| 37 | Re1xe3 | |

But this cannot be disregarded.

| 37 | ... | Kd4xe3 |

Suddenly White's King is in a quasi-stale-mate position—and vulnerable!

| 38 | b4xa5 | c5-c4 |
| 39 | **White Resigns** | |

Merenyi could have a Queen for the

Game 45

asking (one move ahead of Black) but does not care to continue—as he knows how to count moves.

The play would go: 39 a5-a6 c4-c3 40 a6-a7 c3-c2 41 a7-a8(Q) c2-c1(Q) check and checkmate.

GAME 45

White A. Steiner
Black J. R. Capablanca
Budapest, 1928

Ruy López

A full-bodied game, interesting in the opening, exciting in the mid-game, and precise in the ending. For lovers of combination play, it is a game replete with diabolical pitfalls.

A great deal of activity takes place on the King-side and in the center, but the final decision comes about on the Queen-side.

Another of those great Capablanca games which are almost unknown, but which offer a goodly measure of entertainment and instruction.

1	e2-e4	e7-e5
2	Ng1-f3	Nb8-c6
3	Bf1-b5	a7-a6
4	Bb5-a4	d7-d6
5	c2-c3	f7-f5

Deceptively titled the Siesta Variation, this is far from a sleepy line of play.

6 e4xf5

Réti tried 6 d2-d4 against Capablanca a month later at Berlin, but was smashed to smithereens in 18 moves, like this:

6 d2-d4 f5xe4 7 Nf3-g5 e5xd4

8 Ng5xe4 Ng8-f6 9 Bc1-g5 Bf8-e7 10 Qd1xd4 b7-b5 11 Ne4xf6+ g7xf6 (three of White's pieces are now under attack) 12 Qd4-d5 b5xa4 13 Bg5-h6 (if 13 Qd5xc6+, Bc8-d7 wins for Black) 13 ... Qd8-d7 (definitely *not* 13 ... Bc8-d7 14 Qd5-h5 mate!) 14 0-0 Bc8-b7 15 Bh6-g7 0-0-0 16 Bg7xh8 Nc6-e5 (Black's pieces spring into action) 17 Qd5-d1 (guards his f3 square, as 17 Qd5-d4 runs into quick loss by 17...Ne5-f3+ 18 g2xf3 Rd8-g8+ 19 Kg1-h1 Bb7xf3 mate) 17 ... Bb7-f3! 18 g2xf3 Qd7-h3, and the two threats 19 ... Rd8-g8+ and 19 ... Ne5xf3+ cannot both be parried.

6	...	Bc8xf5
7	d2-d4	e5-e4
8	Bc1-g5	

Instead of this, 8 Nf3-g5! keeps Black on the run, a possible continuation being 8 ... Bf8-e7 9 0-0 Be7xg5 10 Qd1-h5+ Bf5-g6 11 Qh5xg5 Qd8xg5 12 Bc1xg5 Ng8-e7 13 Nb1-d2 b7-b5 14 Ba4-b3 d6-d5 15 Ra1-d1.

| 8 | ... | Bf8-e7 |

Page 194

9	Nf3-h4	Bf5-e6!
10	Bg5xe7	Ng8xe7
11	Qd1-h5+	g7-g6
12	Qh5-h6	Ne7-g8!

Delightful! The Knight leaps backward as the best way to drive off the troublesome Queen.

It is reminiscent of a similar move made by Steinitz in a famous game against Anderssen at Vienna in 1873, where this startling undevelopment of the Knight must have startled Anderssen out of his skin!

13   Qh6-f4

Against 13 Qh6-g7, Capablanca's analysis goes thus: 13 . . . Qd8xh4! 14 Ba4xc6+ b7xc6 15 Qg7xh8 0-0-0 16 Nb1-a3 e4-e3 17 0-0-0 e3-e2 18 Rd1-e1 Ng8-f6 19 Qh8-g7 Qh4-f4+ 20 Kc1-b1 Rd8-g8 21 Qg7-e7 Rg8-e8 22 Qe7-g7 Qf4xf2, and White's game is untenable.

13	. . .	Ng8-f6
14	Nb1-d2	0-0

This is the position:

Position after 14 . . . 0-0

15   0-0

On 15 Nd2xe4 instead, Black has the pleasant choice of winning by:

(a) 15 . . . Nf6xe4 16 Qf4xe4 Rf8-e8 17 0-0-0 (if 17 0-0, Be6-c4 wins the exchange) 17 . . . Qd8-g5+ 18 Rd1-d2 d6-d5, and White must abandon the Knight to its fate,

(b) 15 . . . Nf6-h5 16 Qf4-g5 Rf8-f4, and one of the Knights is marked for death.

15   . . .   d6-d5

Protects the e-Pawn, thereby threatening to win the offside Knight by 16 . . . Nf6-h5.

16   Qf4-g5

Practically forced, as 16 g2-g3 (which protects the Knight and provides it with a flight-square) costs the Queen after 16 . . . Nf6-g4 in reply.

But now White threatens 17 Nh4xg6 h7xg6 18 Qg5xg6+ Kg8-h8 19 Qg6-h6+ Kh8-g8 (if 19 . . . Nf6-h7 20 Qh6xe6) 20 Qh6-g6+, and forces a draw by perpetual check.

16	. . .	Nf6-h5
17	Qg5xd8	Nc6xd8!

This way of capturing is preferable to 17 . . . Ra8xd8, which allows 18 Ba4xc6, breaking up Black's Queen-side Pawns.

18   g2-g3

White secures a retreat for the Knight against the threat of winning it by 18 . . . g6-g5.

Of course this creates holes at h3 and f3 (weaknesses on the white squares) but as Nimzowitsch says, 'One cannot always be happy.'

18 ... Be6-h3

Capablanca doesn't wait for a second invitation!

19 Nh4-g2 Nd8-e6

The Knight leaps into the fray, with a view to further invasion by 20 . . . Ne6-g5 and 21 . . . Ng5-f3+.

Should White now try to free his game by 20 Rf1-e1, Black responds by doubling Rooks on the f-file, and concentrating his attack on the f-Pawn—which could not last long.

20 Ba4-b3 c7-c6

21 Bb3-d1 Ra8-e8

22 Bd1xh5 g6xh5

Black has been saddled with doubled Pawns—a temporary liability, as he cleverly undoubles them.

Meanwhile, Steiner has further weakened his white squares, by giving up the Bishop, their chief guardian.

23 f2-f4

A plausible attempt to free himself, obtain some counterplay, and prevent 23 . . . Ne6-g5. One drawback though, is that it transforms Black's e-Pawn into a passed Pawn.

23 ... h5-h4!

Not only does this get rid of a doubled isolated Pawn, but it initiates an exchange which further weakens White's Pawn position on the King-side.

24 Rf1-e1

Best, as 24 g3xh4 loses by 24 . . . e4-e3! 25 Nd2-b3 (if 25 Nd2-f3 Ne6xf4 is good enough

to win) 23 . . . Bh3xg2 26 Kg1xg2 Ne6xf4+ 27 Kg2-h1 e3-e2 28 Rf1-g1+ Kg8-h8 29 Nb3-c5 (to prevent 29 . . . Nf4-d3) 29 . . . Nf4-h3 30 Rg1-e1 Rf8-g8, and the Knight threatens mate next move (if 31 Nc5-d3 Re8-e3 wins).

Ending 45

Position after 24 Rf1-e1

Capablanca to move

Steiner

Black has slightly the better of it. His passed Pawn has a lust to expand, and he has a couple of Rooks with a great deal of potential power.

Capablanca plans to rip away the barrier protecting the adverse King, and expose him to a withering attack. Failing that would still leave him with the superior endgame.

24 ... h4xg3

25 h2xg3 Bh3xg2

The Knight must be destroyed! Otherwise it moves to e3, setting up a strong blockade of the passed Pawn.

26	Kg1xg2	Re8-e7
27	Nd2-f1	

Now *this* Knight is headed for the blockading square e3!

27	...	Re7-g7!

Puts an end to that little scheme, as he threatens 28 . . . Ne6xf4+, winning a Pawn.

28	Kg2-h1	h7-h5

New perils loom up, as 29 . . . h5-h4 next move would yield Black a Pawn or two.

Defence being difficult, White whips up an ingenious counter-attack to divert his opponent from the business in hand.

29	c3-c4	Ne6xd4
30	Re1-d1	Nd4-f3
31	c4xd5	h5-h4

Capablanca had originally planned to force a win by the brilliant 31 . . . Rf8xf4, but analysis showed that the move he actually played (31 . . . h5-h4) was more effective.

The sequel to 31 . . . Rf8xf4 would probably have been 32 c5xd6 (definitely not 32 g3xf4 when 32 . . . Rg7-g1 mates instantly) 32 . . . Rg7xg3 (threatens mate on the move with one Rook, and mate in two with the other) 33 Nf1xg3 Rf4-h4+ 34 Kh1-g2 Rh4-h2+ 35 Kg2-f1 e4-e3 (threat: 36 . . . Rh2-f2 mate) 36 Rd1-d8+ Kg8-f7 37 Rd8-d7+ Kf7-e6 38 Rd7-e7+! Ke6xe7 39 Ng3-f5+ Ke7-e6 40 Nf5xe3, b7xc6 41 Ne3-d1 Rh2-c2, 'and while Black should win, this line of play cannot be considered superior to

the method actually adopted in the game'.

(As Capablanca himself said once, 'It is not the prettiest move that should be played, but the most effective one, the move that will make your opponent resign the soonest.')

32	d5-d6	h4xg3

Threatens nothing less than immediate mate!

33	Kh1-g2	Nf3-h4+
34	Kg2-g1	g3-g2
35	Nf1-h2	Rf8xf4

White must choose his next move with the utmost care.

This is the position:

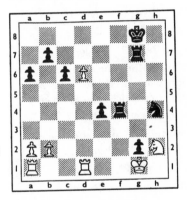

Position after 35 . . . Rf8xf4

36	Rd1-d4!

Steiner avoids the natural Pawn push 36 d6-d7, which loses by 36 . . . Rf4-f1+ 37 Nh2xf1 (if 37 Rd1xf1 g2xf1(Q)+ 38 Kg1xf1 Rg7xd7, and Black, with two extra Pawns, wins easily) 37 . . . Nh4-f3+ 38 Kg1-f2 g2-g1(Q)+ 39 Kf2-e2 Rg7-g2 mate.

36	...	Rg7-d7
37	Ra1-e1	Nh4-f5
38	Rd4xe4	

Obviously better than 38 Re1xe4 Nf5xd4 39 Re4xf4 Nd4-e2+, and Black gets his Rook back with heavy interest.

38	...	Rf4xe4
39	Re1xe4	Rd7xd6
40	Nh2-f3!	

Keeping the enemy Rook out of the seventh rank is clearly preferable to playing 40 Kg1xg2, when 40 ... Rd6-d2+ followed by 41 ... Rd2xb2 leaves Black in sight of a win.

40	...	Rd6-g6
41	Re4-e5	Nf5-d6
42	Re5-e2	Kg8-f8
43	Re2xg2	Rg6-f6

Keeping Rooks on the board offers more winning chances than reducing it to a Knight-and-Pawn ending.

44	Nf3-e5	Kf8-e7

The King comes towards the center, and the enemy Pawns.

45	Rg2-f2	Rf6-e6
46	Ne5-d3	Re6-e3
47	Nd3-f4	Nd6-c4
48	b2-b3	Nc4-e5
49	Nf4-g2	

There was more fight in 49 Rf2-e2 Re3-g3+ 50 Kg1-f2 Rg3-f3+ 51 Kf2-e1 Ke7-d6 52 Nf4-g2 Rf3-d3 53 Re2-e3 Rd3-d4 54 Ke1-e2 b7-b5 55 Re3-c3, and Black must work hard to break through.

49	...	Re3-c3
50	Rf2-e2	Ke7-d6
51	Kg1-f1	

A diagram for the last phase:

Position after 51 Kg1-f1

51	...	Rc3-c1+

This keeps the King from approaching the Queen-side, and also affords White two chances of going wrong: If

(a) 52 Ng2-e1 Ne5-d3 53 Re2-e3 Rc1xe1 54 Re3xe1 Nd3xe1 55 Kf1xe1 Kd6-c5, and Black wins an easy Pawn ending, or if

(b) 52 Re2-e1 Ne5-d3 53 Re1xc1 Nd3xc1, and Black wins another Pawn.

52	Kf1-f2	Ne5-d3+
53	Kf2-e3	Nd3-b4
54	a2-a3	

Necessary to save the Pawn, Black's threat being 54 ... Rc1-a1 55 a2-a4 Ra1-b1, and the b-Pawn falls.

54	...	Rc1-c3+!
55	Ke3-d4	Rc3-c2!

A nice finishing touch.

56	Re2-e1	c6-c5+
57	Kd4-e4	Rc2xg2
58	a3xb4	Rg2-g4+
59	Ke4-d3	Rg4xb4
60	Kd3-c3	

'A hope beyond the shadow of a dream.'

60	. . .	a6-a5
61	Re1-a1	b7-b6
62	Ra1-a2	Kd6-c6

63	Ra2-a1	Kc6-b5
64	Ra1-a2	a5-a4
65	b3xa4+	Rb4xa4
66	Ra2-b2+	Ra4-b4
67	Rb2-h2	Rb4-g4
68	**White Resigns**	

A masterly performance by Capablanca, this game was the theme of his last radio discussion given in December 1941.

GAME 46

White J. R. Capablanca
Black A. Rubinstein
Berlin, 1928

Queen's Pawn Game

Undaunted by Tartakover's aphorism, 'An isolated Pawn spreads gloom all over the chessboard,' Rubinstein cheerfully accepts an isolated Queen Pawn early in the game.

Capablanca's treatment of the situation is unusually instructive. In line with accepted strategy, he starts an attack against the isolated Pawn and its defenders.

Then he suddenly switches the form of his attack. He exchanges Queens, though it permits the Queen Pawn to be united with its fellows.

Characteristically, Capablanca has given up one advantage to secure another—for he now has a Rook posted on the seventh rank, behind the lines, a circumstance generally fatal for the Pawns in its sight.

Rubinstein cannot hold out long, but strangely enough, when he does resign, the miserable Queen Pawn is still on the board!

An outstanding performance by Capablanca, who avenges his defeat by the Polish Grandmaster in their first encounter in 1911.

1	d2-d4	d7-d5
2	Ng1-f3	c7-c5

With this move, recommended by Tarrasch, Black plays the Queen's Gambit, a move behind.

3	d4xc5	e7-e6
4	e2-e4	Bf8xc5

Of course not 4 . . . d5xe4 5 Qd1xd8+ Ke8xd8 6 Nf3-g5 Kd8-e8 7 Ng5xe4, with the better game for White.

5	e4xd5	e6xd5

Game 46

Black has a fine, free development to compensate for his isolated Queen Pawn—whose existence is justified by the fact that it dominates the center.

It is noteworthy that many players do not consider such a Pawn to be a weakness, but agree with Tarrasch, who said, 'He who fears to have an isolated Queen's Pawn should give up chess.'

6   Bf1-b5+

Capablanca is in a hurry to castle, and then get to work on the isolated Pawn.

6	...	Nb8-c6
7	0-0	Ng8-e7
8	Nb1-d2!	

Developing the Queen Knight at d2 instead of at c3 is Standard Operating Procedure in attacking the isolated Pawn. The Knight will swing over to b3 to restrain the Pawn, then to d4 to blockade it.

8	...	0-0
9	Nd2-b3	Bc5-b6
10	Rf1-e1	

The annotators find fault with this move, suggesting these alternatives instead:

(a) 10 h2-h3, to hinder the development of Black's Queen Bishop,

(b) 10 Bc1-f4 followed by 11 c2-c3,

(c) 10 h2-h3, in order to continue with c2-c3, Nb3-d4, and Bc1-e3, followed by pressure on the isolated Queen Pawn.

Capablanca disagrees with the annotators, stating that the object

of his move is to take control of the open file, and also prepare the eventual Bc1-e3, to get rid of the powerful enemy dark-squared Bishop.

'The text move,' he says, 'is an excellent move which could hardly be improved on in this position.'

10   ...   Bc8-g4

Threatens to win a Pawn by 11 ... Bb6xf2+ 12 Kg1xf2 Qd8-b6+.

11   Bb5-d3

This move is a mistake, according to Capablanca. He should have played 11 h2-h3, after which 11 ... Bg4xf3 12 Qd1xf3 gives White the best of it, or if 11 ... Bg4-h5 12 c2-c3 is strong, as Black's Knight may not go to g6 or f5 because of the reply 13 g2-g4 winning a piece.

Capablanca does not analyze the effects of 11 h2-h3 Bb6xf2+, but the continuation would probably be: 12 Kg1xf2 Qd8-b6+ 13 Bc1-e3 Bg4xf3 14 Be3xb6 Bf3xd1 15 Bb6-c5, and White wins.

Meanwhile . . .

White has just played 11 Bb5-d3, and is threatening 12 Bd3xh7+ Kg8xh7 13 Nf3-g5+, winning a Pawn.

11	...	Ne7-g6
12	h2-h3	Bg4xf3
13	Qd1xf3	Nc6-e5
14	Qf3-f5	Ne5xd3

Black must eliminate one of those dangerous Bishops!

15   Qf5xd3

The positions seem fairly even.

Black has lost the services of his light-squared Bishop, chief guardian of the weak d-Pawn, but to offset this, White's dark-squared Bishop is still at home, and his f-Pawn is a tender spot.

Black should now play 15 ... Qd8-f6, with this probable continuation: 16 Bc1-e3 Qf6xb2 17 Qd3xd5 Bb6xe3 18 Re1xe3, with a draw in the offing.

Rubinstein's next move indicates that he may have thought he had winning chances—and proceeds to make a strategic error!

15 ... d5-d4

Situations of this sort call to mind Nimzowitsch's acute observation, 'The isolated Pawn has the choice of becoming weak at d5 or d4.'

While the Pawn now impedes the free development of White's Bishop, and renders his c-Pawn backward, it does cut down the mobility of Black's Bishop, which now must devote itself to guarding the Pawn.

16 Bc1-d2

The Bishop finally makes its début. Its development is modest, but withal to good effect, as its entrance signals the attack in earnest on the d-Pawn, a fixed target.

16 ... Qd8-f6

This is the position:

Position after 16 ... Qd8-f6

17 Re1-e4 Ra8-d8

The Pawn should have been defended by the King Rook, after which 18 ... Ra8-c8 would exert pressure on the c-Pawn, but Black evidently expected an exchange of Rooks.

18 Ra1-e1

Threatens to win at once by 19 Bd2-b4 (the Bishop's revenge!).

18 ... Qf6-c6

Covers the square e8, and clears the way for an exchange of Rooks.

Black also has a pretty little trap set up: If 19 Bd2-a5 f7-f5 20 Re4-e6 Ng6-f4, and he wins the exchange.

19 g2-g3

A very fine move, whose strategic justification is that it restrains the action of Black's Knight, and vacates a square for the King. The weakening of the white squares is of no moment, as Black has no Bishop controlling the white squares.

19 ... Rf8-e8

20   Bd2-a5!

Since White cannot attack the d-Pawn directly with his Bishop, he plays to remove its defending Bishop.

Capturing the d-Pawn instead would not do, as after 20 Re4xe8+ Rd8xe8 21 Re1xe8+ Qc6xe8 22 Nb3xd4 Ng6-e5 23 Qd3-b5 (if 23 Qd3-e4, Bb4xd4 wins a piece) 23 . . . Qe8xb5 24 Nd4xb5 Ne5-f3+, and Black wins the Bishop.

20   . . .   Re8xe4

21   Qd3xe4

Renews the threat of winning the d-Pawn, this time by 22 Ba5xb6 Qc6xb6 23 Re1-d1,

21   . . .   Ng6-f8

Black entertains vague hopes of posting this Knight at e6 to defend the unfortunate d-Pawn. He takes comfort in the fact that an exchange of Queens would unite his Pawns, lessening the dangers now facing the isolani.

Alas, Fate (and Capablanca) have other plans in store for him!

Ending 46

Position after 21 . . . Ng6-f8

Rubinstein

Capablanca to move

Black has a weakness in his isolated d-Pawn, and the fact that his pieces are tied down to its defence.

One would therefore expect Capablanca to concentrate on this vulnerable point, and worry it to death.

Instead, Capablanca, who is not hide-bound by convention, does not hesitate to alter the status of the Pawn. In effect he sacrifices one advantage (in the midgame) to secure another one (in the end-game).

22   Qe4xc6!   b7xc6

23   Re1-e7

Seizes the seventh rank! From this influential position, the Rook is able to attack all the Pawns on the rank directly, and to menace the lives of any Pawns that have advanced, by moving behind them.

Meanwhile White already threat-

ens to win a Pawn by 24 Re7xa7
Bb6xa7 25 Ba5xd8.

23 ...   Rd8-d5

Besides this manner of parrying the
threat, Black had two other plausible defences: If

(a) 23 . . . Nf8-e6 (to protect the
Rook, and also bring the Knight
into play) 24 Ba5xb6 a7xb6
25 Re7-b7 b6-b5 26 Rb7-b6 Rd8-c8
27 Nb3-a5 Ne6-d8 28 Kg1-f1
Kg8-f8 29 Kf1-e2 Kf8-e7
30 Ke2-d3, and White wins a Pawn.

(b) 23 . . . d4-d3 24 c2xd3 Rd8xd3
(threatens 25 . . . Rd3xb3, winning
two pieces for a Rook, as well as
25 . . . Rd3xg3+) 25 Ba5xb6 a7xb6
26 Re7-b7 Rd3-d1+ 27 Kg1-g2
Rd1-b1 (or 27 . . . b6-b5 28 Nb3-a5
Rd1-b1 29 Na5xc6 Rb1xb2
30 Nc6-e7+ Kg8-h8 31 Rb7-b8 and
White wins the Knight and the
game) 28 Rb7xb6 Rb1xb2
29 a2-a4 c6-c5 30 a4-a5 c5-c4
31 Nb3-d4 c4-c3 (or 31 . . . Rb2xb6
32 a5xb6 Nf8-d7 33 b6-b7
Kg8-f8 34 Kg2-f1 Nd7-b8
35 Kf1-e2 Kf8-e7 36 Ke2-d2
Ke7-d7 37 Kd2-c3 Kd7-c7
38 Kc3xc4 Kc7xb7 39 Nd4-f5
g7-g6 40 Nf5-d6+, and White wins
a Pawn and the game) 32 Rb6-c6
Rb2-a2 33 a5-a6 g7-g6 34 Nd4-b5
c3-c2 35 a6-a7! Nf8-d7 36 Rc6xc2,
and wins.

A long piece of analysis, and
while lengthy analysis may be sus-
pect, as Dr. Lasker once remarked,
there is no doubt that Capablanca
would have found the win after
23 . . . d4-d3 without any difficulty.

24   Ba5xb6   a7xb6

25   Re7-b7   Nf8-d7

The only way to rescue his Queen-
side Pawns, but it leaves him in a
passive position, whereas White can
combine an attack on the Pawns
with threats of mate on the last
rank, to compel something to give
way.

The alternative 25 . . . b6-b5
yields to 26 Rb7-c7 Rd5-d6
27 Nb3-a5, and White wins a Pawn.

26   Rb7-c7   Rd5-d6

If 26 . . . c6-c5 27 Rc7-c8+ Nd7-f8
(oh for a flight-square!) 28 Rc8-b8
c5-c4 29 Nb3-d2 d4-d3 30 c2xd3,
and White wins a Pawn.

27   Rc7-c8+   Nd7-f8

28   Nb3-d2   c6-c5

If 28 . . . b6-b5 29 Nd2-b3 followed
by 30 Nb3-a5 wins the c-Pawn,
while an attempt to stir up some
counterplay by 28 . . . d4-d3 is
defeated by 29 c2xd3 Rd6xd3
30 Nd2-c4 b6-b5 31 Nc4-e5
Rd3-d2 32 Ne5xc6, and Black
may not capture the b-Pawn on
pain of mate in two.

29   Nd2-c4   Rd6-e6

30   Rc8-b8   Re6-e1+

31   Kg1-g2   g7-g5

Black must give his King some air
before pursuing his attack.
If 31 . . . Re1-e2 32 Nc4xb6
compels Black to guard against the
threat of 33 Nb6-d7, winning a
piece.

32   a2-a4   Re1-a1

33   Nc4xb6

At last something tangible! a real
live Pawn as reward for all the

previous exertions.

33	. . .	Kg8-g7
34	Rb8-c8	Nf8-e6
35	Nb6-d7	

Though he gives up his passed Pawn, White is content to simplify by exchanging one Pawn for another.

35	. . .	Ra1xa4
36	Nd7xc5	

Behold! A new passed Pawn appears!

This is the position:

Position after 36 Nd7xc5

36	. . .	Ra4-b4

Black may not play 36 . . . Ra4-c4, as 37 Nc5xe6+ would cost his Rook, while an exchange of

Knights would lose this way: 36 . . . Ne6xc5 37 Rc8xc5 Kg7-f6 (White was threatening 38 Rc5xg5+) 38 b2-b3 (simpler than 38 Kg2-f3 Ra4-b4 39 b2-b3 d4-d3) 38 . . . Ra4-b4 39 Rc5-c4 Rb4xc4 40 b3xc4 Kf6-e5 41 Kg2-f3 f7-f5 42 Kf3-e2 Ke5-e4 43 f2-f3+ Ke4-e5 44 Ke2-d3, and White wins.

37	Nc5-d3	Rb4-b5
38	Kg2-f3	h7-h6
39	b2-b4	h6-h5
40	g3-g4	h5xg4+
41	h3xg4	f7-f6
42	Rc8-c4	Kg7-f7
43	Nd3-c5	Ne6-d8

Black could double White's Pawns by exchanging Knights, but the passed Pawn, plus the King's increased mobility, would assure White of an easy win, somewhat as follows: 43 . . . Ne6xc5 44 b4xc5 Rb5-b8 45 c5-c6 Rb8-c8 46 c6-c7 Kf7-e6 47 Kf3-e4 Ke6-e7 48 Rc4-c6 Ke7-d7 49 Ke4-d5 Kd7-e7 50 Kd5-c5 Ke7-d7 51 Kc5-b6 Kd7-e7 52 Kb6-b7 Ke7-d7 53 Rc6-d6+, and White will Queen his Pawn.

44	Nc5-b3	**Black Resigns**

Magnificent endgame play!

GAME 47

White Van den Bosch
Black J. R. Capablanca
Budapest, 1929

Caro-Kann Defence
Capablanca never concerned himself with maintaining an even-

looking Pawn-structure. The power exerted by his pieces and Pawns outweighed the picture they presented on the board.

In this game Capablanca acquires doubled Pawns on the f-file and an isolated Pawn on the d-file as early as the twelfth move.

Peu importe! He has good play for his pieces, and that is what counts.

Nevertheless, his opponent puts up a sturdy fight, seemingly having none the worst of it for about thirty moves. Not content with remaining passive though, and awaiting developments, he makes a hasty King move—and Capablanca (like the god Thor) hurls a bolt of lightning—and the game is over!

1	e2-e4	c7-c6
2	d2-d4	d7-d5
3	e4xd5	c6xd5
4	Bf1-d3	

Quiet development, but the Panov-Botvinnik attack by 4 c2-c4, which almost destroyed the Caro-Kann Defence, had not yet been discovered.

One early game with this attack, which influenced chess theory, and also displayed the abilities of the then little-known Botvinnik in an attractive light was his ninth match game against Flohr in 1933, which continued as follows: 4 c2-c4 Ng8-f6 5 Nb1-c3 Nb8-c6 6 Bc1-g5 d5xc4 7 d4-d5 Nc6-e5 8 Qd1-d4 Ne5-d3+ 9 Bf1xd3 c4xd3 10 Ng1-f3 g7-g6 11 Bg5xf6 e7xf6 12 0-0 Qd8-b6 13 Rf1-e1+ Ke8-d8 14 Qd4-h4 g6-g5 15 Qh4-h5 Bf8-d6 16 Qh5xf7 Rh8-f8 17 Qf7xh7 g5-g4 18 Nf3-d2, and White won on the 33rd move.

Mirabile dictu, Black's frail Queen Pawn, that seemed destined for an early death, remained on the board, still alive at the end of the game!

4	. . .	Nb8-c6
5	c2-c3	Ng8-f6
6	Bc1-g5	Bc8-g4
7	Ng1-e2	e7-e6
8	Qd1-b3	Qd8-d7
9	Ne2-g3	

Threatens 10 Bg5xf6 g7xf6 11 h2-h3 Bg4-f5 12 Bd3xf5 e6xf5, and Black is burdened with a tripled Pawn—a tower of weakness.

9	. . .	Nf6-h5
10	f2-f3	Nh5xg3
11	h2xg3	Bg4-f5
12	Bd3xf5	e6xf5
13	Nb1-d2	f7-f6
14	Bg5-e3	Nc6-a5
15	Qb3-c2	0-0-0
16	0-0-0	

White does not care to venture on the complications arising from 16 c3-c4, when such possible replies as 16 . . . Qd7-c7, or 16 . . . Rd8-e8, or 16 . . . Kc8-b8, or 16 . . . Na5-c6, would furnish too much food for thought.

16	. . .	Rd8-e8
17	Rd1-e1	

Not at once 17 Be3-f4, as 17 . . . g7-g5 in reply ends the Bishop's brief career.

17	. . .	Bf8-d6
18	Be3-f4	Bd6xf4

| 19 | g3xf4 | g7-g6 |

Protects the f5 Pawn, in order to free the Queen from that duty.

| 20 | Nd2-b3 | Na5xb3 |
| 21 | Qc2xb3 | h7-h5 |

Stablizes the King-side Pawns against even a hint of attack, and prepares to start a Pawn-roller by 22 . . . Re8xe1+ 23 Rh1xe1 h5-h4, followed by 24 . . . g6-g5 and 25 . . . g5-g4.

22	Qb3-d1	Kc8-d8
23	Re1xe8+	Rh8xe8
24	Rh1-e1	Re8xe1
25	Qd1xe1	

Ending 47

Position after 25 Qd1xe1

Capablanca to move

Van den Bosch

Black and White are evenly matched in material, and neither side seems to have any advantage in position. In fact, Black's isolated d-Pawn might place him at a disadvantage.

Despite this, in only nine magic moves, Capablanca transforms the position, renders his opponent helpless, and compels him to turn down his King!

Remarkable!

| 25 | . . . | Qd7-d6 |
| 26 | Qe1-d2 | |

If White defends the f-Pawn by 26 Qe1-e3, the reply 26 . . . Qd6-a6, attacking the Rook Pawn while at the same time threatening to win the King Knight Pawn by 27 . . . Qa6-f1+ nets Black a Pawn, while if 26 Qe1-g3 g6-g5! and White's Queen is tied down to the defence of the f4 Pawn.

| 26 | . . . | Qd6-a6 |
| 27 | b2-b3 | |

This is harmless enough, as the alternative 27 a2-a3 accentuates White's weaknesses on the white squares, while 27 Kc1-b1 permits this line of play: 27 . . . Qa6-f1+ 28 Kb1-c2 h5-h4 29 b2-b3 h4-h3 30 g2xh3 Qf1xf3, and White is reduced to passivity.

| 27 | . . . | Qa6-f1+ |
| 28 | Kc1-b2 | Kd8-d7 |

'Black's Queen dominates the situation,' says Hooper in his *Practical Chess Endgames*. 'Black threatens to attack on the King-side by advancing his h-Pawn, and he has the advantage of an "outside" Pawn majority (in this case because the Kings are on the Queen-side, this means a King-side majority). White tries to make a passed Pawn on the Queen-side, but he comes to grief through exposing his King.'

29   Qd2-c2

Partly a waiting move, and partly
to support the advance 30 c3-c4,
which might afford some counter-
play.

29   ...   b7-b5!

Capablanca promptly suppresses
any such ambitions.

As Reuben Fine so aptly puts it,
'Capablanca's games always retain-
ed a flavour of their own. In the
defence he was almost unparalleled;
where others let the attack come on
and then parried it, he smelled the
threats, so to speak, while they
were still no more than the gleam in
the other fellow's eye, and so,
before his opponent could really
get an offensive started, his position
was smashed.'

30   a2-a4   a7-a6

31   a4xb5   a6xb5

32   Kb2-a3

Apparently the idea is to move on
to b4, in order to enforce 34 c3-c4.

Or was White already playing for
self-mate?

32   ...   Kd7-c6

This is not an attempt to lure the
King into a trap. Capablanca wants
to secure the position on the
Queen's wing before starting the
Pawns rolling on the King-side.

33   Ka3-b4

This loses promptly, instantaneous-
ly, on the double, and *tout de suite*!

This is the position:

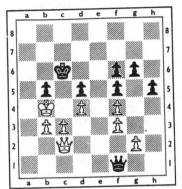

Position after 33 Ka3-b4

33   ...   Qf1-e1!

Tremendous! One little move by
the Queen, and suddenly the King
faces disaster!

The immediate threat is mate
in two by 34 ... Qe1-e7+
35 Kb4-a5 Qe7-a3 mate.

If White guards his a3 square by
playing 34 Qc2-a2, then
34 ... Qe1-e7+ 35 Kb4-a5 Qe7-a7+
wins the Queen, or if he guards his
a3 square by 34 Qc2-b2, then
34 ... Qe1-e7+ 35 Kb4-a5 Qe7-a7+
36 Ka5-b4 Kc6-b6 37 Qb2-a3 (to
prevent 37 ... Qa7-a5 mate)
37 ... Qa7-e7 mate—a problem-like
finish.

Finally, if 34 Kb4-a3 Qf1-a1+
35 Qc2-a2 (carefully avoiding
35 Ka3-b4 Kc6-b6 and mate comes
by 36 ... Qa1-a5) 35 ... Qa1xa2+
(much prettier than the prosaic,
materialistic 35 ... Qa1xc3)
36 Ka3xa2 h5-h4 37 Ka2-b2
g6-g5 38 f4xg5 f6xg5 39 Kb2-c2
g5-g4 40 f3xg4 (if 40 Kc2-d2,

h4-h3 wins) 40 . . . f5xg4
41 Kc2-d2 h4-h3 42 g2xh3 g4xh3,

and Black wins—artistically

34   White Resigns

GAME 48

White E. Canal
Black J. R. Capablanca
Budapest, 1929

Queen's Indian Defence

Canal surprises Capablanca by a combination that wins two pieces for a Rook. Or was it a surprise— something overlooked by Capablanca in his nonchalance?

Judging by the subsequent play, Capablanca had apparently anticipated the combination and, looking further into the position than Canal, saw resources that were not revealed to his opponent.

The endgame that follows is a fascinating study, and illustrates a 'domination' theme rarely found in actual play.

There is a Pawn to be queened, but it would take an eagle eye to find the particular Pawn that will be crowned.

The Canal-Capablanca game is a game for the dilettante to enjoy, and for the connoisseur to savour to the full.

1	d2-d4	Ng8-f6
2	c2-c4	e7-e6
3	Ng1-f3	b7-b6
4	g2-g3	Bc8-b7
5	Bf1-g2	Bf8-b4+
6	Bc1-d2	Bb4xd2+

Simple and sound, though Black has good alternatives in

6 . . . Bb4-e7 and 6 . . . Qd8-e7.

7	Nb1xd2	

The theorists recommend 7 Qd1xd2, so that the Queen Knight may develop at c3, its natural square—but the players insist on capturing as *they* please.

7	. . .	0-0
8	0-0	c7-c5

Challenging the center is almost imperative in Queen Pawn openings.

9	d4xc5	

This looks questionable, as it opens the b-file for Black, but what else is there? Protecting the Pawn by 9 Nd2-b3 leaves the Knight badly placed, while 9 e2-e3 is deplorably passive.

9	. . .	b6xc5
10	Qd1-c2	Nb8-c6

Intensifies the pressure on d4.

11	Rf1-d1	

The advance 11 e2-e4 looks inviting, but after the reply 11 . . . e6-e5 followed by 12 . . . Qd8-e7 and 13 . . . Nc6-d4, Black would enjoy a decided advantage.

11	. . .	Qd8-b6

The Queen is beautifully placed

here, bearing down on the b-file, as well as on the central point d4.

12	a2-a3	Ra8-b8
13	Ra1-b1	Rf8-c8
14	e2-e4	e6-e5
15	Qc2-d3	

White hopes for some play along the d-file, say by 16 Qd3-d6.

Meanwhile he prevents Black from playing 15 . . . Nc6-d4, the response to which being 16 Nf3xe5, removing a loose Pawn.

| 15 | . . . | d7-d6! |

A witty, almost impudent reply. Black guards the e-Pawn (so that he can play 16 . . . Nc6-d4) with a Pawn which is itself unprotected!

White of course must not touch the d-Pawn, the penalty for 16 Qd3xd6 being 16 . . . Rc8-d8, winning the Queen.

| 16 | Nd2-f1 | |

The Knight is on its way to d5 (or so White thinks).

| 16 | . . . | Nc6-d4! |

Establishes a strong outpost in the center, and prevents White from doing likewise!

Should White insist on stationing his Knight at d5, this is what could occur: 17 Nf1-e3 Bb7xe4 18 Ne3-d5 Be4xd3 19 Nd5xb6 Nd4xf3+ 20 Bg2xf3 Rb8xb6 21 Rd1xd3 e5-e4, and the Pawn fork wins a piece.

| 17 | Nf3xd4 | |

White is understandably anxious to remove the annoying beast.

| 17 | . . . | e5xd4 |

Black is more than pleased with the exchange, as he now has a protected passed Pawn. In addition, the Pawn guards the exit at e3, and puts an end to the Knight's dream of reaching d5.

| 18 | b2-b4! | |

Bayonet attack! White's chief threat is 19 b4xc5 Qb6xc5 (Black must capture with the Queen, which is doubly attacked) 20 Rb1xb7 Rb8xb7 21 e4-e5, and the discovered attack nets White two pieces for a Rook.

Black cannot meet the threat with 18 . . . c5xb4, as 19 Rb1xb4 gives White the advantage, while if 18 . . . Qb6-c7 19 b4xc5 d6xc5 20 f2-f4 (or the combination actually played), with the threat of 21 f4-f5 or 21 e4-e5 follows, and White's pieces spring to life.

Herewith a diagram of the critical position:

Position after 18 b2-b4!

| 18 | . . . | Qb6-c6! |

Triple attack on the King Pawn!

White must either meekly defend the Pawn, or go ahead with his intended combination.

19 b4xc5

The temptation to win two pieces for a Rook is irresistible!

19 ... d6xc5

20 Rb1xb7 Qc6xb7

21 e4-e5

Discovered attack on the Queen, and direct attack on the Knight.

21 ... Qb7-b3!

A master move, this remarkable offer to exchange Queens! Generally, it is the side that is ahead in material (in this case White) that tries to clear the board and simplify the ending.

22 e5xf6

This is preferable to 22 Qd3xb3 Rb8xb3 23 e5xf6 Rb3xa3, and Black has two passed Pawns raring to go.

22 ... Qb3xd3

The idea behind the exchange is to force the capturing Rook off the back rank, which then makes it available to Black's Rook as a point of entry, enabling it to get behind White's Pawns.

23 Rd1xd3

Ending 48

Position after 23 Rd1xd3

Capablanca to move

Canal

White's two pieces for a Rook give him a material advantage.

Black's control of the important open b-file, and his protected passed Pawn, give him a positional advantage.

Capablanca plans to exploit the passive state of White's minor pieces to effect an exchange of Rooks. His remaining Rook could then terrorize the isolated Pawns on White's Queen-side. The loss of either of them would provide Black with another passed Pawn.

23 ... Rb8-b1!

The first step in attempting to win the a-Pawn is to take advantage of the crowded state of White's King-side pieces.

Capablanca pins the Knight, and now threatens 24 ... Rc8-e8 followed by 25 ... Re8-e1 and 26 ... Re1-c1. This would attack and win the important c-Pawn,

as White could not protect it by
27 Bg2-d5 without abandoning the
Knight. After capturing the Pawn,
Black would have two dangerous
connected Pawns rushing down to
become Queens.

24   Bg2-d5

Anticipating this possibility, White
protects the vulnerable Pawn immediately, intending to continue
with 25 Kg1-g2, and release the
Knight from the pin.

24   . . .   Rc8-b8

Institutes two threats. The tactical
one is 25 . . . Rb1-c1 followed by
26 . . . Rb8-b1 with a double
attack on the Knight. This would
compel the Bishop's return to g2,
whereupon Black removes the c-
Pawn.

The strategic threat is simply
25 . . . Rb8-b3, forcing an exchange of Rooks, to Black's benefit.

25   Kg1-g2

Unpins the Knight, which has been
hors de combat for the last ten
moves.

25   . . .   Rb8-b3!

Daring, in view of the fact that the
exchange favours White in letting
him remain with two pieces to
Black's one Rook!

26   Rd3xb3   Rb1xb3

27   Nf1-d2

Unable to save the Pawn (if
27 a3-a4 Rb3-b4 28 a4-a5 Rb4-a4)
White sends the Knight out after a
Black Pawn.

27   . . .   Rb3xa3

Wins a Pawn, and creates a candidate for promotion in the a-Pawn.

28   Nd2-e4

The Knight leaps into the fray
with the dire threat of removing
the valuable c-Pawn. This would
not only regain the Pawn he lost,
but would knock the props out
from under the d-Pawn, and as a
further result provide him with a
passed Pawn as well.

Wouldn't you think that Capablanca would meet this threat by
28 . . . Ra3-a5, defending the
precious Pawn?

28   . . .   a7-a5!

Not at all! The Rook must not be
tied down to defending a Pawn,
making its role in the ending a
subordinate one.

*The Rook must be aggressive in
the endgame.*

This is the state of affairs:

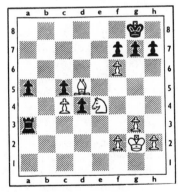

Position after 28 . . . a7-a5

29   Ne4xc5   g7xf6

This is less to win a Pawn (as
Capablanca was never a Pawn-
snatcher) than to enable the King
to take a hand in the game. If at
once 29 . . . Kg8-f8, the reply
30 Nc5-d7+ forces the King's

return to g8, as 30 . . . Kf8-e8 allows 31 f6xg7, winning for White.

Advancing the d-Pawn instead would be premature, as after 29 . . . d4-d3, the reply 30 Kg2-f3 followed by 31 Kf3-e3 summarily ends the Pawn's career.

30 Kg2-f1

The King returns, ready to head off the d-Pawn.

30 . . .   a5-a4

Black does not fear 31 Bd5-c6 (double attack on the Pawn) as he simply responds with 31 . . . Ra3-a1+ followed by 32 . . . a4-a3, and the Pawn has made more progress.

31 Kf1-e2

This may halt the d-Pawn in its tracks, but Black has other resources, as he demonstrates.

31 . . .   Ra3-a1!

Such as queening the passed a-Pawn instead! The idea is: 32 . . . a4-a3 followed by 33 . . . a3-a2 and 34 . . . Ra1-e1+ (to make way for the Pawn without loss of time) and 35 . . . a2-a1(Q).

32 Nc5-d3!

Excellent! At one stroke the Knight blockades an adverse passed Pawn while clearing the way for the advance of his own passed Pawn.

32 . . .   a4-a3

Is this the most likely candidate for promotion, now that the d-Pawn is unable to move?

Maybe, but there are some surprises in store for the reader.

33 c4-c5   a3-a2

Threatens to win in a hurry by 34 . . . Ra1-e1+ followed by queening the Pawn, a threat strong enough to win a piece for the Pawn.

34 Ke2-f3

This avoids the check, but a piece must be lost in any event.

34 . . .   Ra1-d1

35 Bd5xa2

The dangerous Pawn must be destroyed at once!

35 . . .   Rd1xd3+

(This is removing the blockader with a vengeance, Mr. Nimzowitsch.)

36 Kf3-e4

But not 36 Kf3-e2, to keep the Rook off the seventh rank, as then 36 . . . Rd3-c3 would lose his passed Pawn.

36 . . .   Rd3-d2

37 Ba2-c4   Kg8-f8!

Far better to bring the King over to hold back the Pawn, than the Pawn-grubbing 37 . . . Rd2xf2, after which 38 c5-c6 follows and the Rook cannot return to the first rank to stop the Pawn! (If 38 . . . Rf2-c2 39 Ke4-d5, or if 38 . . . Rf2-b2 39 c6-c7 is decisive.)

38 f2-f3

Clearly, if 38 c5-c6 Kf8-e7, and the Pawn poses no danger to Black.

38 . . .   Rd2xh2

Capablanca is content to simplify, instead of grimly holding on to the passed Pawn, confident that his superiority, however small, is sufficient to secure the win.

This requires a belief in justice on the chessboard, and faith in one's ability to mete it out properly.

39 Ke4xd4   Kf8-e7

The King is on his way to blockade the Pawn.

40 Bc4-d3

The idea is to centralize the Bishop at e4. There it would guard the f-Pawn, prevent the advance of Black's doubled Pawns, and be in position to protect his c-Pawn when it reaches c6.

Meanwhile, Black's passed Pawns have disappeared, and his prospects do not look prepossessing, what with his isolated and doubled Pawns to depend on.

How conjure up winning chances?

This is the position:

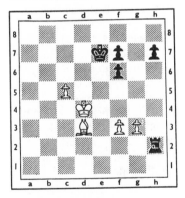

Position after 40 Bc4-d3

40 ...   h7-h5!

Voilà! In no time at all Black has whipped up a threat of obtaining a passed Pawn by continuing with 41 ... Rh2-g2 42 g3-g4

h5-h4, and the Pawn is on its way to glory.

Will the h-Pawn be the one that becomes a Queen?

41 Kd4-e3   Rh2-g2

42 Ke3-f4

Rescues the g-Pawn, but the King has been lured away from his passed Pawn. (The King, unfortunately, cannot be in two places at once.)

The alternative 42 g3-g4 loses quickly by 42 ... h5-h4 43 Bd3-f1 Rg2-c2 44 Ke3-d4 Rc2-f2 45 Bf1-h3 Rf2xf3 46 Bh3-g2 Rf3-g3 47 Bg2-f1 h4-h3, and White will. have to surrender his Bishop.

42 ...   Rg2-g1

Obviously, the Rook's aim is to get behind the passed Pawn. From there its power to strike extends all along the line, so that *no matter how far the Pawn moves up the file, it can never escape the Rook's attack.*

43 Bd3-e4   Rg1-c1

This may look strange, since it compels the Pawn to move up the board. The idea though is to force the Pawn to advance to a white square, and thus tie the Bishop down to its protection.

44 c5-c6

Time for a diagram:

Position after 44 c5-c6

44 ...   Rc1-c3!

A tremendously effective move! It
reduces White to a state of *zugzwang*, the compulsion to move,
when any move he makes either
loses some material, or is fatal.

45   c6-c7

Voluntarily gives up the Pawn,
which he cannot retain.

Consider the consequences of
these interesting alternatives:

(a) 45 Kf2-f5 Rc3-c5+ 46 Kf5-f4
Ke7-e6 47 Kf4-e3 (a Bishop move
loses the Pawn at once, while
47 g3-g4 allows Black to secure a
passed Pawn by 47 ... h5-h4)
47 ... f6-f5 48 Ke3-d4 Ke6-d6
49 Be4-d3 Kd6xc6 50 Bd3-c4
Rc5xc4+! 51 Kd4xc4 f5-f4
52 g3xf4 h5-h4, and Black wins,

(b) 45 Be4-d5 Rc3-c5 46 Kf4-e4
f6-f5+ 47 Ke4-d4 Rc5xd5+
48 Kd4xd5 f5-f4! 49 Kd5-c5 (or
49 g3xf4 h5-h4 50 Kd5-c5 Ke7-d8
51 Kc5-b6 Kd8-c8, and wins)
49 ... f4xg3 50 Kc5-b6 g3-g2
51 c6-c7 g2-g1(Q)+ 52 Kb6-b7

Qg1-b1+ 53 Kb7-c8 Qb1-b6
54 f3-f4 Qb6-a7 55 f4-f5 Qa7-a8
mate.

45   ...   Rc3xc7

Removes a potential danger. The
ending still requires winning, and
the manner of its doing is an illustration of smooth, flawless technique.

The solution is as lucid and
accurate as though it were the
solution of a composed endgame
study.

46   Be4-d5   Rc7-c5

The attack on the Bishop is the
first step in driving it away from
the diagonal leading to e6, a square
that Black wants for his King.

47   Bd5-a2

The Bishop intends to stay on the
critical diagonal. If instead
47 Bd5-b3 Rc5-b5 forces
48 Bb3-a2 (on 48 Bb3-c4 Rb5-b4
pins the Bishop, or if 48 Bb3-a4
Rb5-b4+ wins the Bishop)
48 ... Rb5-b2 49 Ba2-d5 Rb2-b4+!
50 Kf4-f5 (if 50 Bd5-e4 Ke7-e6
51 Kf4-e3 f6-f5 wins, or if
50 Kf4-e3 f6-f5 followed by
51 ... Ke7-f6 wins) 50 ... Rb4-b5
51 Kf5-e4 f6-f5+ 52 Ke4-d4
Rb5xd5+ 53 Kd4xd5 f5-f4
54 g3xf4 h5-h4, and the Pawn cannot be stopped.

47   ...   Rc5-b5!

Complete domination! The Bishop
has no moves!

48   Kf4-e3

If 48 Kf4-e4, the procedure is
48 ... f6-f5+ 49 Ke4-f4 Ke7-f6
50 Kf4-e3 (the Bishop still may
not move, and 50 g3-g4 succumbs

to 50 . . . h5xg4 51 f3xg4 Rb5-b4+
followed by 52 . . . f5xg4)
50 . . . Rb5-b4 51 Ba2-d5 f5-f4+
52 g3xf4 h5-h4 53 Ke3-f2 Rb4-b2+
54 Kf2-g1 Kf6-f5 55 Bd5xf7
Kf5xf7 56 Bf7-d5 Kf4-g3
57 Bd5-e4 Rb2-a2 58 Kg1-f1
h4-h3, and Black wins.

48	. . .	Rb5-a5
49	Ba2-c4	

Just about the only square left to
the Bishop on the diagonal. If
instead 49 Ba2-b3 Ra5-a3 pins the
Bishop, and if 49 Ba2-b1 (reluc-
tantly leaving the diagonal)
49 . . . Ke7-e6 50 Ke3-f4 Ra5-a4+
51 Kf4-e3 (but not 51 Bb1-e4,
when f6-f5 wins the Bishop)
51 . . . f6-f5 52 Bb1-c2 f5-f4+
53 g3xf4 (or 53 Ke3-d2 f4xg3
54 Bc2xa4 g3-g2 wins)
53 . . . Ra4-a3+ 54 Ke3-d2 Ra3-a2
55 Kd2-c1 Ra2xc2+, and Black
wins.

49	. . .	Ra5-c5
50	Bc4-a6	

The alternatives are 50 Ke3-d4
Rc5-g5, winning a Pawn, or
50 Bc4-a2 f6-f5, vacating the
square f6 for the King.

50	. . .	Ke7-e6
51	Ke3-f4	Rc5-c3!
52	Ba6-f1	

White is running short of moves!
On 52 Kf4-e4 (the only square
open to the King) 52 . . . f6-f5+
53 Ke4-f4 Ke6-f6 enables Black to
make further progress.

52	. . .	f6-f5!

At last! The Pawn makes room for
the King to·occpy f6.

This is the position:

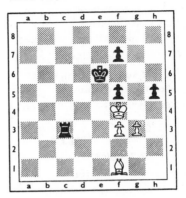

Position after 52 . . . f6-f5!

53	Bf1-a6	

White has little choice. If 53 g3-g4
f5xg4 54 f3xg4 h5-h4 55 g4-g5
h4-h3 56 Kf4-g4 h3-h2 57 Bf1-g2
Rc3-c1, and White will have to give
up his Bishop for the Pawn, or if
53 Kf4-g5 Rc3xf3 54 Bf1-c4+
Ke6-e5 55 Kg5-h4 f5-f4, and Black
wins easily.

53	. . .	Ke6-f6
54	Ba6-b7	

Or 54 Ba6-e2 Rc3-b3 followed by
55 . . . Rb3-b4+ drives White's King
back, while Black's will be enabled
to advance.

54	. . .	Rc3-c4+
55	Kf4-e3	Kf6-g5

With this neat little win in mind:
56 . . . f5-f4+ 57 Ke3-d3 (on
57 g3xf4+ Rc4xf4 gives Black a
passed Pawn, or if 57 Ke3-f2
Rc4-c2+ 58 Kf2-g1 f4xg3 gives
him two passed Pawns)
57 . . . f4xg3 58 Kd3xc4 Kg5-f4!,
and wins nicely, as the Bishop is
shut off from the g2 square.

Game 49

56   Ke3-f2

The King retreats in order to head off the potential passed Pawn—whichever one that may be!

56 ...   f5-f4!

This is the key move in all cases!
The immediate threat is
57 ... Rc4-c2+ 58 Kf2-g1 f4xg3.

57   Kf2-g2

Now the check would be met by 58 Kg2-h3, saving one Pawn.

57 ...   f7-f5!

Passed Pawns must be pushed!
The Pawn which has waited patiently at its home base for 56 moves, is destined, believe it or not, to become the passed Pawn that wins the game!

58   White Resigns

White does not require proof. After 58 Kg2-h3 f4xg3 59 Kh3xg3 h5-h4+ (a likely-looking candidate, but not the final choice) 60 Kg3-h3 Rc4-c3 61 Bb7-d5 Kg5-f4 62 Kh3xh4 Rc3xf3 63 Bd5xf3 Kf4xf3 64 Kh4-h3 f5-f4 65 Kh3-h2 Kf3-e2, and the Pawn marches straight through to the coronation.

'The speed with which the White position fell apart is rather surprising,' says Fine, 'but there does not seem to be anything that he could have done.'

A great game all the way through, and a fascinating ending, abounding in quiet brilliancies.

GAME 49

White K. Havasi
Black J. R. Capablanca
Budapest, 1929

Nimzo-Indian Defence

From the artistic standpoint: I can do no better than quote Golombek, who says, in his admirable *Capablanca's 100 Best Games of Chess*, 'A bright and flawless gem, played with the usual Capablanca elegance.'

From the technical standpoint: a superb specimen of position play, featuring the art of squeezing the utmost out of a tiny advantage.

Capablanca secures a Pawn majority on the Queen-side, and then sets to work to translate it into a passed Pawn. This he accomplishes by obtaining control of the open c-file. He then exploits the weaknesses of his opponent's white squares, infiltrating them with his pieces.

The rest consists of escorting the passed Pawn safely to the queening square.

1   d2-d4   Ng8-f6

2   c2-c4   e7-e6

3   Nb1-c3   Bf8-b4

Pins the Knight, and thereby prevents the formation of a strong Pawn center by 4 e2-e4.

4 Qd1-c2 d7-d5

Restrains White's e-Pawn for a long time, meanwhile taking control of e4, a key square.

5 Ng1-f3

Rather lack-lustre, a preferable line of play being 5 c4xd5 Qd8xd5 6 Ng1-f3 c7-c5 7 Bc1-d2 Bb4xc3 8 Bd2xc3 c5xd4 9 Nf3xd4 e6-e5 10 Nd4-f5 Bc8xf5 11 Qc2xf5 Nb8-c6, and White's two Bishops should offset Black's lead in development.

5 ... c7-c5!

'Black equalizes in any Queen Pawn opening,' says Reuben Fine, 'where he can play both . . . d7-d5 and . . . c7-c5 with impunity.'

6 c4xd5 Qd8xd5

7 a2-a3 Bb4xc3+

There is no choice, as after 7 . . . Bb4-a5 8 b2-b4 c5xb4 9 Nc3xd5 b4-b3+ 10 Bc1-d2 b3xc2 11 Nd5xf6+ g7xf6 12 Bd2xa5, and White has won a piece.

8 b2xc3 Nb8-c6

9 e2-e3

Shuts in the Queen Bishop, but if instead 9 c3-c4 Nc6xd4 10 Qc2-a4+ Qd5-d7 wins a Pawn for Black.

9 ... 0-0

10 Bf1-e2

Much too respectful of his opponent's reputation, Havasi develops timidly. Far better is this vigorous continuation, adopted by Alekhine in his match against Euwe in 1937: 10 c3-c4 Qd5-d6 11 Bc1-b2 c5xd4 12 e3xd4 b7-b6 13 Bf1-d3 Bc8-b7

14 0-0, and Alekhine won on the 40th move.

10 ... c5xd4

11 c3xd4

Of course not 11 Nf3xd4 Qd5xg2 12 Be2-f3 Nc6xd4, and Black wins a piece.

Somewhat preferable though, was to capture by 11 e3xd4, releasing the dark-squared Bishop.

11 ... b7-b6

Black now has a two-for-one Pawn advantage on the Queen-side, and an open c-file that is made to order for his Rooks.

12 Nf3-d2 Bc8-b7

Obviously, snatching the g-Pawn would be a dreadful blunder, the reply 13 Be2-f3 winning a piece on the spot.

13 Be2-f3 Qd5-d7

A superficial assessment would indicate that White has the better game. He has the two Bishops, a well-supported center Pawn, pressure (so far) on the c-file, and no visible weaknesses.

All that Black seems to have is a Pawn majority on the Queen-side, and the possibility of wresting control of the c-file.

But there is hidden strength in Black's position—as we shall see!

14 0-0

Efforts to advance the e-Pawn are premature, as 14 e3-e4 Nc6xd4 costs a Pawn, while 14 Bf3xc6 Bb7xc6 15 e3-e4 Qd7xd4 16 Qc2xc6 Qd4xa1 is even more expensive.

14 ... Ra8-c8

With the transparent threat of
15 . . . Nc6xd4, Black banishes the
enemy Queen from the c-file.

15   Qc2-b1   Nc6-a5!

The Knight brings pressure to bear
on the sensitive white squares.

16   Bf3xb7

White feared the consequences of
16 Bf3-e2 Nf6-d5 followed by
17 . . . Nd5-c3, but exchanging
Bishops simplifies the position, and
accentuates Black's positional superiority.

16   . . .   Qd7xb7

Black is now ready to exploit the
circumstance that his opponent's
white squares are vulnerable to
invasion.

These squares have been weakened by the disappearance of the
Bishop operating on those squares.
This advantage, together with that
of Black's Pawn majority on the
Queen-side (a situation which,
when Capablanca is driving, generally results in the creation of a
passed Pawn), should be enough to
forecast a win for him.

Which is not to say that the
procedure is easy! It still requires
skill of the highest order to attain
the desired result.

From this point on, we will see
the Capablanca technique at its
best, in the art of winning a won
game.

17   Bc1-b2   Qb7-a6

The Queen's presence on this
diagonal increases the pressure on
the white squares. She now threatens to come in strongly at e2.

18   Rf1-e1

If 18 Rf1-c1 (to dispute possession
of the c-file) there follows
18 . . . Qa6-e2 19 Nd2-f3 Na5-b3
20 Rc1xc8 Rf8xc8 21 Ra1-a2
Rc8-c1+, and Black must give up
his Queen to avoid mate (22 Bb2xc1
Qe2-d1+, and mate next).

18   . . .   Nf6-d5

19   Ra1-a2

A strange-looking move. White
intends either to oppose Rooks by
20 Bb2-a1 followed by 21 Ra2-c2,
or to continue with 20 Qb1-a1, in
order to prevent 20 . . . Nd5-c3.

Ending 49

Position after 19 Ra1-a2

Capablanca to move

Havasi

Black enjoys certain advantages:

(1) his Queen Rook controls the
important c-file,

(2) his Queen commands an imposing diagonal,

(3) his Pawn majority on the Queen-

side presages the creation of a passed Pawn.

Capablanca plans to increase the pressure on the c-file by doubling Rooks on the file. He also intends to utilize the circumstance that his opponent's white squares are weak to insinuate his pieces with decisive effect into the enemy's territory, availing himself particularly of the square c4, on which three of his pieces concentrate their power.

19 ...   Rc8-c6

20   e3-e4

This looks attractive, as it builds up an impressive Pawn center.

Such Pawn centers may bear within them the seeds of their own destruction, and that they may be peculiarly vulnerable to attack was graphically demonstrated by Alekhine, when he introduced a new concept, the Alekhine Defence, into tournament practice in 1921.

20   ...   Nd5-c3!

A genuine master move in all respects! One would expect 20 ... Nd5-f4 almost as a matter of routine, as there the Knight assumes a commanding post, but hardly to c3, where this fine, healthy Knight is given up for an impotent, ineffectual Bishop.

But it is characteristic of Capablanca to be ready to yield one advantage for the sake of securing another, which turns out to have more lasting benefit.

21   Bb2xc3   Rc6xc3

22   Nd2-f3

If White disputes the c-file by 22 Re1-c1, there follows

22 ... Rc3xc1+ 23 Qb1xc1 Qa6-d3 24 Qc1-b2 Rf8-d8, and White must lose one of his center Pawns.

22   ...   Rf8-c8

Black now has a powerful grip on the Bishop file, and cannot be easily driven off.

23   h2-h3

Provides a flight-square for the King, while awaiting the turn of events.

A move such as 23 Re1-e3 is of course useless, as 23 ... Rc3-c1+ in reply wins the Queen.

23   ...   Na5-c4

Suddenly White's a-Pawn is under attack by three pieces!

24   a3-a4

This is the position:

Position after 24 a3-a4

24   ...   Nc4-a3!

Neat! At one blow the Knight attacks the Queen, and cuts off the Rook from its protection of the a-Pawn.

25   Qb1-b2

It is futile to try to save the Pawn, as 25 Qb1-d1 would be met by 25 . . . Rc8-c4, striking at the Pawn once more—and winning it.

| 25 | . . . | Qa6xa4 |

The first tangible gain.

Now watch the greatest genius that the game ever produced demonstrate the art of turning a passed Pawn into a Queen.

Notice how any combinations, no matter how attractive, which do not relate to that objective, are sedulously avoided.

Such intensity of purpose is truly frightening (especially to one who has to face it!).

| 26 | Re1-e2 |

What else is there? If 26 Qb2-e2, Rc3-c2 simplifies the position to Black's advantage, while 26 Re1-a1, attacking the pinned Knight a third time, is deftly countered by 26 . . . Qa4-b5, extricating the Knight from his predicament.

| 26 | . . . | b6-b5 |

Passed Pawns must be pushed—at every available opportunity!

| 27 | d4-d5 | e6xd5 |

Black is content to exchange, as the recapture burdens White with an isolated center Pawn.

| 28 | e4xd5 |

The exchange suits White as well, since it opens the e-file for his Rook, and enables him to threaten a mate in two by 29 Qb2xc3 Rc8xc3 30 Re2-e8 mate.

| 28 | . . . | b5-b4! |

Perhaps an obvious move, but brilliant nevertheless in the number of things that a little Pawn push accomplishes:

(a) it nullifies White's threat, the square e8 being now covered by the Queen,

(b) it threatens to win the d-Pawn by 29 . . . Qa4-d1+ 30 Re2-e1 Qd1xd5, after which White may not capture the Rook, which is now protected by the Pawn,

(c) it advances the Pawn one step nearer the goal, the eighth square.

| 29 | Qb2-d2 |

Brings the Queen into more active play, and prepares to advance his own passed Pawn.

| 29 | . . . | b4-b3 |

The Pawn moves up another step, thereby complying with the Manhattan Chess Club epigram, 'Black passed Pawns travel faster than White.'

| 30 | Ra2-b2 |

Blockading the Pawn offers more resistance than 30 Ra2-a1 Rc3-c2 31 Qd2-e3 b3-b2, and White can resign.

| 30 | . . . | Rc3-c2 |

Black's play is crystal-clear. Since (a) the passed Pawn must be pushed, and (b) its path is blocked by a Rook, therefore (c) the blockader must be removed!

| 31 | Qd2-e3 |

The alternative 31 Rb2xc2 b3xc2 followed by 32 . . . Rc8-b8 and 33 . . . Rb8-b1 offers no hope at all; so White tries to complicate matters.

| 31 | . . . | Rc2xb2 |

Begins some neat finishing touches.

32   Re2xb2

This is the situation:

Position after 32 Re2xb2

32   ...   Na3-c4!

Double attack on Queen and Rook! How does White avoid loss of the exchange?

33   Qe3-c1

Answer: by pinning the impertinent Knight!

Instead of this, had White played 33 Qe3xb3, the response would simply be 33 ... Nc4xb2, thereby protecting his Queen with the Knight.

33   ...   Qa4-a3!

Beautiful! Black parries the pin of his Knight by applying a pin of his own—on the Rook, which he now threatens to remove with the Queen.

34   Rb2-b1

The Rook slips out of the pin, only to encounter other troubles.

34   ...   Qa3xc1+!

The *coup de grâce!* This compels White to concede, as after 35 Rb1xc1 b3-b2 (the Pawn pushes on) 36 Rc1-b1 Rc8-b8 37 Kg1-f1 Nc4-a3 (drives off the last blockader) 38 Rb1-d1 b2-b1(Q) and the passed Pawn wins the game for Black.

35   White Resigns

Capablanca's moves flow along smoothly and easily, but behind them is a force that is irresistible.

GAME 50

White J. R. Capablanca
Black G. A. Thomas
Hastings 1929—30

Queen's Indian Defence
Impeccable opening play yields Capablanca a slight advantage in position, which he cleverly carries over into the midgame.

As a result, Sir George's pieces are crowded together, and have little scope to display their prowess.

In fact, at that stage, not one of them dares venture a step beyond the third rank.

The last part of the game is described by Euwe and Prins as, *'Ein ausgezeichnetes Endspiel.'*

And if you gather from that,

that Capablanca's endgame play was outstanding, splendid, artistic, or just plain elegant, you get the picture from any of these adjectives.

1	Ng1-f3	Ng8-f6
2	c2-c4	e7-e6
3	d2-d4	Bf8-b4+
4	Nb1-d2	

Varies from the customary 4 Bc1-d2, an interesting continuation being: 4 . . . Qd8-e7 5 g2-g3 Nb8-c6 6 Bf1-g2 Bb4xd2+ 7 Nb1xd2 d7-d6 8 0-0 0-0 8 e2-e4 e6-e5 10 d4-d5 Nc6-b8 11 b2-b4 Bc8-g4 12 Qd1-c2 c7-c6 13 Nf3-h4, as occurred in 1938 at the Avro Tournament, Euwe (with White) smashing Flohr.

4	. . .	b7-b6
5	e2-e3	Bc8-b7
6	Bf1-d3	Nf6-e4
7	a2-a3	Bb4xd2+
8	Nf3xd2	Ne4xd2
9	Bc1xd2	f7-f5

Naturally, 9 . . . Bb7xg2 10 Rh1-g1 Bg2-b7 11 Rg1xg7 isn't worth a second thought.

Castling on the King-side being dangerous, Black temporizes. Meanwhile, he prevents the advance of White's e-Pawn.

10 Qd1-h5+

The purpose of this is to compel the advance of another Pawn to a white square.

10	. . .	g7-g6
11	Qh5-h6	

Threatens to win by 12 Qh6-g7— which Black promptly prevents.

11	. . .	Qd8-e7
12	f2-f3	

Prepares to build up a broad Pawn center by 13 e3-e4 next move.

12	. . .	d7-d6
13	e3-e4	Nb8-d7
14	0-0-0	0-0-0
15	e4xf5	e6xf5

On 15 . . . g6xf5 16 Bd2-g5 could hurt a bit. Black would have nothing better than 16 . . . Qe7-f8, after which 18 Qh6xe6 Rd8-e8 18 Qe6xf5 wins two Pawns for White.

16 Bd2-g5

This is the position:

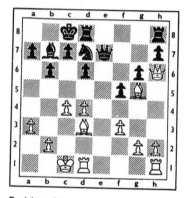

Position after 16 Bd2-g5

16	. . .	Qe7-f8

The saving move, the sequel to interposing by 16 . . . Nd7-f6 being 17 Qh6-h4 Rd8-f8 (or Variation a) 18 Rh1-e1 Qe7-f7 19 Bg5xf6 Qf7xf6 20 Re1-e8+ (taking advantage of the overworked Rook) 20 . . . Kc8-d7 21 Qh4xf6 Rf8xf6 22 Re8xh8, and White has won a Rook.

(a) 17 ... Rh8-f8 18 Rh1-e1
Qe7-f7 19 d4-d5 (threatens
20 Re1-e6) 19 ... Rd8-e8
20 Bg5xf6 Re8xe1 (if
20 ... Qf7xf6 21 Qh4xf6 wins a
Rook) 21 Rd1xe1 Qf7xf6
22 Qh4xf6 Rf8xf6 23 Re1-e7,
and White is in sight of a win.

17	Qh6-h4	Rd8-e8
18	Rh1-e1	Qf8-f7
19	Kc1-c2	a7-a5
20	b2-b3	Bb7-a6
21	Kc2-c3	h7-h5
22	Re1xe8+	

Clearing away the heavy pieces will
accentuate the superiority of the
two Bishops in the ending.

22	...	Rh8xe8
23	Rd1-e1	Ba6-b7
24	Qh4-f2	Kc8-b8

Black is curiously helpless to prevent the forthcoming exchange of
Rooks.

Running away by 24 ... Re8-g8
leads to this: 25 Re1-e7 Qf7-f8
26 Qf2-e3 (threatens to win a Rook
by 27 Qe3-e6 Qf8-d8 28 Re7xd7
Qd8xg5—or 28 ... Qd8xd7
29 Qe6xg8+ and mate next—
29 Rd7-g7+) 26 ... Rg8-h8
27 Bg5-h6 Qf8-d8 (but not
27 ... Qf8xh6 28 Re7-e8+ and
mate next, nor 27 ... Rh8xh6
28 Re7-e8+ and mate next)
28 Bh6-g7 Rh8-g8 29 Qe3-e6
Bb7-c6 30 d4-d5, and Black is out
of moves.

| 25 | Re1xe8+ | Qf7xe8 |

Ending 50

Thomas

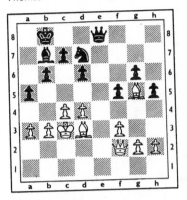

Capablanca to move

White's game is incontestably
superior.

He has the two Bishops; his
King is closer to the center for the
coming endgame; his Pawns have
freedom of movement, Black's
Pawns being unable to move without incurring loss.

Capablanca plans to simplify the
position by exchanging Queens.
Then by reducing the mobility of
Black's remaining pieces, he will
make the way clear for his King to
march over to Black's King-side
Pawns, which will lack adequate
protection, and if necessary, remove them from circulation.

| 26 | Qf2-e2! | Qe8xe2 |

Avoiding the exchange would allow
White to play 27 Qe2-e7 with
paralyzing effect.

| 27 | Bd3xe2 | Bb7-c8 |
| 28 | Bg5-e7!! | |

Two exclamation marks for this move!

One, for fixing the Knight so that it cannot move.

Two, for vacating the square g5 for the King, who can wander over there, and pick off the neighboring Pawns at his leisure.

28 ...   **b6-b5**

Black sacrifices a Pawn to enable his Knight to get into play on the Queen-side.

29 c4xb5   Nd7-b6

Which it does—with a threat of winning the Bishop by 30 . . . Nb6-d5+.

30 Be2-c4   Nb6xc4

The Knight is happy to remove one of the dangerous Bishops, especially as the resulting ending with Bishops of opposite colours usually leads to a draw, even with a Pawn or two less.

31 b3xc4   Kb8-b7

32 d4-d5!

Nails down the position on the Queen-side before starting the King march.

32 ...   f5-f4

This will cost a Pawn, but he must give his Bishop some elbow-room to get some counterplay, or else slowly succumb.

33 a3-a4   Bc8-f5
34 Be7-g5   Kb7-c8
35 Bg5xf4   Kc8-b7
36 h2-h3   Bf5-b1
37 g2-g4   h5xg4
38 h3xg4   Kb7-a7

39 Bf4-d2

With a concealed attack on the a-Pawn.

39 ...   Ka7-b6
40 f3-f4   Bb1-e4
41 f4-f5!

A neat finesse to obtain a passed Pawn.

41 ...   g6xf5
42 g4-g5   f5-f4

Black hastens to return the gift, so that he can blockade the dangerous Pawn.

43 Bd2xf4   Be4-g6
44 Bf4-e3+   Kb6-b7

This is the situation:

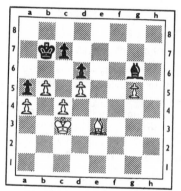

Position after 44 . . . Kb6-b7

45 c4-c5!   d6xc5

Refusing to capture is worse, as after 45 . . . Bg6-f7 instead, this would occur: 46 c5-c6+ Kb7-c8 47 Kc3-c4 and White can continue either with 48 Be3-d2 picking off the Rook Pawn, or with 48 b5-b6, winning easily in either case.

46 Kc3-c4   Bg6-c2

47	Kc4xc5	Bc2xa4

The Bishop does not hesitate to capture, as he can still get back to h7, in time to head off the g-Pawn.

48	Be3-d2	Ba4-c2
49	Bd2xa5	Bc2-g6
50	d5-d6	

Nicely creating another passed Pawn.

50	...	c7xd6+
51	Kc5xd6	**Black Resigns**

Sir George does not care to see the dénouement, but to dispel any doubts, this is how the win could be completed: 51 . . . Bg6-e8 52 Kd6-c5 Be8-g6 53 Ba5-c3 Bg6-e8 54 Bc3-e5 Be8-g6 55 b5-b6 Bg6-e8 56 Be5-c7, after which the King walks over to the King-side, wins the Bishop for the g-Pawn, then returns to the Queen-side, and helps the last Pawn become a Queen.

Exquisite play, and devilishly instructive as well.

As Goethe once said, 'Seeing someone accomplishing arduous things with ease gives an impression of witnessing the impossible.'

GAME 51

White J. R. Capablanca
Black F. D. Yates
Hastings, 1930

Queen's Gambit Declined
Rook endings are important, as they are the ones that occur most often in the game of chess.

One can recognize the touch of a master in the way Capablanca handles Rook endings. They are delicate affairs in which the work of hours may be ruined by one hasty move.

I believe that a proper study of the fine points of such magnificent Rook endings of Capablanca's as the one against Duras in 1913 (Game 15), the one against Tartakover in 1924 (Game 36), and the one that follows against Yates, will go far to improve a player's strength.

The difficulties are heightened when the Pawns are all on one side of the board. The acquisition of a passed Pawn requires the utmost care and attention, such as Capablanca lavishes on the fifty moves of his ending against Yates, in the following game.

1	d2-d4	d7-d5
2	c2-c4	e7-e6
3	Ng1-f3	Ng8-f6
4	Bc1-g5	Nb8-d7
5	e2-e3	Bf8-e7
6	Nb1-c3	0-0
7	Ra1-c1	

Probably best at this point, judging

from the fact that it was played about 20 times in the Capablanca-Alekhine World Championship match in 1927.

The Rooks' influence will be felt on the c-file after the inevitable exchange of Pawns.

7	...	c7-c6
8	Bf1-d3	d5xc4
9	Bd3xc4	a7-a6

Black's idea is to continue with 10 ... b7-b5, 11 ... Bc8-b7, and an eventual ... c6-c5.

The best specific for Black's cramped game is Capablanca's freeing maneuver, 9 ... Nf6-d5, which forces the exchange of a couple of pieces.

A model continuation would go something like this: 9 ... Nf6-d5 10 Bg5xe7 Qd8xe7 11 0-0 Nd5xc3 12 Rc1xc3 e6-e5 13 d4xe5 Nd7xe5 14 Nf3xe5 Qe7xe5 15 f2-f4 Qe5-e4!, with a satisfactory game.

There are perils of course, even in this innocent-looking position. For example, if Black plays 15 ... Qe5-e7 (instead of his last move), there is this neat possibility: 16 f4-f5 Rf8-d8 17 f5-f6 Rd8xd1 18 f6xe7 Rd1xf1+ 19 Bc4xf1 Bc8-f5 (if 19 ... Bc8-e6 20 Rc3-d3!) 20 e3-e4 Bf5-g6 (or 20 ... Bf5xe4 21 Rc3-e3 f7-f5 22 Bf1-c4+ Kg8-h8 23 Bc4-f7 wins) 21 Rc3-d3 Ra8-e8 22 Rd3-d8 f7-f6 23 Bf1-c4† Kg8-h8 24 Bc4-e6, and 25 Be6-d7 next move assures the win for White (Tartakover).

10	0-0	b7-b5
11	Bc4-e2	Bc8-b7
12	Qd1-c2	Ra8-c8

13	Rf1-d1	c6-c5
14	d4xc5	Rc8xc5
15	b2-b4	Rc5-c8
16	Qc2-b1	Nf6-d5
17	Nc3xd5	Be7xg5

Clearly, not 17 ... Bb7xd5 18 Rc1xc8 Qd8xc8 19 Bg5xe7 winning a piece, nor 17 ... Rc8xc1 18 Nd5xe7+ Qd8xe7 19 Bg5xe7 Rc1xb1 20 Rd1xb1, and White has won a piece.

| 18 | Rc1xc8 | Bb7xc8 |

And of course not 18 ... Qd8xc8 19 Nf3xg5, and the threats of 20 Qb1xh7 mate, and 20 Nd5-e7+ winning the Queen, cannot both be parried.

| 19 | Nf3xg5 | Qd8xg5 |
| 20 | Nd5-c3 | Bc8-b7 |

Threatens mate on the move. There is always some satisfaction in that, even if it's short-lived.

This is the picture on the board:

Position after 20 ... Bc8-b7

| 21 | Nc3-e4 | Qg5-g6 |

Ready to meet 22 Rd1xd7 with

22 . . . Bb7xe4–a devastating recapture which forces 23 Qb1-f1, and a passive position.

22	Be2-f3	Bb7-d5
23	Ne4-c3	Qg6xb1
24	Nc3xb1	Nd7-f6

If 24 . . . Bd5xa2 25 Nb1-c3 Ba2-d5 26 Nc3xd5, and White regains his Pawn with the better ending.

| 25 | Nb1-c3 | Rf8-c8 |

Black becomes ambitious! Or does he overlook a fairly easy draw by 25 . . . Bd5xf3 26 g2xf3 Rf8-c8 27 Rd1-d6 Kg8-f8?

26	Nc3xd5	Nf6xd5
27	Bf3xd5	e6xd5
28	g2-g3	g7-g6

On 28 . . . Rc8-d8 29 Rd1-d4 fixes the Pawn and 30 e3-e4 wins it.

29	Rd1xd5	Rc8-c2
30	a2-a4!	b5xa4
31	Rd5-a5	

Alert, and assures White of remaining a Pawn ahead.

31	. . .	Rc2-a2
32	Ra5xa6	Kg8-g7
33	Kg1-g2	a4-a3
34	b4-b5	Ra2-b2
35	Ra6xa3	Rb2xb5

Ending 51

Position after 35 . . . Rb2xb5

Yates

Capablanca to move

Though White is a Pawn ahead, the position is a theoretical draw, as the Pawns are all on one side of the board.

But there are winning chances—especially if White is Capablanca!

Capablanca plans to place his Rook in a dominating position, and force a favorable exchange of Pawns—one that will split up Black's Pawns, and isolate them.

After that a long, careful King-march up the board, sheltering and being sheltered by the advancing Pawns.

All this is carried out by Capablanca in flawless style, in an ending that ranks as one of the grandest in the entire literature of chess.

36	Ra3-a6	Rb5-b4
37	h2-h3	Rb4-c4
38	Kg2-f3	

White is in no hurry to play

38 g3-g4, when 38 . . . Rc4-c5
followed by 39 . . . h7-h5 offers
good drawing chances.

| 38 | ... | Rc4-b4 |
| 39 | Ra6-a5! | Rb4-c4 |

There was still time for
39 . . . h7-h5.

40 g3-g4!

But this prevents it once and for all!

| 40 | ... | h7-h6 |

This *may* be the cause of his loss,
though the authorities are divided
here. Had Yates played otherwise
and lost, the critics might have said,
'Why not 40 . . . h7-h6 at this
point?'

Kashdan, in the *American Chess
Bulletin,* says, 'This natural-looking
move is bad in this position, and is
probably the cause of his loss.

White will eventually play h3-h4,
h4-h5, and h5xg6. If Black recaptures with the Pawn, he allows a
passed King Pawn, or if, as in the
game, with the King, the remaining
Pawns are isolated. With the Pawn
still at h7, White's h4-h5 would
involve no threat, and if he ever
played g4-g5, then . . . h7-h6
could come, and the exchange of
Pawns could lead to a book draw.'

Reuben Fine in *Basic Chess
Endings* views it thus, 'This move is
not necessary to prevent g4-g5,
since it could always be played
then. But it does come in handy
against the advance of the enemy
Rook Pawn, e.g., if Black plays
passively, White may play h3-h4,
h4-h5, Kf3-g3, f2-f4, Kg3-f3, and
finally Ra5-a7, threatening e3-e4,
e4-e5, f4-f5, and h5-h6+. In that

event, . . . h7-h6 at some future
date would certainly be forced.'

41 Kf3-g3

Prepares to advance the Bishop
Pawn—or the Rook Pawn!

41	...	Rc4-c1
42	Kg3-g2	Rc1-c4
43	Ra5-d5	

The position at this stage:

Position after 43 Ra5-d5

| 43 | ... | Rc4-a4 |

Against the plausible 43 . . . g6-g5,
White builds up this formation:
44 f2-f3, 45 e3-e4, 46 Rd5-f5,
and 47 h3-h4. If then 47 . . . g5xh4
48 Kg2-h3 or if 47 . . . f7-f6
48 Rd5-a5, threatening 49 Ra5-a7+
and 50 h4-h5.

44 f2-f4!

Now the threat of 45 h3-h4 and
46 h4-h5 begins to take definite
form.

44	...	Ra4-a2+
45	Kg2-g3	Ra2-e2
46	Rd5-e5	Re2-e1
47	Kg3-f2	Re1-h1

48	Kf2-g2	Rh1-e1
49	h3-h4!	Kg7-f6

'More exact,' says Fine, 'was
49 . . . Re1-a1 50 h4-h5 g6xh5
51 Re5xh5 f7-f6 52 Rh5-b5
Kg7-g6 53 Kg2-f3 Ra1-a4 with
equality.'

I believe though that White
has excellent winning chances, as
the two isolated Pawns can inspire
no confidence in Black's prospects.

50	h4-h5	Re1-e2+

If instead 50 . . . g6xh5 51 Kg2-f2
followed by 52 Re5xh5, with a
position similar to that which
occurred in the game, while on
50 . . . g6-g5, the continuation
51 Re5-f5+ Kf6-g7 52 Kg2-f2
Re1-a1 53 f4xg5 wins a Pawn for
White.

51	Kg2-f3	Re2-e1
52	Re5-a5	Kf6-g7
53	h5xg6	Kg7xg6

If Black avoids Scylla (53 . . . f7xg6,
which lets White have a passed Pawn
on the e-file) he falls into Charybdis
(53 . . . Kg7xg6, which splits up his
Pawns).

The capture by 53 . . . f7xg6
could lead to this pretty win:
54 Ra5-a7+ Kg7-g8 55 e3-e4!
Re1-f1+ 56 Kf3-e3 Rf1-g1
57 f4-f5! Rg1xg4 58 f5-f6! and
White's Pawns, being further advanced, will secure the win for him.

Or if 53 . . . f7xg6 54 Ra5-a7+
Kg7-f6 55 Ra7-h7! Re1-f1+
56 Kf3-g2 Rf1-e1 57 Kg2-f2
Re1-h1 58 Rh7xh6!, and White
wins.

54	e3-e4

'*Sehr fein,*' says Becker in the
Wiener Schachzeitung.

Other critics, though, suggest as
more forceful this line of play:
54 Ra5-d5! Re1-f1+ 55 Kf3-g2
Rf1-e1 56 Kg2-f2 Re1-a1 57 e3-e4
and now the threat of 58 Rd5-d6+
followed by 59 e4-e5 comes in with
greater effect; if then 57 . . . Ra1-a4
58 Kf2-e3 Ra4-a3+ 59 Rd5-d3, and
the Pawns are ready to move forward.

54	. . .	Re1-f1+
55	Kf3-g3	Rf1-g1+
56	Kg3-h3	Rg1-f1

But not 56 . . . Rg1-h1+ 57 Kh3-g2.

57	Ra5-f5

White protects the Pawn properly,
avoiding such impulsive moves as
57 f4-f5+ when 57 . . . Kg6-g5 lets
the opponent out of his clutches.

The diagram shows the position:

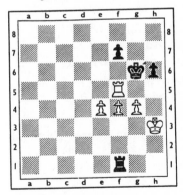

Position after 57 Ra5-f5

57	. . .	Rf1-e1

Black misses a golden opportunity:
he must prevent 58 e4-e5!
He should have proceeded as

follows: 57 . . . f7-f6 58 Kh3-g2
Rf1-e1 59 e4-e5 f6xe5 60 Rf5xe5
Re1xe5 61 f4xe5 h6-h5 62 g4xh5+
Kg6xh5 63 Kg2-f3 Kh5-g6
64 Kf3-e4 Kg6-f7 65 Ke4-d5
Kf7-e7, and the position is a book
draw.

| 58 | e4-e5! | Re1-e3+ |
| 59 | Kh3-g2! | |

Capablanca, as usual, is on the *qui
vive*, and does not fall into
59 Kh3-h4, after which the play
would go this way: 59 . . . Re3-c3!
60 Rf5-f6+ (just about the only
move) 60 . . . Kg6-g7 61 g4-g5 (if
f4-f5 Rc3-e3 wins a Pawn)
61 . . . h6xg5+ 62 Kh4xg5 (on
62 f4xg5 Rc3-e3 63 Rf6-f5 Kg7-g6
draws) 62 . . . Rc3-e3 63 Rf6-a6
Re3-e1 64 Ra6-a4 Re1-e2
65 Kg5-f5 Re2-e1 66 Ra4-a7
Re1-e2 67 Ra7-e7 Re2-a2
68 e5-e6 Ra2-a5+ 69 Kf5-g4
Kg7-f6, and Black forces a draw.

59	. . .	Re3-a3
60	Rf5-f6+	Kg6-g7
61	Rf6-b6	Ra3-e3

Restrains the Pawns from advancing—*pour le moment!*

| 62 | Rb6-b4 | |

This move and the next is intended
to drive the Rook off the e-file.

62	. . .	Re3-c3
63	Kg2-f2	Rc3-a3
64	Rb4-b7	

Threatens to win a Pawn by
65 e5-e6.

| 64 | . . . | Kg7-g8 |

But not 64 . . . Kg7-g6, when
65 f4-f5+ Kg6-g5 66 Rb7xf7

Kg5xg4 67 e5-e6 wins for
White.

| 65 | Rb7-b8+ | Kg8-g7 |
| 66 | f4-f5 | |

Threatens 67 f5-f6+ Kg7-h7 (if
67 . . . Kg7-g6 68 Rb8-g8+ Kg6-h7
69 Rg8-g7+ Kh7-h8 70 Rg7xf7
wins) and now White can choose
one of two wins, either 68 e5-e6
(which seems to do the trick) or
68 Rb8-f8 Ra3-a7 69 Kf2-g3
Ra7-b7 70 Kg3-h4 Rb7-a7
71 Kh4-h5 Ra7-b7 72 g4-g5
(threatens 73 Rf8xf7+) 72 . . .
h6xg5 73 e5-e6! f7xe6 74 Rf8-e8!
Rb7-f7 75 Re8-e7 Kh7-g8
76 Kh5-g6 Rf7-f8 77 Re7-g7+
Kg8-h8 78 f6-f7, and the Rook
threatens mate on the next move.

| 66 | . . . | Ra3-a2+ |
| 67 | Kf2-e3 | |

Begins one of the great King
wanderings of master play.

67	. . .	Ra2-a3+
68	Ke3-e4	Ra3-a4+
69	Ke4-d5!	

Brilliant! Black may not take the
Pawn, as after 69 . . . Ra4xg4
70 f5-f6+ Kg7-h7 71 Rb8-f8
Kh7-g6 72 Rf8-g8+ Kg6-f5
73 Rg8xg4 Kf5xg4 74 e5-e6!;
and one of White's Pawns crashes
through.

69	. . .	Ra4-a5+
70	Kd5-d6	Ra5-a6+
71	Kd6-c7	

The position at this point:

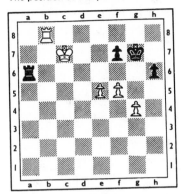

Position after 71 Kd6-c7

71 ...   Kg7-h7

on 71 ... Ra6-a1 instead, White
wins with a flourish, thus: 72 f5-f6+
Kg7-h7 73 Rb8-f8 Ra1-a7+
74 Kc7-d8 Kh7-g6 75 Rf8-g8+
Kg6-h7 76 Rg8-g7+ Kh7-h8
77 g4-g5! h6xg5 78 Kd8-e8 Ra7-a5
79 Rg7xg5 Ra5-a7 60 e5-e6!
f7xe6 81 f6-f7 Ra7-a8+ 82 Ke8-e7
Ra8-a7+ 83 Ke7-f6 Ra7-a8
84 Rg5-h5 mate!

72 Kc7-d7!   Ra6-a7+

73 Kd7-d6   Kh7-g7

Continuing to check instead leads
to this: 73 ... Ra7-a6+ 74 Kd6-e7
Ra6-a7+ (or 74 ... Kh7-g7
75 f5-f6+) 75 Ke7-f6, and the f-
Pawn is doomed.

74 Rb8-d8

White is now ready to meet
74 ... Ra7-a6+ with 75 Kd6-e7
Ra6-a7+ 76 Rd8-d7 Ra7-a5
77 e5-e6! f7xe6 (or 77 ... Ra5-e5
78 Ke7-e8!) 78 f5-f6+ Kg7-g6
79 f6-f7, and wins.

74 ...   Ra7-a5

The waiting move: 74 ... Ra7-b7
meets with this fate: 75 f5-f6+
Kg7-g6 (or 75 ... Kg7-h7
76 Rd8-d7 Rb7-b6+ 77 Kd6-c5
and White wins a Pawn) 76 Kd6-c6
Rb7-a7 77 Kc6-b6! Ra7-a4
78 Rd8-g8+ Kg6-h7 79 Rg8-g7+,
and the unfortunate Pawn falls.

75 f5-f6+   Kg7-h7

76 Rd8-f8

It shouldn't take long now, but
Yates hangs on like grim death!

76 ...   Ra5-a7

Nothing is to be gained from
76 ... Ra5-a6+ 77 Kd6-d7 Ra6-a7+
78 Kd7-e8.

Another diagram please, Mr. Printer!

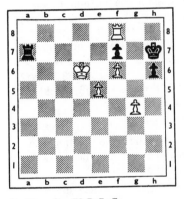

Position after 76 Ra5-a7

77 Kd6-c6!

Magnificent! Black is in *zugzwang*—
that unfortunate state where one
must move, though every move
loses.

77 ...   Kh7-g6

All that is left, there being no point
in 77 ... Ra7-a6+ 78 Kc6-d7
Ra6-a7+ 79 Kd7-e8, etc.

78	Rf8-g8+	Kg6-h7
79	Rg8-g7+	Kh7-h8
80	Kc6-b6!	

Accurate to the last detail! Playing 80 e5-e6 seems to win, but after 80 . . . Ra7-a6+ 81 Kc6-d7 Ra6xe6 82 Rg7xf7 Re6-a6!, the position is only a draw!

| 80 | . . . | Ra7-d7 |
| 81 | Kb6-c5! | |

Now the threat (which has been hanging fire for hours) becomes acute.

| 81 | . . . | Rd7-c7+ |
| 82 | Kc5-d6 | Rc7-a7 |

There are still some delightful finesses in the position. For example, if White tries 83 g4-g5, this could happen: 83 . . . h6xg5 84 Rg7xg5 Kh8-h7 85 Rg5-g7+ Kh7-h8 86 e5-e6 Ra7-a6+ 87 Kd6-e7 Ra6xe6+! 88 Ke7xf7 Re6xf6+! 89 Kf7xf6, and Black has been stalemated.

| 83 | e5-e6! | |

Finally, the move that has been poised over Yates's head like the Sword of Damocles!

| 83 | . . . | Ra7-a6+ |
| 84 | Kd6-e7 | Ra6xe6+ |

Or he could lose in glorious style by 84 . . . f7xe6 85 f6-f7 Ra6-a7+ 86 Ke7-f6 Ra7-a8 87 Kf6-g6, and White mates next move.

| 85 | Ke7xf7 | Re6-e4 |

Or 85 . . . Re6-e5 86 g4-g5! Re5xg5 (on 86 . . . h6xg5 87 Kf7-g6 wins, the threat being 88 Rg7-e7—which Black cannot counter by

87 . . . Re5-e8, as 88 Rg7-h7+ Kh8-g8 89 f6-f7+ wins the Rook) 87 Rg7xg5 h6xg5 88 Kf7-e8 and White wins.

| 86 | g4-g5! | |

An elegant finish.

| 86 | . . . | h6xg5 |
| 87 | Kf7-g6 | Black Resigns |

A last diagram:

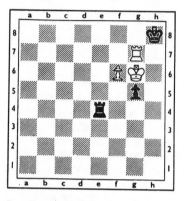

Position after 87 Kf7-g6

The threat of 88 Rg7-h7+ Kh8-g8 89 f6-f7+ Kg8-f8 90 Rh7-h8+ can only be countered by 87 . . . Re4-h4 (preventing the check) or by 87 . . . Re4-e6 (pinning the Pawn).

Both these moves succumb at once to 88 Rg7-e7!

A magnificent ending, one that is outstanding even among the many great ones created by Capablanca.

It offers more instruction in strategy and tactics than the student will discover in a dozen brilliant King-side attacks.

GAME 52

White V. Menchik
Black J. R. Capablanca
Hastings, 1931

Queen's Indian Defence
Nothing exciting seems to happen
in this game, yet it is a joy to play
through. In it we see an interesting
aspect of Capablanca's wondrous
technique—his inimitable flair for
extracting an advantage from the
most routine of procedures.

For example, Miss Menchik
tries to force a draw by exchanging
as many pieces as possible. Far
from avoiding these attempts to
simplify the game, Capablanca
welcomes the exchanges, and
emerges from each of them with
a slightly superior position.

By the time most of the pieces
have been cleared away, his positional advantage is strong enough
to yield a Pawn.

One extra Pawn is all Capablanca needs, and since he had an
incomparable faculty for making
all endings look easy, it is a treat
to watch him win this one.

1	d2-d4	Ng8-f6
2	Ng1-f3	b7-b6
3	e2-e3	Bc8-b7
4	Bf1-d3	c7-c5

Black naturally strikes a blow at
the center.

5	0-0	Nb8-c6
6	c2-c3	e7-e6
7	Nf3-e5	

White is eager to exchange pieces,
even at the cost of neglecting
development!

Preferable was 7 Nb1-d2, bringing another piece into play, or
7 e3-e4, releasing the dark-squared
Bishop.

| 7 | ... | d7-d6 |
| 8 | Ne5xc6 | Bb7xc6 |

Black has benefited by the exchange, as White's Knight has disappeared, but *Black's Knight has
been replaced by another piece.*

Black already has two pieces in
play against one of White's (though
admittedly the latter has castled).

The Art of Exchanging Unwisely
was known as far back as the
Morphy era.

Take as instance the first few
moves of the famous game Morphy
against the Duke of Brunswick and
the Count Isouard, which went as
follows: 1 e2-e4 e7-e5 2 Ng1-f3
d7-d6 3 d2-d4 Bc8-g4 4 d4xe5
Bg4xf3 5 Qd1xf3 (Black's Bishop
has disappeared from the board,
while White's Knight has been replaced by another piece)
5 ... d6xe5 6 Bf1-c4, and Morphy,
with two pieces in the field against
none of Black's, already threatens
mate!

| 9 | Qd1-e2 | Bf8-e7 |
| 10 | Bd3-b5 | |

For the second time, White moves a
piece twice in the opening merely
for the sake of forcing an exchange
of pieces.

Such violation of principles is

bound to bring punishment.

| 10 | ... | Qd8-d7 |
| 11 | Bb5xc6 | Qd7xc6 |

Black's superiority in position is now apparent. He has three pieces in the field against two of White's—considering the process of castling as a developing move.

| 12 | Nb1-d2 | 0-0 |
| 13 | d4xc5 | |

This opens the d-file for the convenience of Black's Rooks, but if 13 e3-e4 at once, then 13 . . . c5xd4 14 c3xd4 Ra8-c8 (or 14 . . . Qc6-c2) is strong for Black, while 13 Qe2-f3 (angling for an exchange of Queens) is countered by 13 . . . d6-d5 and Black exerts strong pressure on e4.

| 13 | ... | d6xc5 |
| 14 | e3-e4 | |

White's pieces need room!

This is the position:

Position after 14 e3-e4

| 14 | ... | Ra8-d8 |
| 15 | e4-e5 | |

The Pawn advances so that the Knight, which was tied down to protecting it, may be enabled to move. The Knight will move next, freeing the Bishop, which in turn will move, letting the Queen Rook come into play.

(The process is reminiscent of the children's story *The House that Jack Built*.)

15	...	Nf6-d5
16	Nd2-f3	Rd8-d7
17	Rf1-d1	Rf8-d8
18	Bc1-d2	

Just about the only spot for the Bishop, as 18 Bc1-e3 Nd5xe3 19 Rd1xd7 Qc6xd7 leaves Black in possession of the d-file, while 18 Bc1-g5 loses quickly by 18 . . . Be7xg5 19 Nf3xg5 Nd5-f4 (attacks the Queen and also threatens mate) 20 Qe2-g4 Rd7-d1+ 21 Ra1xd1 Rd8xd1+ 22 Qg4xd1 Qc6xg2 mate.

| 18 | ... | b6-b5! |

Initiates activity on the Queen-side. The square b6 is vacated so that the Knight can leap there and then to c4 or a4, either square serving as a strong outpost.

| 19 | Kg1-f1 | Nd5-b6 |
| 20 | Bd2-f4 | h7-h6 |

A quiet little move, which accomplishes a great deal:

(a) it provides a flight-square for the King,

(b) it restricts the activity of White's Knight and Bishop,

(c) it prepares the way for a possible attack by . . . g7-g5.

| 21 | Rd1xd7 | Rd8xd7 |

22	Ra1-d1	Rd7xd1+
23	Qe2xd1	

Ending 52

Position after 23 Qe2xd1

Capablanca to move

Menchik

Black's Queen and Knight are poised for the kill. In just a couple of moves Black manages to win a Pawn, and the rest for the skilled master, is 'just a matter of technique'.

And it is Capablanca's smooth, flawless technique, his incomparable faculty for making the most effective moves—the ones that make the opponent resign the soonest—that endow this ending with a particular radiance.

23	...	Qc6-e4

This attack on the unprotected Bishop, combined with threat of 24 ... Qe4-c4+ followed by 25 ... Qc4xa2, assures Black of winning a Pawn.

24	Bf4-g3	

As good as any, the other unhappy choices being:

(a) 24 Bf4-e3 (or 24 Bf4-d2) 24 ... Nb6-c4, and Black wins the e-Pawn or the b-Pawn.

(b) 24 ... Bf4-c1 (protecting the b-Pawn) Qe4-c4+ 25 Qd1-e2 Qc4xa2 26 Qe2xb5 Qa2-b1, and Black wins the hapless Bishop.

24	...	Qe4-c4+
25	Qd1-e2	Qc4xe2+

The right way, whereas 25 ... Qc4xa2 26 Qe2xb5 Qa2-c4+ 27 Qb5xc4 Nb6xc4 28 b2-b3 Nc4-a5 29 Nf3-d2 finds all points protected.

26	Kf1xe2	Nb6-a4

Attacks the b-Pawn, which must not stir, as after 27 b2-b3 Na4xc3+ wins two Pawns instead of one.

27	Ke2-d2	Na4xb2
28	Kd2-c2	Nb2-c4
29	Nf3-d2	

An offer to exchange pieces, which Black is happy to accept.

29	...	Nc4xd2
30	Kc2xd2	

The position at this stage:

Position after 30 Kc2xd2

30	...	c5-c4!

This complies of course with the principle that Pawns should not occupy squares of the same colour as the Bishop, as then they restrict the Bishop's range of activity.

Note that White's Bishop is hampered in its movements by the fact that the square e5 is occupied by a Pawn.

This principle of endgame strategy governs all cases, except for the 23rd match game between Capablanca and Marshall (see Game 4). There Marshall complied with this convention, while Capablanca disregarded it—but Capablanca nevertheless won the game!

(It pays to be a genius!)

31	Bg3-f4	

The object is to get the Bishop back into the game, perhaps along another diagonal.

Meanwhile, White sets a trap to catch an over-eager opponent.

The idea is this: if Black plays to exchange Bishops and bring the position to a simple Pawn-ending, this could happen:
31 . . . Be7-g5 32 Bf4xg5 h6xg5 33 Kd2-e3 Kg8-f8 34 Ke3-d4 Kf8-e7 35 Kd4-c5 a7-a6 36 a2-a3 and White has at least a draw.

Capablanca hardly even glances at the trap!

He goes about his business, leaving the Bishop at e7, where it prevents White's King from reaching c5, and plays

31	...	a7-a6
32	Bf4-e3	Kg8-f8

'The King, a purely defensive piece during the opening and middle-game,' says Capablanca himself, 'very often becomes an offensive piece in the ending. In endings of one or two minor pieces, the King should generally be marched forward towards the center of the board. In King-and-Pawn endings, almost invariably so.'

Elsewhere, Capablanca states it as clearly and simply as possible, 'In King-and-Pawn endings, it is imperative that the King be advanced to the center of the board.'

33	Be3-b6	Kf8-e8
34	Kd2-e3	Ke8-d7
35	Ke3-d4	Kd7-c6
36	Bb6-a7	

The only decent move left to the Bishop, as 36 Bb6-a5 loses the f-Pawn by 36 . . . Be7-c5+.

36	...	f7-f5!

Tightens his grip! Now neither King nor Bishop dare move. If 37 Ba7-b8 (other Bishop moves subject it to immediate capture) 37 . . . Be7-c5 is mate, or if the King moves to e3 (his only move) then 37 ... Be7-c5+ forces an exchange of Bishops, leaving an easily won Pawn-ending.

If White tries 37 e5xf6 *en passant,* then 37 ... Be7xf6+ 38 Kd4-e4 Bf6xc3 leaves Black two Pawns ahead.

What to do?

This is the position:

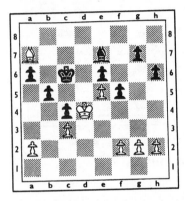

Position after 36 ... f7-f5!

| 37 | a2-a4 | |

This may look like suicide, but White is in a state of near-*zugzwang,* and is running short of moves.

Advancing the King-side Pawns

is only delaying the inevitable, while any move of King or Bishop is fatal.

Incidentally, I would venture to say that Capablanca has won more games by *zugzwang* than has any other master.

37	...	g7-g6
38	f2-f4	h6-h5
39	a4xb5+	Kc6xb5

The right way to recapture, as Black thereby acquires a passed Pawn ...

| 40 | g2-g3 | a6-a5 |

... which starts out on the road to success.

| 41 | Kd4-e3 | |

Absolutely necessary, or the Pawn could not be headed off.

41	...	Be7-c5+
42	Ba7xc5	Kb5xc5
43	**White Resigns**	

The rest could go like this: 43 Ke3-d2 Kc5-d5 44 Kd2-e3 a5-a4 45 Ke3-d2 a4-a3 46 Kd2-c2 Kd2-e4 47 Kc2-b1 Ke4-d3, finis.

The moral is: play for a win, and you might draw.

GAME 53

White A. Kevitz
Black J. R. Capablanca
New York, 1931

Réti's Opening
Naturally enough, the opening is a Réti, this being Kevitz's speciality, but it soon takes an original turn,

when Capablanca gives up a Pawn (or did he possibly overlook something and lose it?).

Whatever the case, he proceeds to weave a Queen-side attack, leading to a winning ending, from the skimpiest of materials—one might say from nothing at all.

Capablanca's 31st move drives a wedge in the enemy's Queen-side position, his next breaks up a little army of Pawns, while his brilliant 36th move forces the win in problem style.

A delightful gem, with a piquant finish.

1	Ng1-f3	d7-d5
2	c2-c4	c7-c6
3	b2-b3	Bc8-f5
4	g2-g3	Ng8-f6
5	Bf1-g2	e7-e6
6	0-0	Nb8-d7
7	Bc1-b2	Bf8-d6
8	d2-d3	0-0
9	Nb1-d2	Qd8-e7

Very good, as the Queen not only backs up an expansion in the center by 10 . . . e6-e5, but also supports the wing thrust . . . Bd6-a3, to eliminate White's strongly-placed dark-squared Bishop.

10   Rf1-e1

Develops with a threat of winning a piece by 11 e2-e4 and 12 e4-e5.

10	. . .	e6-e5
11	c4xd5	c6xd5
12	e2-e4!	d5xe4

Practically forced, to prevent the opening of the e-file.

13	d3xe4	Bf5-e6
14	Qd1-e2	Ra8-c8
15	Nd2-f1	Bd6-a3

Speculation, calculation, or a deep feeling for positional considerations?

Safer of course is the stodgy 15 . . . Rf8-d8, waiting for White to declare his intentions.

A diagram of the position:

Position after 15 . . . Bd6-a3

16   Nf3xe5

The right way to capture, as 16 Bb2xe5 loses material by 16 . . . Nd7xe5 17 Nf3xe5 Ba3-b4 18 Re1-c1 Bb4-c3, and Black wins the exchange.

16	. . .	Ba3xb2
17	Qe2xb2	Nd7xe5
18	Qb2xe5	Qe7-a3

Black is a Pawn behind, but he does exert some pressure on the Queen-side, which serves as part payment for the Pawn.

His Queen is strongly placed, and his Rook, in full control of the c-file, threatens to swoop down to the seventh rank, and win the a-Pawn.

19   Nf1-e3   Nf6-g4

Renews the threat against the Pawn, by 20 . . . Ng4xe3 followed by 21 . . . Rc8-c2.

20	Ne3xg4	Be6xg4
21	h2-h3	Bg4-e6
22	Re1-e2	

Ending 53

Capablanca to move

Kevitz

Guards against the intrusion and the consequent loss of the a-Pawn, but this (forced) loss of a tempo gives Black the opportunity to seize another open file.

22	. . .	Rf8-d8
23	Qe5-b2	

Kevitz hastens to exchange pieces, not having learned a lesson from the game Menchik-Capablanca (Game 52), where this strategy failed badly.

One is tempted to offer this piece of advice, 'Never exchange pieces with Capablanca even if you are a Rook ahead!'

'Timidity is out of place,' says Golombek acutely, 'when one is a Pawn up with an excellent position.'

23	. . .	Qa3-c5
24	Re2-d2	Rd8xd2
25	Qb2xd2	b7-b6
26	Ra1-d1	g7-g6
27	Kg1-h2	

Capablanca is behind in material, having sacrificed a Pawn to acquire an advantage in position.

This advantage (hardly visible to the naked eye) consists of a stronger grip on the c-file than his opponent exerts on the d-file. Efforts to dispute this control are not easily initiated, as after Black's next move (27 . . . a7-a5) the reply 28 Qd2-d6 loses the f-Pawn, while 28 Qd2-d4 also costs a Pawn by 28 . . . Qc5xd4 29 Rd1xd4 Rc8-c2.

Black's positional superiority is admittedly slight, but Capablanca has an original plan for winning, which is distinguished by a pretty problem-move, which we shall see as the endgame unfolds.

27	. . .	a7-a5!

A quiet little move, it is the forerunner of a strong Queen-side attack.

28 Qd2-e2

Anticipating 28 . . . Qc5-c2 followed by 29 . . . b6-b5 and
30 . . . a5-a4, White seeks to prevent it by threatening to play
29 Rd1-d2, the moment Black's
Queen moves down to the
seventh.

28	...	b6-b5
29	f2-f4	a5-a4
30	b3xa4	b5xa4

Clearly indicating that he intends
to play 31 . . . a4-a3 next move,
nailing down the a-Pawn, thus
making it a fixed target for attack.

The fall of this important Pawn
would leave Black with a passed
Pawn only two steps away from the
queening square.

But it is not so easy as it sounds!

31 Rd1-d2

Kevitz must have been blissfully
ignorant of danger, or he would
have sacrificed a Pawn by 31 f4-f5
g6xf5 32 e4xf5 Be6xf5.

This would have the merit of
opening the long diagonal for his
Bishop, as well as disrupting the
Pawn position of Black's King-side.

31 ... a4-a3!

Fixes the adverse a-Pawn and
establishes support for an outpost
at b2 for one of Black's pieces.

32 g3-g4

This attempt to get in 33 f4-f5
without giving up a Pawn gives
Capablanca the opportunity to
wind up the game with a couple of
surprise moves.

The position at this point:

Position after 32 g3-g4

32 ... g6-g5!

Not only does this permit 33 f4-f5,
it practically urges Kevitz to play it!

He resists the temptation as the
consequences would be: 33 f4-f5
Qc5-e5+, and (a) 34 Kh2-g1
Rc8-c1+ 35 Rd2-d1 (if 35 Bg2-f1
Be6-c4 wins) 35 . . . Qe5-d4+, and
Black wins a Rook; (b) 34 Kh2-h1
Rc8-c1+ 35 Rd2-d1 Qe5-b2
36 Qe2-e1 Rc1xd1 (safer than such
adventures as 36 . . . Rc1-c2
37 f5xe6 Rc2xg2 38 e6xf7+
Kg8xf7 39 Qe1-f1+ Rg2-f2
40 Qf2-c4+, and the intended
victim might become the victor)
37 Qe1xd1 Be6xa2, and Black
wins.

33 Qe2-f2 Qc5xf2

Confident in the superiority of his
position, Capablanca does not hesitate to exchange Queens.

34	Rd2xf2	g5xf4
35	Rf2-f3	

The Rook is not interested in the
f-Pawn, but sets his sights on the

a-Pawn, the most dangerous Pawn on the board.

Indeed there is no time for 35 Rf2xf4, as there would follow 35 . . . Be6xa2 36 Rf4-f3 Rc8-a8 (threatens 37 . . . Ba2-b1 and 38 . . . a3-a2) 37 Rf3-f1 Ba2-c4 38 Rf1-a1 a3-a2, after which 39 . . . Ra8-b8 and 40 . . . Rb8-b1 would force the win.

35   . . .   Rc8-a8

36   Rf3-f2

Protects the a-Pawn, after which Black can apparently make no progress, as 36 . . . Ra8-b8 (attempting to come in at b2) is parried by 37 Rf2-f3, attacking the Pawn once more, and forcing Black's Rook to return to a8 to protect it.

So much for normal winning attempts, but Black has a surprise move in reserve.

36   . . .   f4-f3!

Beautiful! This pretty Pawn sacrifice interferes with the action of White's Rook and Bishop at the f3 square.

If 37 Bg2xf3, *the Bishop occupies f3 and prevents the Rook's return to that square*, Black would then continue by 37 . . . Ra8-b8 and 38 . . . Rb8-b2, winning the a-Pawn and the game, e.g., if after 37 . . . Ra8-b8 38 Bf3-d1 Rb8-b2 39 Kh2-g3 Rb2xf2 40 Kg3xf2 Be6xa2 41 Bd1-c2 Ba2-c4 42 Bc2-b1 a3-a2, and White must give up his Bishop.

Or if the Rook captures the troublesome Pawn, the play goes (after 37 Rf2xf3) 37 . . . Be6xa2 38 Rf3-f1 Ba2-c4, and wins as in an earlier note.

37   Bg2-f1   Ra8-b8

38   Rf2xf3   Rb8-b2+

Another neat point (the kick at the end of this combination) is that the forced removal of White's Bishop from the second rank enables Black's Rook to come in on the seventh *with check*, thus giving him time to capture the white a-Pawn and protect his own Pawn.

39   Kh2-g3   Rb2xa2

40   Rf3-c3   Ra2-a1

41   White Resigns

White sees no hope in 41 Bf1-c4 Be6xc4 42 Rc3xc4 a3-a2 43 Rc4-a4 Ra1-g1+, nor in 41 Kg3-f2 a3-a2 42 Rc3-a3 Ra1-c1, and Black wins.

An unusual game, marked by nice, original touches.

GAME 54

White G. M. Lissitzin
Black J. R. Capablanca
Moscow, 1935

Réti's Opening
Lissitzin's early initiative lets him put on pressure. This is augmented when an early advance of his Queen-side minority of Pawns splits

up Capablanca's Pawns, rendering them vulnerable to attack.

Unfortunately for Lissitzin though, he loses the thread of the game, and misses his chance for glory.

He lets Capablanca escape from the toils!

The ensuing endgame finds Capablanca in his element. Handling it with his usual cool efficiency, he centralizes his Queen, so that her attack radiates in three directions at once.

The task of protecting three Pawns is too much for Lissitzin, who is gradually drawn into a semi-*zugzwang* position, and into an inevitable exchange of Queens—which is fatal.

1	Ng1-f3	d7-d5
2	c2-c4	c7-c6
3	e2-e3	Ng8-f6
4	Nb1-c3	Bc8-g4
5	c4xd5	Nf6xd5

Better than 5 . . . c6xd5 6 Qd1-b3 (attacks the d-Pawn, as well as the b-Pawn weakened by the absence of the Bishop) 6 . . . Bg4-c8 (retreat is practically forced, as 6 . . . Qd8-d7 fails after 7 Nf3-e5) 7 Bf1-b5+ Nb8-c6 8 Nf3-e5 Qd8-c7 9 d2-d4 e7-e6 10 Qb3-a4, with advantage to White.

6	Bf1-e2	e7-e6
7	d2-d4	Nb8-d7
8	0-0	Qd8-c7
9	Bc1-d2	Bf8-d6

The better course was 9 .'. . Bf8-e7, Black's present threat of winning a Pawn by 10 . . . Bf4xf3 followed by

11 . . . Bd6xh2+ being easily parried.

10	Nc3-e4	Nd7-f6
11	Ne4xd6+	Qc7xd6
12	Nf3-e5	Bg4xe2
13	Qd1xe2	0-0
14	Ra1-c1	Nd5-b6
15	Ne5-d3	Rf8-e8
16	Rf1-d1	Nb6-d7
17	h2-h3	

A diagram of the position:

Position after 17 h2-h3

| 17 | . . . | Qd6-d5 |

The attractive freeing maneuver 17 . . . e6-e5 is thwarted by 18 d4xe5 Nd7xe5 19 Nd3xe5 Re8xe5 (best, as White has good chances after 19 . . . Qd6xe5 20 Bd2-c3 Qe5-e6 21 Bc3xf6 Qe6xf6 22 Rd1-d7) 20 Bd2-c3 Re5-d5 (the only move) 21 Bc3xf6 Rd5xd1+ (if 21 . . . Qd6xf6 22 Rd1xd5 c6xd5 23 Qe2-b5 Qf6-b6 24 Qb5-d7 g7-g6 25 Rc1-c7 with a winning position) 22 Rc1xd1 Qd6xf6 23 Qe2-d2, and White's control of the d-file

assures him of the better ending
(Lissitzin).

18	b2-b3	Qd5-b5
19	Bd2-c3	Nf6-d5
20	Qe2-d2	Nd5xc3
21	Qd2xc3	Ra8-d8
22	a2-a4	Qb5-b6
23	b3-b4	Nd7-f6
24	Qc3-c4	

Little by little White gains ground,
and his Queen-side minority attack
begins to look dangerous.

24 ... Nf6-e4

Black's difficulties begin with this
move.

Lissitzin suggests 24 ... a7-a6
instead, with this possible continuation: 25 Qc4-c5 Nf6-d7
26 Qc5xb6 Nd7xb6 27 Nd3-c5
Rd8-b8 28 b4-b5 a6xb5 29 a4xb5
Re8-c8 30 Rc1-b1 Nb6-d5
31 b5xc6 b7xc6, with a probable
draw.

25	a4-a5!	Qb6-c7
26	a5-a6!	Rd8-c8
27	a6xb7	Qc7xb7

Lissitzin has managed to disrupt
Black's Pawn position on the Queen-
side, leaving him with two isolated
Pawns to watch over, and is in sight
of a win.

28 Rc1-a1

Threatens 29 Qc4-a6 Qb7xa6
30 Ra1xa6 Rc8-c7 31 Rd1-c1
Re8-c8 32 Nd3-e5, and White wins
the c-Pawn.

28	...	Rc8-c7
29	Rd1-c1	Re8-b8
30	Qc4-c2	

Initiates this subtle threat: 31 f2-f3
Ne4-f6 32 Nd3-c5 Qb7xb4 (other
Queen moves do not help)
33 Nc5-a6, and White wins the exchange by a mighty Knight fork.

30 ... Qb7-c8

This is how the board looks:

Position after 30 ... Qb7-c8

31 Ra1-a5

White misses his chance to win a
Pawn, and possibly the game, by
31 Nd3-e5!. If then 31 ... Ne4-d6
32 Ne5xc6 Kg8-h8 (if 32 ... Kg8-f8
33 Qc2-c5!) 33 Ra1xa7 Rc7xa7
34 Nc6xa7 Qc8xc2 35 Rc1xc2
Rb8xb4 36 Rc2-c6, and the threat
of mate wins a piece for White.

31 ... Rb8-b6

32 Qc2-a4

Here too 32 Nd3-e5 is strong, e.g.,
if 32 ... Ne4-d6 33 Ra5-c5
Rb6xb4 34 Ne5xc6 Rb4-b7
35 Nc6-e7+, and White wins. Or if
32 ... Ne4-f6 33 Ra5-c5 Nf6-d7
34 Ne5xd7 Qc8xd7 35 b4-b5,
and White wins a Pawn.

32 ... Qc8-b8

33	f2-f3	Ne4-f6
34	Ra5-c5	Nf6-d5
35	Rc5xc6	Rc7xc6
36	Rc1xc6	Rb6xc6
37	Qa4xc6	Nd5xe3
38	Nd3-c5	

White has missed his golden opportunity, and must run for the draw. The text looks good, as it threatens 39 Nc5xe6 f7xe6 40 Qc6xe6+, but it is inferior to 38 Qc6-d7 with this probable continuation:
38 . . . Ne3-d5 39 Nd3-e5 Qb8-f8 40 b4-b5 Nd5-c3 41 Kg1-f2.

38	. . .	Ne3-d5
39	b4-b5	Nd5-b6!
40	Nc5-d7	Qb8-d8!
41	Nd7xb6	a7xb6

Black of course could have forced a draw by 41 . . . Qd8xd4+ 42 Kg1-h2 Qd4-e5+ 43 Kh2-h1 Qe5-e1+ 44 Kh1-h2 Qe1-e5+—but, relying on his extraordinary skill in the endgame, goes gunning for a win.

| 42 | Qc6-c4 | |

Ending 54

Position after 42 Qc6-c4

Capablanca to move

Lissitzin

Material is even, but White does have a couple of isolated Pawns to worry about. The natural result should probably be a draw, as it usually is in Queen-endings of this sort, but—

Capablanca centralizes his King, and maneuvers his Queen so that she blockades one Pawn while attacking two others.

Lissitzin defends ably, but Capablanca draws the coils tighter, and soon forces his opponent into semi-*zugzwang*.

This results in loss of a Pawn, and shortly thereafter the game.

42	. . .	h7-h5
43	Kg1-f1	

White decides on passive resistance. More to the point was 43 Kg1-f2, ready to meet 43 . . . Qd8-d6 with 44 Kf2-e3 followed possibly by 45 Qc4-c6. Of if 43 . . . Qd8-f6

44 d4-d5 disposes of a weakness.

43	...	g7-g6
44	Kf1-g1	Kg8-g7
45	Kg1-f1	Qd8-d6
46	Kf1-g1	Qd6-f4

Pins the d-Pawn.

47 Qc4-c3

Unpins the Pawn and threatens
48 d4-d5+ followed by an exchange
of Pawns, thereby getting rid of one
weakness.

47	...	Kg7-h7
48	Kg1-f1	Qf4-f5
49	Qc3-c4	Kh7-g7

The King tries to get to the center.

50	Kf1-f2	Qf5-g5
51	Qc4-e2	

Now if Black plays 51 ... Qg5-d5
hastily, the reply 52 Qe2-e5+ lets
White escape with a draw.

51 ... Kg7-f6

The King approaches the center,
and renders 52 Qe2-e5+ impossible.

52 Qe2-b2

Not content with returning to c4
and probably drawing, White becomes over-ambitious and tries to
regain the initiative.

52 ... Qg5-d5!

Blockade! If it does not win, this
sort of move effectively curbs
aggressive tendencies.

53 Kf2-e3

According to Capablanca, White
still had drawing chances with
53 Qb2-b4 instead.

This is the state of affairs:

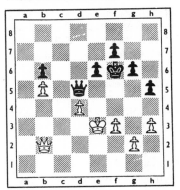

Position after 53 Kf2-e3

53 ... e6-e5!

Exclamation point because the move
has winning chances, and keeps the
draw in hand.

The tournament book gives the
move a question mark, and suggests
53 ... Qd5-c4 instead, after which
54 d4-d5+ loses by 54 ... e6-e5.

Fine agrees with this and adds
this line of play (after
53 ... Qd5-c4!) 54 Qb2-b1 Kf6-e7
55 Qb1-b2 Ke7-d7 56 Qb2-b1
Kd7-d6 57 Qb1-b2 Kd6-d5, and
White is in *zugzwang*.

This seems plausible, but Euwe,
in *Das Schachphänomen 'Capablanca'*,
disagrees, and commenting that the
game suffers from faulty annotation
gives 53 ... e6-e5! an exclamation
point, and says that Black makes no
progress with 53 ... Qd5-c4, as
after 54 f3-f4 in reply Black's King
cannot reach d5 easily
(54 ... Kf6-e7 55 Qb2-a3+, or if
54 ... Qc4-d5 55 Qb2-c3 Qd5xb5
56 d4-d5+, and again White draws).

Very well, doctors may disagree,
but Euwe contradicts himself in a

later book *A Guide to Chess Openings* (written with David Hooper) when he says apropos the position discussed, that 53 . . . Qd5-c4 is correct, when White is in danger of running out of moves.

My own belief is that Capablanca's move is best, and offers more winning prospects than does 53 . . . Qd5-c4.

54   f3-f4

White avoids 54 d4xe5+ Qd5xe5+ 55 Qb2xe5+ Kf6xe5, which loses the b-Pawn and the game, but the move he makes also lands him in difficulties.

He might still have saved the game with 54 Qb2-b4 e5xd4+ 55 Qb4xd4+ Qd5xd4+ (or 55 . . . Qd5-e5+ 56 Ke3-d3!) 56 Ke3xd4 Kf6-e6! 57 f3-f4 f7-f6 58 Kd4-c4!, and White draws.

54   . . .   e5xf4+

55   Ke3xf4   Kf6-e6

This is the situation:

Position after 55 . . . Kf6-e6

The position is deceptive. One might think that White, with a passed Pawn in the center, has the better game.

In reality though, Black has the advantage. His Queen, beautifully posted in the center, not only blockades the passed Pawn, but attacks two other Pawns as well, a circumstance that renders the adverse Queen almost helpless to do anything but stay at b2 to guard the three Pawns.

Black meanwhile can give his attention to acquiring a passed Pawn on the King-side, where he has a Pawn majority.

In these circumstances it will be seen that White will be quickly driven into *zugzwang*.

'The ending might be abandoned at this point,' says Euwe, 'except that the course it takes illustrates graphically the simplicity and elegance that is characteristic of the Cuban's style and perception.'

56   h3-h4

Sidesteps this loss: 56 Qb2-e2+ Ke6-d6 57 Kf4-e3 (or 57 Qe2-e5+ Qd5xe5+ 58 d4xe5+ Kd6-d5 followed by 59 . . . Kd5-d4—if necessary—to win the e-Pawn, not the b-Pawn, and the game) 57 . . . Qd5-e6+ 58 Ke3-d2 Qe6xe2+ 59 Kd2xe2 Kd6-d5, and Black will obtain a passed Pawn on the King-side while White is occupied with defending his isolated Pawns.

56   . . .   f7-f6

57   Kf4-e3

The tempting 57 Qb2-e2+ Ke6-d6 58 Qe2-e4 succumbs to 58 . . . g6-g5 59 h4xg5 Qd5xg5+ 60 Kf4-f3 Qg5xb5 61 Qe4-f4+

Kd6-d7!, and White suddenly discovers that he may not play 62 Qf4xf6 to regain the Pawn he lost, on pain of losing his Queen by 62 . . . Qb5-f1+.

57 . . . Qd5-c4!

58 g2-g3

Temporarily delaying 58 . . . Ke6-d5, when 59 Qb2-g2+ would compel the King to retreat to d6.

58 . . . g6-g5

59 h4xg5 f6xg5

60 Qb2-h2

Just about all that is left, as 60 Qb2-b1 loses the d-Pawn or the g-Pawn by 60 . . . Qc4-c3+, and 60 Qb2-e2 by 60 . . . Qc4xe2+ 61 Ke3xe2 Ke6-d5.

Finally, on 60 Ke3-e4 g5-g4 (threatens 61 . . . Qc4-d5+) 61 Ke4-f4 Ke6-f6 62 Kf4-e4 Qc4-e6+ 63 Ke4-d3 Qe6-d5 64 Qb2-f2+ Kf6-g6, and Black wins.

60 . . . Qc4-b3+

61 Ke3-e4 g5-g4

With two powerful threats! One against the King by 62 . . . Qb3-f3—instant mate!

The other, if the King tries to flee by 62 Ke4-f4, against the Queen, thus: 62 . . . Qb3-f3+ 63 Kf4-g5 Qf3-f6+ 64 Kg5xh5

Qf6-h8+, and the Queen falls victim to a skewer attack.

62 Qh2-e2

The Queen can protect one Knight Pawn only at the expense of the other.

62 . . . Qb3xg3

63 Qe2-c4+ Ke6-e7

Black now threatens to force a winning exchange of Queens by 64 . . . Qg3-f3+ 65 Ke4-e5 Qf3-f6+ 66 Ke5-e4 (66 Ke5-d5 Qf6-e6 mate) 66 . . . Qf6-e6+, and easily wins the Pawn ending once the Queens are gone.

64 Qc4-c8

A desperate try for a perpetual check but there is no avoiding the inevitable. Nor is there any escape by 64 Qc4-g8, to which there would follow 64 . . . Qg3-f3+ 65 Ke4-e5 Qf3-f6+ 66 Ke5-d5 Qf6-f7+.

64 . . . Qg3-f3+

65 Ke4-e5 Qf3-f6+

66 Ke5-d5 Qf6-d6+

67 White Resigns

After 67 Kd5-c4 (or 67 Kd5-e4) Qd6-e6+ forces the exchange of Queens and wins for Black.

A fine example of the power exerted by the Queen occupying the center of the board.

GAME 55

White J. R. Capablanca
Black A. Lilienthal
Moscow, 1936

Réti's Opening
Capablanca handles the Réti in a
way that would have delighted the
originator himself, even unto the
placing of his Queen in the lower
left corner of the board, the move
that startled the natives when Réti
first played it in 1924.

Capablanca whips up an attack
on the Queen-side. In the course of
it, his Knight takes up a strong post
at a5, only to sacrifice himself for
the sake of securing a different
advantage—the penetration of a
Rook to the seventh and eighth
ranks. This all-powerful Rook cuts
down every Pawn in sight.

Curiously enough, after all the
activity which nets Capablanca two
passed Pawns on the Queen-side,
the decision is brought about by
the threat of a Pawn queening on
the King-side!

1	Ng1-f3	d7-d5
2	c2-c4	c7-c6
3	b2-b3	Bc8-f5
4	Bc1-b2	e7-e6
5	g2-g3	Ng8-f6
6	Bf1-g2	Nb8-d7
7	0-0	h7-h6

Preserves his Bishop against the
threat of its exchange by 8 Nf3-h4
Bf5-g6 9 Nh4xg6, though this was
not much of a threat, as after
9 . . . h7xg6 in reply, Black would
have an open file against the King
as compensation.

A good alternative was
7 . . . Bf8-d6 8 d2-d3 0-0
9 Nb1-d2 e6-e5 10 c4xd5 c6xd5
11 Ra1-c1 Qd8-e7 12 Rc1-c2
a7-a5, as in the famous Réti-
Lasker New York 1924 game (see
The Golden Dozen, p. 243).

8	d2-d3	Bf8-e7

Developing the Bishop at d6 as in
the Réti-Lasker game (with a view
to castling followed by . . . e6-e5) is
now not so effective. After 9 e2-e4
in reply (threatening to win a piece
by 10 e4-e5) 9 . . . d5xe4
10 d3xe4 Nf6xe4 11 Bb2xg7
ruins Black's prospects of castling
on the King-side.

9	Nb1-d2	0-0
10	Ra1-c1	a7-a5
11	a2-a3	

Ready to meet Black's threat of
opening the Rook file with
11 . . . a5-a4, by replying 12 b3-b4.

11	. . .	Rf8-e8
12	Rc1-c2	Bf5-h7
13	Qd1-a1!	

There are fine points to this move.
White dominates the long diagonal,
bears down from a distance on the
central square e5, and establishes
communication between the two
Rooks.

More could hardly be expected
from one move!

13	. . .	Be7-f8

Black sits back to await developments. More aggressive of course is 13 . . . Be7-d6 followed by 14 . . . e6-e5, to free his position and increase the range of his pieces.

14   Rf1-e1

Capablanca is never lured into premature action, such as 14 Nf3-e5, when the continuation 14 . . . Nd7xe5 15 Bb2xe5 Nf6-d7 followed by 16 . . . f7-f6 and 17 . . . e6-e5 repulses White's untimely foray.

14   . . .   Qd8-b6

It was still not too late for counterplay in the center by 14 . . . Bf8-d6 followed by 15 . . . Qd8-b8 and the advance of the e-Pawn.

15   Bg2-h3   Bf8-c5

16   Re1-f1   Bc5-f8

17   Rc2-c1

Removes the Rook from the line of fire of the Bishop at h7, allowing White to play d3-d4 at the proper time.

17   . . .   Ra8-d8

18   Rf1-e1   Bf8-c5

Black is trying to provoke 19 d3-d4 —a tempting move, but a positional blunder. It would shut in White's dark-squared Bishop, render the advance of the e-Pawn difficult, and lengthen the scope of Black's light-squared Bishop, poised hopefully at h7.

19   Re1-f1   Bc5-f8

Both sides are jockeying for position, trying not to commit themselves to definite action.

   (Capablanca is not underestimating his opponent, as Lilienthal

had beaten him two years earlier at Hastings—even throwing in his Queen for good measure!)

20   Bh3-g2   Bf8-d6

Finally! Black is now ready to advance his e-Pawn—but Capablanca won't allow it!

21   Nf3-e5!   Bd6xe5

22   Bb2xe5   Nd7xe5

23   Qa1xe5

This is the position:

Position after 23 Qa1xe5

23   . . .   Nf6-d7

Blocking the center instead by . . . d5-d4 in either of the following lines of play would be to White's advantage, according to Capablanca, as his Knight could then get to d6 by way of c4 with great effect, thus:

(a) 23 . . . d5-d4 24 c4-c5 Qb6-b5 25 Nd2-c4 Re8-e7 26 Nc4-d6 Qb5xb3 27 Rc1-b1 Qb3xa3 28 Nd6xb7 Rd8-c8 29 Rb1-a1 Qa3-b4 30 Nb7xa5, or,

(b) 23 . . . Nf6-g4 24 Qe5-b2 d5-d4 25 b3-b4 followed by 26 c4-c5, Nd2-c4, and Nc4-d6.

24   Qe5-b2   Nd7-f6

More to the point was 24 . . . c6-c5 (after which White may not capture twice at d5, his King Pawn being *en prise*) followed by . . . Nd7-b8 and . . . Nb8-c6, where the Knight would have some influence on the center, and also restrain White's Queen-side Pawns from any ambitious thoughts of advancing.

25   b3-b4!

Begins the decisive action, aimed at breaking down the barriers, and acquiring a passed Pawn—or two!

25   . . .   a5xb4

26   Qb2xb4   Qb6xb4

If 26 . . . Qb6-c7 27 Rc1-b1 Re8-e7 28 Rb1-b3 followed by 29 Rf1-b1, with unremitting pressure on the b-Pawn.

27   a3xb4   Rd8-a8

28   Rc1-a1

This is the position that Capablanca had visualized.

His Knight is headed for a fine outpost at c5 or a5, while his Bishop exerts pressure on the three Pawns lined up on the long diagonal, in contradistinction to Black's Bishop, which is biting on granite (in Nimzowitsch's felicitous phrase).

28   . . .   Nf6-d7

Black hastens to prevent White's Knight from settling down at c5.

Ending 55

Position after 28 . . . Nf6-d7

Lilienthal

Capablanca to move

Capablanca has a wee bit of an advantage in position.

His Bishop exerts a good deal of pressure on the Queen-side Pawns. This pressure will be intensified, according to Capablanca's plan, by exchanging Rooks and then maneuvering his Knight over to a5. Thence it can bear down strongly on the vulnerable b- and c-Pawns.

Black's remaining Rook, tied down to the defence of the Pawns, will be unable to dispute possession of the open d-file.

Such positions are usually ripe for combination play, the culmination of which is generally a decisive material advantage for the attacking player.

29   Nd2-b3   Kg8-f8

30   Ra1-a5   d5xc4

'This loses because of the opening of the long diagonal, permitting the

"Réti Bishop" to make his presence felt,' says one annotator, 'Correct' (he continues glibly) 'was 30 ... Kg8-e7, and 31 ... Ke7-d6, when the outcome would be doubtful.'

It is easy for an annotator to draw against Capablanca (analysing the game years after it was played).

The procedure against 30 ... Kf8-e7, according to Capablanca himself, would have been as follows: 31 Rf1-a1 Ra8xa5 32 Ra1xa5 Ke7-d6 33 Ra5-a7 Kd6-c7 34 Nb3-a5 Re8-b8 35 c4-c5, continuing with d3-d4, Bg2-f1, e2-e3, and Bf1-a6, and White wins (and even then the annotator may fail to draw).

The position of White's three pieces concentrating their fire on the b-Pawn is reminiscent of similar strategy that Capablanca turned to account in his magnificent game against Treybal at Carlsbad in 1929 (see particularly the diagram on p. 324 of *The Golden Dozen*).

31	d3xc4	Nd7-b6
32	Ra5xa8	Re8xa8
33	Nb3-a5	

This attack on the b-Pawn compels Black to defend it with his Rook— thereby condemning it to a miserable post.

33	...	Ra8-a7

On the alternative 33 ... Ra8-b8, the play might go this way: 34 b4-b5 c6xb5 35 c4xb5 Nb6-d5 36 Bg2xd5 e6xd5 37 Rf1-d1 Rb8-d8 (on 37 ... Bh7-e4, the reply 38 f2-f3 dislodges the Bishop) 38 Na5xb7 Rd8-b8 39 Nb7-d6

Kf8-e7 40 Rd1xd5 Rb8-d8 41 Nd6-f5+, and White wins.

34	Rf1-d1

Threatens to win some material by this pretty idea: 35 Bg2xc6 b7xc6 36 Rd1-d8+ Kf8-e7 37 Na5xc6+ Ke7-f6 38 Nc6xa7, and White is the exchange and a Pawn ahead.

34	...	Kf8-e8

No satisfactory defence is offered by 34 ... Kf8-e7, as that allows 35 Bg2xc6 (and if 35 ... b7xc6 36 Na5xc6+ removes the Rook) while 34 ... f7-f6 yields to 35 Rd1-d8+ followed by 36 Rd8-b8.

A diagram shows the position:

Position after 34 ... Kf8-e8

35	Na5xb7!

This fine combination is the logical consequence of White's exemplary opening play.

With this move and the next, the obstructions on the long diagonal are ripped away, and the Bishop is free to express itself.

35	...	Ra7xb7
36	Bg2xc6+	Rb7-d7

37	c4-c5	Ke8-e7

This offers stout resistance, as Black will be left with two minor pieces for a Rook (though the Rook turns out to be a holy terror).

Other defences are found wanting. For example, if 37 . . . Bh7-e4 38 Rd1xd7! Be4xc6 39 Rd7-c7 and White wins a piece. Or if 37 . . . Nb6-d5 38 b4-b5 Ke8-e7 39 Bc6xd7 Ke7xd7 40 Rd1-a1 followed by 41 Ra1-a7+, and the two passed Pawns should assure the victory.

38	Bc6xd7	Nb6xd7
39	c5-c6	Nd7-b6
40	c6-c7	

Indicating that he intends to play 41 Rd1-d8 followed by queening the Pawn, a contingency which Black's next move is designed to forestall.

40	. . .	Bh7-f5

The Bishop emerges, after lingering in the background for the last 28 moves.

41	Rd1-d8

Instead of this, the play could go as follows: 41 e2-e4 Bf5-g4 (if 41 . . . Bf5xe4 42 Rd1-d8 Be4-b7 43 Rd8-b8, and White wins one of the loose pieces) 42 f2-f3 Bg4xf3 43 Rd1-d8 Bf3xe4 44 c7-c8(Q) Nb6xc8 45 Rd8xc8, and White wins.

Capablanca undoubtedly saw this possibility. Why didn't he go in for it? Evidently, because he had already visualized a line of play leading to a win, and there was no reason to analyze other means of procedure.

41	. . .	e6-e5
42	Rd8-b8	Nb6-c8
43	b4-b5	Ke7-d6
44	b5-b6	Nc8-e7

Or 44 . . . Kd6-c6 45 b6-b7 Kc6xc7 46 b7xc8(Q)+ Bf5xc8 47 Rb8-a8, and the advantage of the exchange ahead is decisive.

45	Rb8-f8

Again White could force the game by 45 c7-c8(Q) Ne7xc8 (or Bf5xc8) 46 b6-b7, and White wins the piece at c8, as moving it allows 47 Rb8-d8+ followed by queening the Pawn.

Capablanca sticks to his original plan, which just as surely wins, and wins, and wins.

45	. . .	Bf5-c8

Black must prevent 46 b6-b7.

46	Rf8xf7	Ne7-d5
47	Rf7xg7	

While Black is busy restraining the passed Pawns on the Queen-side, the Rook removes everything in sight on the King-side.

47	. . .	Nd5xb6
48	Rg7-h7	Nb6-d5
49	Rh7xh6+	Kd6xc7
50	e2-e4	Nd5-e7
51	f2-f3	Kc7-d7
52	h2-h4	Kd7-e8
53	Rh6-f6	Ne7-g8
54	Rf6-c6	Black Resigns

Any move by the Bishop allows 55 Rc6-c5, and the last Black Pawn comes off.

This beautiful game was awarded a special prize.

GAME 56

White I. Kann
Black J. R. Capablanca
Moscow, 1936

Vienna Game
Before half-a-dozen moves have
been made, White has managed
to acquire the two-Bishop advantage.

The open a-file accruing to his
opponent as a result of the exchange of Knight for Bishop
might seem to be small consolation for the missing Bishop, but it
serves as a marvelous jumping-off
place for the Rook, which is enabled to penetrate into the heart
of the adverse position.

Both Capablanca's Rooks, in
fact, leap gaily over the board, in
the ending that is quickly reached,
with the grace and abandon of
adagio dancers.

The entire ending is replete
with absorbing play, and is one of
the finest endings in the entire
literature of chess.

The whole game itself was selected as the best game of the tournament.

1	e2-e4	e7-e5
2	Nb1-c3	

This perfectly good opening is so
rarely played nowadays, that it is
not even mentioned in some of the
recent opening books. But opinions
change, and the Vienna may yet
come into vogue, as did the Tarrasch
Defence to the Queen's Gambit.

And after all, didn't Kann (Capablanca's opponent in this game)

beat Botvinnik in 26 moves with a
Vienna one year earlier at Moscow?

2	...	Bf8-c5
3	Ng1-f3	d7-d6

Better than 3 ... Nb8-c6 4 Nf3xe5!

4	Nc3-a4	Bc5-b6
5	Na4xb6	a7xb6
6	d2-d4	e5xd4
7	Qd1xd4	Qd8-f6

Best, as routine development by
7 ... Ng8-f6 lets White put on the
pressure with 8 Bc1-g5.

8	Bc1-g5	Qf6xd4
9	Nf3xd4	

'White has a respectable position,'
says Euwe, 'thanks to his two
Bishops and his center Pawn, which
ensure for him a little more terrain.

Black's task is now, above all,
to prevent his opponent's posting
his pieces aggressively, and Capablanca is just the man for this.'

9	...	Bc8-d7
10	Bf1-c4	Ng8-e7
11	0-0	Ne7-g6

Capablanca not only prepares to
castle, but is ready to penalize an
impetuous 12 f2-f4 by 12 ... h7-h6
13 f4-f5 Ng6-e5, winning one of the
precious Bishops.

12	a2-a3	0-0
13	Ra1-d1	Nb8-c6!

The position at this point:

Position after 13 . . . Nb8-c6!

Black now threatens 14 . . . Ra8-a4, after which this could follow: 15 Nd4xc6 Bd7xc6 16 Bc4-d5 (if 16 Bc4-d3, Bc6xe4 17 b2-b3 Be4xd3) 16 . . . Bc6xd5, and White has had to part with a Bishop.

How does White proceed now? The attractive 14 Nd4-b5 runs into this: 14 . . . Nc6-e5 15 Bc4-e2 Bd7xb5 16 Be2xb5 Ra8-a5 17 Bb5-e2 Ne5-f3+ 18 Be2xf3 Ra5xg5, and the threat of 19 . . . Ng6-h4 assures Black of good winning chances in the ending.

14   Nd4xc6

Not best, though understandable, in view of the fact that exchanges clear the board and allow more scope to the Bishops.

(Little did Kann reckon that he was in for a hard Rook-ending with nary a Bishop in sight!)

Capablanca himself suggested 14 Bg5-c1, defending the a-Pawn, so that 14 . . . Ra8-a4 could be met by 15 b2-b3 followed by 16 a3-a4.

14   . . .   b7xc6

The exchange is to Black's benefit, as he now has a Pawn at c6, guarding the important central square d5 against invaders.

15   Bg5-d2

There was still time for 15 Bg5-c1.

15   . . .   Ra8-a4!

This will ultimately kill off one of the Bishops.

16   Bc4-d3   Ng6-e5

17   Bd2-c3   f7-f6

Black is in no hurry to give up his Knight, which justifies its existence merely by standing proudly in the center and looking fierce!

18   f2-f3   Rf8-e8

19   Rf1-f2   Bd7-c8

20   Bd3-f1   Bc8-a6!

Now we see what Capablanca is getting at! An earlier exchange by . . . Ne5xd3 would have left Bishops of opposite colour, and good drawing chances, whereas this exchange of Bishop for Bishop removes that possibility.

21   Bf1xa6   Ra4xa6

22   Bc3xe5

It was either that (which improves Black's Pawn position) or worry about the Knight moving to c4, whenever it pleased him to do so.

22   . . .   f6xe5

23   Rd1-d3

Ending 56

Position after 23 Rd1-d3

Capablanca to move

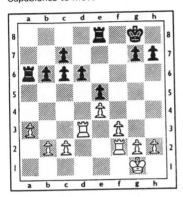

Kann

Black has good chances in the endgame. His Rooks have more maneuvering space, and his Pawns control more central squares than do White's.

Capablanca plans to utilize these advantages to bring his King to the center, advance his King-side Pawns for a breakthrough at g4, and establish a Rook at d4, where it will exert unremitting pressure on the adverse position.

23   ...   b6-b5!

An important move, if only to prevent 24 c2-c4.

24   Rf2-d2

Fine dismisses 24 f3-f4 e5xf4 25 Rf2xf4 Ra6-a4 26 Rd3-e3 Ra4-c4 27 c2-c3 d6-d5, with the comment that it loses a Pawn.

24   ...   c6-c5

25   Kg1-f2   Ra6-a4

Black increases the pressure on the e-Pawn, to discourage any freeing attempts by f3-f4.

26   Kf2-e2   Kg8-f7

27   Rd2-d1   Kf7-e6

28   Ke2-d2   Re8-b8

Before taking any decisive action on the King-side, Black indicates that he might try 29 ... b5-b4, a breakthrough on the Queen-side.

29   Rd3-c3

Prevents 29 ... b5-b4 30 a3xb4 c5xb4, as 31 Rc3xc7 would follow.

29   ...   g7-g5

Capablanca prepares a breakthrough on the King-side, an important decision, as the opening up of the game will afford White counterplay.

30   h2-h3   h7-h5

Position after 30 ... h7-h5

31   Rd1-h1

'The first inaccuracy,' says Euwe in *Das Schachphänomen 'Capablanca'*. 'The Rook is placed unfortunately at h1, so that White has practically lost a move, and will have to lose another.'

Euwe reverses himself though in
Meet the Masters, where he says of
31 Rd1-h1, 'A good move. White
threatens 32 h3-h4, after which
Black would either have to remain
with a weak Pawn on the Rook's file
(if he plays 32 . . . g5xh4, or lets White
capture by 33 h4xg5), or to concede his opponent a strong passed
Pawn on the same file (after
32 h3-h4) by 32 . . . g5-f4
33 f3xg4 h5xg4 34 h4-h5.'

('You pays your money and you
takes your choice,' commented
Punch, away back in 1846.)

| 31 | . . . | Ra4-d4+ |
| 32 | Kd2-e2 | Rb8-g8 |

Not only to further his own fell
designs, but to forestall 33 h3-h4,
after which there would come
33 . . . g5-g4 34 f3xg4 Rg8xg4,
and the Rook's simultaneous attack
on the e-Pawn and the g-Pawn
would net Black a couple of Pawns.

| 33 | Rc3-d3 | Rd4-a4 |

Black is not yet ready to exchange.

| 34 | Rh1-d1 | g5-g4! |

This will assure Black of an open
file for his King Rook.

| 35 | h3xg4 | h5xg4 |
| 36 | Ke2-e3 | |

White, on the other hand, may not
avail himself of the h-file, as after
36 Rd1-h1, the continuation
36 . . . g4xf3+ 37 g2xf3 (if
37 Ke2xf3, Rg8-f8+ 38 Kf3-e3
Rf8-f4 wins the e-Pawn for Black)
37 . . . Rg8-g2+ 38 Ke2-d1 Rg2-f2,
and the threat of 39 . . . b5-b4,
followed by 40 . . . c5-c4 and
41 . . . c4-c3, is bound to win Black

some material.

| 36 | . . . | Rg8-h8! |

There being nothing in 36 . . . g4xf3
37 g2xf3 Rg8-g2 38 Rd3-d2, Black
seizes the open file.

| 37 | Rd3-b3 | |

This attempt to get some counter-
play is preferable to 37 f3xg4
Rh8-g8 38 Ke3-f3 Rg8-f8+
39 Kf3-e3 Rf8-f4, and White's
Pawns begin to fall like the pro-
verbial ripe apples.

A diagram would be helpful:

Position after 37 Rd3-b3

| 37 | . . . | Rh8-h2 |

Far better to establish a Rook on
the seventh rank, and meet
38 Rb3xb5 with 38 . . . Rh2xg2,
than to play the meek
37 . . . c7-c6. This would protect
the b-Pawn at the expense of weakening the d-Pawn—which would require immediate defence after
38 Rb3-d3.

| 38 | Rd1-d2 | Ra4-d4 |
| 39 | Rd2-e2 | |

The alternative (to exchange Rooks

instead of running away)
39 Rd2xd4 c5xd4+ 40 Ke3-f2
g4xf3 41 Kf2xf3 c7-c6 is in Black's
favour.

Meanwhile, Black must look to
his Pawns, two of them being *en
prise*.

39 ...   c7-c6

Saves the b-pawn, and is ready to
meet 40 f3xg4 with 40 ... c5-c4
41 Rb3-c3 Ke6-f6 and 42 ... Kf6-g5.

40 Rb3-c3   g4-g3

Capablanca has strengthened his
position skilfully and systematically,
and with this last move threatens
to gain a decisive advance by
41 ... Rh2-h1

But for the moment his g-Pawn
is weak, a circumstance which
allows White a rare opportunity
to obtain a draw, as Capablanca
himself pointed out.

The play to do so would go thus:
41 f3-f4! (threatens to win the g-
Pawn by 42 Ke3-f3) 41 ... Rh2-h4
42 f4xe5 Rd4xe4+ 43 Ke3-f3
Rh4-f4+ 44 Kf3xg3 Rf4-g4+
45 Kg3-f3 Re4xe2 46 Kf3xe2
Rg4xg2+ 47 Ke2-f3 Rg2-h2
48 Kf3-g3! (prevents
48 ... Rh2-h3+ followed by
49 ... Rh3xc3) 48 ... Rh2-e2
49 e5xd6, and the game is drawn.

41 Rc3-d3   Rh2-h1

Black has a strong grip on the
position, which he threatens to
strengthen by 42 ... Rh1-f1 or
42 ... d6-d5.

42 f3-f4

Too late! Too late! Now the move
fails in its object, as White dis-

covers to his sorrow.

42 ...   Rh1-f1

This keeps the King away from the
Pawn.

43 f4-f5+

If instead 43 f4xe5, Ke6xe5
44 Rd3xd4 (or 44 Ke3-d2 c5-c4
45 Rd3xd4 Ke5xd4 46 Re2-e3
Rf1-d1+ wins) 44 ... c5xd4+
45 Ke3-d2 c6-c5 and the continuation 46 ... Rf1-f4 will win the
e-Pawn.

43 ...   Ke6-f6

Now the threat is a breakthrough
in the center by ... d6-d5—and
this threat is irresistible.

44 c2-c3   Rd4xd3+
45 Ke3xd3   d6-d5!

Threatens to win a Pawn by
46 ... d5xe4+ followed by
47 ... Rf1xf5, as well as by
46 ... c5-c4+ followed by
47 ... Rf1-f4.

46 b2-b3   c5-c4+
47 b3xc4   b5xc4+
48 Kd3-e3

Hope springs eternal! There is a
faint chance that Capablanca will
play 48 ... Rf1-c1, to which
White would reply 49 Re2-a2,
followed by advancing his passed
Pawn.

Truth to tell, there was nothing
better, as 48 Kd3-d2 loses the
Rook Pawn after 48 ... Rf1-a1,
while 48 Kd3-c2 allows
48 ... d5-d4 in reply, giving
Black two dangerous connected
passed Pawns.

48	...	Rf1-a1!
49	Ke3-f3	Ra1xa3
50	Kf3xg3	

On 50 Re2-e3 to protect the c-Pawn, there comes 50 . . . Ra3-b3 51 Kf3xg3, and d5-d4 is painful.

50	...	Ra3xc3+
51	Kg3-h4	Rc3-c1!

Black is in no hurry to advance his d-Pawn, as after 51 . . . d5-d4 52 g2-g4 Rc3-c1 53 g4-g5+, and White still needs subduing.

52	g2-g4	Rc1-h1+

53	Kh4-g3	d5-d4
54	Re2-a2	d4-d3
55	Kg3-g2	Rh1-e1
56	Kg2-f2	Re1xe4
57	Kf2-f3	

Kann resigned without waiting for Black to play 57 . . . Re4-f4+, after which 58 Kf3-g3 loses by . . . c4-c3, or 58 . . . Kf6-f5, and all his Pawns come off the board.

A difficult, highly instructive endgame, conducted by Capablanca in a mannner which is perfection itself.

GAME 57

White Em. Lasker
Black J. R. Capablanca
Moscow, 1936

Sicilian Defence
Capablanca's blending of logic and force could serve as a model for this line of the Sicilian.

Capablanca counters White's threats on the King-side with vigorous play on the Queen-side, culminating, after careful preparation, in the advance of his d-Pawn. This advance, bearing out thé principle that 'wing attack is best met by play in the center', is strategically decisive, as Lasker's threats are rendered harmless, and his pieces left stranded on the sidelines.

The Queen ending is handled impeccably by Capablanca, noteworthy being the quiet little 39 . . . h7-h6 move that suddenly brings about *zugzwang*, just as

25 . . . h7-h6 did in the famous Samisch-Nimzowitsch immortal *zugzwang* game, Copenhagen, 1923 (*The Golden Dozen*, p. 8).

1	e2-e4	c7-c5

Capablanca rarely resorted to the Sicilian, but he was out for blood, as he had to avenge his defeat by Lasker the previous year.

2	Ng1-f3	Nb8-c6
3	d2-d4	c5xd4
4	Nf3xd4	Ng8-f6
5	Nb1-c3	d7-d6
6	Bf1-e2	

The popular line nowadays is 6 Bc1-g5, the Rauzer System, which restrains counter-action in the center, and prepares for Queen-side castling, and a Pawn advance by f2-f4 and an eventual e4-e5.

6	...	Bc8-d7
7	Bc1-e3	

Lasker varies from 7 0-0 a7-a6 8 Bc1-e3 Qd8-c7 9 f2-f4 Nc6-a5 10 f4-f5, with which he had smashed Pirc in 20 moves one year earlier at Moscow.

7	...	e7-e6

There is no hurry about playing 7 ... a7-a6, as 8 Nd4-b5 Qd8-b8 9 Be3-f4 is easily parried by 9 ... Nc6-e5.

8	Qd1-d2	

Now there is a definite threat against the d-Pawn by 9 Nd4-b5 Qd8-b8 10 0-0-0.

8	...	a7-a6
9	f2-f4	Qd8-c7

With a view to deploying his Queen Knight to c4 by way of a5, in order to kill off a Bishop.

10	Nd4-b3	

Which White promptly prevents!

10	...	b7-b5

Customary expansion on the Queen-side, one effect of which is to curb any ambitions White's Queen Knight might harbor of moving to a4, and then anchoring itself, or the Bishop, at b6.

11	Be2-f3	Ra8-b8
12	Nc3-e2	Bf8-e7
13	0-0	0-0
14	Ne2-g3	

Lasker launches a King-side attack, which should have been prefaced

(Capablanca suggests) by 14 g2-g4.

14	...	a6-a5!

Capablanca counterattacks on the Queen-side—the usual specific in the Scheveningen line of the Sicilian.

15	Nb3-d4	a5-a4
16	Ra1-e1	Rf8-c8
17	Rf1-f2	Nf6-e8

The position on the board:

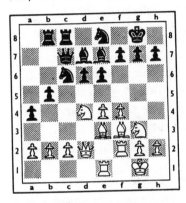

Position after 17 ... Nf6-e8

18	Nd4xc6	

White must exchange Knights if he wants to play 18 f4-f5 without permitting 18 ... Nc6-e5 in reply. In doing so, though, he facilitates the advance of the d-Pawn, a vital move for Black.

18	...	Bd7xc6
19	f4-f5	

A risky move, which enables Black, after suitable preparation, to gain control of the center.

19	...	e6-e5!

'What about the backward Pawn?' shrieks the pious student, brought

up on sound positional principles.
The answer is that there ain't goin'
to be no backward Pawn (Purdy).

| 20 | Ng3-h5 | Qc7-b7 |

This, and Black's 22nd and 23rd
moves are directed to support the
all-important advance of the d-
Pawn, one effect of which will be
to weaken the base of White's
f-Pawn.

| 21 | Be3-g5 | f7-f6 |
| 22 | Bg5-e3 | Ne8-c7 |

Capturing the e-Pawn results in
material loss, thus: 22 . . . Bc6xe4
23 Bf3xe4 Qb7xe4 24 Be3-a7, and
White wins the exchange.

23	Qd2-d1	Rc8-d8
24	Rf2-d2	Kg8-h8
25	a2-a3	Rb8-c8

Now there is a threat against the e-
Pawn.

| 26 | Be3-f2 | d6-d5! |

With this move, a *sine qua non* in
almost all Black defences, Capablanca seizes the initiative—and
doesn't let go!

27	e4xd5	Nc7xd5
28	Bf3xd5	Rd8xd5
29	Qd1-g4	

This is the situation:

Position after 29 Qd1-g4

Threatens instant mate, and sets up
a pretty little trap as well, to wit:
if Black tries to forestall mate and
win a Rook by 29 . . . g7-g6
30 f5xg6 Rd5xd2, he falls into
31 g6-g7+ Kh8-g8 32 Qg4-e6 mate!

29	. . .	Be7-c5!
30	Re1-d1	Bc5xf2+
31	Kg1xf2	Rc8-d8
32	Rd2xd5	Rd8xd5
33	Rd1xd5	Bc6xd5

Black's advantage evidences itself
in his passed Pawn on the e-file, the
long lines of attack open to his
Queen and Bishop, and in the target
he has in the adverse King who is
exposed to attack.

| 34 | Qg4-b4 | |

Indirectly protects the g-Pawn by
the threat of mate on the move.

Ending 57

Capablanca to move

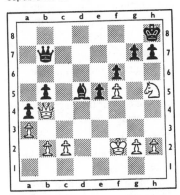

Lasker

White's King is out in the open, exposed to wintry blasts, and his Knight is on the sidelines, away from the theater of action. His Queen, however, poised for attack, looks menacing.

To compensate for this, Capablanca possesses what Bronstein calls the most powerful weapon in chess—the right to make the next move!

34   ...   Qb7-a7+!

Capablanca is precise to the last detail! It is important that the Queen check at a7 and not at b6 (a square nearer the King, while also protecting the b-Pawn), as will be seen from the subsequent play.

35   Kf2-e2

Sudden death follows 35 Kf2-g3 by 35 . . . Qa7-e3+ 36 Kg3-g4 Qe3-g5+ 37 Kg4-h3 Bd5xg2 mate, while 35 Kf2-e1 loses by

35 . . . Qa7-g1+ 36 Ke1-e2 Qg1xg2+ 37 Ke2-e1 Qg2-g1+ 38 Ke1-e2 Qg1xh2+, and the Knight comes off next move. (No, White does not mate by 40 Qb4-f8+.)

35   ...   Bd5-c4+

36   Ke2-f3

This is forced, as 36 Ke2-e1 allows a mate in five beginning with 36 . . . Qa7-e3+ 37 Ke1-d1 Bc4-e2+, while other moves lose the Knight.

36   ...   Qa7-a8+!

Again this, and not the nearer square b7, is the proper square from which to check.

A diagram would not be amiss:

Position after 36 . . . Qa7-a8+!

37   Kf3-f2

The alternative 37 Kf3-g3 is not enticing, as this would be the sequel: 37 . . . Qa8-e8 38 Kg3-h4 (on 38 Kg3-g4 Bc4-e2+ wins the Knight) 38 . . . g7-g5+ 39 f5xg5 *en passant* h7xg6 40 Nh5-g3 (or 40 Nh5xf6 Qe8-d8 41 Kh4-g5 Kh8-g7, and Black wins the Knight) 40 . . . Qe8-d8 (threatens

41 ... f6-f5+ 42 Kh4-h3 f5-f4
43 Ng3-e4 Bc4-e6 mate) 41 Qb4-c3
(of course not 41 Kh4-g4 Qd8-d4+
42 Kg4-f3 Qd4-f4 mate)
41 ... f6-f5+ 42 Kh4-h3 Qd8-e7,
and the threats of 43 ... f5-f4
followed by 44 ... Bc4-e6 mate,
as well as 43 ... Qe7-h7+ winning
the Knight, are decisive.

37   ...   Qa8-d8!

The point of Capablanca's previous
moves. The Queen is beautifully
placed for defence against intrusion by the enemy Queen, and for
attack as well, the immediate threat
being capture of the indiscreet
Knight, as follows: 38 ... Qd8-d4+
39 Kf2-g3 (if 39 Kf2-e1 Qd4-e3+
forces mate, or if 39 Kf2-f3
Qd4-d1+ wins the Knight)
39 ... Qd4-e3+ 40 Kg3-g4 (or to
h4) 40 ... Qe3-g5+, and the Knight
comes off with check.

38   Qb4-c3

Nipping at the Bishop instead loses
in a flash, thus: 38 b2-b3 Qd8-d4+
39 Kf2-f3 Bc4-d5+ 40 Kf3-e2
Qd4xb4 41 a3xb4 a4-a3, and the
Pawn promotes to a Queen.

Capablanca suggests as White's
best line of defence the following:
38 Kf2-e1 h7-h6 39 b2-b3 a4xb3
40 c2xb3 Bc4-f7 41 Qb4-g4
Qd8-f8 42 b3-b4 Bf7-d5, though
Black's passed Pawn could still
present White with some problems.

Lasker's last move, whose object
is to bring the Queen to the aid of
the King, gives Capablanca the
opportunity (which he seizes
instantly!) to force his opponent
into *zugzwang*, that dreadful
paralyzing state where one must

move but cannot do so without
incurring loss of some kind.

38   ...   Qd8-d1!

39   Nh5-g3   h7-h6

A quiet little move, but deadly
none the less. Suddenly, White is
out of moves! The proof!

(a) a Queen move allows Black to
capture the c-Pawn with check,

(b) a Knight move to h5, h1, f1, or
e2 lets the Knight be snapped off,
while 40 Ng3-e4 loses the Knight
by 40 ... Qd1-e2+,

(c) a move by the King (40 Kf2-e3
is the only move) yields to
40 ... Qd1-g1+ 41 Ke3-f3 Bc4-d5+
(stronger than the petty
41 ... Qg1xh2) 42 Kf3-g4 (on
42 Ng3-e4 Qg1-f1+ 43 Kf3-e3
Qf1-f4+ wins the Knight)
42 ... Qg1xg2, and Black threatens
43 ... h6-h5+! 44 Kg4xh5 (or
44 Kg4-h4 Qg2xh2 mate)
44 ... Qg2-h3+ 45 Kh5-g6 Qh3-h7
mate,

(d) moves by the h-Pawn are quickly exhausted, Black's King simply
moving to and fro until they are.

White has only one move on the
board!

40   b2-b3   a4xb3

41   c2xb3   Bc4xb3

The first tangible gain—but Lasker
still needs subduing!

42   Ng3-f1   Qd1-b1

43   g2-g4

Protecting the f-Pawn by 43 Nf1-e3
allows 43 ... Qb1-a2+, followed by
44 ... Qa2xa3, and Black acquires
another passed Pawn.

The text move is intended to protect the a-Pawn indirectly, as after 43 ... Qb1-a2+ 44 Nf1-d2, and Black may not capture the Pawn, on pain of losing his Bishop, which is doubly attacked.

43 ...   Bb3-c4

44 Nf1-e3

If 44 Nf1-g3 (to prevent 44 ... Qb1-h1) 44 ... Qb1-a2+ 45 Kf2-g1 Bc4-d5 is conclusive.

44 ...   Qb1-h1

This is the position:

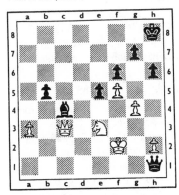

Position after 44 ... Qb1-h1

45 Ne3xc4

White pins his last hope on the passed Pawn that he will have as a result of this exchange.

Had White tried 45 Kf2-g3 instead, he would have succumbed to some pretty play, as witness this: 45 Kf2-g3 Bc4-e2, and White is practically in *zugzwang*:

If the Knight moves to g2, 46 ... Be2xg4 wins a Pawn, or if it moves to c2, then 46 ... Qh1-g1+ and 47 ... Qg1xg4 mate.

If the Queen moves, say, to c5 to keep in touch with the Knight, then 46 ... Qh1-g1+ 47 Kg3-h3 (if 47 Kg3-h4, Qg1xh2 is mate) 47 ... Be2-f1+ 48 Kh3-h4 (the Knight is pinned) 48 ... Qg1xh2 is mate.

Or if 46 Qc3-d2 (instead of 46 Qc3-c5) 46 ... Qh1-f3+ 47 Kg3-h4 Qf3-f2+ 48 Kh4-h5 (or to h3) 48 ... Be2xg4+, and Black wins the Queen.

If (after 45 Kf2-g3 Bc4-e2) White tries for a perpetual check by 46 Qc3-c8+ Kh8-h7 47 Qc8-e8, then 47 ... Qh1-f3+ 48 Kg3-h4 Qf3-f2+ 49 Kh4-h3 (or 49 Kh4-h5 Qf2xh2 mate) 49 ... Qf2xe3+ 50 Kh3-h4 Qe3-f2+ and mate next move.

45 ...   Qh1xh2+

46 Kf2-e1

On 46 Kf2-e3, Capablanca would definitely *not* exchange Queens, as after 46 ... Qh2-g3+ 47 Ke3-d2 Qg3xc3+ 48 Kd2xc3 b5xc4 49 a3-a4, and wins, Black's King being miles away.

46 ...   Qh2-g1+

47 Ke1-d2   Qg1-f2+

48 Kd2-c1   Qf2-f1+

49 Kc1-d2   b5xc4

50 a3-a4   Qf1-f4+

51 Kd2-c2

Against 51 Kd2-e1, Capablanca intended to continue with 51 ... Qf4-e4+ 52 Ke1-d2 Qe4xg4 53 a4-a5 Qg4-g2+ 54 Kd2-e3 Qg2-g3+ 55 Ke3-d2 Qg3-f2+ 56 Kd2-c1 Qf2-a2, and Black wins, as the a-Pawn is stopped.

51 ...   Qf4xg4

Game 58

52	a4-a5	Qg4xf5+
53	Kc2-c1	

A diagram of the position:

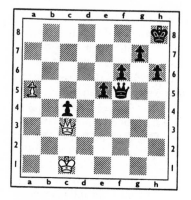

Position after 53 Kc2-c1

In this critical situation, Capablanca took a half-hour before deciding on the clearest way to win.

One line which included letting White promote his Pawn to a Queen went as follows: 53 . . . e5-e4 54 a5-a6 Qf5-c5 55 Qc3-b2 c4-c3 56 Qb2-b8+ Kh8-h7 57 a6-a7 Qc5-e3+ 58 Kc1-b1 Qe3-d3+ 59 Kb1-a2 c3-c2 60 a7-a8(Q) (on 60 Ka2-b2 Qd3-d2 wins) 60 . . . Qd3-c4+ and wins.

However, Capablanca discarded this line and chose another which secures the win in simpler but no less forceful manner.

53	. . .	Qf5-f2!
54	Qc3-a3	

Lasker's suggestion (after the game) of 54 Qc3-c2 is beaten easily by 54 . . . Qf2-c5, while against 54 Qc3xc4 Capablanca was prepared to win this way: 54 . . . Qf2-e1+ 55 Kc1-c2 Qe1xa5 56 Qc4-c8+ Kh8-h7 57 Qc8-f5+ Kh7-g8 58 Qf5-e6+ Kg8-f8 59 Qe6-d6+ Kf8-e8 60 Qd6-e6+ Ke8-d8 61 Qe6-g8+ Kd8-e7 62 Qg8xg7+ Ke7-e6 63 Qg7-g8+ Ke6-d6 64 Qg8-f8+ Kd6-d5 65 Qf8xf6 Qa5-a4+, and Black wins.

54	. . .	Kh8-h7

Lasker resigned, as 55 a5-a6 is met by 55 . . . c4-c3! 56 Qa3xc3 Qf2-f1+ 57 Kc1-c2 Qf1xa6, and the last Pawn, and with it White's last hope, is gone.

This was the last great battle of these two giants of the chess world.

They met across the board for the last time at Nottingham, but the game resulted in an uneventful draw.

GAME 58

White J. R. Capablanca
Black E. Eliskases
Moscow, 1936

Giuoco Piano
Capablanca evolves an endgame win from a position that is truly fantastic.

Picture, if you will, a line-up of two Kings, two Queens, and four Rooks crowded together along two files of the King-side of the board, with hardly any breathing space between the pieces!

In a trice Capablanca solves the problem of simplying the position!

He clears away four of the heavy pieces, and brings it to a Rook-ending where he gives it the winning touch—the sacrifice of a Pawn that lets his King become active.

The play that follows—the queening of a Pawn—is easily understood, but nevertheless a pleasure to watch.

1	e2-e4	e7-e5
2	Ng1-f3	Nb8-c6
3	Bf1-c4	Bf8-c5
4	Nb1-c3	Ng8-f6
5	d2-d3	d7-d6
6	Bc1-g5	

The Canal Variation, introduced by the Peruvian master into tournament play at Carlsbad in 1929, breathed new life into the staid Giuoco Piano (the quiet game).

6	. . .	h7-h6

Black must do *something* to forestall 7 Nc3-d5 followed by 8 Nd5xf6+, breaking up the King-side Pawn structure.

There is an alternative of course in 6 . . . Nc6-a5 7 Bc4-b3 c7-c6, but the text is the most effective way for Black to obtain the two Bishops.

7	Bg5xf6	

Inferior would be 7 Bg5-h4 g7-g5 8 Bh4-g3, when the Bishop is impotent. (Black's broken Pawn position on the King-side does not matter as he can castle on the Queen-side.)

7	. . .	Qd8xf6
8	Nc3-d5!	

The point of the variation!

The Knight dominates the center, with an immediate attack on the Queen, and a threat of a Knight fork winning the Queen Rook.

8	. . .	Qf6-d8

It is noteworthy that none of Canal's opponents ventured on the counterattack by 8 . . . Qf6-g6, to which White could respond 9 Qd1-e2 or 9 Nf3-h4 Qg6-g5 10 g2-g3 with a good game.

9	c2-c3	Nc6-e7

Black's idea, naturally, is to get rid of White's strongly-placed Knight.

It is also worthy of note that this position came up five times at the Carlsbad tournament, and the players of Black made five different replies, with the following results (though of course these results are not meant to be conclusive so far as the value of each move is concerned).

They are interesting though in showing that five masters looking at a position that is new to them, may find different 'best' moves.

(1) Treybal played 9 . . . a7-a6 against Canal, and lost.
(2) Capablanca played 9 . . . 0-0 against Canal, and drew.
(3) Becker played 9 . . . Bc8-e6 against Canal, and lost.
(4) Johner played 9 . . . Nc6-e7 against Canal, and lost.
(5) Treybal played 9 . . . a7-a5 against Tartakover, and drew.

Besides this proliferation of possible moves, 9 . . . Bc5-b6 and 9 . . . Nc6-a5 are worth considering —which shows that new ideas in the opening are still far from being exhausted.

10   Nd5-e3

This Capablanca innovation, which leads to a quiet positional struggle, suitable to the Cuban's style, is stronger than the usual line 10 d3-d4 Ne7xd5 11 Bc4xd5 e5xd4 12 Nf3xd4 0-0, which can create undesirable complications.

10   . . .   Bc8-e6

Somewhat preferable to this, which sets up targets for attack, was 10 . . . 0-0 11 0-0 Bc5-b6 12 d3-d4 Ne7-g6, holding the strong point e5.

11   Bc4xe6   f7xe6

12   Qd1-b3   Qd8-c8

The position at this point:

Position after 12 . . . Qd8-c8

13   d3-d4

White does not try to win a Pawn by 13 Nf3xe5 d6xe5 14 Qb3-b5+, as Black simply interposes

13 . . . Bc5xe3 instead and wins a piece.

Capablanca's move seizes control of the center.

13   . . .   e5xd4

14   Nf3xd4   Bc5xd4

But not 14 . . . e6-e5 15 Nd4-e6, to White's advantage.

15   c3xd4   0-0

At the end of the opening phase, Capablanca enjoys a slight superiority in position. His Queen is aggressively placed, whereas Black's Queen is restricted to defence, and he (Capa) has a fine open c-file for the concenience of his Rooks.

16   0-0   Qc8-d7

17   Ra1-c1

Not at once 17 Qb3xb7 Rf8-b8, when Black regains his Pawn and (to add insult to injury) posts a Rook on the seventh rank.

After the text move, though, there is a threat of 18 Qb3xb7 followed by 19 Qb7xc7.

17   . . .   Ra8-b8

18   Rc1-c3

White consolidates his forces, rather than go in for direct (and possibly premature) attack by 18 f2-f4, with the threat of 19 f4-f5.

18   . . .   d6-d5

19   Qb3-c2

Attacks the c-Pawn, while protecting his own e-Pawn as well.

There was nothing in 19 e4-e5, the simplest reply to which was 19 . . . Ne7-c6, nor in 19 Ne3-g4 Rf8-f4 20 Rc3-g3 Kg8-h7.

| 19 | ... | c7-c6 |

Fortifies the center at the expense of taking a good square away from the Knight.

Capablanca suggests instead 19 ... Ne7-c6 20 e4xd5 e6xd5 21 Rc3-c5 Nc6xd4 22 Qc2-d3, with White having the edge.

20	e4-e5	Rf8-f4
21	Qc2-d1	Rb8-f8
22	f2-f3	

The plan is to continue with 23 g2-g3 Rf4-f7 24 f3-f4.

| 22 | ... | Qd7-d8 |

Black's best defence, according to Capablanca, was 22 ... Rf4-f7! 23 g2-g3 Ne7-f5 24 Ne3xf5 Rf7xf5 25 f3-f4 g7-g5.

23	g2-g3	Rf4-f7
24	f3-f4	Ne7-f5
25	Ne3xf5	Rf7xf5

Ending 58

Position after 25 ... Rf7xf5

Eliskases

Capablanca to move

Capablanca's advantage, as in so many of his endings, is almost imperceptible.

His Pawn majority on the King-side looks imposing, and his e-Pawn seems destined for greatness. Two barriers stand in the way though—Black's e-Pawn, and the Rook occupying f5.

The Rook must be dislodged and a breakthrough made at that key square.

To do so requires patience and delicate handling, as endings featuring the heavy pieces are notoriously difficult and respond only to skilful treatment.

| 26 | h2-h4 | |

A move that not only frightens off the opponent from playing 26 ... g7-g5, but convinces the commentators as well.

One of them writes, 'If 26 ... g7-g5 27 h4xg5 h6xg5 28 Qd1-g4 with a winning game.'

Another says, 'If 26 ... g7-g5 27 h4xg5 h6xg5 28 Kg1-g2 followed by 29 Rf1-h1'.

A third suggests this winning line after 26 ... g7-g5: 27 Qd1-h5 Qd8-e8 28 Qh5xe8 Rf8xe8 29 f4xg5 Rf5xf1+ 30 Kg1xf1 Re8-f8+ 31 Kf1-g2 h6xg5 32 h4xg5 Rf8-f5 33 Rc3-b3, and White wins a Pawn.

Capablanca however, who was objective in his analysis (a trait few masters possess) recommended 26 ... g7-g5 for Black, as after the continuation 27 h4xg5 h6xg5 28 Qd1-h5 (if 28 Qd1-g4 Rf8-f7 followed by 29 ... Rf7-g7) 28 ... Qd8-e8 29 Qh5xe8 Rf8xe8 30 f4xg5 Re8-f8 31 Rf1xf5

Rf8xf5 32 Kg1-g2 Rf5xg5
33 Rc3-f3 c6-c5! (but not
33 . . . Rg5-g4 34 Rf3-f4) Black
should obtain a draw.

26	. . .	g7-g6
27	Kg1-g2	Qd8-e7
28	a2-a3	

Not so much to prevent
28 . . . Qe7-b4, as that were adequately answered by 29 Rc3-b3,
but to prepare for b2-b4 and put
a stop to . . . c6-c5 once and for
all.

28	. . . Qe7-g7	

'My opponent should consider
28 . . . g6-g5,' says Capablanca, 'as
after 29 Qd1-g4 Qe7-g7 30 Rc3-f3
g5xf4 31 Rf3xf4 Rf5xf4
32 Qg4xg7+ Kg8xg7 33 g3xf4,
the resulting Rook ending is not
unfavourable to Black.'

29	Rc3-f3	Qg7-e7!

A clever move, it anticipates
30 g3-g4, the reply to which is
30 . . . Rf5-f7, and Black has a tactical threat in 31 . . . Qe7xh4, and
a strategic one in 31 . . . c6-c5.

Note that it was too late for
29 . . . g6-g5, as after 30 f4xg5
h6xg5 31 Rf3xf5 Rf8xf5
32 Rf1xf5 e6xf5 33 Qd1-h5!
g5xh4 34 Qh5xh4, and White
should win.

30	Qd1-c2!	

Black's move elicits an equally
clever reply!
White not only prevents
30 . . . c6-c5, but also threatens
31 g3-g4, winning the Pawn at g6.

30	. . .	Kg8-g7

An alternative was 30 . . . h6-h5
(to hinder 31 g3-g4) but that meant
renouncing the possibility of freeing his game by . . . g6-g5.

This fixing of the King-side
Pawn position would permit White
to switch the attack to the other
wing, where he could institute a
minority Pawn attack by means of
b2-b4, Rf3-b3, Rf1-c1, a3-a4, and
b4-b5.

Capablanca's comments in the
Book of the Tournament are
skimpy from this point on, as though
he considered the game as strategically won, and further explanations superfluous.

31	g3-g4	

Capablanca utilizes the power of his
Pawn majority—first by driving the
Rook away.

31	. . .	Rf5-f7
32	Kg2-h3	Qe7-d7

Black must not allow a breakthrough by 33 f4-f5.

33	b2-b4	

White must not be tempted into
Pawn-hunting, lest he suffer this
misadventure: 33 h4-h5 g6xh5
34 g4xh5 Rf7-f5 35 Qc2-g2+
Kg7-h8 36 Qg2-g6 Rf8-f7
37 Qg6xh6+ Rf7-h7 38 Qh6-g6
Rf5xh5+ 39 Kh3-g2. (If 39 Kh3-g4
Rh5-h6 40 Qg6-c2 Qd7-g7+ and
mate next move.) Rh7-g7, and
White must give up his Queen.

33	. . .	Rf8-g8

A diagram of the position:

Position after 33 ... Rf8-g8

34   Rf1-g1

A concealed attack on the King, by virtue of which White is enabled to threaten 35 f4-f5, and if then 35 ... e6xf5 36 g4xf5 Rf7xf5 37 Qc2xf5, and Black may not capture by 37 ... Qd7xf5 as 38 Rf3xf5 leaves him unable to recapture.

34   ...   Kg7-h8

The King's safest escape from the pin, as 34 ... Kg7-f8 loses the a-Pawn by the Queen check at c5, while 34 ... Kg7-h7 allows 35 h4-h5 to White's advantage.

35   Qc2-d2

Now the threat is 36 f4-f5 followed by 37 Qd2xh6+.

35   ...   Rf7-h7

36   Qd2-f2   h6-h5

Black strikes at the g-Pawn, as its disappearance from the scene would greatly lessen the possibility of White's effecting a breakthrough at f5.

37   g4xh5   Rh7xh5

This capture is preferable to 37 ... g6xh5 (removing the Pawn's influence on f5) 38 Rg1-g5! Rg8-f8 39 f4-f5 e6xf5 40 Kh3-h2, with great advantage to White.

38   Rg1-g5   Qd7-h7

39   Qf2-g3   Qh7-h6

A slight inexactitude (39 ... Qh7-f7 being safer) and Capablanca immediately seizes the opportunity to make things uncomfortable for Eliskases.

40   Qg3-g4

Though there is no threat, as 41 Rg5xh5 is met by 41 ... g6xh5 (attacking and winning the Queen) while 41 Qg4xe6 permits 41 ... Rh5xh4+ and a counter-attack ... The point is that Black can hardly stir!

For instance, if:

(a) 40 ... Qh6-g7 41 Qg4xe6,

(b) 40 ... Qh6-h7 41 Rg5xh5 Qh7xh5 (or 41 ... g6xh5 42 Qg4xe6) 42 Qg4xh5 g6xh5 43 f4-f5 with advantage.

40   ...   Rg8-g7

41   Rf3-g3   Kh8-h7

If 41 ... Rg7-h7 42 Rg5xh5 Qh6xh5 (of course not 42 ... g6xh5 43 Qg4-g8 mate) 43 Qg4xh5 g6xh5 44 Rg3-g6 Rh7-e7 45 Rg6-h6+, and White wins a Pawn.

This unusual position, with eight pieces crowded on two files, deserves a diagram:

Ending 58

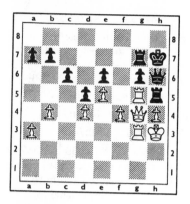

Position after 41 . . . Kh8-h7

42   Rg3-g2

The idea is to transfer the Rook to
the h-file to protect the Pawn, thereby releasing the Queen that is now
tied down to its defence.

42   . . .   Kh7-h8

43   Kh3-g3   Kh8-h7

44   Rg2-h2

Now there is a threat of taking the
e-Pawn—which Black promptly
wards off.

44   . . .   Rg7-e7

45   Rh2-h3   Kh7-g7

Instead of this, Eliskases thought
that 45 . . . Re7-e8 might occasion
White more trouble, but Capablanca (ready for this defence)
demonstrated the following win:
46 Kg3-f3 Re8-e7 47 Rh3-g3!
Rh5xh4 48 Rg5xg6 Rh4xg4
49 Rg6xh6+ Kh7xh6 50 Rg3xg4
Re7-g7 51 Rg4-h4+ Kh6-g6
52 Rh4-h8 Rg7-e7 53 Kf3-g4
Kg6-g7 54 Rh8-a8 a7-a6
55 Kg4-g5 Kg7-f7 56 Kg5-h6, and
White wins by the force of *zugzwang.*

After Black's actual move, four
heavy pieces come flying off the
board, and the dénouement comes
quickly.

46   Rg5xh5   Qh6xh5

47   Qg4xh5   g6xh5

48   f4-f5!!

The winning shot, the culmination
of all of Capablanca's previous
strategical maneuvering.

White will acquire a passed Pawn
(whether Black captures or not) and
his King will come strongly into the
game.

48   . . .   e6xf5

49   Kg3-f4   Re7-e6

Against 49 . . . Re7-f7, the procedure is: 50 Rh3-g3+ Kg7-h6
51 Rg3-g5 followed either by
52 e5-e6 or 52 Rg5xf5, winning
easily.

50   Kf4xf5   Re6-g6

Black must avoid this contretemps:
50 . . . Kg7-f7 51 Rh3-g3 (threatens
52 Rg3-g7+!) 51 . . . Re6-h6
52 Rg3-g5 Rh6-h8 (Black must give
way somewhere) 53 e5-e6+ Kf7-e7
54 Rg5-g7+ Ke7-d6 55 Rg7-d7
mate!

51   e5-e6!

'Capa's winning line is simplicity
itself,' says Reuben Fine admiring-
ly.

51   . . .   Rg6-g4

53   Kf5-e5   Rg4-e4+

53   Ke5-d6   Re4xd4

If 53 . . . Kg7-f8 54 Kd6-d7 followed by 55 Rh3-f3+ and 56 e6-e7,
forcing Black to give up his Rook
for the Pawn.

| 54 | Rh3-e3 | **Black Resigns** |

After 54 . . . Rd4-e4 55 Re3xe4 d5xe4 56 e6-e7 Kg7-f7 57 Kd6-d7, and the Pawn becomes a Queen

and wins.

(Strange that nothing at all happened on the Queen-side of the board for the last 35 moves!)

GAME 59

White A. Ilyin-Genevsky and
I. L. Rabinovich
Black J. R. Capablanca
Consultation Game, Leningrad, 1936

Queen's Indian Defence
In this, as in many of his games, Capablanca seems to be toying with his opponents, winning in just about any way he pleases.

It calls to mind what Lodewijk Prins once wrote:

'For a lover of chess it was a real delight to see Capablanca play. Playing over his brilliant games, one would hardly believe that this man would sit at the board as if some comedy were being performed before his eyes, and would seize any opportunity to rise and walk around with a smile on his face. It is remarkable how accurately Capablanca's combinations are calculated. Twist and turn as you will, test all the possibilities, and inevitably you come to the conclusion that everything has been taken into account with the utmost care and precision.'

1	d2-d4	Ng8-f6
2	Ng1-f3	b7-b6
3	g2-g3	Bc8-b7
4	Bf1-g2	c7-c5

Capablanca favoured the Queen's

Indian (over the King's Indian) as a defence to the Queen's Pawn Opening, playing it twenty-nine times in his tournament and match career, with the result that he won twenty games, drew seven, and lost two (to Sultan Khan and Euwe).

His last move is intended to do away with White's center Pawn, or compel its exchange for the c-Pawn.

5	0-0	c5xd4
6	Nf3xd4	Bb7xg2
7	Kg1xg2	d7-d5

Black has good alternatives in 7 . . . Qd8-c8, or 7 . . . g7-g6, whereas the text move served Alekhine badly in his third match game against Capablanca. Their game continued this way:
7 . . . d7-d5 8 c2-c4! e7-e6
9 Qd1-a4+ Qd8-d7 10 Nd4-b5
Nb8-c6 11 c4xd5 e6xd5 12 Bc1-f4
Ra8-c8 13 Rf1-c1 (threatens to win by 14 Nb5-c7+) 13 . . . Bf8-c5
14 b2-b4! Bc5xb4 15 Rc1xc6
Rc8xc6 16 Qa4xb4, and Capa as White won at the 42nd move after a series of sparkling combinations.

8   c2-c4   Qd8-d7

Capablanca improves on Alekhine's play, given in the previous note.

9   c4xd5   Nf6xd5

This is better than 9 . . . Qd7xd5+ 10 Kg2-g1 e7-e5 11 Qd1-a4+ Qd5-d7 12 Nd4-b5, which is in White's favour.

10   e2-e4   Nd5-c7

Preferable to 10 . . . Nd5-f6, as the Knight now guards the tender square b5 against invasion.

11   Nb1-c3   e7-e5

12   Nd4-f5   Qd7xd1

13   Rf1xd1

A diagram of the situation:

Position after 13 Rf1xd1

13   . . .   Nb8-a6

This is better than the routine (though natural) development of the Knight at c6, Capablanca foreseeing that the Knight is destined to have a brilliant future at c5.

14   Bc1-e3   Ra8-d8

15   Rd1xd8+   Ke8xd8

16   a2-a4

This is to support the entry of the Knight which is headed for b5 and the capture of the a-Pawn.

16   . . .   Kd8-d7

Strangely enough, the King makes no effort to save the threatened Pawn, but is on his way to the King-side!

Centralizing the King in the endgame is more important than the life of a mere Pawn—especially if the opponent must make some effort to capture it.

17   Nc3-b5

A safer continuation was 17 a4-a5, but White could hardly have anticipated that winning the Pawn would involve him in difficulties, as he can only get the Knight back into play at the cost of being saddled with isolated doubled Pawns.

17   . . .   g7-g6

18   Nf5-h4

White's last chance to obtain equality was with this line of play: 18 Ra1-d1+ Kd7-e6 19 Nf5-d6 Nc7xb5 20 Nd6xb5 Bf8-c5! 21 Be3-h6.

Ending 59

Position after 18 Nf5-h4

Capablanca to move

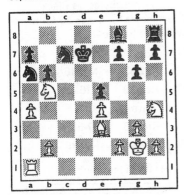

Allies

Black has the advantage for the endgame, as his position is superior.

His King is closer to the center than is White's.

His King-side pieces, though undeveloped, have a great deal of potential power. They can come into play quickly, and occupy important squares.

White's pieces, on the other hand, are scattered over the board, making it difficult for them to co-operate properly.

| 18 | ... | Bc8-c5 |
| 19 | Nb5xa7 | |

White is intent on winning a Pawn, even at the cost of ruining his Pawn structure. The allies may have been influenced by Steinitz's observation, 'A Pawn is worth a little trouble.'

The prudent course was to exchange Bishops, and follow that up with 20 Nb5-c3 and 21 Kg2-f3.

| 19 | ... | Bc5xe3 |
| 20 | f2xe3 | Na6-c5! |

Threatens to win a Pawn by 21 ... Nc6xe4, and also to trap the Knight by 21 ... Rh8-a8 (22 Na7-b5 Nc7xb5 23 a4xb5 Ra8xa1).

| 21 | Na7-b5 | Nc7xb5 |
| 22 | a4xb5 | Kd7-e6 |

Capablanca is never in a hurry! Lesser mortals would grab the Pawn and philosophize later. Capablanca does not care to allow counterplay after 22 ... Nc5xe4 by 23 Ra1-a7+ Kd7-e6 24 Ra7-b7.

White is a Pawn ahead, but Black's centralized King and Knight go far to make up the disadvantage in wordly goods.

This is in accordance with Capablanca's dictum, 'Position comes first, material next. Space and Time are complementary factors of Position.'

Capablanca not only expressed this principle—he lived by it!

| 23 | Kg2-f3 | |

If White plays 23 Ra1-d1 instead, taking control of the d-file, Black replies 23 ... Rh8-a8 followed by 24 ... Ra8-a4 and 25 ... Ra4-b4, and plays havoc with the helpless Pawns, while the enemy Rook can accomplish nothing along the d-file.

The position at this point:

Position after 23 Kg2-f3

23	...	Rh8-d8

Indicates his intention to continue by 24 ... Nc5-b3 and 25 ... Nb3-d2+, winning an e-Pawn.

24	b2-b4	Nc5-b3
25	Ra1-a7	

Attacking the b-Pawn instead would have this sequel: 25 Ra1-a6 Nb3-d2+ 26 Kf3-e2 Rd8-d6 27 Nh4-f3 Nd2xe4, and after Black plays 28 ... h7-h6 (to keep the Knight out of g5) there are threats of winning a Pawn by 29 ... Ne4-c3+, as well as threats of a more serious nature by 29 ... g6-g5, 30 ... g5-g4, and 31 ... Rd6-d2+.

25	...	Nb3-d2+
26	Kf3-g2	Nd2xe4
27	Nh4-f3	Rd8-d5
28	Ra7-a8	

Unable to save his Queen-side Pawn, White tries to get at his opponent's King-side Pawns.

28	...	Rd5xb5
29	Ra8-e8+	Ke6-f6
30	g3-g4	Ne4-g5
31	Nf3xg5	

There's little choice, as Black threatened 31 ... Ng5-e6 followed by 32 ... Rb5xb4.

31	...	Kf6xg5
32	Kg2-g3	Kg5-f6
33	Re8-h8	Kf6-g7

'Not a button!'

34	Rh8-e8	h7-h6
35	h2-h4	Kg7-f6

The picture on the board:

Position after 35 ... Kg7-f6

The attack on the King-side was short-lived. An attempt to continue it would lead to this finish: 36 Re8-h8 Rb5xb4 37 Rh8xh6 Kf6-g7 (the unfortunate Rook is now out of play for a while) 38 g4-g5 Rb4-e4 (clears the way for the Pawn) 39 Kg3-f3 Re4-c4 40 Kf3-g3 b6-b5 41 h4-h5 b5-b4 42 h5xg6 f7xg6 43 Rh6-h2 b4-b3 44 Rh2-b2 Rc4-b4 45 Kg3-f2 Kg7-f7 46 Kf2-e2 Kf7-e6

47 Ke2-d3 Ke6-d5 48 Kd3-c3
Rb4-b6 49 Rb2-d2+ Kd5-e4
50 Rd2-e2 (on 50 Kc3-b2 Ke4xe3
wins) 50 . . . b3-b2 and Black wins
easily.

36	Re8-c8	Rb5xb4
37	Rc8-c6+	Kf6-g7
38	g4-g5	h6-h5
39	Rc6-c8	Rb4-g4+
40	Kg3-h3	Rg4-e4
41	Rc8-c3	b6-b5

42   White Resigns

After 42 Rc3-b3 b5-b4 43 Kh3-g3
Kg7-f8 44 Kg3-h3 Kf8-e7 (threatens
to wander over to c4, drive the
Rook off, and escort the Pawn up
the board) 45 Rb3-d3 Re4-c4, and
now the threat of winning by
46 . . . Rc4-c3 forces the Rook to
return to b3, whereupon the King
advances to d6, c5, etc., and wins.

A beautifully played ending, one
that nourishes the soul.

GAME 60

White J. R. Capablanca
Black S. Reshevsky
Nottingham, 1936

Queen's Gambit Accepted
Reshevsky seizes the initiative early
in the game, and throws Capablanca
on the defence.

It takes skill and patience to
equalize, but Capablanca has a
plentiful supply of both, and is not
easily overwhelmed.

The position levels out, but
gradually he gains a whisper of an
advantage, and lures Reshevsky into
an ending of Knight against Bishop.

The ending is played exquisitely
by Capablanca, whose agile, high-
stepping Knight dances rings around
the bewildered Bishop.

1	d2-d4	d7-d5
2	Ng1-f3	Ng8-f6
3	c2-c4	d5xc4
4	Qd1-a4+	Nb8-d7
5	Qa4xc4	

Since White can take the Pawn at
his leisure, a good alternative is
5 g2-g3, and if then 5 . . . a7-a6,
6 Nb1-c3 brings another piece into
play.

5	. . .	e7-e6
6	g2-g3	a7-a6
7	Bf1-g2	b7-b5
8	Qc4-c6	

This holds back 8 . . . c7-c5, but
only temporarily.

8	. . .	Ra8-a7
9	Bc1-f4	

Capablanca later suggested 9 Bc1-e3
as better, with this probable continuation: 9 . . . Nf6-d5 10 Be3-g5
Bf8-e7 11 Bg5xe7 Qd8xe7 12 0-0
Bc8-b7 13 Qc6-c2, with an even
game.

9	. . .	Bc8-b7
10	Qc6-c1	

The Pawn of course is taboo, as after 10 Qc6xc7 Qd8xc7 11 Bf4xc7 Bb7xf3 wins a piece for Black.

10	. . .	c7-c5

This freeing move is almost a must for Black in Queen Pawn openings.

11	d4xc5	Bf8xc5
12	0-0	0-0

Black has more space on the Queen-side, and the prospect of annoying White's uncomfortably-placed Queen with his minor pieces.

13	Nb1-d2	Qd8-e7
14	Nd2-b3	Bc5-b6
15	Bf4-e3	

Aiming at simplication, White tries to rid the board of his opponent's powerful dark-squared Bishop, even if he has to lose several moves with his Queen to do so.

15	. . .	Rf8-c8
16	Qc1-d2	Nf6-e4
17	Qd2-d3	Ne4-c5
18	Nb3xc5	Nd7xc5
19	Qd3-d1	

The Queen, having been driven from pillar to post, returns home from her wanderings.

This is the position:

Position after 19 Qd3-d1

19	. . .	Bb7-a8

Alekhine considers this as one of several indifferent moves, and suggests instead as best 19 . . . Bb7-d5, and if 20 b2-b3 Ra7-d7 21 Qd1-e1 Rd7-d8, followed eventually by . . . Qe7-b7, with a still freer position.

20	Ra1-c1	Ra7-c7

Reshevsky's development of the Queen Rook to c7 by way of a7 is reminiscent of Janowsky's similar insinuation of the Queen Rook into active play in his 1911 encounter with Capablanca at San Sebastian, where he also got the mighty Cuban in hot water (see Game 7).

21	b2-b3	Nc5-d7

Reshevsky could have temporized with 21 . . . f7-f6, but relying on his great skill in the endgame, forces a couple of exchanges.

22	Rc1xc7	Rc8xc7
23	Be3xb6	Nd7xb6
24	Qd1-d4!	Nb6-d5

| 25 | Rf1-d1 |

Threatens 26 e2-e4 Nd5-f6
27 Qd4-d8+, winning the Bishop.

25	. . .	f7-f6
26	Nf3-e1	Ba8-b7
27	Bg2xd5	e6xd5

Undoubtedly weak, as it limits the
scope of the Bishop, and relegates
it to defence.

The better way was to capture
by 27 . . . Bb7xd5, but Reshevsky
may not have wanted to allow
28 e2-e4 in response.

| 28 | e2-e3 | Qe7-e4 |

Hoping for 29 Qd4xe4 d5xe4,
which allows the Bishop a bit
more freedom—but Capablanca
does not oblige!

| 29 | h2-h4 | a6-a5 |
| 30 | f2-f3 | Qe4xd4 |

Capablanca welcomes the exchange
of Queens on his terms, which
include keeping the Bishop confined behind the d-Pawn.

Alekhine suggests '30 . . . Qe4-e5
instead, and after 31 Kg1-f2, b5-b4
offers better chances.'

But if we continue by
32 Qd4-b6, defence may be difficult for Black.

(Life is not easy facing Capablanca over the board!)

| 31 | Rd1xd4 | Rc7-c1 |

Reshevsky plays for further exchanges—which is suicidal.

The proper strategy was to
bring the King to the center.

32	Kg1-f2	Rc1-a1
33	Rd4-d2	a5-a4
34	Ne1-d3	Ra1-b1

Ending 60

Position after 34 . . . Ra1-b1

Reshevsky

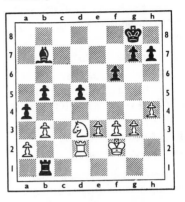

Capablanca to move

A cursory glance at the situation
would seem to indicate a routine
win for White.

His Knight, a stronger piece in
this position than the Bishop, can
occupy such important squares as
d4, c5, and b4, without fear of
being driven off by the Bishop,
whose influence is restricted to the
white squares.

The Bishop, on the other hand,
is not only restrained in its movements by the two weak isolated
Pawns at d5 and b5, but has the
thankless task of protecting them
from capture.

Capablanca's initial procedure is
simple enough. He forces an exchange of Rooks (to clarify the
position) and maneuvers his King
and Knight to dominating squares,
and then acquires a passed Pawn.

Complications present themselves when his ingenious opponent

creates a passed Pawn of his own.
The problem of rendering this
menacing Pawn harmless requires
precise timing on the part of Capablanca.

The finish, with both sides rushing to queen their Pawns, is truly
exciting.

35	Rd2-b2	Rb1xb2

Black must exchange, as
35 . . . Rb1-d1 36 Kf2-e2 Rd1-h1
37 b3xa4 wins a Pawn (or two) for
White.

36	Nd3xb2	Bb7-c6
37	Nb2-d3	g7-g5

Reshevsky is always dangerous, and
puts up a hard fight in positions
that appear hopeless. Here he begins
a dangerous counter-attack that
offers good chances of succeeding.

Passive play would let White
bring his Knight to b4 and his King
to d4, after which he could exploit
Black's two weaknesses, the Pawns
at d5 and b5, with relative ease.

Black could have embarked on
another course (instead of the line
he chose, beginning with
37 . . . g7-g5) with no better result
though, as Fine indicates in his
book *Basic Chess Endings*, thus:
37 . . . Kg8-f7 38 Nd3-b4 Bc6-b7
39 Nb4-c2 Bb7-c6 40 Nc2-d4
Bc6-d7 41 Kf2-e2 Kf7-e7
42 Ke2-d3 a4xb3 43 a2xb3 Ke7-d6
44 Kd3-c3 Kd6-c5 45 b3-b4+
Kc5-d6 46 Nd4-e2 Kd6-e5
47 Ne2-c1 Bd7-c6 48 Nc1-d3+
Ke5-d6 49 Kc3-d4 Bc6-e8
50 Nd3-f4 Be8-f7 51 Nf4-e2·
Bf7-e8 52 Ne2-c3 Be8-c6 53 g3-g4
(this reduces Black to Pawn moves)

53 . . . g7-g5 54 h4-h5 h7-h6
55 f3-f4 g5xf4 56 e3xf4 Bc6-d7
57 Nc3xd5 Bd7xg4 58 Nd5xf6
Bg4-f5 59 Nf6-g8 Bf5-g4
60 Ng8xh6 Bg4xh5 61 Nh6-f5+
Kd6-d7 (unfortunately he may not
play 61 . . . Kd6-e6) 62 Kd4-e5,
and the rest is simple.

38	h4xg5	f6xg5
39	Nd3-b4	a4xb3
40	a2xb3	

Clearly, 40 Nb4xc6 is unthinkable,
as Black replies 40 . . . b3xa2 and
gets a new Queen to repay him for
loss of the Bishop.

40	. . .	Bc6-b7
41	g3-g4!	

It is important to discourage any
thoughts of getting a passed Pawn
by means of 41 . . . h7-h5 followed
eventually by . . . h5-h4.

41	. . .	Kg8-g7
42	Kf2-e2	Kg7-g6
43	Ke2-d3	h7-h5

The impetuous 43 . . . d5-d4 is met
by 44 e3-e4, and the d-Pawn is lost.

44	g4xh5+	Kg6xh5
45	Kd3-d4	Kh5-h4
46	Nb4xd5	

Wins a Pawn at the cost of freeing
the Bishop, but—a Pawn's a Pawn
for a' that and a' that.

46	. . .	Kh4-g3
47	f3-f4	

This is how the board looks:

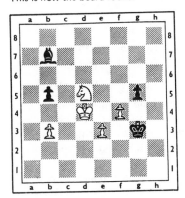

Position after 47 f3-f4

Should Black exchange pieces first before going for a Queen, the play would go as follows: 47 . . . Bb7xd5 48 Kd4xd5 g5-g4 (if 48 . . . g5xf4 49 e3xf4 Kg3xf4 50 Kd5-c5, and the win is elementary) 49 f4-f5 Kg3-h3 (the King must make way for the Pawn, and moving to the f-file lets White queen his Pawn with check) 50 f5-f6 g4-g3 51 f6-f7 g3-g2 52 f7-f8(Q) g2-g1(Q) 53 Qf8-h6+ Kh3-g2 54 Qh6-g5+, and White exchanges Queens and wins.

Returning to the diagram . . .

47	. . .	g5-g4
48	f4-f5	Bb7-c8
49	Kd4-e5	

Not at once 49 f5-f6 when 49 . . . Bc8-e6 stops the Pawn in its tracks, and makes a win for White difficult at best.

Now there is a threat of queening the Pawn in a hurry.

| 49 | . . . | Bc8-d7 |
| 50 | e3-e4 | |

The proper touch. The tempting 50 Nd5-f6 fails in its object, as after 50 . . . Kg3-h3 51 Nf6xd7 g4-g3 52 f5-f6 g3-g2 53 f6-f7 g2-g1(Q) 54 f7-f8(Q) Qg1xe3+ 55 Ke5-f6 Qe3xb3, and White has no more than a draw.

| 50 | . . . | Bd7-e8 |
| 51 | Ke5-d4 | |

Make way for the e-Pawn!'

51	. . .	Kg3-f3
52	e4-e5	g4-g3
53	Nd5-e3	

A diagram shows the situation:

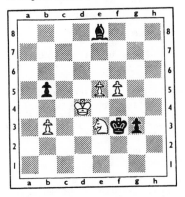

Position after 53 Nd5-e3

The position is remarkable. Black seems to have a good defence in 53 . . . Be8-d7, but White can force a win with the aid of a Knight that does some fancy stepping in attack and defence, as Capablanca thus demonstrated: 53 . . . Be8-d7 54 e5-e6 Bd7-c8 55 e6-e7 Bc8-d7 56 f5-f6 Bd7-e8 57 Ne3-f5! (the key square—the Bishop must be destroyed!) 57 . . . g3-g2 (if 57 . . . Kf3-g4 58 Nf5xg3 Kg4xg3

59 Kd4-e5 Be8-f7 60 Ke5-d6 and
wins) 58 Nf5-h4+ Kf3-f4 (or
58 . . . Kf3-g3 59 Nh4xg2)
59 Nh4xg2+ Kf4-f5 60 Ng2-e3+
Kf5xf6 61 Ne3-d5+ Kf6-f7
62 Nd5-c7 Be8-d7 (or
62 . . . Kf7xe7 63 Nc7xe8 Ke7xe8
64 Kd4-c5 and wins) 63 e7-e8(Q)+
Bd7xe8 64 Nc7xe8 Kf7xe8
65 Kd4-c5 Ke8-d7 66 Kc5xb5
Kd7-c7 67 Kb5-a6 Kc7-c6
68 b3-b4 Kc6-c7 69 b4-b5 Kc7-b8
70 Ka6-b6! (this placing of the
King in front of the Pawn, wins
with or without the move)
70 . . . Kb8-a8 71 Kb6-c7 and
White wins.

| 53 | . . . | Kf3-f4 |
| 54 | e5-e6 | g3-g2 |

The last hope, as the Bishop cannot hold back the enemy Pawns indefinitely.

55	Ne3xg2+	Kf4xf5
56	Kd4-d5	Kf5-g4
57	Ng2-e3+	Kg4-f4
58	Kd5-d4	Black Resigns

There is no defence against
59 e6-e7 followed by 60 Ne3-d5
and 61 Nd5-c7, forcing Black to
give up his Bishop for the passed
Pawn.

An ending in the grand manner, impressive in its aristocratic elegance.

It is masterly play of this sort that moved Alekhine to say, 'Until the end, Capablanca could still evolve true pearls of chess art.'

Index of openings

Principal themes in the endings

The references are to game numbers

Capablanca has	Opponent has
Pawns	Pawns, 21, 30, 40
Pawns	Bishop, 38
Knight	Bishop, 43, 60
Bishop	Knight, 1, 41
Bishop	Bishop (same colour), 23, 52
Bishop	Bishop (opposite colour), 16, 18, 28, 50
Knight	Rook, 44
Rook	Bishop, 48
Rook	Rook, 9, 12, 13, 15, 26, 36, 39, 51, 59
Rook	Knight and Bishop, 55
Rook	Rook and Knight, 14
Queen	Queen, 47, 54
Queen	Queen and Bishop, 3
Bishop and Knight	Rook, 2
Two Bishops	Two Bishops, 8
Rook and Bishop	Rook, 4
Rook and Knight	Rook and Knight, 32, 45, 46
Rook and Knight	Rook and Bishop, 31, 35
Rook and Bishop	Rook and Bishop, 33, 53
Rook and Bishop	Rook and Knight, 19
Two Rooks	Rook and Bishop, 24
Two Rooks	Two Rooks, 5, 10, 56
Two Rooks	Rook and two Bishops, 6
Queen and Knight	Queen and Knight, 7
Queen and Bishop	Queen and Knight, 11, 57
Queen and Knight	Rook, Bishop, and two Pawns, 22
Queen and Rook	Queen and Rook, 20, 42
Rook and two Knights	Rook, Knight, and Bishop, 34, 37
Two Rooks and Bishop	Two Rooks and Knight, 25, 27
Two Rooks and Bishop	Two Rooks and Bishop, 29
Queen, Rook, and Knight	Queen, Rook, and Knight, 49
Queen and two Rooks	Queen and two Rooks, 17, 58

Index of Capablanca's opponents

The references are to game numbers

Capablanca's tournament and match record

Tournament record

Event	Rank	P	W	L	D
New York State, 1910	1	7	6	0	1
New York, 1911	2	12	8	1	3
San Sebastian, 1911	1	14	6	1	7
New York, 1913	1	13	10	1	2
Havana, 1913	2	14	8	2	4
*New York, 1913	1	13	13	0	0
St. Petersburg, 1914	2	18	10	2	6
New York, 1915	1	14	12	0	2
New York, 1916	1	17	12	1	4
New York, 1918	1	12	9	0	3
Hastings, 1919	1	11	10	0	1
London, 1922	1	15	11	0	4
New York, 1924	2	20	10	1	9
Moscow, 1925	3	20	9	2	9
Lake Hopatcong, 1926	1	8	4	0	4
New York, 1927	1	20	8	0	12
Bad Kissingen, 1928	2	11	4	1	6
Budapest, 1928	1	9	5	0	4
Berlin, 1928	1	12	5	0	7
Ramsgate, 1929	1	7	4	0	3
Carlsbad, 1929	2–3	21	10	2	9
Budapest, 1929	1	13	8	0	5
Barcelona, 1929	1	14	13	0	1
Hastings, 1929–30	1	9	4	0	5
Hastings, 1930–1	2	9	5	1	3
New York, 1931	1	11	9	0	2
Hastings, 1934–5	4	9	4	2	3
Moscow, 1935	4	19	7	2	10
Margate, 1935	2	9	6	1	2
Margate, 1936	2	9	5	0	4
Moscow, 1936	1	18	8	0	10
Nottingham, 1936	1–2	14	7	1	6

*Beihoff (½–3½) and Stapfer (0–1) retired, all their games being scored against them.

Event	Rank	P	W	L	D
Semmering,1937	3--4	14	2	1	11
Paris, 1938	1	10	6	0	4
AVRO, 1938	7	14	2	4	8
Margate, 1939	2—3	9	4	0	5
Buenos Aires, 1939	—	16	7	0	9
Totals		**485**	**271**	**26**	**188**

Match record

Corzo, 1901		13	4	3	6
Marshall, 1909		23	8	1	14
Kostics, 1919		5	5	0	0
Lasker, 1921		14	4	0	10
Alekhine, 1927		34	3	6	25
Euwe, 1931		10	2	0	8
Totals		**99**	**26**	**10**	**63**
Grand Totals		**584**	**297**	**36**	**251**

Bibliography

General Works

Alekhine, Alexander-*Deux Cents Parties D'Échecs*

Alexander, C. H. O'D.-*A Book of Chess*

Bisguier, Arthur and Solits, Andrew-*American Chess Masters from Morphy to Fischer*

Bogolyubov, Ewfim-*Klassische Schachpartien aus modernen Zeiten*

Capablanca, José R.-*My Chess Career*
—*Chess Fundamentals*
—*A Primer of Chess*
—*Last Lectures*
—*Uchevnik Schachmatnoy Igri*

Chernev, Irving-*The Golden Dozen*
—*Logical Chess Move by Move*
—*The Chess Companion*
—*The Most Instructive Games of Chess Ever Played*
—*Combinations: The Heart of Chess*
—*Wonders and Curiosities of Chess*

Chernev, Irving and Reinfeld, Fred-*The Fireside Book of Chess*

Euwe, Max-*Meet the Masters*
—*Judgment and Planning in Chess*
—*From Steinitz to Fisher*

Euwe, Max and Prins, Lodewijk-*Das Schachphänomen 'Capablanca'*

Fine, Reuben-*The Middle Game in Chess*
—*The World's Great Chess Games*

Gelabert, José A.-*Glorias del Tablero 'Capablanca'*

Gilchrist, J. and Hooper, David-*Weltgeschichte des Schachs 'Capablanca'*

Golombek, Harry-*Capablanca's 100 Best Games of Chess*

Goetz, Alphonse-*Cours d'Échecs*

Hooper, David and Brandreth, Dale-*The Unknown Capablanca*

König, Imre-*Chess from Morphy to Botvinnik*

Kotov, Alexander-*Think Like a Grandmaster*

Lasker, Edward-*Chess Strategy*
—*The Adventure of Chess*
—*Chess and Checkers*
—*Chess Secrets I Learned from the Masters*

Lasker, Emanuel-*Manual of Chess*

Lionnais, François L.-*Les Prix de Beauté aux Échecs*

Lionnais, François L. and Maget, Ernst-*Dictionnaire des Échecs*

Müller, Hans-*Vom Element zur Planning*

Napier, William E.-*Amenities and Background of Chess* (3 Vols.)

Pachman, Ludek-*Modern Chess Strategy*

Page 286

Pachman, Ludek-*Complete Chess Strategy*
—*Entscheidungspartien*
Palau, Luis-*Joyas del Ajedrez*
Panov, Vasily-*Capablanca*

Reinfeld, Fred-*The Immortal Games of Capablanca*
—*Great Games by Chess Prodigies*
—*The Human Side of Chess*
Reinfeld, Fred and Chernev, Irving-*Chess Strategy and Tactics*
Réti, Richard-*Modern Ideas in Chess*
—*Masters of the Chessboard*

Soltis, Andrew-*The Great Chess Tournaments and Their Stories*
Stahlberg, Gideon-*Chess and Chess Masters*
Sunnucks, Anne-*The Encyclopaedia of Chess*

Tarrasch, Siegbert-*Die moderne Schachpartie*
Tartakover, Savielly-*Die hypermoderne Schachpartie*
—*Führende Meister*
Tartakover, Savielly and du Mont, Julius-*500 Master Games of Chess*

Vuković, Vladimir-*The Art of Attack in Chess*

Winter, William-*Kings of Chess*
—*Chess for Match Players*

Yates, F. D. and Winter, William-*Modern Master Play*

Znosko-Borovsky, Eugène-*The Middle Game in Chess*

Tournament Books

Alekhine, Alexander-*The New York International Tournament 1924*
—*Das New Yorker Schachturnier 1927*
—*The Book of the Nottingham International Chess Tournament 1936*

Bogolyubov, Ewfim-*Das Internationale Schachturnier Moskau 1925*

Capablanca, José R.-*Torneo Internacional de Ajedrez 1913*

Helms, Hermann-*International Masters' Tournament of the Manhattan Chess Club 1918*

Kmoch, Hans (ed.)-*Internationales Schachmeisterturnier Karlsbad 1929*

Levenfisch, Grigory (ed.)-*Tretii Mezhdunarodny Schachmatny Turnir Moskva 1936*

Maroczy, Geza (ed.)-*The Book of the London International Chess Congress 1922*
Mieses, Jacques and Lewitt, Dr. M.-*Internationales Schachturnier zu San Sebastian 1911*

Rabinovich, I.L. (ed.)-*Vtoroi Mezhdunarodny Schachmatny Turnir Moskva 1935*

Tarrasch, Siegbert-*Das Grossmeister Turnier zu St. Petersburg 1914*
Tartakover, Savielly-*Internationales Schachturnier Bad Kissingen 1928*

Endgame Manuals

Averbach, Yuri-*Lehrbuch der Endspiele* (4 Vols.)

Barden, Leonard-*How to Play the Endgame in Chess*

Chéron, André-*Lehr-und Handbuch der Endspiele* (3 Vols.)

Euwe, Max and Hooper, David-*A Guide to Chess Endings*

Fine, Reuben-*Basic Chess Endings*

Gawlikowski, Stanislaw-*Koncowa Gra Zachowa*

Hooper, David-*How to Play Chess Endgames*

Levenfisch, Grigori and Smyslov, Vasily-*Rook Endings*

Rabinovich, I. L.-*Toren Eindspelen –Pard en Loper Eindspelen*
Radulescu, Mihai-*Finulari Complexe in Sah*

Znosko-Borovsky, Eugène-*How to Play Chess Endings*

Magazines

American Chess Bulletin 1909–1942
Chess Review 1933–1942
L'Échiquier 1925–1937
Les Cahiers de L'Échiquier Français 1925–1936
Wiener Schachzeitung 1909–1915, 1924–1933

A CATALOG OF SELECTED
DOVER BOOKS
IN ALL FIELDS OF INTEREST

A CATALOG OF SELECTED DOVER
BOOKS IN ALL FIELDS OF INTEREST

DRAWINGS OF REMBRANDT, edited by Seymour Slive. Updated Lippmann, Hofstede de Groot edition, with definitive scholarly apparatus. All portraits, biblical sketches, landscapes, nudes. Oriental figures, classical studies, together with selection of work by followers. 550 illustrations. Total of 630pp. 9⅛ × 12¼.
21485-0, 21486-9 Pa., Two-vol. set $25.00

GHOST AND HORROR STORIES OF AMBROSE BIERCE, Ambrose Bierce. 24 tales vividly imagined, strangely prophetic, and decades ahead of their time in technical skill: "The Damned Thing," "An Inhabitant of Carcosa," "The Eyes of the Panther," "Moxon's Master," and 20 more. 199pp. 5⅜ × 8½. 20767-6 Pa. $3.95

ETHICAL WRITINGS OF MAIMONIDES, Maimonides. Most significant ethical works of great medieval sage, newly translated for utmost precision, readability. Laws Concerning Character Traits, Eight Chapters, more. 192pp. 5⅜ × 8½.
24522-5 Pa. $4.50

THE EXPLORATION OF THE COLORADO RIVER AND ITS CANYONS, J. W. Powell. Full text of Powell's 1,000-mile expedition down the fabled Colorado in 1869. Superb account of terrain, geology, vegetation, Indians, famine, mutiny, treacherous rapids, mighty canyons, during exploration of last unknown part of continental U.S. 400pp. 5⅜ × 8½.
20094-9 Pa. $6.95

HISTORY OF PHILOSOPHY, Julián Marías. Clearest one-volume history on the market. Every major philosopher and dozens of others, to Existentialism and later. 505pp. 5⅜ × 8½.
21739-6 Pa. $8.50

ALL ABOUT LIGHTNING, Martin A. Uman. Highly readable non-technical survey of nature and causes of lightning, thunderstorms, ball lightning, St. Elmo's Fire, much more. Illustrated. 192pp. 5⅜ × 8½.
25237-X Pa. $5.95

SAILING ALONE AROUND THE WORLD, Captain Joshua Slocum. First man to sail around the world, alone, in small boat. One of great feats of seamanship told in delightful manner. 67 illustrations. 294pp. 5⅜ × 8½. 20326-3 Pa. $4.95

LETTERS AND NOTES ON THE MANNERS, CUSTOMS AND CONDITIONS OF THE NORTH AMERICAN INDIANS, George Catlin. Classic account of life among Plains Indians: ceremonies, hunt, warfare, etc. 312 plates. 572pp. of text. 6⅛ × 9¼. 22118-0, 22119-9 Pa. Two-vol. set $15.90

ALASKA: The Harriman Expedition, 1899, John Burroughs, John Muir, et al. Informative, engrossing accounts of two-month, 9,000-mile expedition. Native peoples, wildlife, forests, geography, salmon industry, glaciers, more. Profusely illustrated. 240 black-and-white line drawings. 124 black-and-white photographs. 3 maps. Index. 576pp. 5⅜ × 8½.
25109-8 Pa. $11.95

THE BOOK OF BEASTS: Being a Translation from a Latin Bestiary of the Twelfth Century, T. H. White. Wonderful catalog real and fanciful beasts: manticore, griffin, phoenix, amphivius, jaculus, many more. White's witty erudite commentary on scientific, historical aspects. Fascinating glimpse of medieval mind. Illustrated. 296pp. 5⅜ × 8¼. (Available in U.S. only) 24609-4 Pa. $5.95

FRANK LLOYD WRIGHT: ARCHITECTURE AND NATURE With 160 Illustrations, Donald Hoffmann. Profusely illustrated study of influence of nature—especially prairie—on Wright's designs for Fallingwater, Robie House, Guggenheim Museum, other masterpieces. 96pp. 9¼ × 10¾. 25098-9 Pa. $7.95

FRANK LLOYD WRIGHT'S FALLINGWATER, Donald Hoffmann. Wright's famous waterfall house: planning and construction of organic idea. History of site, owners, Wright's personal involvement. Photographs of various stages of building. Preface by Edgar Kaufmann, Jr. 100 illustrations. 112pp. 9¼ × 10.
23671-4 Pa. $7.95

YEARS WITH FRANK LLOYD WRIGHT: Apprentice to Genius, Edgar Tafel. Insightful memoir by a former apprentice presents a revealing portrait of Wright the man, the inspired teacher, the greatest American architect. 372 black-and-white illustrations. Preface. Index. vi + 228pp. 8¼ × 11. 24801-1 Pa. $9.95

THE STORY OF KING ARTHUR AND HIS KNIGHTS, Howard Pyle. Enchanting version of King Arthur fable has delighted generations with imaginative narratives of exciting adventures and unforgettable illustrations by the author. 41 illustrations. xviii + 313pp. 6⅛ × 9¼. 21445-1 Pa. $5.95

THE GODS OF THE EGYPTIANS, E. A. Wallis Budge. Thorough coverage of numerous gods of ancient Egypt by foremost Egyptologist. Information on evolution of cults, rites and gods; the cult of Osiris; the Book of the Dead and its rites; the sacred animals and birds; Heaven and Hell; and more. 956pp. 6⅛ × 9¼.
22055-9, 22056-7 Pa., Two-vol. set $21.90

A THEOLOGICO-POLITICAL TREATISE, Benedict Spinoza. Also contains unfinished *Political Treatise*. Great classic on religious liberty, theory of government on common consent. R. Elwes translation. Total of 421pp. 5⅜ × 8½.
20249-6 Pa. $6.95

INCIDENTS OF TRAVEL IN CENTRAL AMERICA, CHIAPAS, AND YUCATAN, John L. Stephens. Almost single-handed discovery of Maya culture; exploration of ruined cities, monuments, temples; customs of Indians. 115 drawings. 892pp. 5⅜ × 8½. 22404-X, 22405-8 Pa., Two-vol. set $15.90

LOS CAPRICHOS, Francisco Goya. 80 plates of wild, grotesque monsters and caricatures. Prado manuscript included. 183pp. 6⅜ × 9⅜. 22384-1 Pa. $4.95

AUTOBIOGRAPHY: The Story of My Experiments with Truth, Mohandas K. Gandhi. Not hagiography, but Gandhi in his own words. Boyhood, legal studies, purification, the growth of the Satyagraha (nonviolent protest) movement. Critical, inspiring work of the man who freed India. 480pp. 5⅜ × 8½. (Available in U.S. only)
24593-4 Pa. $6.95

CATALOG OF DOVER BOOKS

ILLUSTRATED DICTIONARY OF HISTORIC ARCHITECTURE, edited by Cyril M. Harris. Extraordinary compendium of clear, concise definitions for over 5,000 important architectural terms complemented by over 2,000 line drawings. Covers full spectrum of architecture from ancient ruins to 20th-century Modernism. Preface. 592pp. 7½ × 9⅜.
24444-X Pa. $14.95

THE NIGHT BEFORE CHRISTMAS, Clement Moore. Full text, and woodcuts from original 1848 book. Also critical, historical material. 19 illustrations. 40pp. 4⅝ × 6.
22797-9 Pa. $2.50

THE LESSON OF JAPANESE ARCHITECTURE: 165 Photographs, Jiro Harada. Memorable gallery of 165 photographs taken in the 1930's of exquisite Japanese homes of the well-to-do and historic buildings. 13 line diagrams. 192pp. 8⅜ × 11¼.
24778-3 Pa. $8.95

THE AUTOBIOGRAPHY OF CHARLES DARWIN AND SELECTED LETTERS, edited by Francis Darwin. The fascinating life of eccentric genius composed of an intimate memoir by Darwin (intended for his children); commentary by his son, Francis; hundreds of fragments from notebooks, journals, papers; and letters to and from Lyell, Hooker, Huxley, Wallace and Henslow. xi + 365pp. 5⅜ × 8.
20479-0 Pa. $5.95

WONDERS OF THE SKY: Observing Rainbows, Comets, Eclipses, the Stars and Other Phenomena, Fred Schaaf. Charming, easy-to-read poetic guide to all manner of celestial events visible to the naked eye. Mock suns, glories, Belt of Venus, more. Illustrated. 299pp. 5¼ × 8¼.
24402-4 Pa. $7.95

BURNHAM'S CELESTIAL HANDBOOK, Robert Burnham, Jr. Thorough guide to the stars beyond our solar system. Exhaustive treatment. Alphabetical by constellation: Andromeda to Cetus in Vol. 1; Chamaeleon to Orion in Vol. 2; and Pavo to Vulpecula in Vol. 3. Hundreds of illustrations. Index in Vol. 3. 2,000pp. 6⅛ × 9¼.
23567-X, 23568-8, 23673-0 Pa., Three-vol. set $37.85

STAR NAMES: Their Lore and Meaning, Richard Hinckley Allen. Fascinating history of names various cultures have given to constellations and literary and folkloristic uses that have been made of stars. Indexes to subjects. Arabic and Greek names. Biblical references. Bibliography. 563pp. 5⅜ × 8½.
21079-0 Pa. $7.95

THIRTY YEARS THAT SHOOK PHYSICS: The Story of Quantum Theory, George Gamow. Lucid, accessible introduction to influential theory of energy and matter. Careful explanations of Dirac's anti-particles, Bohr's model of the atom, much more. 12 plates. Numerous drawings. 240pp. 5⅜ × 8½.
24895-X Pa. $4.95

CHINESE DOMESTIC FURNITURE IN PHOTOGRAPHS AND MEASURED DRAWINGS, Gustav Ecke. A rare volume, now affordably priced for antique collectors, furniture buffs and art historians. Detailed review of styles ranging from early Shang to late Ming. Unabridged republication. 161 black-and-white drawings, photos. Total of 224pp. 8⅜ × 11¼. (Available in U.S. only) 25171-3 Pa. $12.95

VINCENT VAN GOGH: A Biography, Julius Meier-Graefe. Dynamic, penetrating study of artist's life, relationship with brother, Theo, painting techniques, travels, more. Readable, engrossing. 160pp. 5⅜ × 8½. (Available in U.S. only)
25253-1 Pa. $3.95

HOW TO WRITE, Gertrude Stein. Gertrude Stein claimed anyone could understand her unconventional writing—here are clues to help. Fascinating improvisations, language experiments, explanations illuminate Stein's craft and the art of writing. Total of 414pp. 4⅝ × 6⅜.   23144-5 Pa. $5.95

ADVENTURES AT SEA IN THE GREAT AGE OF SAIL: Five Firsthand Narratives, edited by Elliot Snow. Rare true accounts of exploration, whaling, shipwreck, fierce natives, trade, shipboard life, more. 33 illustrations. Introduction. 353pp. 5⅜ × 8½.   25177-2 Pa. $7.95

THE HERBAL OR GENERAL HISTORY OF PLANTS, John Gerard. Classic descriptions of about 2,850 plants—with over 2,700 illustrations—includes Latin and English names, physical descriptions, varieties, time and place of growth, more. 2,706 illustrations. xlv + 1,678pp. 8½ × 12¼.   23147-X Cloth. $75.00

DOROTHY AND THE WIZARD IN OZ, L. Frank Baum. Dorothy and the Wizard visit the center of the Earth, where people are vegetables, glass houses grow and Oz characters reappear. Classic sequel to Wizard of Oz. 256pp. 5⅜ × 8.
24714-7 Pa. $4.95

SONGS OF EXPERIENCE: Facsimile Reproduction with 26 Plates in Full Color, William Blake. This facsimile of Blake's original "Illuminated Book" reproduces 26 full-color plates from a rare 1826 edition. Includes "The Tyger," "London," "Holy Thursday," and other immortal poems. 26 color plates. Printed text of poems. 48pp. 5¼ × 7.   24636-1 Pa. $3.50

SONGS OF INNOCENCE, William Blake. The first and most popular of Blake's famous "Illuminated Books," in a facsimile edition reproducing all 31 brightly colored plates. Additional printed text of each poem. 64pp. 5¼ × 7.
22764-2 Pa. $3.50

PRECIOUS STONES, Max Bauer. Classic, thorough study of diamonds, rubies, emeralds, garnets, etc.: physical character, occurrence, properties, use, similar topics. 20 plates, 8 in color. 94 figures. 659pp. 6⅛ × 9¼.
21910-0, 21911-9 Pa., Two-vol. set $15.90

ENCYCLOPEDIA OF VICTORIAN NEEDLEWORK, S. F. A. Caulfeild and Blanche Saward. Full, precise descriptions of stitches, techniques for dozens of needlecrafts—most exhaustive reference of its kind. Over 800 figures. Total of 679pp. 8⅛ × 11. Two volumes.   Vol. 1 22800-2 Pa. $11.95
                                                     Vol. 2 22801-0 Pa. $11.95

THE MARVELOUS LAND OF OZ, L. Frank Baum. Second Oz book, the Scarecrow and Tin Woodman are back with hero named Tip, Oz magic. 136 illustrations. 287pp. 5⅜ × 8½.   20692-0 Pa. $5.95

WILD FOWL DECOYS, Joel Barber. Basic book on the subject, by foremost authority and collector. Reveals history of decoy making and rigging, place in American culture, different kinds of decoys, how to make them, and how to use them. 140 plates. 156pp. 7⅞ × 10¾.   20011-6 Pa. $8.95

HISTORY OF LACE, Mrs. Bury Palliser. Definitive, profusely illustrated chronicle of lace from earliest times to late 19th century. Laces of Italy, Greece, England, France, Belgium, etc. Landmark of needlework scholarship. 266 illustrations. 672pp. 6⅛ × 9¼.   24742-2 Pa. $14.95

ILLUSTRATED GUIDE TO SHAKER FURNITURE, Robert Meader. All furniture and appurtenances, with much on unknown local styles. 235 photos. 146pp. 9 × 12. 22819-3 Pa. $7.95

WHALE SHIPS AND WHALING: A Pictorial Survey, George Francis Dow. Over 200 vintage engravings, drawings, photographs of barks, brigs, cutters, other vessels. Also harpoons, lances, whaling guns, many other artifacts. Comprehensive text by foremost authority. 207 black-and-white illustrations. 288pp. 6 × 9. 24808-9 Pa. $8.95

THE BERTRAMS, Anthony Trollope. Powerful portrayal of blind self-will and thwarted ambition includes one of Trollope's most heartrending love stories. 497pp. 5⅜ × 8½. 25119-5 Pa. $8.95

ADVENTURES WITH A HAND LENS, Richard Headstrom. Clearly written guide to observing and studying flowers and grasses, fish scales, moth and insect wings, egg cases, buds, feathers, seeds, leaf scars, moss, molds, ferns, common crystals, etc.—all with an ordinary, inexpensive magnifying glass. 209 exact line drawings aid in your discoveries. 220pp. 5⅜ × 8½. 23330-8 Pa. $4.50

RODIN ON ART AND ARTISTS, Auguste Rodin. Great sculptor's candid, wide-ranging comments on meaning of art; great artists; relation of sculpture to poetry, painting, music; philosophy of life, more. 76 superb black-and-white illustrations of Rodin's sculpture, drawings and prints. 119pp. 8⅜ × 11¼. 24487-3 Pa. $6.95

FIFTY CLASSIC FRENCH FILMS, 1912–1982: A Pictorial Record, Anthony Slide. Memorable stills from Grand Illusion, Beauty and the Beast, Hiroshima, Mon Amour, many more. Credits, plot synopses, reviews, etc. 160pp. 8¼ × 11. 25256-6 Pa. $11.95

THE PRINCIPLES OF PSYCHOLOGY, William James. Famous long course complete, unabridged. Stream of thought, time perception, memory, experimental methods; great work decades ahead of its time. 94 figures. 1,391pp. 5⅜ × 8½. 20381-6, 20382-4 Pa., Two-vol. set $19.90

BODIES IN A BOOKSHOP, R. T. Campbell. Challenging mystery of blackmail and murder with ingenious plot and superbly drawn characters. In the best tradition of British suspense fiction. 192pp. 5⅜ × 8½. 24720-1 Pa. $3.95

CALLAS: PORTRAIT OF A PRIMA DONNA, George Jellinek. Renowned commentator on the musical scene chronicles incredible career and life of the most controversial, fascinating, influential operatic personality of our time. 64 black-and-white photographs. 416pp. 5⅜ × 8¼. 25047-4 Pa. $7.95

GEOMETRY, RELATIVITY AND THE FOURTH DIMENSION, Rudolph Rucker. Exposition of fourth dimension, concepts of relativity as Flatland characters continue adventures. Popular, easily followed yet accurate, profound. 141 illustrations. 133pp. 5⅜ × 8½. 23400-2 Pa. $3.50

HOUSEHOLD STORIES BY THE BROTHERS GRIMM, with pictures by Walter Crane. 53 classic stories—Rumpelstiltskin, Rapunzel, Hansel and Gretel, the Fisherman and his Wife, Snow White, Tom Thumb, Sleeping Beauty, Cinderella, and so much more—lavishly illustrated with original 19th century drawings. 114 illustrations. x + 269pp. 5⅜ × 8½. 21080-4 Pa. $4.50

SUNDIALS, Albert Waugh. Far and away the best, most thorough coverage of ideas, mathematics concerned, types, construction, adjusting anywhere. Over 100 illustrations. 230pp. 5⅜ × 8½. 22947-5 Pa. $4.50

PICTURE HISTORY OF THE NORMANDIE: With 190 Illustrations, Frank O. Braynard. Full story of legendary French ocean liner: Art Deco interiors, design innovations, furnishings, celebrities, maiden voyage, tragic fire, much more. Extensive text. 144pp. 8⅜ × 11¼. 25257-4 Pa. $9.95

THE FIRST AMERICAN COOKBOOK: A Facsimile of "American Cookery," 1796, Amelia Simmons. Facsimile of the first American-written cookbook published in the United States contains authentic recipes for colonial favorites— pumpkin pudding, winter squash pudding, spruce beer, Indian slapjacks, and more. Introductory Essay and Glossary of colonial cooking terms. 80pp. 5⅜ × 8½. 24710-4 Pa. $3.50

101 PUZZLES IN THOUGHT AND LOGIC, C. R. Wylie, Jr. Solve murders and robberies, find out which fishermen are liars, how a blind man could possibly identify a color—purely by your own reasoning! 107pp. 5⅜ × 8½. 20367-0 Pa. $2.50

THE BOOK OF WORLD-FAMOUS MUSIC—CLASSICAL, POPULAR AND FOLK, James J. Fuld. Revised and enlarged republication of landmark work in musico-bibliography. Full information about nearly 1,000 songs and compositions including first lines of music and lyrics. New supplement. Index. 800pp. 5⅜ × 8¼. 24857-7 Pa. $14.95

ANTHROPOLOGY AND MODERN LIFE, Franz Boas. Great anthropologist's classic treatise on race and culture. Introduction by Ruth Bunzel. Only inexpensive paperback edition. 255pp. 5⅜ × 8½. 25245-0 Pa. $5.95

THE TALE OF PETER RABBIT, Beatrix Potter. The inimitable Peter's terrifying adventure in Mr. McGregor's garden, with all 27 wonderful, full-color Potter illustrations. 55pp. 4¼ × 5½. (Available in U.S. only) 22827-4 Pa. $1.75

THREE PROPHETIC SCIENCE FICTION NOVELS, H. G. Wells. *When the Sleeper Wakes, A Story of the Days to Come* and *The Time Machine* (full version). 335pp. 5⅜ × 8½. (Available in U.S. only) 20605-X Pa. $5.95

APICIUS COOKERY AND DINING IN IMPERIAL ROME, edited and translated by Joseph Dommers Vehling. Oldest known cookbook in existence offers readers a clear picture of what foods Romans ate, how they prepared them, etc. 49 illustrations. 301pp. 6⅛ × 9¼. 23563-7 Pa. $6.50

SHAKESPEARE LEXICON AND QUOTATION DICTIONARY, Alexander Schmidt. Full definitions, locations, shades of meaning of every word in plays and poems. More than 50,000 exact quotations. 1,485pp. 6½ × 9¼. 22726-X, 22727-8 Pa., Two-vol. set $27.90

THE WORLD'S GREAT SPEECHES, edited by Lewis Copeland and Lawrence W. Lamm. Vast collection of 278 speeches from Greeks to 1970. Powerful and effective models; unique look at history. 842pp. 5⅜ × 8½. 20468-5 Pa. $11.95

THE BLUE FAIRY BOOK, Andrew Lang. The first, most famous collection, with many familiar tales: Little Red Riding Hood, Aladdin and the Wonderful Lamp, Puss in Boots, Sleeping Beauty, Hansel and Gretel, Rumpelstiltskin; 37 in all. 138 illustrations. 390pp. 5⅜ × 8½. 21437-0 Pa. $5.95

THE STORY OF THE CHAMPIONS OF THE ROUND TABLE, Howard Pyle. Sir Launcelot, Sir Tristram and Sir Percival in spirited adventures of love and triumph retold in Pyle's inimitable style. 50 drawings, 31 full-page. xviii + 329pp. 6½ × 9¼. 21883-X Pa. $6.95

AUDUBON AND HIS JOURNALS, Maria Audubon. Unmatched two-volume portrait of the great artist, naturalist and author contains his journals, an excellent biography by his granddaughter, expert annotations by the noted ornithologist, Dr. Elliott Coues, and 37 superb illustrations. Total of 1,200pp. 5⅜ × 8.
Vol. I 25143-8 Pa. $8.95
Vol. II 25144-6 Pa. $8.95

GREAT DINOSAUR HUNTERS AND THEIR DISCOVERIES, Edwin H. Colbert. Fascinating, lavishly illustrated chronicle of dinosaur research, 1820's to 1960. Achievements of Cope, Marsh, Brown, Buckland, Mantell, Huxley, many others. 384pp. 5¼ × 8¼. 24701-5 Pa. $6.95

THE TASTEMAKERS, Russell Lynes. Informal, illustrated social history of American taste 1850's–1950's. First popularized categories Highbrow, Lowbrow, Middlebrow. 129 illustrations. New (1979) afterword. 384pp. 6 × 9.
23993-4 Pa. $6.95

DOUBLE CROSS PURPOSES, Ronald A. Knox. A treasure hunt in the Scottish Highlands, an old map, unidentified corpse, surprise discoveries keep reader guessing in this cleverly intricate tale of financial skullduggery. 2 black-and-white maps. 320pp. 5⅜ × 8½. (Available in U.S. only) 25032-6 Pa. $5.95

AUTHENTIC VICTORIAN DECORATION AND ORNAMENTATION IN FULL COLOR: 46 Plates from "Studies in Design," Christopher Dresser. Superb full-color lithographs reproduced from rare original portfolio of a major Victorian designer. 48pp. 9¼ × 12¼. 25083-0 Pa. $7.95

PRIMITIVE ART, Franz Boas. Remains the best text ever prepared on subject, thoroughly discussing Indian, African, Asian, Australian, and, especially, Northern American primitive art. Over 950 illustrations show ceramics, masks, totem poles, weapons, textiles, paintings, much more. 376pp. 5⅜ × 8. 20025-6 Pa. $6.95

SIDELIGHTS ON RELATIVITY, Albert Einstein. Unabridged republication of two lectures delivered by the great physicist in 1920–21. *Ether and Relativity* and *Geometry and Experience.* Elegant ideas in non-mathematical form, accessible to intelligent layman. vi + 56pp. 5⅜ × 8½. 24511-X Pa. $2.95

THE WIT AND HUMOR OF OSCAR WILDE, edited by Alvin Redman. More than 1,000 ripostes, paradoxes, wisecracks: Work is the curse of the drinking classes, I can resist everything except temptation, etc. 258pp. 5⅜ × 8½. 20602-5 Pa. $4.50

ADVENTURES WITH A MICROSCOPE, Richard Headstrom. 59 adventures with clothing fibers, protozoa, ferns and lichens, roots and leaves, much more. 142 illustrations. 232pp. 5⅜ × 8½. 23471-1 Pa. $3.95

PLANTS OF THE BIBLE, Harold N. Moldenke and Alma L. Moldenke. Standard reference to all 230 plants mentioned in Scriptures. Latin name, biblical reference, uses, modern identity, much more. Unsurpassed encyclopedic resource for scholars, botanists, nature lovers, students of Bible. Bibliography. Indexes. 123 black-and-white illustrations. 384pp. 6 × 9. 25069-5 Pa. $8.95

FAMOUS AMERICAN WOMEN: A Biographical Dictionary from Colonial Times to the Present, Robert McHenry, ed. From Pocahontas to Rosa Parks, 1,035 distinguished American women documented in separate biographical entries. Accurate, up-to-date data, numerous categories, spans 400 years. Indices. 493pp. 6½ × 9¼. 24523-3 Pa. $9.95

THE FABULOUS INTERIORS OF THE GREAT OCEAN LINERS IN HISTORIC PHOTOGRAPHS, William H. Miller, Jr. Some 200 superb photographs capture exquisite interiors of world's great "floating palaces"—1890's to 1980's: *Titanic, Ile de France, Queen Elizabeth, United States, Europa*, more. Approx. 200 black-and-white photographs. Captions. Text. Introduction. 160pp. 8⅜ × 11¾. 24756-2 Pa. $9.95

THE GREAT LUXURY LINERS, 1927–1954: A Photographic Record, William H. Miller, Jr. Nostalgic tribute to heyday of ocean liners. 186 photos of Ile de France, Normandie, Leviathan, Queen Elizabeth, United States, many others. Interior and exterior views. Introduction. Captions. 160pp. 9 × 12. 24056-8 Pa. $9.95

A NATURAL HISTORY OF THE DUCKS, John Charles Phillips. Great landmark of ornithology offers complete detailed coverage of nearly 200 species and subspecies of ducks: gadwall, sheldrake, merganser, pintail, many more. 74 full-color plates, 102 black-and-white. Bibliography. Total of 1,920pp. 8⅜ × 11¼. 25141-1, 25142-X Cloth. Two-vol. set $100.00

THE SEAWEED HANDBOOK: An Illustrated Guide to Seaweeds from North Carolina to Canada, Thomas F. Lee. Concise reference covers 78 species. Scientific and common names, habitat, distribution, more. Finding keys for easy identification. 224pp. 5⅜ × 8½. 25215-9 Pa. $5.95

THE TEN BOOKS OF ARCHITECTURE: The 1755 Leoni Edition, Leon Battista Alberti. Rare classic helped introduce the glories of ancient architecture to the Renaissance. 68 black-and-white plates. 336pp. 8⅜ × 11¼. 25239-6 Pa. $14.95

MISS MACKENZIE, Anthony Trollope. Minor masterpieces by Victorian master unmasks many truths about life in 19th-century England. First inexpensive edition in years. 392pp. 5⅜ × 8½. 25201-9 Pa. $7.95

THE RIME OF THE ANCIENT MARINER, Gustave Doré, Samuel Taylor Coleridge. Dramatic engravings considered by many to be his greatest work. The terrifying space of the open sea, the storms and whirlpools of an unknown ocean, the ice of Antarctica, more—all rendered in a powerful, chilling manner. Full text. 38 plates. 77pp. 9¼ × 12. 22305-1 Pa. $4.95

THE EXPEDITIONS OF ZEBULON MONTGOMERY PIKE, Zebulon Montgomery Pike. Fascinating first-hand accounts (1805–6) of exploration of Mississippi River, Indian wars, capture by Spanish dragoons, much more. 1,088pp. 5⅜ × 8½. 25254-X, 25255-8 Pa. Two-vol. set $23.90

A CONCISE HISTORY OF PHOTOGRAPHY: Third Revised Edition, Helmut Gernsheim. Best one-volume history—camera obscura, photochemistry, daguerreotypes, evolution of cameras, film, more. Also artistic aspects—landscape, portraits, fine art, etc. 281 black-and-white photographs. 26 in color. 176pp. 8⅜ × 11¼. 25128-4 Pa. $12.95

THE DORÉ BIBLE ILLUSTRATIONS, Gustave Doré. 241 detailed plates from the Bible: the Creation scenes, Adam and Eve, Flood, Babylon, battle sequences, life of Jesus, etc. Each plate is accompanied by the verses from the King James version of the Bible. 241pp. 9 × 12. 23004-X Pa. $8.95

HUGGER-MUGGER IN THE LOUVRE, Elliot Paul. Second Homer Evans mystery-comedy. Theft at the Louvre involves sleuth in hilarious, madcap caper. "A knockout."—Books. 336pp. 5⅜ × 8½. 25185-3 Pa. $5.95

FLATLAND, E. A. Abbott. Intriguing and enormously popular science-fiction classic explores the complexities of trying to survive as a two-dimensional being in a three-dimensional world. Amusingly illustrated by the author. 16 illustrations. 103pp. 5⅜ × 8½. 20001-9 Pa. $2.25

THE HISTORY OF THE LEWIS AND CLARK EXPEDITION, Meriwether Lewis and William Clark, edited by Elliott Coues. Classic edition of Lewis and Clark's day-by-day journals that later became the basis for U.S. claims to Oregon and the West. Accurate and invaluable geographical, botanical, biological, meteorological and anthropological material. Total of 1,508pp. 5⅜ × 8½.
21268-8, 21269-6, 21270-X Pa. Three-vol. set $25.50

LANGUAGE, TRUTH AND LOGIC, Alfred J. Ayer. Famous, clear introduction to Vienna, Cambridge schools of Logical Positivism. Role of philosophy, elimination of metaphysics, nature of analysis, etc. 160pp. 5⅜ × 8½. (Available in U.S. and Canada only) 20010-8 Pa. $2.95

MATHEMATICS FOR THE NONMATHEMATICIAN, Morris Kline. Detailed, college-level treatment of mathematics in cultural and historical context, with numerous exercises. For liberal arts students. Preface. Recommended Reading Lists. Tables. Index. Numerous black-and-white figures. xvi + 641pp. 5⅜ × 8½.
24823-2 Pa. $11.95

28 SCIENCE FICTION STORIES, H. G. Wells. Novels, *Star Begotten* and *Men Like Gods,* plus 26 short stories: "Empire of the Ants," "A Story of the Stone Age," "The Stolen Bacillus," "In the Abyss," etc. 915pp. 5⅜ × 8½. (Available in U.S. only)
20265-8 Cloth. $10.95

HANDBOOK OF PICTORIAL SYMBOLS, Rudolph Modley. 3,250 signs and symbols, many systems in full; official or heavy commercial use. Arranged by subject. Most in Pictorial Archive series. 143pp. 8⅛ × 11. 23357-X Pa. $5.95

INCIDENTS OF TRAVEL IN YUCATAN, John L. Stephens. Classic (1843) exploration of jungles of Yucatan, looking for evidences of Maya civilization. Travel adventures, Mexican and Indian culture, etc. Total of 669pp. 5⅜ × 8½.
20926-1, 20927-X Pa., Two-vol. set $9.90

CATALOG OF DOVER BOOKS

DEGAS: An Intimate Portrait, Ambroise Vollard. Charming, anecdotal memoir by famous art dealer of one of the greatest 19th-century French painters. 14 black-and-white illustrations. Introduction by Harold L. Van Doren. 96pp. 5⅜ × 8½.
25131-4 Pa. $3.95

PERSONAL NARRATIVE OF A PILGRIMAGE TO ALMANDINAH AND MECCAH, Richard Burton. Great travel classic by remarkably colorful personality. Burton, disguised as a Moroccan, visited sacred shrines of Islam, narrowly escaping death. 47 illustrations. 959pp. 5⅜ × 8½. 21217-3, 21218-1 Pa., Two-vol. set $17.90

PHRASE AND WORD ORIGINS, A. H. Holt. Entertaining, reliable, modern study of more than 1,200 colorful words, phrases, origins and histories. Much unexpected information. 254pp. 5⅜ × 8½. 20758-7 Pa. $5.95

THE RED THUMB MARK, R. Austin Freeman. In this first Dr. Thorndyke case, the great scientific detective draws fascinating conclusions from the nature of a single fingerprint. Exciting story, authentic science. 320pp. 5⅜ × 8½. (Available in U.S. only) 25210-8 Pa. $5.95

AN EGYPTIAN HIEROGLYPHIC DICTIONARY, E. A. Wallis Budge. Monumental work containing about 25,000 words or terms that occur in texts ranging from 3000 B.C. to 600 A.D. Each entry consists of a transliteration of the word, the word in hieroglyphs, and the meaning in English. 1,314pp. 6⅝ × 10.
23615-3, 23616-1 Pa., Two-vol. set $27.90

THE COMPLEAT STRATEGYST: Being a Primer on the Theory of Games of Strategy, J. D. Williams. Highly entertaining classic describes, with many illustrated examples, how to select best strategies in conflict situations. Prefaces. Appendices. xvi + 268pp. 5⅜ × 8½. 25101-2 Pa. $5.95

THE ROAD TO OZ, L. Frank Baum. Dorothy meets the Shaggy Man, little Button-Bright and the Rainbow's beautiful daughter in this delightful trip to the magical Land of Oz. 272pp. 5⅜ × 8. 25208-6 Pa. $4.95

POINT AND LINE TO PLANE, Wassily Kandinsky. Seminal exposition of role of point, line, other elements in non-objective painting. Essential to understanding 20th-century art. 127 illustrations. 192pp. 6½ × 9¼. 23808-3 Pa. $4.50

LADY ANNA, Anthony Trollope. Moving chronicle of Countess Lovel's bitter struggle to win for herself and daughter Anna their rightful rank and fortune—perhaps at cost of sanity itself. 384pp. 5⅜ × 8½. 24669-8 Pa. $6.95

EGYPTIAN MAGIC, E. A. Wallis Budge. Sums up all that is known about magic in Ancient Egypt: the role of magic in controlling the gods, powerful amulets that warded off evil spirits, scarabs of immortality, use of wax images, formulas and spells, the secret name, much more. 253pp. 5⅜ × 8½. 22681-6 Pa. $4.50

THE DANCE OF SIVA, Ananda Coomaraswamy. Preeminent authority unfolds the vast metaphysic of India: the revelation of her art, conception of the universe, social organization, etc. 27 reproductions of art masterpieces. 192pp. 5⅜ × 8½.
24817-8 Pa. $5.95

CHRISTMAS CUSTOMS AND TRADITIONS, Clement A. Miles. Origin, evolution, significance of religious, secular practices. Caroling, gifts, yule logs, much more. Full, scholarly yet fascinating; non-sectarian. 400pp. 5⅜ × 8½.
23354-5 Pa. $6.50

THE HUMAN FIGURE IN MOTION, Eadweard Muybridge. More than 4,500 stopped-action photos, in action series, showing undraped men, women, children jumping, lying down, throwing, sitting, wrestling, carrying, etc. 390pp. 7⅞ × 10⅝.
20204-6 Cloth. $19.95

THE MAN WHO WAS THURSDAY, Gilbert Keith Chesterton. Witty, fast-paced novel about a club of anarchists in turn-of-the-century London. Brilliant social, religious, philosophical speculations. 128pp. 5⅜ × 8½. 25121-7 Pa. $3.95

A CEZANNE SKETCHBOOK: Figures, Portraits, Landscapes and Still Lifes, Paul Cezanne. Great artist experiments with tonal effects, light, mass, other qualities in over 100 drawings. A revealing view of developing master painter, precursor of Cubism. 102 black-and-white illustrations. 144pp. 8¾ × 6⅜. 24790-2 Pa. $5.95

AN ENCYCLOPEDIA OF BATTLES: Accounts of Over 1,560 Battles from 1479 B.C. to the Present, David Eggenberger. Presents essential details of every major battle in recorded history, from the first battle of Megiddo in 1479 B.C. to Grenada in 1984. List of Battle Maps. New Appendix covering the years 1967–1984. Index. 99 illustrations. 544pp. 6½ × 9¼.
24913-1 Pa. $14.95

AN ETYMOLOGICAL DICTIONARY OF MODERN ENGLISH, Ernest Weekley. Richest, fullest work, by foremost British lexicographer. Detailed word histories. Inexhaustible. Total of 856pp. 6½ × 9¼.
21873-2, 21874-0 Pa., Two-vol. set $17.00

WEBSTER'S AMERICAN MILITARY BIOGRAPHIES, edited by Robert McHenry. Over 1,000 figures who shaped 3 centuries of American military history. Detailed biographies of Nathan Hale, Douglas MacArthur, Mary Hallaren, others. Chronologies of engagements, more. Introduction. Addenda. 1,033 entries in alphabetical order. xi + 548pp. 6½ × 9¼. (Available in U.S. only)
24758-9 Pa. $11.95

LIFE IN ANCIENT EGYPT, Adolf Erman. Detailed older account, with much not in more recent books: domestic life, religion, magic, medicine, commerce, and whatever else needed for complete picture. Many illustrations. 597pp. 5⅜ × 8½.
22632-8 Pa. $8.95

HISTORIC COSTUME IN PICTURES, Braun & Schneider. Over 1,450 costumed figures shown, covering a wide variety of peoples: kings, emperors, nobles, priests, servants, soldiers, scholars, townsfolk, peasants, merchants, courtiers, cavaliers, and more. 256pp. 8⅜ × 11¼.
23150-X Pa. $7.95

THE NOTEBOOKS OF LEONARDO DA VINCI, edited by J. P. Richter. Extracts from manuscripts reveal great genius; on painting, sculpture, anatomy, sciences, geography, etc. Both Italian and English. 186 ms. pages reproduced, plus 500 additional drawings, including studies for *Last Supper, Sforza* monument, etc. 860pp. 7⅞ × 10¾. (Available in U.S. only) 22572-0, 22573-9 Pa., Two-vol. set $25.90

THE ART NOUVEAU STYLE BOOK OF ALPHONSE MUCHA: All 72 Plates from "Documents Decoratifs" in Original Color, Alphonse Mucha. Rare copyright-free design portfolio by high priest of Art Nouveau. Jewelry, wallpaper, stained glass, furniture, figure studies, plant and animal motifs, etc. Only complete one-volume edition. 80pp. 9⅜ × 12¼.   24044-4 Pa. $8.95

ANIMALS: 1,419 COPYRIGHT-FREE ILLUSTRATIONS OF MAMMALS, BIRDS, FISH, INSECTS, ETC., edited by Jim Harter. Clear wood engravings present, in extremely lifelike poses, over 1,000 species of animals. One of the most extensive pictorial sourcebooks of its kind. Captions. Index. 284pp. 9 × 12.
23766-4 Pa. $9.95

OBELISTS FLY HIGH, C. Daly King. Masterpiece of American detective fiction, long out of print, involves murder on a 1935 transcontinental flight—"a very thrilling story"—NY Times. Unabridged and unaltered republication of the edition published by William Collins Sons & Co. Ltd., London, 1935. 288pp. 5⅜ × 8½. (Available in U.S. only)   25036-9 Pa. $4.95

VICTORIAN AND EDWARDIAN FASHION: A Photographic Survey, Alison Gernsheim. First fashion history completely illustrated by contemporary photographs. Full text plus 235 photos, 1840–1914, in which many celebrities appear. 240pp. 6½ × 9¼.   24205-6 Pa. $6.00

THE ART OF THE FRENCH ILLUSTRATED BOOK, 1700–1914, Gordon N. Ray. Over 630 superb book illustrations by Fragonard, Delacroix, Daumier, Doré, Grandville, Manet, Mucha, Steinlen, Toulouse-Lautrec and many others. Preface. Introduction. 633 halftones. Indices of artists, authors & titles, binders and provenances. Appendices. Bibliography. 608pp. 8⅜ × 11¼.   25086-5 Pa. $24.95

THE WONDERFUL WIZARD OF OZ, L. Frank Baum. Facsimile in full color of America's finest children's classic. 143 illustrations by W. W. Denslow. 267pp. 5⅜ × 8½.   20691-2 Pa. $5.95

FRONTIERS OF MODERN PHYSICS: New Perspectives on Cosmology, Relativity, Black Holes and Extraterrestrial Intelligence, Tony Rothman, et al. For the intelligent layman. Subjects include: cosmological models of the universe; black holes; the neutrino; the search for extraterrestrial intelligence. Introduction. 46 black-and-white illustrations. 192pp. 5⅜ × 8½.   24587-X Pa. $6.95

THE FRIENDLY STARS, Martha Evans Martin & Donald Howard Menzel. Classic text marshalls the stars together in an engaging, non-technical survey, presenting them as sources of beauty in night sky. 23 illustrations. Foreword. 2 star charts. Index. 147pp. 5⅜ × 8½.   21099-5 Pa. $3.50

FADS AND FALLACIES IN THE NAME OF SCIENCE, Martin Gardner. Fair, witty appraisal of cranks, quacks, and quackeries of science and pseudoscience: hollow earth, Velikovsky, orgone energy, Dianetics, flying saucers, Bridey Murphy, food and medical fads, etc. Revised, expanded In the Name of Science. "A very able and even-tempered presentation."—The New Yorker. 363pp. 5⅜ × 8.
20394-8 Pa. $6.50

ANCIENT EGYPT: ITS CULTURE AND HISTORY, J. E Manchip White. From pre-dynastics through Ptolemies: society, history, political structure, religion, daily life, literature, cultural heritage. 48 plates. 217pp. 5⅜ × 8½.   22548-8 Pa. $4.95

CATALOG OF DOVER BOOKS

SIR HARRY HOTSPUR OF HUMBLETHWAITE, Anthony Trollope. Incisive, unconventional psychological study of a conflict between a wealthy baronet, his idealistic daughter, and their scapegrace cousin. The 1870 novel in its first inexpensive edition in years. 250pp. 5⅜ × 8½. 24953-0 Pa. $5.95

LASERS AND HOLOGRAPHY, Winston E. Kock. Sound introduction to burgeoning field, expanded (1981) for second edition. Wave patterns, coherence, lasers, diffraction, zone plates, properties of holograms, recent advances. 84 illustrations. 160pp. 5⅜ × 8¼. (Except in United Kingdom) 24041-X Pa. $3.50

INTRODUCTION TO ARTIFICIAL INTELLIGENCE: SECOND, ENLARGED EDITION, Philip C. Jackson, Jr. Comprehensive survey of artificial intelligence—the study of how machines (computers) can be made to act intelligently. Includes introductory and advanced material. Extensive notes updating the main text. 132 black-and-white illustrations. 512pp. 5⅜ × 8¼. 24864-X Pa. $8.95

HISTORY OF INDIAN AND INDONESIAN ART, Ananda K. Coomaraswamy. Over 400 illustrations illuminate classic study of Indian art from earliest Harappa finds to early 20th century. Provides philosophical, religious and social insights. 304pp. 6⅜ × 9⅜. 25005-9 Pa. $8.95

THE GOLEM, Gustav Meyrink. Most famous supernatural novel in modern European literature, set in Ghetto of Old Prague around 1890. Compelling story of mystical experiences, strange transformations, profound terror. 13 black-and-white illustrations. 224pp. 5⅜ × 8½. (Available in U.S. only) 25025-3 Pa. $5.95

ARMADALE, Wilkie Collins. Third great mystery novel by the author of The Woman in White and The Moonstone. Original magazine version with 40 illustrations. 597pp. 5⅜ × 8½. 23429-0 Pa. $9.95

PICTORIAL ENCYCLOPEDIA OF HISTORIC ARCHITECTURAL PLANS, DETAILS AND ELEMENTS: With 1,880 Line Drawings of Arches, Domes, Doorways, Facades, Gables, Windows, etc., John Theodore Haneman. Sourcebook of inspiration for architects, designers, others. Bibliography. Captions. 141pp. 9 × 12. 24605-1 Pa. $6.95

BENCHLEY LOST AND FOUND, Robert Benchley. Finest humor from early 30's, about pet peeves, child psychologists, post office and others. Mostly unavailable elsewhere. 73 illustrations by Peter Arno and others. 183pp. 5⅜ × 8½. 22410-4 Pa. $3.95

ERTÉ GRAPHICS, Erté. Collection of striking color graphics: Seasons, Alphabet, Numerals, Aces and Precious Stones. 50 plates, including 4 on covers. 48pp. 9⅜ × 12¼. 23580-7 Pa. $6.95

THE JOURNAL OF HENRY D. THOREAU, edited by Bradford Torrey, F. H. Allen. Complete reprinting of 14 volumes, 1837–61, over two million words; the sourcebooks for Walden, etc. Definitive. All original sketches, plus 75 photographs. 1,804pp. 8½ × 12¼. 20312-3, 20313-1 Cloth., Two-vol. set $80.00

CASTLES: THEIR CONSTRUCTION AND HISTORY, Sidney Toy. Traces castle development from ancient roots. Nearly 200 photographs and drawings illustrate moats, keeps, baileys, many other features. Caernarvon, Dover Castles, Hadrian's Wall, Tower of London, dozens more. 256pp. 5⅜ × 8¼. 24898-4 Pa. $5.95

CATALOG OF DOVER BOOKS

AMERICAN CLIPPER SHIPS: 1833–1858, Octavius T. Howe & Frederick C. Matthews. Fully-illustrated, encyclopedic review of 352 clipper ships from the period of America's greatest maritime supremacy. Introduction. 109 halftones. 5 black-and-white line illustrations. Index. Total of 928pp. 5⅜ × 8½.
25115-2, 25116-0 Pa., Two-vol. set $17.90

TOWARDS A NEW ARCHITECTURE, Le Corbusier. Pioneering manifesto by great architect, near legendary founder of "International School." Technical and aesthetic theories, views on industry, economics, relation of form to function, "mass-production spirit," much more. Profusely illustrated. Unabridged translation of 13th French edition. Introduction by Frederick Etchells. 320pp. 6⅛ × 9¼. (Available in U.S. only)
25023-7 Pa. $8.95

THE BOOK OF KELLS, edited by Blanche Cirker. Inexpensive collection of 32 full-color, full-page plates from the greatest illuminated manuscript of the Middle Ages, painstakingly reproduced from rare facsimile edition. Publisher's Note. Captions. 32pp. 9⅜ × 12¼.
24345-1 Pa. $4.95

BEST SCIENCE FICTION STORIES OF H. G. WELLS, H. G. Wells. Full novel *The Invisible Man,* plus 17 short stories: "The Crystal Egg," "Aepyornis Island," "The Strange Orchid," etc. 303pp. 5⅜ × 8½. (Available in U.S. only)
21531-8 Pa. $4.95

AMERICAN SAILING SHIPS: Their Plans and History, Charles G. Davis. Photos, construction details of schooners, frigates, clippers, other sailcraft of 18th to early 20th centuries—plus entertaining discourse on design, rigging, nautical lore, much more. 137 black-and-white illustrations. 240pp. 6⅛ × 9¼.
24658-2 Pa. $5.95

ENTERTAINING MATHEMATICAL PUZZLES, Martin Gardner. Selection of author's favorite conundrums involving arithmetic, money, speed, etc., with lively commentary. Complete solutions. 112pp. 5⅜ × 8½.
25211-6 Pa. $2.95

THE WILL TO BELIEVE, HUMAN IMMORTALITY, William James. Two books bound together. Effect of irrational on logical, and arguments for human immortality. 402pp. 5⅜ × 8½.
20291-7 Pa. $7.50

THE HAUNTED MONASTERY and THE CHINESE MAZE MURDERS, Robert Van Gulik. 2 full novels by Van Gulik continue adventures of Judge Dee and his companions. An evil Taoist monastery, seemingly supernatural events; overgrown topiary maze that hides strange crimes. Set in 7th-century China. 27 illustrations. 328pp. 5⅜ × 8½.
23502-5 Pa. $5.95

CELEBRATED CASES OF JUDGE DEE (DEE GOONG AN), translated by Robert Van Gulik. Authentic 18th-century Chinese detective novel; Dee and associates solve three interlocked cases. Led to Van Gulik's own stories with same characters. Extensive introduction. 9 illustrations. 237pp. 5⅜ × 8½.
23337-5 Pa. $4.95

Prices subject to change without notice.
Available at your book dealer or write for free catalog to Dept. GI, Dover Publications, Inc., 31 East 2nd St., Mineola, N.Y. 11501. Dover publishes more than 175 books each year on science, elementary and advanced mathematics, biology, music, art, literary history, social sciences and other areas.